THE SARI

STYLES ~ PATTERNS ~ HISTORY ~ TECHNIQUES

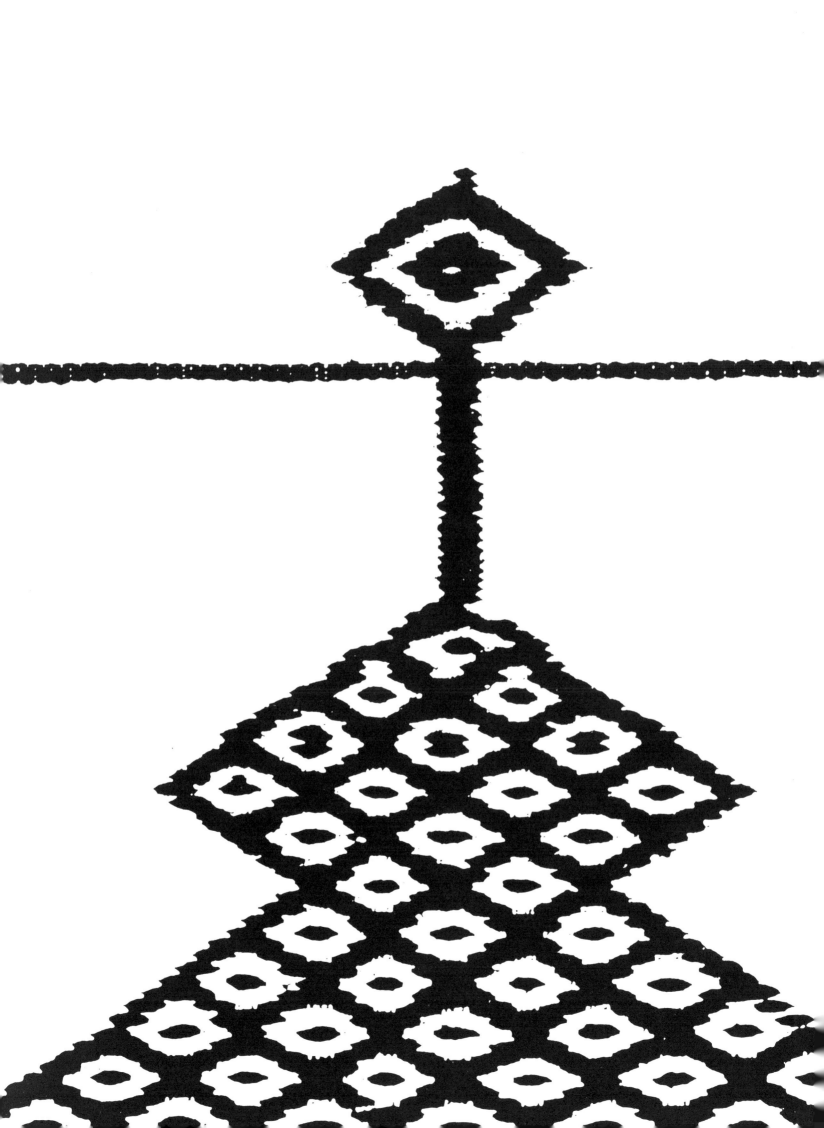

THE SARI

STYLES ~ PATTERNS ~ HISTORY ~ TECHNIQUES

WITH OVER 470 ILLUSTRATIONS, 206 IN COLOUR

LINDA LYNTON

photographs by SANJAY K. SINGH

THAMES AND HUDSON

This book is dedicated to our
parents: George and Edna Lynton,
and Sarojini and D. K. N. Singh

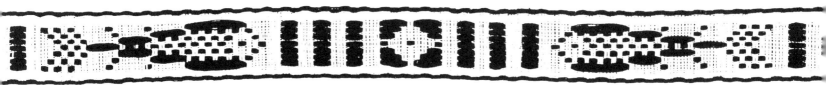

p. 1 A Boro textile motif from the endpiece of an
Assamese sari.

p. 2 A *phool cheeta chauk* design on a Gond
ganda (wedding sari) from Koraput, Orissa.

This page, and opposite   Details from a Gadaba
kerong, Koraput, Orissa.

© 1995 Thames and Hudson Ltd, London

Design by Avril Broadley

British Library Cataloguing-in-Publication Data
A catalogue record for this book is available from
the British Library

ISBN 0-500-01672-0

Printed and bound in Singapore by C.S. Graphics

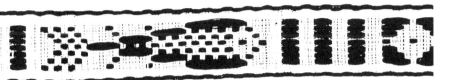

CONTENTS

1   Lifting the Veil 7

2   The Western Region 25

3   The Eastern Region 41

4   The North-East and the Himalayas 73

5   The Eastern Deccan 89

6   The South 121

7   The Western Deccan 145

8   Iconography 161

Notes on the Text 181

Glossary of Indian Terms 190

Glossary of Textile Terms 196

'Sari' in Indian Languages 198

Table of Sari Measurements 199

Chronology 200

Museum Collections 200

Bibliography 202

Acknowledgments 204

Index 205

Lifting the Veil

The sari is the quintessential Indian female garment. Nothing identifies a woman as being Indian so strongly as the sari, although women also wear saris in many other countries, especially in Bangladesh, Nepal and Sri Lanka. Saris come in all shapes and sizes, from textured handwoven fabrics created in remote mountain areas to sheer luxurious silks, once exclusively royal. Even today, after two centuries of disruptions caused by colonialism and industrialization, a multiplicity of traditional saris still exists, created in a wide range of fabrics and designs, reflecting the subcontinent's great cultural diversity. There are tribal (*adivasi*)[1] peoples whose ancestors were probably South Asia's original inhabitants; many ethnic groups[2] who may live in remote rural areas or in the heart of big cities but who still maintain their cultural identities; and sophisticated urbanites[3] whose ancestors were India's aristocrats, intellectuals and traders. Most of them possess traditional saris which they still wear today.

India's saris evolved out of a complex physical, historical and cultural environment that differs from region to region and community to community. In order to gain some understanding of why its regional saris diversified in the ways they have, we first need to take a comprehensive look at this geo-historical complexity before we can consider the sari itself.

Covering a landmass of over 1.6 million square kilometres (over 600,000 square miles),[4] the Indian subcontinent is bounded to the north by the Himalayas, where conditions are arctic in the high peaks, while in the alpine plateaux and valleys microclimates range from temperate to subtropical. About 2560 kilometres (1600 miles) to the south, at Cape Comorin, the climate is tropical with heavy rainfall, rich soils and lush vegetation. Immediately south of the Himalayas, the wide, fertile plains of the Indus, Ganga and Brahmaputra rivers and their tributaries stretch for 3200 kilometres (2000 miles) from west to east, making up most of northern India, Pakistan and Bangladesh. These verdant plains are prone to heavy flooding, unlike the Thar Desert and semi-arid areas of the Sind that lie to the west

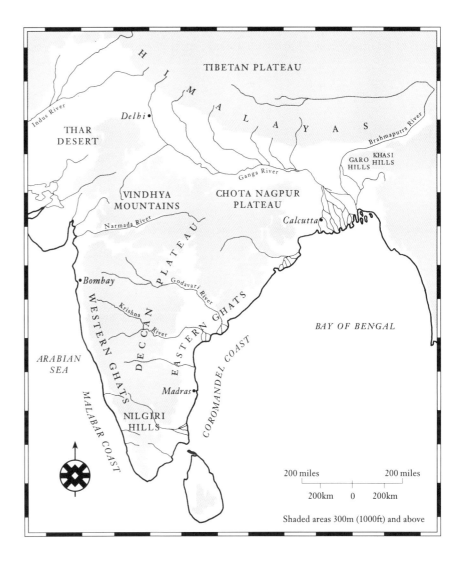

Opposite A *kalga* motif on a Baluchar sari from Bankura, West Bengal [Pl. 62].

Punjab
Haryana
DELHI
Nepal
Rajasthan
Uttar Pradesh
Sikkim
Arunchal Pradesh?
Assam
Nagaland
Meghalaya
Bihar
Bangladesh
Manipur
Gujarat
Tripura
Mizoram
Madhya Pradesh
West Bengal
CALCUTTA•
Maharashtra
Orissa
•BOMBAY
Andhra Pradesh
Goa
Karnataka
MADRAS•
Tamil Nadu
Kerala
Sri Lanka

TRADITIONAL
SARI-WEARING
AREAS

200 miles   200 miles
200km   0   200km

between India and Pakistan. The Deccan plateau juts against the Ganga plain and covers most of peninsular India with an often arid landscape in the north that becomes more hospitable further south. Mountain ranges and steep forested hills – the Eastern and Western Ghats – border both sides of the Deccan, descending to narrow coastal plains in the west and broad estuarine valleys in the east.

India's seasons are equally extreme. In most areas, about two thirds of the year are dry, with cool or warm winters, hot dry summers, and monsoon rains falling between June and early September. The seasons often start with sudden violence. Relentless summer heat encourages drought, while the monsoon rains may last for weeks, creating devastating floods, with cyclones and hurricanes in their wake.

The subcontinent's political history has been just as turbulent, with waves of new conquerors uprooting entire communities,[5] and artisans and weavers often moving from one area to another in search of work.[6] Each change has added something new to sari-weaving and -wearing traditions where these communities settled down. We now also know that the subcontinent's regional cultures have very deep roots. Archaeologists have found distinctive regional variations in stone tools fashioned as early as 50,000 years ago,[7] while by 2000 BC many differences were well established: the people of the Indus Valley civilization (*c.* 3500–1700 BC) in the north-west were making bread from wheat, possibly the *nans* and *chapatis* still eaten today, and may have been wearing dyed cotton clothes just as local people do now; while a thousand miles to the east, the Neolithic inhabitants of present-day Bihar were growing and eating rice, and cotton had not yet appeared as a crop.[8] At the same time, however, a recognizably Indian cultural homogeneity was also evolving. From our point of view, the Indus Valley civilization left one of the most significant legacies, namely the domestication of cotton (*Gossypium arboreum*) and the technology to dye it. We know that cotton was being grown in the western region as early as 4000 BC as its seeds have been found at a Neolithic site near Mehrgarh, northern Baluchistan, while the remains of dyed cotton cloth excavated at Mohenjo-daro were dated about 2000 BC.[9]

Although the southern coastal areas have had well-developed maritime traditions for millennia, many of India's cultural changes were instigated by new invaders and settlers descending from the Iranian plateau via the north-west 'corridor', rather than by sea. As early as 2000 BC nomadic, horse-rearing, Indo-European-speaking

Opposite Tumpals in the endpiece patterning of a nineteenth-century Gujarati *patolu*, a textile traditionally exported to Indonesia as well as worn as saris by wealthy local communities.

tribes (called Indo-Aryans to distinguish them from other Indo-Europeans) passed through this corridor and spread south and east into India from the central Asian steppes.[10] About the same time, tribes from southern China travelled through Tibet and Burma to enter India from the north-east,[11] but they never had the cultural impact of the Indo-Aryans. The latter are believed to have pushed the Austro-Asiatic-speaking[12] tribes (which are now only found in the Eastern Ghats and Meghalaya) to the remoter areas of the Deccan plateau and the north-east, and the Dravidian-speaking[13] peoples of the subcontinent to the south.

Today there are well over one hundred different languages spoken in India,[14] and, it could be argued, an equal number of distinct cultures that arrived and evolved at different times. After the Indo-Aryans settled, the Greeks from Europe (*c.* 300 BC), the Scythians and Kushans from Central Asia (*c.* 50 BC–AD 200), and then different Islamic groups from Afghanistan and further west (*c.* AD 700–1200) pushed their way into South Asia from the north-west.[15] The early Islamic invasions resulted in various Muslim dynasties ruling northern India, culminating in the Mughal Empire (1526–*c.* 1765) whose court textiles influenced the fabrics worn by most north and central Indian aristocrats until the early twentieth century. Mughal political and military power was superseded by the British in the late eighteenth century. The British were originally only one among several European nations trading in the subcontinent since the sixteenth century, snatching a piece of India's then-enormous textile export industry. But by the early nineteenth century the British East India Company's business practices had already produced severe economic imbalances. It coerced many South Asians into exporting commodities in exchange for manufactured goods, resulting in the widespread pauperization of India's once-flourishing agricultural and artisan classes. Weavers and other skilled textile craftspeople were further impoverished by the establishment of cotton mills in Bombay and Ahmedabad in the 1850s and the growth of India's now-thriving industrial textile business.

The Swadeshi movement was founded in the late nineteenth century in rebellion against unfair British trade practices (which put high tariffs on locally made textiles). Gandhi expanded the movement in the early twentieth century by encouraging hand-spinning and weaving as a political symbol as well as a means of giving the poor an income. Popularly known as *khadi* (see p. 52), this handmade cloth has been an important symbol since the early 1920s and is still worn by politicians and intellectuals today, but it failed to halt the flood of inexpensive factory-made textiles issuing from India's mills (see p. 152). Unlike many fine aristocratic saris, which started disappearing in the early twentieth century in response to changing upper-class fashions, many tribal and ethnic saris were not seriously threatened until the late 1950s when India's mills began producing high volumes of low-priced mass-market textiles.[16] Since India's Independence in 1947 the government has encouraged the continuation and revival of its crafts heritage, including the creation of traditional regional saris. However, handloom weavers today are forced to change and adapt

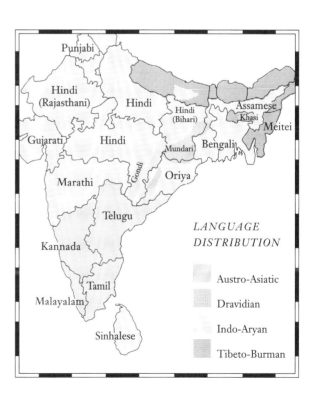

LANGUAGE
DISTRIBUTION

Austro-Asiatic

Dravidian

Indo-Aryan

Tibeto-Burman

Above A Shunga terracotta, *c.* 100 BC. The garment this woman is wearing appears to be draped between the legs, in the *kachchha* style, as well as over the left shoulder. (Ashmolean Museum, X201)

Opposite, above A Gupta terracotta, *c.* 400 AD. The attendant is wearing what would appear to be a full-body sari draped in the Dravidian style. (Brooklyn Museum, 1990.226)

Opposite, below Detail of a Gandharan frieze showing the birth of the Buddha, *c.* 200 AD. The Buddha's mother is wearing a sari-type drape. Her attendant has a *kachchha dhoti* or wrap under an upper garment that is either a tunic or an untailored cloth pinned at the shoulders. (Freer Gallery of Art, Arthur M. Sackler Gallery, 49.9)

many traditional textiles in an effort to compete with the mills and India's fashion industry.

History of the Sari

The sari's origins are obscure, in part because there are so few historical records in India compared to most other major civilizations. Yet we know that Indians were wearing lengths of unsewn cloth draped around their bodies long before tailored clothes arrived. One of the earliest depictions of a sari-like drape covering the entire body dates back to about 100 BC. A north Indian terracotta (Shunga period, *c.* 200–50 BC)[17] depicts a woman wearing a sari wound tightly around her entire body in the *kachchha* style (see p. 14). This elaborate, body-hugging style represented in the terracotta may have evolved among India's temple dancers in ancient times to allow their limbs freedom of movement while at the same time maintaining their societies' standards of modesty.[18]

Saris draping the entire body may have also been worn by various regional and ethnic groups at the turn of the first millennium AD. Many sculptures of the Graeco-Indian Gandharan civilization (50 BC–AD 300)[19] show a variety of different sari draping styles. In addition, a terracotta from eastern India, dated to AD 300–550 (from the Gupta period, which takes its name from the major ruling dynasty of the time) and which is in the Brooklyn Museum,[20] depicts a woman wearing a full-skirted sari draped around her entire body. She is holding a fan of unusual type, suggesting she may be from a 'foreign' place.[21]

The overall lack of historical data, however, makes it difficult to assess the origins of the sari in India as a whole, for Gandhara was in the extreme north-west and this hardly makes it culturally representative of the entire subcontinent. Also, we can be confident in assuming that most ancient artwork depicted the social elite and their dress, telling us little about what ordinary people wore. Yet even within these limited parameters, there are indications that in some regions the sari as we know it today may have had humble origins. Among the many gods, demi-gods and mortals depicted in the murals at the Ajanta Caves (late fifth century AD) in western Maharashtra[22] are two representations of women wearing saris covering the entire body. Cave One shows a woman sitting with a man (who is wearing a loose, tailored top) looking up at the courtly scene around her.[23] She is wearing a short sari with narrow warp-wise borders and weft-wise stripes draped over her left shoulder. In Cave Eight an old woman looking around a door is draped in a voluminous sari in the *kachchha* style.[24] Both these women are clearly not participants in the central activities, which suggests that they were of quite low status.

In the millennium that passed between the painting of the Ajanta murals and the miniatures of the Mughal period, very few pictorial representations even of royal women, let alone commoners, have survived. Apart from some Gujarati manuscripts created by the Jain sect (*c.* AD 1200–1500), most paintings are no older than the sixteenth century. They usually show members of the ruling elite, who by then were often wearing the tailored styles of upper-class Muslims, not the untailored clothes of Hindus (who felt that cloth cut and pierced by needles was impure). Only some seventeenth- and eighteenth-century paintings from the Hindu courts of the Deccan and south India[25] show women wearing saris draped in a variety of ways.

This dearth of pictorial representation makes it difficult to assess the age of most types of traditional regional saris, and the problem is compounded by the fact that very few saris survive even from the early nineteenth century.[26] In terms of studying India's regional saris, the anthropological museum collections amassed during the twentieth century have proved the best resource, as well as the often-extensive private collections of many South Asian women throughout the subcontinent.

Mention must also be made of tailored women's clothes, be they the *ghaghras* (full gathered skirts) of the western region, the *salwar kameez* (gathered trousers and loose tailored top) once associated with western-region Muslims but now popular among young urban women throughout India, or the *choli* (blouse) worn under the sari. All of these were later introductions. The Scythians and other ancient horse-riding warrior groups wore tailored clothes, but it was probably not until the arrival of the Huns (*c.* AD 450–600) and various Middle Eastern peoples at the turn of the millennium (*c.* AD 1000–1200) that most women in India's western region began wearing tailored clothes. The sari-like *odhni* (a large veil about 2.7 metres – nearly 9 feet – long), commonly worn with the *ghaghra* [Pls. 26, 30], may have been an adaptation of the older Gandharan sari to this newer form of dress.

It is commonly believed in India that today's ubiquitous petticoat, worn under the sari, came with the Muslims in the form of the *ghaghra*, and the tailored *choli* with the British, despite the fact that blouses were often mentioned in classical Sanskrit poetry.[27] Increasing numbers of upper-class women in the early twentieth century did adopt such items of European-style clothing as the fitted blouse and slim petticoat, however, in part because transparent chiffon saris became fashionable. In fact today's modern style, with its clinging blouse, long petticoat and fine, sheer sari draped in the *nivi* style (see p. 14) is as modern as the movies; for although the wives of India's rajas draped their chiffon saris – which were made by Paris designers in the 1920s and 1930s[28] – in the *nivi* style, it was not until the stars of the Bombay film world started emulating their dress that mainstream India became aware of it. Even now, India's movie stars dictate fashion, and the introduction of cable and satellite television is bound to have an

Above A painted wall-hanging from the Madras/Golconda region depicting a court scene, 1630–40. The saris are shown draped in a complicated seventeenth-century southern style that produced the 'fishtail' effect in the front. All the saris here have very narrow borders.

Opposite Assamese sari border with tribal patterning [Pl. 93].

impact on the middle-class sari as we know it today.

What the Sari Is

The sari is a length of cloth measuring from about 4 to 8 metres by about 120 centimetres (13 to 26 feet by about 4 feet), which is draped around the entire body. Most of this fabric is pleated at the waist and then wound round to make a skirt or pair of trousers, with the remaining few yards swept across the upper half of the body, covering at least one shoulder and sometimes veiling the head. In some regions, a woman traditionally wears a shorter length of fabric draped below the waist only, rather like an Indonesian sarong, except unlike the sarong the fabric is not sewn to form a tube. This lower garment has many different regional names,[29] although throughout India the male (as well as female Punjabi) version is called a *lungi*,[30] a term used in this book as a generic name for this type of wrap.

Saris are either woven by hand – there are over three million handlooms in India employing more than six million people[31] – or by powerlooms in textile mills. The creation of both types of sari is big business: sari production accounts for an estimated 25.5 per cent of all textile production in India,[32] and most Indian women, excepting the very poorest, buy both kinds. Handwoven saris (or 'handloom' saris, as they are known), are highly prized, and most women can still recognize the finer details of good handloom weaving, although for everyday wear the usually less expensive mill-made saris are now commonly worn.

A woman's ethnicity and class or caste background usually influence her choice of fabrics, colour and pattern, and all of these will in turn be affected by the social norms found in the region in which she lives. These differences are still noticeable today, though they are not as distinct as a century or even thirty years ago. For example, in northern India a widow is expected to wear white, the colour of mourning, since bright colours are regarded as the prerogative of young married women, with bright red being seen as the colour of joy, energy and marital bliss (which is why it is worn by brides) [Pls. 15, 16]. Older married women are expected to wear dark blues and other 'dull' tones. In the Dravidian south, however, these colour 'rules' do not apply. North Indian women are expected to cover their heads [Pl. 10]. Some scholars attribute this to Islamic domination, but ancient Sanskrit texts, such as the *Mahabharata* (compiled between 800 and 700 BC),[33] indicate that high-caste women were expected to be veiled before their elders and social superiors more than a millennium before Islam was even founded.[34] Again, women in the south are less likely to cover their heads, and those who can afford it add garlands of fresh flowers to their hair [Pl. 1].

Yet below the various layers of local tradition and history lie certain general rules about what a sari is and is not, and regional peculiarities are all variations on certain basic themes – namely, its dimensions and design structure.

A Sari's Dimensions

The actual length and width of the sari varies by region and by quality. A good quality sari made of expensive fabric, like a dense silk or fine cotton muslin, will often be both broader and longer than one that is less costly; the least expensive mill-made saris worn by peasants and the urban poor are noticeably short in length and width [Pl. 186]. Many traditional heavy cotton saris worn by tribal, peasant and low-caste working women have always been short in order to facilitate movement [Pl. 115], but among middle-class and wealthier women saris are expected to sweep the floor because exposed ankles are a sign of belonging to the labouring poor.

Traditional sari dimensions are also influenced by regional and community draping styles. In the Dravidian south, for instance, many poorer low-caste and tribal women, as well as some conservative orthodox Brahmins,[35] still wear saris 7 to 9 metres (23 to 30 feet) long that are draped in various trouser-like forms traditional to their communities. Such draping styles, and saris, are rarely worn by today's urban middle classes as they have adopted the now ubiquitous *nivi* style, which during the last century was only worn in the western Deccan and some areas of Dravidian India.

Sari Design Structure

Although the sari is an untailored length of cloth, the fabric is highly structured and its design vocabulary very sophisticated. It is divided into three areas: the longitudinal borders; the endpiece; and the field. Traditionally, each area communicated a woman's social and family status, as well as her regional identity, for certain colours and motifs were region- and community-specific. Its size and elaboration also indicated a family's wealth because added ornamentation takes more weaving time, and so adds to the sari's cost.

Borders usually extend the full (longitudinal) length of the sari either (1) as a woven design created by contrasting supplementary-warp or -weft weaving [Pl. 53]; (2) through the warp threads being a different colour to the warps making the field [Pl. 176]; or (3) by printing or embroidery [Pl. 200]. Most regions, and even towns and villages, had their own traditional distinctive borders,[36] and in some areas, such as Bengal, different weavers in the same town specialized in specific designs (see p. 44). Although today the width of borders tends to follow fashion rather than tradition, the regional origins of many border designs can still be recognized.

The endpiece is the part of the sari that is draped over the shoulder and left to hang over the back or front. The degree of embellishment traditionally depends on how this is draped,[37] as well as for what occasion it is used, because expensive saris tend to have larger and more elaborate endpieces than less costly, everyday ones.

The sari's field is also embellished according to regional rules, and in many parts of India it is traditionally unadorned, with designs

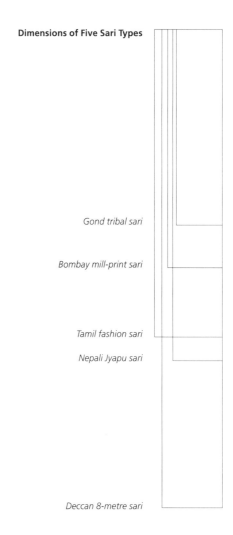

Dimensions of Five Sari Types

Gond tribal sari

Bombay mill-print sari

Tamil fashion sari

Nepali Jyapu sari

Deccan 8-metre sari

Sari Design: Basic Structure

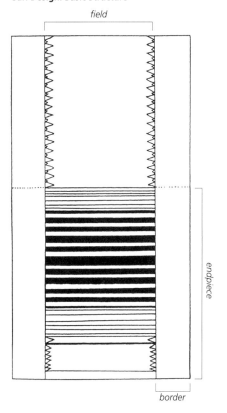

field

endpiece

border

Above Diagram of the layout of an Orissan *hansabali kapta*, a traditional ethnic sari from the eastern Deccan. Its endpiece is about one metre (3 feet) long.

(Note: To-scale diagrams of sari layouts are found throughout Chapters 2–7. Each diagram represents the first 2 metres [6 feet] of the sari, including its endpiece.)

Draping the Sari The diagrams opposite show how three common and simple types of sari drape (the *nivi*, northern and Maharashtran *kachchha*) are created. Front pleating, illlustrated at the top of the page, is the first stage in all of these draping methods. Each can also be draped without the use of a petticoat by tying the sari tightly round the waist, knotting the upper border and the upper inner corner at the front right side.

woven, embroidered or printed onto it only when the sari has been made for weddings.

The Basic Draping Styles

The *nivi*[38] style of draping the sari is now so common among urban middle-class Indian women that many foreigners do not realize that there are other ways of wearing it – whereas in fact there are literally dozens. Different regional, ethnic and tribal communities all have their own sari styles and draping methods, and these can be divided into six major types. Today most saris are tied in place with a string (sometimes to a petticoat), but in the past, the upper border of the first 90 centimetres (3 feet) of the sari was usually knotted firmly round the waist, and the pleats and folds of cloth that formed the skirt (or trousers) would have been tucked into that.[39]

The northern styles have skirt pleats in the front and the free end draped around the back and over the front, so that the endpiece covers the wearer's breasts [Pls. 15, 18]. There are many variations on this style, with the Gujarati, Bihari and Orissan versions being the most well known. The Bengali drape shows elements of both the northern and Dravidian styles [Pls. 8, 9]. Not surprisingly, traditional saris from the northern areas have large decorated endpieces because they are so visible [Pl. 88]. The age of the northern draping styles is revealed by the fact that even today in the north Indian state of Bihar they are called *sidha* (correct, straight, good) draping styles, while the *nivi* style is called an *ulta* (reverse, opposite, bad) style, even by women who have never worn a sari in the *sidha* manner.[40]

The Deccan styles include the *nivi* version, which has various names in the different regions of south and south-west Deccan where it originated (see Note 38). It uses 4.5 to 5.5 metres (15 to 18 feet) of cloth draped to create a skirt with pleats in the front, while the rest is drawn from the right hip across the breasts and left shoulder to hang down the back [Pls. 1, 3]. Another, once more widely distributed type of draping style that is also traditional to the Deccan and parts of south India is the *kachchha*,[41] which creates the practical effect of a pair of trousers [Pls. 11, 12, 186]. There are many ways of tying and draping *kachchha* saris, each giving a different result – from tight to loose around the legs – and each uses a different part of the cloth to begin the often-complicated draping sequence. These styles are associated with Maharashtra, but they are found throughout the Deccan plateau (Maharashtra, Andhra Pradesh, Madhya Pradesh) and the south (Karnataka, Tamil Nadu). Until the 1960s, they were also worn by many tribal groups such as the Bhils of western India and the Ho, Munda and Bhumij of the Chota Nagpur plateau. The most well-known form, however, is the Maharashtran *kachchha* style which is similar to the *nivi* drape except that the free end of the front pleats is drawn between the legs and tucked into the back waist. Unlike the *nivi*, however, all *kachchha* drapes require 8 to 9 metres (26 to 30 feet) of cloth in order to make the trouser-like elements. They also have the distinction of being perhaps the oldest sari style depicted in the archaeological record (the Shunga terracotta illustrated on p. 10 shows a version of it).

Front Pleats The upper, inner edge of the sari is tucked in at the right front hip with the left hand, and the upper border tucked around the waist into the petticoat string-band. One half to two thirds of the cloth are pleated with the left hand, and then tucked into the petticoat waistband.

Northern The remaining cloth is passed round the left hip and draped over the right shoulder from the back. The left corner of the endpiece is tucked into the petticoat waistband at the left back hip. The cloth draping the shoulder and back is pulled over the head so that it rests like a veil.

Nivi The remaining cloth is passed around the left back to the right hip where the endpiece is pleated so that it will be narrow enough to rest on the shoulder. The endpiece is draped over the front left shoulder so the end hangs down the back. In the Tamil version, the hanging end is wrapped round the waist from the right front side and tucked in at the left hip waist.

Maharashtran *kachchha* All *kachchha* drapes require an 8–10 metre sari, and no petticoat is used. The upper border is first tied tightly round the waist before the front pleats are created. The central point of the pleated fabric is pulled backwards at the hem between the legs and tucked into the sari 'waistband'. The remainder is wrapped and draped in a manner similar to the *nivi* style.

Above A *nari* (dancing woman) motif on the border of a nineteenth-century Gujarati *patolu*.

The Dravidian styles are probably indigenous to southern India and Sri Lanka, although Bengali and some tribal drapes (Santhal, Oraon) are similar, being combinations of Dravidian and northern draping styles. The pleats of the skirt are usually created before the sari is wound around the body, and are fixed against the hip on the inside so that they are covered by at least one wrap of cloth. The endpiece is usually thrown over the front of the body and shoulder instead of being wound around the hips, and is often tightly tied around the torso instead of hanging free and loose. The position of the interior pleats differs according to caste and locality, and the length of these saris varies from a couple of metres-long *lungi*-like style to voluminous 9-metre (30-foot) drapes [Pls. 5, 7].

Saris knotted at the shoulder form a distinctive group of drapes and usually require much less cloth than the other styles (one to 2 metres, or about 3 to 7 feet). Many tribal women in both peninsular India and the north-east, such as the Gonds (eastern Deccan) and Hallaki Gauda and Coorgs (southern Karnataka), and Khasi and Jaintia (Meghalaya) use this style [Pls. 20, 22]. The Coorgs[42] wear expensive 5.5-metre (18-foot) silk saris that are pinned rather than knotted, with full pleats at the back rather than at the front, while most tribal women tie short, heavy cotton saris without any pleats in this manner.

Two-piece draping styles are included in this book because many show affinities with the full-body sari. The *mundu veshti*[43] of Kerala consists of two almost identical lengths of cloth which look like a full-body Dravidian sari when draped. Similarly, the *chadar* (shawl) and *mekhla* (*lungi*) of Assam, as well as other north-eastern tribal costumes, often use matching fabrics. Tribal groups in peninsular India, such as the Khonds and some Santhali women, also traditionally wear short, two-piece outfits. In Nepal this concept is reversed: the traditional sari is about 6 metres (20 feet) long, but is only draped around the lower body; it is worn with a tailored, front-tying Tibetan-style blouse [Pl. 23].

***Odhnis* or half-saris** are commonly found in the west, particularly in Gujarat, Rajasthan and Haryana, and are worn with either the *ghaghra* or *lungi*[44] [Pls. 26, 30]. Although increasing numbers of rural, ethnic and tribal women in western and central India are now wearing the full-body sari instead of these outfits,[45] they are often draping them in styles similar to the *odhni* drape, a style normally known as Gujarati. As with the two-piece garments, traditional *odhni* designs and motifs are now being transferred to locally made saris, further blurring the transition from *odhni* to sari.

Draping styles influenced the way India's regional saris were woven and embellished, just as the natural environment, history and culture also had an impact. Now the subcontinent is going through rapid technological, economic and social changes, the sari is proving to be a still-thriving part of Indian material culture. The regional designs, fabrics, and even draping styles of South Asia's saris retain echoes of a past that was possibly ancient when the Indo-Aryans arrived, yet they are as modern today as any clothes being worn by women in New York, Paris or Tokyo.

The *Nivi* Style

The *nivi* style of sari drape is now so ubiquitous among urban and middle-class Indians that many people are not aware that there are hundreds of other ways to drape a sari. In most regions, women only began to adopt this style in the 1920s and 1930s.

1 *Top* Tamil ladies wearing saris draped in the *nivi* style, with garlands of fresh flowers (*kanakambara*) in their hair – a traditional and commonly worn ornament in southern India. Madapuram, south Tamil Nadu.

3 *Bottom* Women cooking food during a festival at the Mahakaliamman Temple in Madapuram, with saris draped in the Tamil version of the *nivi* style: the endpiece is wrapped tightly around the waist.

2 *Left* A heavy silk sari made for the pan-Indian fashion market, containing many traditional south-Indian elements, such as a finely woven border with small supplementary-warp patterns as well as a warp-faced satin-woven band along the selvage. Dharmavaram, Andhra Pradesh.

4 *Below* Is this a depiction of a sari? One of two comic low-status characters depicted in a fifth-century mural at Ajanta is wearing what may be an early (working-class) version of a sari. The narrow fabric is wound around the legs and then thrown over the shoulder.

The Bengali Drape

The Bengali drape is worn by women living in the lower Ganga area, including West Bengal and Bangladesh. It contains both northern Indian and Dravidian draping elements, with the fabric folded in front of the skirt (Dravidian) and the endpiece wound around the head and shoulders (northern).

8 *Above* Santhali women from south-eastern Bihar (Singhbhum district) wearing pink mill-print saris draped in the Bengali manner.

9, 10 *Right* Bengali *jamdani* saris are fine cotton muslins with coloured supplementary-weft threads woven in by hand. The angular patterning is created through using thicker coloured threads for the supplementary work than for the ground. Here it is draped in the traditional Bengali manner, with the house keys tied to a corner of the endpiece.

The Dravidian Style

In the Dravidian style, the pleats of the skirt are created first, so that they hang inside the sari and the skirt fabric wraps around them. This results in the upper end of the pleats being folded outside as a frill around the waist. The remaining few yards of cloth are folded in front to form a large, apron-like drape over the front of the skirt.

5, 7 *Inset above, and left* Ladies at the Mahakaliamman Temple wearing Kornad (wide-bordered) and narrow-bordered saris draped in the traditional Dravidian manner.

6 *Above* A *mubbhagam* sari, a style of Kornad sari where the two borders and field are of the same width. Kanchipuram, 1970.

The *Kachchha* Style

Saris draped so that they look and function like a pair of trousers go by many names, but are often called *kachchha*, literally, 'tucking the sari between the legs'. *Kachchha* drapes vary in complexity, but all require long lengths of cloth. Since the rise of the *nivi* drape, such styles have lost favour among many upper- and middle-class women.

11 *Above* A Maharashtran woman cooking food for tourists in Elephanta, near Bombay. Not only is she wearing her sari in the traditional *kachchha* drape, but she is also wearing the traditional western Deccan blouse known as a *khan*. Her sari is typical of some of the remoter rural areas in the central Deccan, with a plain ground and contrasting supplementary-warp and -weft patterning.

12 *Left* Some *kachchha* drapes are very complicated to tie, such as this 8-metre Vaishnavite Brahmin sari worn in Tamil Nadu and Karnataka. During the draping process, the entire sari is passed between the legs, and tightly wound around the waist. Although younger south-Indian Brahmin ladies rarely wear such complicated saris on a daily basis, they still wear them on religious and special occasions.

19

The Northern Indian Style

Throughout northern India, from Gujarat to Orissa, the sari is traditionally draped with the endpiece falling across the front of the body. In western India and the Ganga plain (where the Muslim cultural influence was strong), women also draped the sari over their heads, hiding the face, a practice still continued in most wedding ceremonies.

13 *Top* The silver *kalga* and *jhaalar zari* patterns in this Banarasi silk sari border show a distinctly Mughal aesthetic.

14 *Left* A *tanchoi* sari worn as a wedding sari in the mid-1970s. The weaving virtuosity of this sari is apparent in its double-faced, wide borders.

16 *Bottom* A gold *kincab* wedding sari woven in Banaras in the mid-1980s.

17 *Left* Artist Chano Devi is a well-known master-painter of Madhubani paintings, which are traditional to the Maithili area of north Bihar. She is painting such a picture on a white muslin sari. In eastern India, white cotton saris are traditional garb; the few coloured embellishments signify a woman recently married (bright red), older with children (blue or black) or widowed (plain white).

15 *Left* The Banaras *kincab* wedding sari of a Punjabi lady living in Uttar Pradesh in 1970, worn in traditional north Indian style, with the endpiece draping the front of the body and covering the head and face. The finely woven brocade with dense floral patterning and *kalga buta*, as well as plenty of *zari*, shows the sari's Mughal design heritage.

18 *Right* Munda women at a festival in Muingutu village, Singhbhum district, southern Bihar. The Munda of southern Bihar wear their traditional sari, the *sangol paria*, draped in the Bihari style (*sidha*). The *sangol paria* is an intricately woven textile with several features making it unique among Indian saris. Still woven in remote areas today, it is a prized family heirloom, and no two *paria* are alike.

19 *Left* This Munda *sangol paria* displays a great deal of weaving virtuosity, despite its heavy threads worked on a simple loom. The supplementary weft triangular motif, called a *singhaulia*, is a typical eastern Deccan tribal sari motif. Chondor village, southern Bihar.

Saris Knotted at the Shoulder

Most of the saris traditionally knotted or pinned at the shoulder are created by women from tribal communities which are found throughout India, such as in southern Karnataka (Coorgs), eastern Madhya Pradesh (Gonds) and Meghalaya (Khasis).

20 *Inset* The Khasi *dhara* ('silk cloth') is cut into two, each half being draped round the body and knotted on opposite shoulders. This particular *dhara* was woven in the late nineteenth century for Sarah Diengdoh, a wealthy Khasi lady who lived in Shillong, Meghalaya, at the turn of the century. It is now a prized family heirloom.

22 *Below left* Two Khasi girls wearing *jainkyrshah* ('chequered cloth'), the daily-wear Khasi garment that is draped under one arm and knotted on the opposite shoulder.

21 *Left* A modern Assamese sari woven in *muga* silk, a highly prized, golden wild silk that is only found in Assam.

The Nepali Style

23 *Below* Jyapu Newari women wearing the traditional *patasi*. Although the woman on the left is wearing the traditional colours (black with a red border) and an equally traditional white shawl, the lady to the right is more fashionable, with modern turquoise *patasi* borders and a matching shawl. Market square, Bhaktapur, Nepal.

Colour in Traditional Saris

Colour and its symbolism has played a major role in the development of traditional saris. Yellow, for instance, has religious and auspicious associations even today.

24 *Right* Santhali ladies from Halubani village in south-eastern Bihar, who celebrate the birth of their children by wearing a yellow sari with red borders.

25 *Below* A Tamil lady is rolling around the Mahakaliamman Temple in order to fulfil a vow to the local deity. She holds leaves of the neem tree in her arms because the tree is sacred to this temple. The religious and protective associations of its colour make her yellow sari the logical choice.

Two-Piece Drapes

In many parts of India a two-piece outfit consisting of a sarong-like *lungi* with a veil or shawl draped around the torso was common, and is probably the precursor to many full-body saris. Women in many communities throughout India (such as in Kerala, Assam and Gujarat) still wear such outfits, often in matching pairs, giving the overall effect of a single piece of cloth.

26 *Right* A mural painted in the Gujarati style, on a wall in the Crafts Museum, New Delhi, showing how the tailored, fully gathered *ghaghra* (skirt) and the large veil or half-sari, the *odhni*, are draped.

23

 The Western Region

The western region consists of the desert states of Gujarat and Rajasthan as well as Haryana, western Uttar Pradesh and western Madhya Pradesh. The more northerly states of Punjab, Jammu and Kashmir, and Himachal Pradesh are for the most part not mentioned in this chapter because saris are not traditionally worn there, although some of their towns have modern sari-producing industries selling to the rest of India.[1] The region is home to a wide variety of people with different religious beliefs and cultures, most of whom have distinctive traditional textiles. They include Jains, Parsis, Hindus and Muslims, as well as tribal groups such as the Bhils and Mina.[2] Yet the dominant characteristic of the traditional saris and *odhnis* of all these communities, as with all western Indian fabrics, is colour. For textile variation in the western region is determined by dyeing rather than weaving techniques, and the three major forms of Indian resist-dyeing evolved here. These are block-printing, tie-dye, and ikat, which culminates in the complex multicoloured *patola* (see p. 30). Western India's extensive embroidery traditions also emphasize colour, usually mixing many bright hues together with metallic thread (*zari* or *jari*) embroidery, and often include sparkling embellishments such as tinsel, sequins and mirrors.

This region's propensity toward colour has deep roots, for it is here that the Indus Valley civilization developed cotton-growing and -dyeing technologies. From at least the early second millennium AD, western India has traded dyed textiles to the Middle East, South-East Asia and the Far East, and later to Europe and the Americas, although most local communities maintained their own textile designs. These usually had Mughal-style or geometric patterns, unlike those created in export cloths. Today, however, modern saris are often created using the resist-dyed *saudagiri* (trade cloth) prints once made solely for the foreign market [Pl. 34].

Block-Printed Saris

No one knows when or where block-printing originated, but the late fifth-century murals at Ajanta showing textiles containing small repeat motifs suggest that such work was already being carried out.[3] It was

Opposite **27** A *patolu* wedding sari with a *popat kanjar* (parrot and elephant) design. It was probably worn by a bride from a Hindu community such as the Brahmins or Bhatia traders. Patan, Gujarat, *c.* 1875–1900.

28 *Below* The field of a *patolu* sari with a *peepal bhat* pattern. The peepal tree, with its distinctive heart-shaped leaves, has traditionally been regarded as special by many devout Hindus. Patan, Gujarat, late nineteenth century.

certainly in existence by the eleventh century because printed Indian textile fragments have been excavated from the rubbish dumps of the medieval Egyptian port of al-Fustat.[4]

Block-printed saris have been created throughout India over the past few centuries, but the western region has remained the primary area of production. Until the early 1960s, in remote and conservative areas in Rajasthan and Madhya Pradesh, various rural and ethnic groups still wore saris printed in specific colours and designs typical of their communities, but now this tradition is almost completely lost, as most women wear lower-priced mill-printed textiles, and only samples found in anthropological museum collections indicate the old diversity. Unlike other traditional textiles, block-printed saris have been almost completely wiped out by the mill-print sari industry, and the few traditional saris and *odhnis* that are still being made are usually created to 'standard' dimensions (5.5-metre, or 18-foot, saris and 2-metre, or 6-foot, *dupattas*), so that they will sell throughout India.[5]

Today, saris make up only a small percentage of India's block-printed textile industry, and most of the major block-print centres create many other kinds of fabrics, including yardage for tailored apparel and home furnishings. The two largest concentrations of block-printing activity centre around Sanganer/Bagru/Jaipur (Rajasthan) and Farukabad/Fatehpur/Allahabad (Uttar Pradesh),[6] with smaller industries in Barmer, Pali and Kota (Rajasthan), Bhairongarh (Madhya Pradesh) and Anjar, Deesa, Dhamadka and Ahmedabad (Gujarat), as well as New Delhi, Haryana, Srinagar and Jammu (Jammu and Kashmir).

Rural and tribal groups, such as the Bhamiyo agricultural community and tribal Bhils and Bhilalas,[7] traditionally wore indigo-dyed dark blue or black saris and *odhnis* [Pls. 29, 31], while higher caste groups favoured red or off-white with red and black printed designs. High-caste Hindus eschewed blue because indigo dyeing involved fermentation, which they regarded as ritually impure, but those who wore it saw blue as protection against the evil eye.[8]

A strong Mughal aesthetic dominates the region's printed sari designs, whether on tribal, rural or upper-class textiles, as well as on modern saris made for the mainstream market [Pls. 29, 32]. Borders and endpieces consist of repeated bands of undulating and intertwining vines (*bel*) of various sizes, which are given different names in different areas. For instance, the printers of Allahabad (Uttar Pradesh) and Bhairongarh (Madhya Pradesh) respectively call the larger bands and motifs *pheta* and *bel-phool-gad* or *-rek*, while narrow geometric borders and scrolls are called *kungri* and *bel-buti-gad/rek*. The term *buti*[9] is given to any small floral or vegetal motif, which is usually scattered against a plain ground, while *gad* and *rek* refer to different types of blocks used during the printing process. Ornamental frills (*jhaalar* or *jhul*) are often printed along inner border and endpiece edges, mimicking woven patterns of the same type. The endpieces may have *bel* bands repeated many times, while sari fields are often covered with a repeat design, varying from small, simple dots or geometric shapes to large complex floral *buta*[10] of the tree-of-life and *kalga* (mango, paisley or Persian *buteh*)[11] types.

Above Western region printed saris.

Top Patterns incorporating *jhaalar*, *bel-phool-gad* and *jowari buti* motifs block-printed on the border of a sari from western Madhya Pradesh.

The endpieces of some traditional saris have no *kalga* or *buta* at all, just repeated rows of *bel* and geometric bands, with or without a *jhaalar* embellishing either side: a black or dark blue sari with a resist-printed endpiece of this type was worn by Bhil women, for instance. Some saris, especially those worn by tribal and poor low-caste groups, traditionally had no obvious endpiece at all. A resist-printed dark blue or black sari, worn by wealthier Bhilalas and Bhils in Gujarat, had multicoloured *buti* in the dark blue body and only a simple line marking the edge [Pl. 31]. This is similar to *odhnis* worn by poor, low-caste women in Jodhpur (western Rajasthan), which have resist-dyed crimson star-like *buti* against the black ground of the field.[12]

Although printed saris were rarely worn as wedding saris by wealthier or high-caste groups, the Bhamiyo women of western Madhya Pradesh once wore red wedding saris with printed (black) *bel* vine bands in the borders and endpiece, and star-like lotus-pod *kamal buti* in the field. The Bhils wore a simple block-printed red sari with very fine, tiny resist-dyed or -printed *buti* (*jowaria*, literally 'barley grain') throughout the field, with a single *bel* vine band for the border and endpiece, often embroidered by its owner before it was worn.

Most of the aristocratic printed saris traditionally worn prior to the twentieth century have also disappeared and are only known through written accounts and the occasional Rajput painting. In a 1903 exhibition catalogue, George Watt[13] describes some of the finer block-printed saris coming out of Rajasthan – then considered the main centre for block-printing and dyeing – which were at that time rapidly disappearing. The village of Sanganer near Jaipur was in the eighteenth and early nineteenth centuries a major centre for very fine block-cutting and -printing, and produced fine muslin saris printed on both sides of the fabric. This elaborate work needed expertly cut mirror-image blocks to print the usually asymmetrical Mughal-style designs. Even as late as 1903 the intricacy and fineness of the blocks and overall quality of the workmanship were considered by Watt to be finer than those being produced anywhere else.[14] Although Sanganer was then well known for producing fine block-printed textiles on off-white or pastel backgrounds, local printers today create a wide range of textiles with both dark and pale grounds [Pl. 34].

Above A block-printed border design from Uttar Pradesh.

Top A *kamal* design block-resist printed on an indigo-dyed sari from Gujarat.

Left A dense *buti* design block-printed in the field of a sari from Uttar Pradesh.

Other distinctive upper-class saris included the muslins of Alwar (Rajasthan), which were printed or brush-dyed in different colours on each face of the fabric.[15] In addition, the fine translucent muslins called *masuria malmal*, for which Kota (Rajasthan) is still famous, were woven in yarn-dyed threads with different colours for warp and weft. Today, Kota's transparent muslins (often called Kota saris), which are a mix of fine cotton and single-filament silk threads, are screen-printed, woven with dyed or unbleached cotton and *zari* threads, tie-dyed or embroidered [Pls. 35, 36]. Kota saris are nationally popular hot-season garments because of their very light weight.

Block-printed silk saris are also created throughout the region as well as in Srinagar, which has a small sericulture industry. Its silk fabrics are often of low quality but they make popular, relatively inexpensive silk saris.

Bandhani Saris

The technique of tie-dyeing cloth so that many small resist-dyed 'spots' produce elaborate patterns over the fabric is called *bandhani* in Gujarat, a name which also refers to the tie-dyed fabric itself.[16] *Bandhani* is believed to have existed in India since at least the late fifth century AD because such work is evident in the fabrics depicted in the Ajanta murals,[17] but many of today's western Indian *bandhej* (*bandhani* craftspeople) trace their ancestry back only two or three hundred years, to Pakistan's Sind and Punjab.[18] Most traditional *bandhej* belong to either the Khatri,[19] Chhipa (printing), Punjabi Chavda, Rangrez (dyer) or Neelgar (indigo dyer) communities. In fact, about nine totally different social groups are involved with the production of traditional *bandhani* textiles, which is perhaps why they are still made for local communities in many areas, and why this particular ethnic craft has not been as badly decimated as the traditional block-printing industry.[20]

Bandhani saris and *odhnis* were worn by women of all religions, castes and tribes, and were made of cotton, mulberry silk, and even wool in the case of some ethnic *odhnis*. The traditional *bandhani* market has shrunk, however, because of the rise of low-cost silk-screened imitations [Pl. 45], and most modern *bandhani* saris are made with larger designs and fewer ties than in the past. Yet even today many different ethnic and tribal groups still wear *odhnis* with specific colours and designs, and *bandhani* saris are traditionally worn by wealthier, often urban, women for special occasions, including weddings.

The most important manufacturing centres are: Jamnagar (Saurashtra), which has a reputation for producing cloths of a very bright red resulting from the quality of the local water; Bhuj (Kutch), where some of the finest knots are still created; Ahmedabad (central Gujarat), one of India's major industrial textile centres where many rural craftspeople migrate for work; and Jhunjhunu, Sikar, Bikaner, Jodhpur and Jaipur (Rajasthan).

Sari and *odhni bandhani* designs fall into five main categories:

    1~ Those of two contrasting colours, with borders, endpieces and one (or more) large central medallion called a *pomcha*

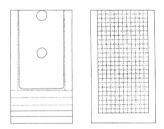

Above A nineteenth-century *panetar* sari (*left*), and a *gharcholu* sari.

Top A nineteenth-century *bandhani* border design with *matichar* and leaf patterning, Gujarat [Pl. 41].

or *padma* (lotus flower). Red and black is the most common colour combination, as in the finely made Khatriya *odhnis* [Pl. 43], but other pairs of colours are found. For instance, the *panetar* sari is a Gujarati Hindu wedding sari of satin-weave *gajji* silk with red borders, central medallions and a white body, which may contain regularly spaced red tie-dyed spots [Pl. 41]. The bright red and yellow *pomcha piliya* ('yellow veil with medallions') is a traditional *odhni* worn by Rajasthani and Haryana groups such as the Jat, and red and yellow medallion saris have also existed since at least the nineteenth century.[21] Some traditional *odhnis* do not have central medallions. For instance, a *gajji* silk *odhni* with black borders and a field containing various foliate and zoomorphic patterns incorporating elephants, peacocks, tigers and dancing women, known as a *shikar* (hunting scene) design [Pl. 40], was worn in Saurashtra in the nineteenth century.[22]

2~ Saris and *odhnis* with a single ground colour and multicoloured tie-dyed spots are common among certain ethnic groups. Their grounds are usually dark blue or black, being dyed in successive indigo baths after the paler dyes have been applied. For instance, the nomadic Kutch Rabaris create a black *odhni* (using wool from their herds) with red spots, in ritual mourning for a late medieval Rajput king who died defending them.[23] The Khoja community of Saurashtra traditionally wear black *odhnis* with yellow, white and occasionally red spots in geometric designs [Pl. 42].[24] The geometric designs and dominantly black with white colour schemes of their *bandhanis* are somewhat similar to *bandhani* fabrics traditionally worn by the Parsi community (see p. 150).

3~ Single-colour saris and *odhnis* with white spots are also common. The most famous of this type is the Gujarati sari called the *gharchola*. It is usually red but occasionally green, and is divided into a network of squares created by rows of white tie-dyed spots or woven bands of *zari*. Single motifs are created within each compartment – usually elephants, dancing girls, parrots and flowers – sometimes with discontinuous supplementary-weft *zari* woven in. The *gharchola* is a traditional Hindu and Jain wedding sari which used to be made of cotton but is now usually silk, and the number of squares in the sari are ritually significant multiples of nine, twelve or fifty-two.[25]

4~ In Rajasthan, a type of *bandhani* created by tying the entire length of cloth rather than tiny sections produces diagonal stripes of bright colours called *lahariya* (waves).[26] These saris were traditionally given as gifts during the festivals of Holi (March or April) and Teej (June or July).

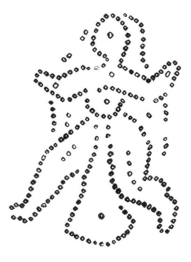

Motifs from a nineteenth-century Gujarati *gajji bandhani* [Pl. 40]: a dancing woman (*above*) and a lion, a peacock and an elephant (*below, left to right*).

5~ Today, many modern *bandhani* saris have multi-coloured stripes (*patadar*) in the border and endpiece, created through successive dip-dyeing into different dye baths. The number of tie-dyed spots in these saris is usually very small.

Bandhani spots are given a variety of different names: some relate more to size than shape, such as very small spots without a dark centre (*bindi*, *bund*); and those with one (*churi*) [Pl. 44]. Other names refer to the shape of the spot, such as *kori* (cowrie shell) for a tear-drop shape, *chundadi* for round spots and *ghatadi* for square (all Gujarati) [Pl. 42]; they are often found in traditional Rajasthani *kaledar odhni* tied in regular geometric patterns. Large square or circular spots with multiple layers of coloured concentric rings called *laddu jalebi* (coloured sweets) or *dabbi* (small box) are also found in the *kaledar*; while a group of small spots tied closely together to form a block of colour is called a *matichar*.[27]

Saris of different colours are traditionally associated with different festivals. For instance, dark blue and pink cloths were once given for Diwali (the post-monsoon Festival of Lights); while *gharchola* and *panetar*-like saris [Pl. 41] with green grounds are still given for Raksha Bandhan (July or August), when a brother reaffirms his filial ties with his sister by giving her a green sari.[28]

Although usually less finely tied and intricately patterned, many modern saris created for the middle-class urban market use traditional ethnic *odhni* and sari patterns. Cotton muslin or light- to medium-weight silk is dyed, since plain *gajji* silk is no longer made. *Gaj* is Gujarati for a yard, and *gajji* silk was originally a 36-inch-wide silk satin cloth that was initially made in China and exported to India, but was later woven in Surat by weavers who learned the technique.[29]

Patola Saris

The most time-consuming and elaborate sari created in the western region is the *patolu* (plural: *patola*), which has intricate five-colour designs resist-dyed into both warp and weft threads before weaving, resulting in a completely reversible fabric. Although they are now only created by two families in Patan (Gujarat), *patola* are believed to have been made since at least the thirteenth century[30] and have always had aristocratic or ritualistic associations. The walls of some south Indian temples, such as at Mattancheri (Kerala), and

Nineteenth-century Gujarati *patola* designs: the *Vohra gaji bhat* motif (*top*) and endpiece *tumpals* with floral vine border patterns (*above and right*)

Padmanabhapuram (southern Tamil Nadu) contain eighteenth-century depictions of *patola* designs.[31] Gujarat is believed to have exported *patola* to South-East Asia since at least the fourteenth century, the trade only dying out in the 1940s. Traditionally created by the Hindu Salvi caste and traded to South-East Asia by the Muslim Vohra community, these costly, high-status saris were worn by the Vohras and well-off Jains and Hindus (Brahmins and Bhatia traders) for weddings and other auspicious occasions.[32]

Their distinctive repetitive, often geometric designs fall into three types: (1) purely geometric forms reminiscent of Islamic architectural embellishments and *ajrak* (complex geometric print designs of the Sind), such as the *navaratna bhat* (nine jewels design); (2) floral and vegetal patterns which, like the former, catered to the needs of the Muslim market which eschewed depictions of animals and people, such as the *Vohra bhat* (Vohra community design), *paan bhat* (paan leaf or peepal tree leaf design) [Pl. 28], and *chhaabdi bhat* (floral basket design); and (3) designs depicting such forms as the *nari* (dancing woman), *kunjar* (elephant) and *popat* (parrot) [Pl. 27]. *Patola* made for the South-East Asian market often had large triangular *tumpals*[33] resist-dyed into the endpiece, a pattern missing from most *patola* made for the Indian market. Only the Vohra Muslims used a version of it in their wedding saris.

A silk ikat sari industry has recently developed in Rajkot (Gujarat) that creates *patola* and modern geometric designs in the weft threads only. Because so much less labour is involved in making these saris, they are considerably cheaper than the double-ikat *patola*.

Embroidered Saris

The western region also has a rich embroidery (*bharat*) tradition, much of which is created by ethnic groups like the Rabari and Sodha Rajputs who do not wear saris, and whose work has not yet been transferred to modern 'designer' saris.[34] Saris with metallic-thread embroidery are commonly found in the west, although most of this type of work is created throughout northern India [Pls. 38, 39]. Originally associated with wealthy (often aristocratic) Muslim communities, metallic embroidered saris are frequently worn by Rajputs, Lohana (Sindi traders), Marwaris (Rajasthani traders), and other wealthier, often urban, women for weddings and special occasions.[35] Some scholars believe that when the Mughal court collapsed in the late eighteenth century, court embroiderers emigrated to the Rajput kingdoms where their work continued and spread.[36] However, the fact that in the thirteenth century Marco Polo praised Gujarat's gold and silver embroidery, albeit on leather, suggests that this tradition may have already been well established prior to Mughal times.

Three types of metallic-thread embroidery are found, two of which use gold-wrapped threads called either *kalabattun* (now considered an old-fashioned term) or *zari*. One style (*muka*) requires thick *zari* to be coiled on the surface and couched with silk, and is usually worked on heavier silks and satins [Pl. 39]. Another style, called *kamdani* and sometimes *kalabattun*, has metallic threads

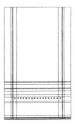

Above A nineteenth-century *patolu* sari.

Top The *chhabdi bhat* (basket design) motif, on a nineteenth-century Gujarati *patolu* sari.

embroidered directly into the fabric with both the *zari* and ground cloth being finer and lighter than in *muka* work – both chiffon and georgette are popular [Pl. 38]. Both types of embroidery are also called *zardozi* or *zardoshi*. The third type of metallic embroidery is easier to distinguish because it uses flattened gold or silver wire (*badla*) that is pulled through the fabric, creating small raised metallic 'dots' or 'knots' distributed over the cloth to form floral and foliate patterns.

Tinsel Saris

An extension, as it were, of metallic-embroidered saris are tinsel saris, generally known as *khari* or, in Saurashtra and Kutch, *roghan* [Pl. 37]. Technically they are block-printed or silk-screened, but instead of the pattern being a dye, a transparent resinous glue is printed onto the fabric and, traditionally, flakes of mica or gold dust scattered over it. Although the Gujarati name *roghan* (resin) is more accurate, the Hindi-Gujarati word *khari* (chalk) is now more commonly used throughout northern India, and *khari* has become almost synonymous with tinsel work. Often the resin is dyed, creating a thick coloured pattern with or without the sparkling particles, and this type is commonly found in inexpensive *odhnis* in the western deserts.[37] Today, synthetic gold-coloured paints and particles are commonly used to create tinsel saris, while a thin white *khari* is silk-screened to form imitation *bandhani* spots on coloured fabrics [Pl. 45].

Khari work is created in most block-printing centres of western India as well as in the Ahmedabad mills, and today most tinsel saris are associated with less affluent women, although in the past wealthier ladies wore *khari* saris sprinkled with gold dust.[38]

Gujarati Brocades

Although there have been recent attempts to revive the Gujarati figured silk ('brocade')[39] industry which once thrived in Surat and Ahmedabad, today it is virtually extinct. It fell victim to early twentieth-century upper-class fashions changing from the Mughal *kincabs* (figured cloths with more *zari* thread than silk) [Pls. 15, 16] to plainer fabrics, as well as to the removal of much of the traditional Muslim client base that used these textiles, as they moved to Pakistan prior to Independence in 1947. Although Surat continued producing figured *zari* yardage into the mid-1950s, the quality and variety had noticeably declined.[40] These silks were still fine enough in 1903 to win all the prizes for brocade fabrics during the exhibition recorded by Watt (see Note 13), yet even then the quality was declining. Watt states that the older eighteenth- and nineteenth-century *kincabs* were 'infinitely superior to the modern glaring colours and wallpaper designs' of early twentieth-century samples.[41]

These old brocades had such distinguishing characteristics as (1) *buti* woven into the field in the warp direction instead of the weft, resulting in their lying horizontally instead of vertically on the sari when draped; and (2) floral designs woven in coloured silks against a golden (*zari*-woven) ground fabric. Although such 'inlay' work is a common feature of many western Deccan figured silks, the Gujarati work usually had leaves, flowers and stems outlined by a fine dark line.

Gujarat   Rajasthan

Opposite **29** *Above* The fact that the traditional designs of many Bhil saris are in the Mughal style shows how well entrenched the Mughal aesthetic is in the western region. Elsewhere in India, most tribal and ethnic saris do not carry this type of pattern. Ahmedabad, Gujarat, 1954.

30 *Inset, below left* Gujarati women wearing the traditional *ghaghra* (gathered skirt) and *odhni* (half-sari, or veil) of the western region. Rajkot, Saurashtra, Gujarat.

31 *Below right* Saris and *odhnis* worn by poorer Bhil and rural women in the western region may not have an endpiece, as is the case with this heavy cotton, resist-printed *odhni* made for the western Gujarati rural market. Rajkot, 1994.

Printed Saris

Most hand-printed saris are today made for mainstream urban markets, as the traditional prints created for rural, ethnic and local communities in western India have been almost completely replaced by factory-made products.

32 *Left* A hand-spun cotton *khadi* sari with a silk-screened pattern typical of the Mughal style, with intricate, three-dimensional floral and vegetal patterns created in intertwining scrolls and the distinctive *kalga buta* motif.

33 *Below left* A silk sari with both resist- and direct-printed designs in the Mughal style, made in Sanganer, Rajasthan, in 1993.

34 *Below right* The design of this modern *saudagiri* ('trade') print sari used to be printed and hand-painted onto cloths exported to Thailand and South-East Asia during the eighteenth and nineteenth centuries.

Kota Muslins

Traditionally from Kota, Rajasthan, Kota muslins are now also made in western Madhya Pradesh and Uttar Pradesh. The cloth is woven with alternating cotton and silk (or synthetic) threads in an open weave ideal for India's hot summers.

35 *Inset* A white Kota muslin sari embellished with coloured *chikankari* embroidery. White is the traditional colour worn by widows in northern India.

36 *Left* This muslin, made in Kota in 1980, was woven with a mixture of yarn-dyed threads and *zari*.

Zardozi and Tinsel Saris

Zardozi is gold-thread embroidery. It has traditionally featured in the wedding saris of aristocrats and other very wealthy people since at least the nineteenth century, and is still used today in the saris of some western Indian communities.

37 *Bottom* A tinsel sari. In the past, wealthy women wore saris embellished with crushed gold leaf sprinkled on resin that had been printed on the cloth in a pattern. The name of the resin, *roghan*, is also given to these saris, and today it is commonly dyed gold or other bright colours. Tinsel-work saris are now usually only worn by poor women.

38 *Below right* Modern *zardozi* saris, such as this wedding sari made in Delhi in 1985, are usually embroidered with finer threads on chiffon and other delicate fabrics.

39 This *zardozi* sari was the wedding sari of Uma Devi, daughter of a wealthy Zamindar (landlord), who was married in 1933, at thirteen. Her family later burned most of the sari to retrieve the gold from which the thread and sequins were made (a common practice throughout much of India until recent years). This section, however, was saved as a memento. The peacocks featured here are actually only 4 centimetres long.

Bandhani Saris

Bandhani (tie-dye) work is traditional in western India and appears in many saris used for special and ritual occasions.

40 *Left* A *bandhani odhni* of silk satin (*gajji*) with a *shikar* (hunting scene) design. Saurashtra, Gujarat, late nineteenth century.

41 *Below* A *raksha bandhan* sari is given to a Gujarati woman by her brother during the festival of the same name (July/August). This sari was created on silk satin in the late nineteenth century, in Saurashtra. The extremely fine dots (*chundadi*) (**44,** *right*) were all tied by hand.

42 *Top, right* An *odhni* traditionally worn by women of the Khoja community. Saurashtra, late nineteenth or early twentieth century.

43 *Top, far right* A *gajji* silk *bandhani odhni* traditionally worn by women of the Khatri community, Gujarat's traditional dyers, weavers and *bandhej* (tiers). Kutch, Gujarat, late nineteenth century.

45 *Far right* A modern Rajasthani sari dyed in traditional local colours with white spots (*churi*) block-printed in the border, and screen-printed in the field. Udaipur, Rajasthan.

The Eastern Region

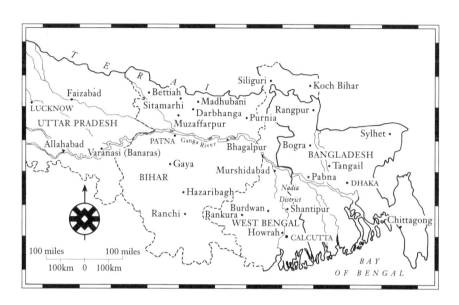

The eastern region covers the lower reaches of the Ganga plain and delta, and consists of the Indian states of West Bengal, Bihar and eastern Uttar Pradesh, as well as the nation of Bangladesh. Two and a half thousand years ago it developed a distinctive culture that dominated most of the subcontinent and profoundly influenced all of Asia, because the prince who became the Buddha lived here.[1] Some two hundred years after his death, the small kingdom of Magadha in central Bihar became the base of the Mauryan and Shunga empires (320–50 BC)[2] and over the following twelve hundred years eastern India remained the centre of Buddhist and classical Hindu culture. It was only with the arrival of Muslim invaders from Afghanistan in the late twelfth century[3] that eastern India lost its political and cultural dominance. Nevertheless, the origins of many of eastern India's traditional regional textiles can be traced back to the pre-Islamic period.[4]

Many of this region's indigenous saris disappeared even before the effects of the British industrial revolution were felt. When the East India Company entrenched itself here during the eighteenth century, its business practices[5] soon reduced once-comfortable peasants and artisans to utter poverty by preventing them from spinning and weaving their own cloth for sale,[6] causing the disappearance of many local textiles. The saris that survived were usually those created for luxury and urban markets like Lucknow and Calcutta.

Although the region was ruled by Muslims from the west since the late twelfth century, saris, rather than cut and stitched garments, always dominated women's clothing; and they were woven with designs and draped in ways that were neither western Indian nor Islamic in origin. India's three major natural fibres, namely cotton, mulberry silk and wild silk (see p. 77), have traditionally been cultivated and woven here, and in contrast to western India, the textile emphasis has always been on texture rather than colour. Even many of the indigenous fibres are textured: most wild silks have irregularly shaped filaments that are difficult to degum, producing a rough fabric, while the traditional Bengali variety of cotton (*deshi*) has a short fibre that is more crimped than most longer-fibred cottons cultivated for mechanical spinning,[7] giving a distinct crepe-like appearance to the woven cloth.

Opposite **46** The bright red colour of this otherwise traditional *jamdani* sari indicates that it is modern, as older saris of this type were dark. Bangladesh, 1980.

Texture is also obtained through supplementary-weft and -warp weaving, with the supplementary threads woven in either contrasting or complementary colours to the ground. Eastern Indian weaving techniques are varied, including (1) several types of figured and inlaid work created through supplementary-warp patterning and discontinuous supplementary-weft weaving; (2) interlocked-weft weaving in sari borders; and (3) twill as well as plain weaves. Interlocked-weft weaving[8] is found throughout the eastern half of India from the north-eastern state of Manipur to the south-eastern state of Tamil Nadu, and is commonly found in older Bengali and Banarasi saris. These saris often had straight borders, but today most are woven with serrations known in English as 'temple motifs', but usually called *kumbh* or *kumbha* (literally, 'clay pot', a fertility symbol) [Pl. 59].

Many traditional eastern-region saris display simple palettes based on the natural colours of the fibres used. Wild silks were rarely dyed, and unbleached, undyed cottons were preferred [Pl. 50]. Likewise, many of the expensive *jamdani* muslins of the nineteenth century (see p. 45) were neither bleached nor dyed; some contained the discontinuous supplementary-weft work created with the golden-coloured *muga* silk of Assam,[9] giving rise to a luxury fabric that was completely 'natural' in terms of its colour scheme. When colour was used in eastern Indian saris, it was usually woven in as yarn-dyed thread, creating contrasting monochromatic designs most often in red, black or blue against a white or natural-coloured ground. Except for expensive mulberry-silk brocades, saris with varied colour palettes were rare, although Muslim women traditionally wore more colourful saris than Hindus. White, unbleached cotton muslins and silks have a long history here; the seventh-century Chinese pilgrim Hsuen Tsang described the local people thus: 'They affect fresh white garments: they esteem little those of mixed colour or ornamented.'[10] This preference hardly changed over the next thirteen hundred years!

In the last quarter of the twentieth century, however, this tradition has almost disappeared as women wear more mill-woven and mill-printed fabrics with their western Indian designs and colours, but the aesthetic of understatement lingers on among urban women of eastern Indian origin, as many regard white silk or fine white muslin saris with ornately figured or inlaid borders as good, conservative attire for special occasions.[11] Only in parts of West Bengal[12] do women still wear traditional undyed, figured or inlaid saris on a daily basis.

Bengali *Deshi* Muslins

Because West Bengal and Bangladesh make up a continuous geographic, cultural and linguistic zone (Bengali is spoken throughout and the Ganga delta spreads across both areas), the traditional textiles are essentially the same for both. Consequently, the term 'Bengali' is here used to refer to the entire Ganga delta region, and the political names are only applied when there is a need to be more geographically specific.

Bengal has been famous for its fine, transparent cotton muslins for millennia. Bengali cotton was mentioned in the ancient legal

West Bengal   Bangladesh

document, the *Arthashastra* (*c*. 200 BC),[13] and in the anonymous first-century AD Roman text, *The Periplus of the Erythrean Sea*, which noted that the finest muslins from India were 'Gangetic muslins' from the delta area.[14] However, the everyday muslins worn by Bengali women, often called *deshi* muslins, were usually heavier and more opaque [Pl. 54], although today many handloom weavers are producing semi-transparent *deshi* saris with relatively high thread counts because mill-made saris have taken over most of the market for cheaper, heavier, daily-wear textiles.

The traditional *deshi* muslin sari is the archetypal sari of the eastern region. Its design is usually simple and understated, with colour added through discrete supplementary-warp or -weft patterning. The body is usually white or unbleached cotton with a narrow border (*kinara*, *kora*) and a short endpiece (*anchal*, *anchala*), woven as a series of narrow stripes of yarn-dyed threads [Pl. 53]. Today, most are woven in Shantipur and Dhaniyakhali (West Bengal), and in Pabna, Tangail, Demra, Bajitpur and Dhaka (Bangladesh). Muslims (Julahas) and Hindus (Tantis) are the traditional weavers, with a poorer Hindu caste, the Jaggis, weaving inexpensive saris made of a mixture of cotton and hemp for local low-income markets.

There are three types of *deshi* muslins: (1) plain-woven fabrics with warp and/or weft stripes created by yarn-dyed fibres;[15] (2) others with decorative, contrasting borders woven with supplementary-warp threads, usually of silk [Pl. 53]; and (3) a more complex type incorporating both of the above, often woven in twill as well as plain weaves [Pl. 51]. Muslin saris with extensive supplementary-warp border designs, often in fine repeat patterns, and sometimes with twill-woven checks and stripes in the body, are characteristic of Tangail, although similar saris are now made in Dhaniyakhali, where they are regarded as daily-wear saris. These 'Tangail saris', incidentally, should not be confused with the modern Indian 'Tangail' *jamdanis* which have a very different appearance.

In Hindu-dominated West Bengal, saris now show a greater range of colours than in the past: bright yellows, greens, reds and blues are present, although they are rarely as saturated as those of the

Above A *bel* design on a *deshi* muslin sari border from Shantipur, West Bengal [Pl. 52].

Bottom A *mor* design on a *kore wali* sari popular in Bihar, 1954 [Pl. 54].

Below A *deshi* muslin sari (*left*) draped in the Bengali style (*right*).

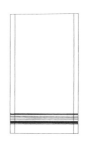

subcontinent's 'colour zones' of the west and south. Until the 1960s, many white or unbleached Bengali muslins were dipped into a wash of grey or grey-blue dye after cleaning to give them a greyish tone.[16] In addition, saris in dark colours, such as dark blue, black and wine red, were made. The locally popular *neelambari* sari[17] is dark blue or black, usually a dark blue muslin with or without woven or embroidered embellishments.[18] The price and quality of *neelambari* saris vary according to the quality of the fabric and its ornamentation, and in the nineteenth century, they ranged from very fine Dacca (Dhaka)[19] muslins (see below) with *zardozi* embroidery to inexpensive *deshi* cottons with brightly coloured cotton flowers woven in.[20]

Today, plastic gilt thread as well as *zari* is commonly found in Bangladeshi muslins, following the traditional north Indian Muslim preference for textiles with metallic-thread embellishments. The Dacca *bhiti* sari is dark (black or blue) with warp border and weft endpiece stripes of *zari* and bright colours. Another dark-coloured sari was created in the Chittagong region in the late nineteenth century, with reversible warp stripes in red, orange and green. Today striped (*duria*) and checked (*charkhana*) saris are commonly made throughout Bengal.

In most *deshi* muslins, border designs fall into three types: Mughal, geometric and Dacca. Mughal designs consist of the typical *kalga*, *bel*, flowers and foliage [Pl. 52]. Of the geometric patterns, the most elaborate were woven in the Shantipur area, with reversible borders containing at least three different batches of coloured threads that were woven to form complex patterns. The rest of the sari was of plain white or unbleached muslin.[21] Because of the complexity of these borders, a weaver would specialize in only one design and women of means would visit different weavers for saris with different border patterns. Because most of these weavers were Muslim and their customers Hindu, the market for these sophisticated saris collapsed after the population shifts caused by Partition and Independence in 1947, and the special skills needed to create them have died out. Fine geometric borders were still being woven in West Bengal as late as the early 1970s [Pl. 49], but these were usually monochromatic; during the last twenty years the quality of this kind of work has deteriorated sharply [Pl. 50].

Dacca border designs are more common in Bangladesh than West Bengal and contain rows of sharp points and zig-zags called *daant* (teeth) [Pl. 50]. They are peculiar to the Ganga delta area and do not show an affinity with designs found elsewhere in South Asia, although some reflect the angular, geometric patterns of tribal north-east India, which is Bangladesh's immediate neighbour to the east.

Dacca Muslins

The Ganga delta, most of which is in Bangladesh, is the indigenous home of the Dacca muslin sari, which was the finest of all Bengali muslins. The very finest have not been made since the late eighteenth century following the decline of the Mughal Empire and its satellite states, whose courts were the major consumers. These muslins had poetic names that were also given to the finer silks and brocades of the

Above A Tangail *jamdani* endpiece design from West Bengal [Pl. 55].

period: *abrawan* (flowing water), *baft-hana* (woven air), *shab-nam* (evening dew) and *malmal khas* (king's muslin, which was believed to have been the finest), all of which refer to the transparency of the fabric. *The Periplus of the Erythrean Sea* may have signified these muslins.[22]

Very fine, sheer fabrics have always been highly prized in India. Sanskrit poetry often describes women's bodies being revealed through the fineness of their clothes. A passage in the seventh-century AD *Harshacharita* by Banabhatta, for instance, describes the goddess Lakshmi as wearing a garment 'so thin and fine [it] shows her limbs... almost as if she is coming out of it'.[23]

By the sixteenth century, these muslins were part of regal diplomatic exchanges as well as items of royal clothing. The seventeenth-century French chronicler Baron Tavernier described such a gift to the Persian Shah Shafy (1628–41) that was 'so fine that you would scarcely know what it was you held in your hand'.[24] Even as late as the mid-nineteenth century, an appropriate test for estimating the fineness of these muslins was to see if they could easily pass through a lady's finger ring. The best of these muslins were so delicate they could only be woven during the monsoon season, when the humidity was high, and even today they cannot be mechanically reproduced because the type of cotton used to create them and the very fine yarn can only be spun by hand.

Jamdani Muslins

The most expensive and exclusive Dacca muslins were those that had a distinctive style of discontinuous supplementary-weft work woven into the fabric [Pl. 10]. It is unclear when these muslins (called *jamdanis*) first appeared, because although the name *jamdani* is believed to be of Persian origin,[25] many Hindi and other north Indian-language textile terms (such as *resham* for silk and *zari* for gold-wrapped thread) had become Persianized after the Islamic invasions, and this may be no exception. The *jamdani* weaving method does not require the use of the Persian-derived drawloom. Instead it employs two weavers sitting side by side at a simple handloom who add every discontinuous supplementary-weft motif separately by hand, using individual spools of thread called *tilis*. No special warp-lifting mechanisms are required (which are necessary in drawlooms), so such weaving could have been created long before the arrival of Persian or Muslim weavers with their drawloom technology.[26]

The labour involved in creating the finest of these fabrics meant that their cost was incredibly high, and although by the late nineteenth century these top-quality *jamdanis* were no longer made, the best that were still being woven were expensive. Watt mentions that a *jamdani* sari which won the bronze medal for muslin-weaving during the 1903 exhibition cost Rs 500 (at a time when it was possible to buy an ordinary silk sari for as little as Rs 5).[27]

Coarser *jamdanis* also probably existed in the eighteenth century because only the finest are documented as being reserved for court use, but there is virtually no recorded information about them until the late nineteenth century. Watt's catalogue gives the prices of a few

Above A Tangail *jamdani* sari.

Top A Tangail *jamdani* endpiece design from West Bengal [Pl. 9].

of these saris, and, tellingly, the least expensive – a *neelambari jamdani* at Rs 40, regarded by him as cheap – reveals that even the coarser versions were expensive textiles. But just as the very fine varieties are no longer woven, so have some of the coarser types disappeared. Many *jamdanis* dating from the 1930s and earlier are woven with heavier, coarser threads than seen today, although their open gauze-like weave often makes them more transparent than some finer modern varieties [Pl. 46]. The only low-count, coarse type still woven is the brightly coloured *tanti* sari, made as a low-cost alternative to mill-prints, short in length and width with only a few supplementary-weft embellishments.

Jamdanis are decorated with floral motifs woven in discontinuous supplementary-weft cotton, or occasionally silk or synthetic fibres, providing an opaque patterning against a transparent ground. Often the supplementary threads are thicker and heavier than the ground [Pl. 10]. In the late nineteenth century, Mughal motifs were usual, although they were often stylized and angular. Today, Bangladeshi *jamdanis* continue the tradition [Pl. 57] but in West Bengali saris more geometric, abstract and zoomorphic forms are more common [Pl. 55].

Although *jamdanis* were traditionally woven by Muslims, Hindu weavers who moved from Tangail during Partition developed India's modern *jamdani* industry. They were probably originally trained in the pre-Partition government school that was founded at Tangail in the 1930s in an effort to revive the then-disappearing craft of *jamdani* weaving. Significantly, West Bengali *jamdanis* are often called 'Tangail *jamdanis*', and they typically have many small *buti* woven throughout the field, often diagonally. They are now woven in many areas of West Bengal, in such villages as Dhatrigram, Samudragarh, Saithia, Phulia and Shantipur (Nadia and Burdwan districts). Those from Shantipur have black or dark blue bodies with bright *buti* suggestive of the inexpensive *neelambari* saris woven there at the beginning of the twentieth century. Today, the 'Tangail *jamdani*' has developed a style of its own with a distinctly Modernist Hindu aesthetic, and it is now acquiring the vibrant colours of southern India and bold animal designs of Andhra Pradesh [Pl. 58]. Many are also made in silk (including the wild silk called *tasar*) instead of cotton because silk is

Below A *jamdani* vine pattern from West Bengal.

Below right Part of the endpiece of a Tangail *jamdani* from West Bengal [Pl. 55].

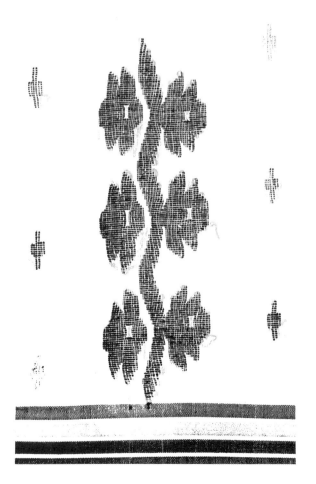

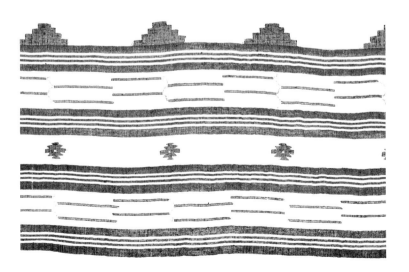

easier and faster to weave, and, ironically, weavers are usually paid more for weaving silk fabric than cotton, despite the extra labour involved in creating the latter.

In terms of colour and design, contemporary *jamdanis* fall into six categories: those with (1) natural-coloured, unbleached cotton grounds with bleached white cotton supplementary work; (2) pastel-coloured grounds with white supplementary work; (3) dark-coloured grounds (usually black, dark blue, dark red) with white supplementary threads [Pl. 56]; (4) any of the above, with coloured threads, either of similar or contrasting tones [Pl. 55]; (5) any of the above combinations with *zari* supplementary threads as part of the mix; or (6) dark grounds with only *zari* supplementary work.

The only town in India where more traditional *jamdanis* are still made is Tanda in Uttar Pradesh. Here, finely patterned white *jamdanis*, usually completely covered with vines and foliate patterns, have been created since at least the nineteenth century. Always white-on-white, the patterning is woven in thicker threads than the ground, producing the typical opaque design against a transparent cloth. Today, most Tanda *jamdanis* are woven into *dupattas* (veils worn with *salwar kameez*) or yardage, although saris of this type were once popular among wealthy older women and widows.

Bengali Silks

Silk saris are woven in regions of West Bengal away from the delta, in the northern (Murshidabad) and south-western districts (Burdwan, Bogra, Bankura and Midnapur). Saris with white, undyed fields and simple coloured borders are common, being known as *gorad*[28] or *puja* saris, the latter because of their ritual associations [Pl. 63]. The wedding robes described in many medieval Sanskrit documents reflect this aesthetic,[29] and until recently red-bordered, white silk saris were often worn by high-caste Bengali women during marriages. Such saris were also traditionally worn on important ceremonial and religious occasions such as the annual Durgapuja held during the autumnal Navaratri (nine-night) festival, which culminates in a clay statue of the goddess Durga being immersed in the Ganga on the tenth day. In some Bengali towns the statue is draped in this sari and, in the past, the local raja would be ritually draped in it during a pivotal part of the festival.[30]

Always of silk, *gorad* saris may be created from either mulberry or *tasar*; the term *gorad*, meaning white, refers to undyed rather than just white silk. Sometimes the triangular *kumbh* are added, especially to those with interlocked-weft borders [Pl. 59], while the endpiece is typically small, consisting of the usual cluster of yarn-dyed weft threads forming stripes. The overall quality of the fibres and weaving is usually what distinguishes different *gorad* saris from each other.[31]

A popular nineteenth-century figured silk was the Baluchar sari [Pl. 62], an elaborately woven brocade known to have been made at least as early as the mid-eighteenth century through to about 1900 in the villages surrounding Baluchar (Murshidabad district). This is the only Bengali sari created on the drawloom, which contains a complicated mechanism for weaving multi-warp and multi-weft

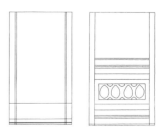

Above A *gorad puja* sari (*left*) and a Baluchar sari.

Top The border of a Baluchar sari from Bankura, West Bengal [Pl. 62].

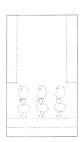

Above A *kantha* embroidered sari.

Top Two kinds of *buti* motif, from a Baluchar
sari, West Bengal [Pl. 62].

figured textiles. It is believed that this loom was developed in Persia in about AD 300, and the technology arrived in India during the influx of immigrants following the Islamic invaders sometime between 700 and 1200. Baluchar saris are similar in appearance and in weaving techniques to many Banaras brocades, although they never contain *zari* threads, only silk. They have intricate supplementary-weft or -warp borders and endpieces created in untwisted silk threads of colours that contrast with the ground, with elaborate floral borders [Pl. 61], *buti* in the field and a row of large floral *kalga* in the centre of the endpiece. The *kalga* are characteristically surrounded by up to three box-like rows containing a repeat motif of human figures usually placed within architectural arcades [Pl. 62]. The figures are commonly involved in such activities as smoking a hookah, riding a train, or smelling a flower, and are often dressed in Mughal-style or European clothes. The grounds of these saris are usually dark (often shot with different-coloured weft and warp threads), with purple, dark brown and dark red being common, while the wide range of colours found in the supplementary threads were always lighter, such as white, yellow, orange and pink.

In 1958, weavers began creating these saris again in Bishnupur. Woven on jacquard looms instead of drawlooms, they were originally replicas of the nineteenth-century originals in terms of the types of threads, colours and designs used [Pl. 61],[32] but now more 'fashionable' versions are woven, depicting, among other things, scenes from the *Ramayana*, flowers and birds, with usually only two colours being used to create the entire sari [Pl. 60].

A traditionally simpler version of these saris, which may have been the ancestor of the ornate Baluchar, is a group of silk saris called *butidar* saris. Like the Baluchar, they are figured silks but usually have supplementary-warp not supplementary-weft borders, and discontinuous supplementary-weft *buti* in the field. The designs were created in contrasting colours to the ground; usually only two colours were used, often a combination of red or dark pink and white (undyed) silk. Because these saris were less expensive and consequently less valued than the Baluchar, very few remain, but those that have found their way into museum collections show finely woven patterns that are a mixture of geometric (often with *daant* borders) and floral patterning. They were called *butidar* because of the volume of small supplementary-weft *buti* woven in the field.[33]

Embroidered Saris

Eastern India also has a strong embroidery tradition. During the sixteenth and early seventeenth centuries the Portuguese imported embroidered quilts from Bengal,[34] while in the eighteenth and nineteenth centuries, cotton and silk appliqués were created in Bihar. Various kinds of cotton-on-muslin, silk-on-muslin and *zardozi* embroideries were also commercially manufactured throughout the region. Yet by the early twentieth century, many of these commercial enterprises had declined because of changes in fashion, and today the most well-known embroideries come from the traditional domestic, as opposed to commercial, arena. It is also these embroideries that government and non-government aid organizations are encouraging as a source of income for poor rural women.

In the second half of the twentieth century, the most famous Bengali embroidery is the *kantha*, a folk-art quilt made from old saris and *dhotis*, created in Bangladesh, West Bengal and parts of Bihar (where they are called *sujani*). The embroidery is a simple running stitch in contrasting colours on a natural-coloured ground, depicting figures, animals and foliage in lively folk-art designs. Since the late 1980s, so-called '*kantha* saris' [Pl. 70] embroidered in the *kantha*-style running stitch have been created by local rural women, usually with stencilled designs supplied by professional designers [Pl. 71]. The embroideries often mimic nineteenth-century *kantha* designs and are created on *tasar* or mulberry silk.

Another type of embroidered sari traditional to Dacca is still produced there. Made of fine *jamdani*-quality muslin embroidered with coloured floss silks, it is called *reshmi karchopi*, literally a silk-embroidered sari. In 1903, Watt described it as being 'done in blue, purple, green, scarlet and gold worked by satin stitch into large rosettes',[35] the same style found in *muga* silk-embroidered samples in J. Forbes-Watson's extensive survey and collection of Indian textiles of the mid-1860s.[36]

In Bihar, embroidered and appliquéd textiles are also known to have been created since at least the seventeenth century;[37] and embroidered wedding saris are traditionally worn by high-caste brides.[38] The embroideries and appliqués emphasize form and texture rather than colour, and although colours often contrast, they are not richly polychromatic as in the west. Traditional Bihari appliqués often have finely detailed white embroidery or appliqué placed against a dark blue or bright red background, with meandering designs [Pl. 66] given extra texture through the addition of raised embroidery stitches, tapes and buttons. Today, however, wider ranges of colour are used, although they are still relatively subdued, such as maroon against olive green, black on green, or grey upon red. Although local cottage industries have developed to create these appliqués for the commercial market [Pl. 68], most are still being sewn by high-caste Bihari women in the northern and north-western parts of the state for family use, and designs are still passed down from mother to daughter.

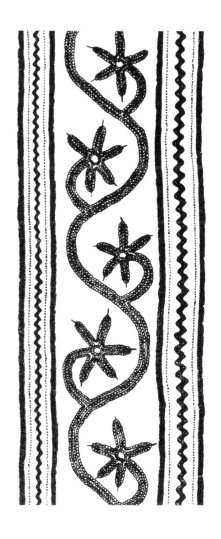

Above A *kachida* (embroidered) border with rickrack appliqué, north Bihar, c. 1914.

Left The border of a *kantha* sari from West Bengal [Pl. 70].

The most common appliqué style worked on saris involves a cloth of contrasting colours cut into repeated motifs. This may be the style mentioned by Grierson in 1885 when he described a form of appliqué called *sorahi* as 'a piece of calico cut into an ornamental shape and appliquéd onto the shoulder of a coat'.[39] The designs are distinctive to the area, with angular shapes and large, intricately convoluted curves, depicting stylized birds, creeping vines, leaves, and even rows of figures, although they are often so abstracted it is difficult to tell at first glance what the shapes represent. The best of these appliqués have a flowing, lyrical quality [Pl. 66].

In addition, a *zari*-embroidered sari with appliquéd gold braid, called a *gota* sari, traditionally played an important role in the higher-caste Bihari bride's wardrobe during the wedding ceremony [Pl. 67]. In fact, Banaras brocades were traditionally not considered the correct wedding apparel among Bihari Bhumihar Brahmins (landowning Brahmins), although they are commonly worn today.[40] *Gota* saris are now made of red silk, although they used to be made of cotton, upon which extensive *zari* embroidery and appliquéd *gota* were added [Pl. 69]. (*Gota* is the name of a narrow braid with a warp of flattened gilded silver wire, known as *badla*, and a weft usually of silk thread.)[41] Unlike the *zardozi* saris of western India, there are no sequins or tinsel, but Western Indian saris are now replacing *gota* saris in local stores.[42] The origin of *gota* saris is unclear, although Patna had a strong commercial *zardozi* embroidery tradition for many years, serving local aristocrats and other wealthy patrons during the nineteenth century. Now, however, only a few families are still engaged in this work, for the local Rajput and Punjabi markets.[43]

The only other commercial embroidery still being created that has an aristocratic history is the *chikankari* embroidery of Lucknow (Uttar Pradesh) [Pl. 64]. Once commonly made for export and commercial sale in many major eastern Indian towns (including Patna and Calcutta), this all-cotton, white-on-white embroidery is also declining. *Chikankari* is believed to have developed in the seventeenth century as a way of mimicking the expensive *jamdani* muslins.[44] The embroidery involves about forty different stitches, with six basic ones on which the others are built. Each stitch has an individual name, involves a specific number of threads and has a specific use; it is never used in another part of the design. *Rahet*, for instance, is a stem stitch worked with six threads producing a solid line of backstitch on the front of the fabric, and is used only as an outlining stitch. Finely detailed, dense floral patterns with knots, pulled network and other textural elements are characteristic of this work [Pl. 65]. In the nineteenth century, *muga* silk was also used as a filler.

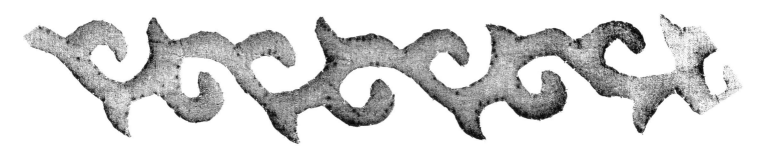

There appear to have been regional variations of *chikankari*, because Grierson noted two types of muslin embroidery in Bihar in the 1880s; one was called *silhahra*, where 'two thicknesses of muslin are sewn together. The under one has holes cut in it which are embroidered and are visible through the upper one';[45] and a second type called *bel* (apparently not to be confused with the vine pattern) where 'patterns of various leaves, etc., and not holes, are cut into the lower muslin'.[46]

Today, the predominant local commercial embroidery [Pl. 72] offered in most towns and markets is machine embroidery. Although it is regarded by purists as of a lower order to handwork, much of it is finely made, in a variety of small detailed patterns chosen by the customer.

Tasar Silk Saris of Bihar

Most of India's *tasar* silk[47] comes from Bihar. Bihar produces about 66 per cent of India's *tasar* silk and 33 per cent of all Indian wild silks,[48] although much of it is woven in West Bengal and Orissa.[49] *Tasar* silk is produced in the hills of the southern and eastern districts of Hazaribagh, Ranchi, Singhbhum, Palamu, Begusarai, Munger, Santhal Parganas and Bhagalpur, with the greatest volumes in Singhbhum and Santhal Parganas.[50] The east Bihar town of Bhagalpur is famous for its *tasar* silk mills, and although nobody knows when this industry began, it was thriving when the first European merchants arrived in the sixteenth century.[51] In about 1800, Francis Buchanan, at one time a British government official, surveyed local textiles for the East India Company and listed five types of *tasar* silk fabric woven there; they were all *tasar*-cotton mixes, usually with a *tasar* warp and mixed *tasar*-cotton weft, and four types were exported out of state. The fifth type, *kharisaris*, consisted of more cotton than *tasar* and was used by local people, being about half the price of the lowest-priced export fabric.[52] Traditionally, *tasar* cultivation and collection was conducted by various tribal groups,[53] but it is now a significant cottage industry for many non-tribal rural villagers and members of weavers' cooperatives.[54]

An eighteenth-century description of textiles offered for sale by local people to Maharashtran Jain pilgrims visiting the central Bihar town of Gaya (a historically important Jain and Buddhist religious centre) suggests how some old Bihari saris might have looked. A pure silk fabric called *sela* and a cotton *dhoti* with a *tasar* border called a *manipuri dhoti* were being sold,[55] the latter apparently similar to traditional cotton-field and *tasar*-border saris created further south in the eastern Deccan. Given the availability of *tasar* in Bihar, it is likely that such saris were also created here.

Two types of *tasar* sari are woven today: plain *tasar* and mixed *tasar*-cotton. Plain *tasar* saris made from reeled (not spun) threads are popular throughout India. Called *sania*, they were traditionally worn by Brahmin and other orthodox Hindu women when cooking and eating meals, and were usually sold by the yard from a bolt (*than*) of

Bihar

Top A negative (reversed photographic) image of all-white *chikankari* embroidery from Lucknow, Uttar Pradesh [Pl. 64].

Opposite Appliqué from a modern Bihari sari.

Uttar Pradesh

Below A screen-printed design from the field of a *khadi* silk sari from Uttar Pradesh [Pl. 47].

cloth approximately 36 to 45 metres (about 39 to 49 yards) long.[56] Traditionally, there was a whole class of *tasar* silk saris woven for the ritually important task of preparing and cooking meals. One group, called *mukta*, was made from a variety of *tasar* silk where the moth had cut through the cocoon and escaped, leaving the silk filament as a mass of short fibres which had to be spun. The same name was also given to cloth made from the waste silk remains of reeled mulberry-silk cocoons, which were also spun. The 'real' *mukta* saris, however, were popular among Jains and other groups who refused to wear ordinary silk because its manufacture caused the death of the silkworm inside the unopened cocoon, which is boiled to loosen the silk filaments.[57] In fact, the name *mukta* means 'freedom' or 'liberation'. The practice of wearing *tasar* silk during meal preparation may also have been practical as well as ritually correct, for *tasar* does not absorb water easily and repels stains more readily than mulberry silk – facts that were probably not lost on frugal housewives.

Today, the tradition of wearing *tasar* saris during meal preparation is rarely maintained, but most plain *tasar* saris woven in Bihar still usually have either no border at all or just a simple stripe created from dyed warp threads. The sari is judged by the quality of its threads and the fineness of its weave, with very fine, densely woven fabrics considered most superior [Pl. 56]. Using this criterion, the standard of many *tasar* saris created in the last half of the twentieth century is consistently poorer than those woven in the nineteenth century,[58] as many modern *tasar* saris use thick, heavily textured threads. (Today, most fine *tasar* cloth is sold as bolts of dyed cloth for the export and tailored-garment market.)

Local saris made from mixed *tasar*-cotton fabric are still being created, although they usually reverse the *tasar*-warp, cotton-weft structure recorded by Buchanan. Many of these modern saris also use ikat-dyed cotton-warp borders imported from Orissa (where they are manufactured in bulk)[59] and have an unadorned field. Today the cheapest *tasar* saris cost more than the lowest-priced mulberry silks,[60] which makes them no longer the 'poor man's silk' that they once were.

Khadi Saris

About 57 per cent of all the people employed in the *khadi* industry live in eastern India, with Uttar Pradesh alone accounting for 39 per cent.[61] *Khadi*, which is a popular abbreviation of *khaddar*, is the handspun, handwoven cloth that became the enduring symbol of the Indian independence movement in the 1920s (the Indian flag depicts the *charkha* spinning wheel). It evolved out of the Swadeshi movement of the late nineteenth century,[62] which emphasized the use of indigenous rather than imported products, in particular cotton cloth, as a means of regaining political and economic autonomy from the British. Gandhi pushed the idea further by including hand-spinning, something that had all but disappeared in

India by the mid-1820s, in order to give employment to poor women as well as to make a political statement.

Most *khadi* saris are difficult to distinguish from other handloom saris, especially today as much of the cotton yarn is mechanically produced rather than handspun. But *khadi* fabrics usually have a slightly 'rough' appearance, partly because they are always woven by hand on simple handlooms without any mechanical aids. The threads of *khadi* silks, however, are still hand-reeled as well as handwoven, so the fabrics have a more obviously textured appearance [Pl. 48]. Because of the amount of labour involved in their manufacture, *khadi* saris of any kind are always relatively expensive, but they have a loyal following because of the textile's political and intellectual associations, in addition to their aesthetic appeal.

Again, in terms of designs, little differentiates *khadi* from other handloom saris as they are usually decorated with local patterns. The exception are the silks which are often block- or silkscreen-printed with modern rather than traditional motifs (such as prints depicting bullock carts driven along the road or the patterns found in traditional appliquéd wall-hangings) [Pl. 47]. So, although preindustrial production methods are used to create these silk saris, their designs root them squarely in twentieth-century India, just as *khadi* itself is very much a twentieth-century textile.

Banaras Brocades

Today Varanasi, still locally known as Banaras, is the undisputed centre of India's *zari* figured-silk weaving industry; indeed, it is the

Above A screen-printed *kalga* motif on a *khadi* silk sari from Uttar Pradesh.

Top The field design of a block-printed *khadi* silk sari from Gaya, Bihar [Pl. 48].

only major centre left since the old western Indian industry has completely disappeared. Its figured silks are called brocades in India, although technically they can be classified as both brocades (fabrics with discontinuous supplementary-weft patterning) and lampas (figured silks with at least two warps and/or two wefts).[63] All of these textiles used to be woven by teams of weavers and assistants using the traditional *naksha* drawlooms, which have now been replaced by jacquard equipment.

Judging from several early first-millennium Buddhist texts that mention Banaras fabrics, Varanasi seems to have been a centre of fine textile weaving for at least two millennia,[64] although it is unclear whether these textiles were of silk or cotton. Nowadays, and during the past few centuries, its weavers are almost exclusively Muslim, belonging to the Julaha community, although they prefer to call themselves 'Ansari', meaning 'weaver'.[65] They are well known for their entrepreneurial spirit and marketing acumen coupled with a high level of technical and aesthetic skill, for they take pride in finding new markets and developing new textiles.[66] No one is really sure when the ancestors of today's weavers first settled here, but they most probably arrived during one of the periodic migrations that have occurred from the Middle East and western India since the early second millennium AD. Some Varanasi weavers trace their history back as far as AD 990,[67] which is about the period that the *naksha* drawloom is believed to have been introduced into India.

Banaras brocade saris vary tremendously because weavers create different products to suit different regional markets and changing fashions, but several weaving and design characteristics distinguish them from other Indian brocades. (1) The supplementary thread designs, including dense border patterns, are almost always woven as discontinuous supplementary-weft with the highly decorated endpiece usually ending abruptly in a strip of unembellished cloth 15 to 40 centimetres (6 to nearly 16 inches) long [Pl. 75]. (2) The designs, and consequently the threads, are usually extremely fine, with thread sizes ranging from medium to the finest on the market [Pl. 85]. (3) There are exceptions, but most brocades usually have strong Mughal design influences, such as intricate intertwining floral and foliate motifs, *kalga* and *bel*. A characteristic motif found along the inner and sometimes outer edges of borders is a narrow fringe-like pattern that often looks like a string of upright leaves, called a *jhaalar* (frill). This is almost a signature of a Banaras brocade, for other weaving centres rarely depict it as finely as do Varanasi looms [Pl. 13]. (4) Most Banaras brocade motifs are densely patterned and look three-dimensional, quite unlike the static, two-dimensional quality of Deccan and south Indian brocades [Pl. 89]. (5) Traditional Banaras brocade saris usually have subtle colours which may be quite pale compared to western and southern Indian silks [Pl. 79]. (6) Throughout the twentieth century there has also been a class of Banaras brocades that is embellished with patterns from distinctly Western (European, American) design schools, ranging from mid-Victorian Naturalist through to late twentieth-century Modernist [Pl. 77]. It appears that during the nineteenth and early twentieth

centuries these styles were not forced onto the weavers by outsiders, as happened with the textile-mill designs introduced in western India and Bombay; rather the weavers themselves picked them up from such sources as British wallpaper sample books.[68]

Keeping all these design characteristics in mind, Banaras brocade saris can be divided into three types:

1~ Opaque *zari* brocades. These are usually divided into two groups based upon the amount of (supplementary-weft) *zari* present. *Kincabs* are heavy gilt brocades with considerably more *zari* visible than underlying silk [Pls. 86, 88]. They are commonly worn as wedding saris today, especially in northern India, although in the eighteenth and nineteenth centuries they were popular dress (yardage) fabrics among the Muslim upper classes.[69] The other kind of *zari* brocades were once known as *pot-than*, *baft-hana* or *bafta*, but are often just called 'brocades' today. These are the classic brocaded saris associated with twentieth-century Banaras, and unlike *kincabs* have considerably less *zari* with more silk fabric showing. The *zari* usually accounts for 50 per cent or less of the fabric surface [Pl. 76].[70]

Fashion usually dictates the weight of the silk and amount of *zari* in these saris; for instance, lightweight, opaque silks with heavy *zari* borders were popular in the 1950s and early 1960s [Pls. 78, 79], whereas in the early 1990s, denser, heavier silks with very narrow borders became more fashionable.

2~ *Amru* brocades. The supplementary-weft patterning of these brocades is woven in silk, not in *zari* thread [Pls. 80, 81]. The threads may be either untwisted, giving a 'thick' line to the woven design, or they may be made of twisted yarns that produce a finer, denser pattern.

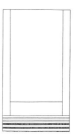

Above A Banaras brocade sari.

Top An Art-Deco style endpiece pattern on a Banaras brocade, woven *c.* 1940–50 [Pl. 77].

Opposite Banaras brocade patterns and motifs: (from top to bottom) a field pattern with *buti*; a *kalga* motif in the *konia* (corner) position, from a late nineteenth-century sari; and an endpiece design in Arts and Crafts Movement style, possibly taken from a wallpaper pattern, *c.* 1950 [Pl. 78].

Opposite, bottom A border from an *amru* sari, Banaras, 1940.

Above A Banaras brocade border pattern, c. 1950, with central floral motifs in the style of damask wallpapers popular in the late nineteenth and early twentieth centuries, and possibly taken from a wallpaper pattern. The border frill is the *jhaalar* [Pl. 78].

Khadi Saris
Khadi silk saris are made as part of the Gandhian Khadi Gram Udyog movement, where village cooperatives are set up under Gandhian principles that place emphasis on hand-spinning, weaving and embellishment. Although market forces have introduced a certain amount of mechanization, especially in cotton cloth production, *khadi* silk saris are still hand-reeled and handwoven.

Opposite **47** *Above* This *khadi* silk sari from Uttar Pradesh features a silk-screened design based on the traditional appliquéd hangings of Uttar Pradesh and western Bihar.

48 *Below* Most designs on *khadi* silk saris are modern and can be rather folksy, as can be seen from this example. Gaya, central Bihar, 1980.

One distinctive type of *amru* brocade is the *tanchoi* [Pl. 14]. This is a figured silk that is technically related to complex weaves like the lampas because it has one or two warp and two to five weft colours often in the same shed. A densely patterned, heavy fabric is created that has no floats on the reverse – the 'unused' threads are woven into the 'foundation' at the back. Traditionally, the face of the fabric has a satin weave ground (warp threads) with small patterns made by the weft threads repeated over the entire surface [Pl. 74].

Tanchoi brocades originated from China, initially being part of the nineteenth-century Parsi trade between India, China and England (see p. 150). They became popular saris among Parsis at that time, and although modern *tanchois* often use pastel or Indianized versions of Chinese colour schemes (such as combinations of yellow and purple) [Pl. 73], the few known Chinese *tanchoi* saris in museum collections[71] (which appear to have been imported into India in about the mid- to-late nineteenth century) show they were woven in very bright colours such as lemon yellow, pink and bright blue. It is believed that in the last half of the nineteenth century, three Parsi brothers called Chhoi learned the technique of weaving these brocades in China and introduced it to Indian weavers in Surat (Gujarat), hence the name *tanchoi*, which literally means 'three Chhois'. A descendant of one of these brothers continued producing *tanchois* in Bombay into the early 1950s, but when Varanasi weavers started making less expensive versions he was forced out of business, leaving Varanasi as the sole supplier of these densely woven figured silks.[72]

3~ The third type of Banaras brocade sari may technically be either a *zari* brocade or an *amru*, but the ground fabric is always a transparent silk muslin or organza with fine coloured silk and/or *zari* supplementary-thread patterning [Pl. 85]. Like the Dacca muslins, they are also called *abrawans*, and as with the opaque silks, the volume of patterning throughout the fabric may vary from barely noticeable additions to extensive supplementary work covering the entire textile. Sometimes the supplementary threads which create the patterning through their contrasting colours are as fine as the ground fabric, resulting in a transparent cloth that at first glance looks lightly printed rather than woven. Obviously, in such cases the silk and (optional) *zari* threads are the finest on the market.

A subgroup of this category is the 'cutwork' brocade. Here, the transparent silk fabric has supplementary-weft patterning woven in heavier, thicker fibres than the ground. Silk, *zari*, synthetic fibres and sometimes even wool may be used to create the supplementary-weft designs, but instead of each motif being separately woven in by hand as a discontinuous weft, the threads extend the entire width of the fabric, leaving floats at the back that are cut away by hand after weaving [Pl. 83].

Another type of *abrawan* is the *tarbana* (literally, 'woven water') or 'tissue' brocade. Like the other *abrawans*, it has a very fine silk warp, but the weft threads of the ground are of *zari* instead of silk, giving the cloth a metallic sheen [Pls. 82, 84]. Several other weights and shades of supplementary-weft *zari* are often used to create the patterning, giving a very rich effect to an extremely fine and delicate cloth.

Deshi Muslins

49 *Above* A *deshi* sari woven about 1970, whose border design is similar to the older reversible, complex geometric patterns created in the Shantipur area of West Bengal prior to 1955. Each weaver once specialized in a single design, but Partition destroyed this market. By 1970, all that was left of this tradition were monochrome border saris with fine geometric patterns. By 1990, it had virtually disappeared.

50 *Left* Two *deshi* muslin saris with traditional border designs. The black sari is woven in simple geometric patterns reminiscent of the older reversible Shantipur designs; the orange sari bears the zig-zag pattern often associated with Dacca muslins. They were made by weavers from Tangail, Bangladesh, now living in Shantipur, Nadia district, West Bengal, in 1993.

51 *Below* Weavers in Dhaniyakali, West Bengal, still create some of the finer *deshi* muslins such as this, woven in 1975. These have large, intricately patterned supplementary-warp silk borders, with field checks and stripes often woven in a twill weave.

54 *Right* Locally called *korawali*, this high-quality cotton muslin sari was made of a fabric known as *tanzeb*, in Ahmedabad, Gujarat, in 1954, for the eastern Indian market.

52, 53 A typical *deshi* muslin sari with a white cotton ground. Its border (*above*) is created with coloured supplementary-warp silk threads in a Mughal-style design, with a scrolling vine and edge pattern based on the *kalga* motif. Shantipur (Nadia district), West Bengal, 1991.

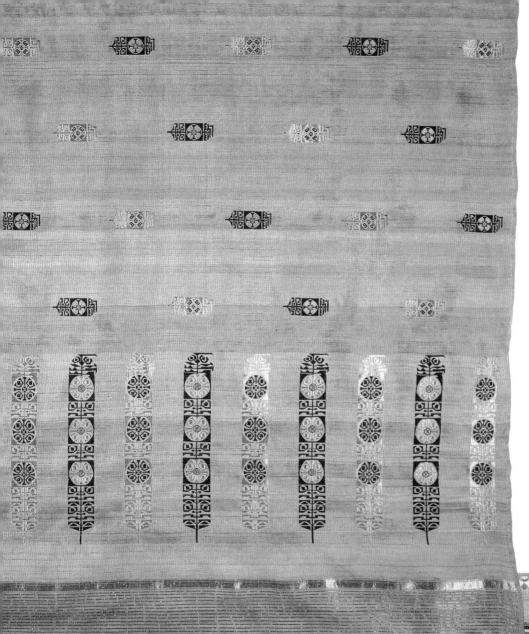

Jamdani Muslins

Jamdani muslins are fine quality, sheer cotton muslins with high thread counts, and extensive supplementary-weft patterning created in coloured cotton yarns thicker than the ground threads. The designs are typically geometric and angular.

Opposite page **55** A modern 'Tangail *jamdani*'. Nadia district, West Bengal, 1990.

This page **57** *Below left* The distinctive angular depiction of the Mughal style designs (scrolling vine and *kalga*) on this Bangladeshi sari, made in 1980, is typical of traditional *jamdani* work.

Tasar Silk Saris

Bihar is India's largest producer of *tasar* silk, and although much is exported out of state, it has a centuries-old *tasar* silk weaving tradition.

56 *Left* A *tasar* silk sari woven in Bhagalpur, Bihar, in the early 1960s.

58 *Below* A modern *jamdani* sari woven in *tasar* silk with cotton supplementary-weft patterns. The large endpiece with its repetitive peacocks and non-existent border indicate that this is a 'fashion' sari of the late 1980s and early 1990s.

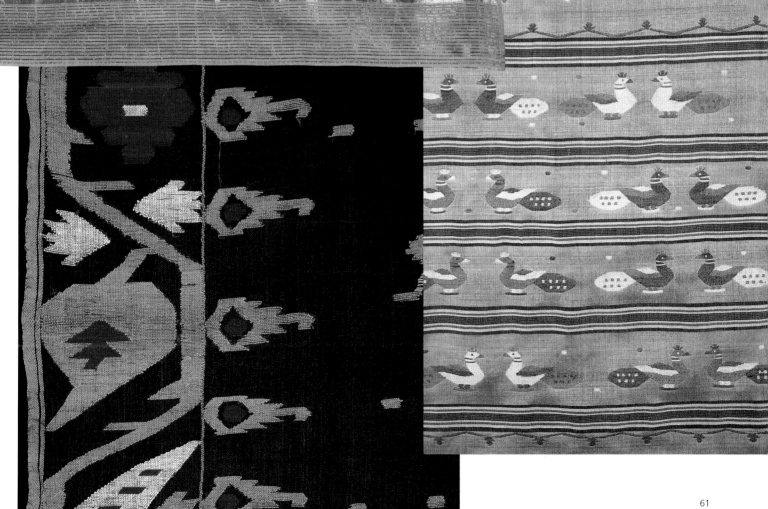

Bengali Silk Saris

This page **59** *Right* This form of *puja* sari, made of *tasar* silk, was traditionally associated with the ritually important task of cooking food. Note the interlocked-weft border of this example, created with a *kumbh* design. Burdwan district, West Bengal, 1990.

60 *Below* The border of a modern Baluchar sari showing scenes from the *Ramayana*. This new style continues the nineteenth-century Baluchar pictorial tradition.

61 *Below right* The border of a traditional Baluchar sari. Only coloured silks, never *zari*, are used to create the patterning, which traditionally shows a strong Mughal aesthetic.

Opposite page **62** A Baluchar sari woven in Bankura, Burdwan district, West Bengal, in 1993. The Baluchar has been made in West Bengal for at least 250 years, although it was originally woven in the Murshidabad/Baluchar area further north, from which it takes its name.

63 The endpiece and satin-woven border of a Bengali *puja* sari. Saris such as this, woven in Bankura in 1993, are also called *maami* saris because today they are usually only worn by older women during major religious festivals, in particular the nine-day Durgapuja (also called the Navaratri) in October.

Embroidered Saris

Opposite page **66** A Bihari appliqué made for family use in the early 1980s by Sarojini Singh, a Bhumihar (landowning) Brahmin's wife from Patna. This sari has a typical repeat design of lotus leaves created in cotton cloth and sewn upon mulberry-silk yardage. The small amounts of embroidery adding texture and highlights are typical of this style, as are subdued colours.

67 The wedding sari of Shankuntala Singh, a Bhumihar Brahmin from the Sitamarhi district of north Bihar, who was married in 1914, at fifteen. The sari, short by today's standards, is made of red gauze-like cotton muslin edged by *gota* braid. In the early twentieth century, Bhumihar Brahmins, who grew most of the world's indigo, were usually very prosperous. The simplicity of such wedding saris belied the wealth of their wearers: the gold jewelry that the bride would have worn at this time would have weighed several kilos. By the 1920s many Bhumihars had lost their wealth owing to the invention of much cheaper synthetic indigo.

68 *Inset* Women making appliqué bedspreads using traditional local motifs, as part of a government-sponsored programme encouraging cottage industries. Patna, Bihar.

64, 65 A cotton muslin sari with *chikankari* embroidery. Developed in the eighteenth century to replicate the more expensive *jamdani* textiles worn by the aristocracy, it became a complex artform with many types of tiny stitches producing various textured effects. This sari, made in Lucknow, Uttar Pradesh, in 1989, utilizes embroidery techniques once commonly used throughout the eastern region. One such is known as 'shadow work', whereby translucent muslin is embroidered with opaque thread: extra 'depth' is given to certain areas by criss-crossing the thread against the back of the cloth, creating a shadow-like effect.

69 *Right* A *gota* wedding sari of the mid-1970s. This *zardozi* embroidered sari was worn by a Bhumihar Brahmin lady from Sitamarhi district. It was made of silk instead of cotton, and most of its gold work was couched *zari* thread instead of the more traditional *gota* braid. Patna, Bihar, 1975.

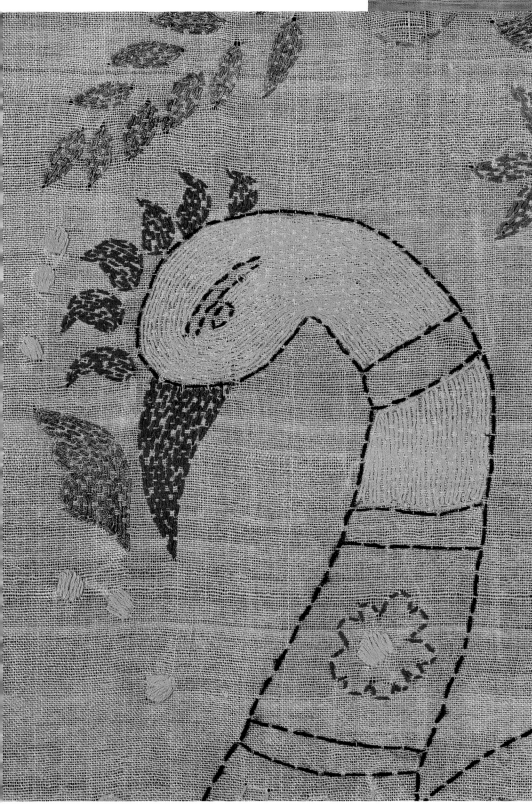

70, 71 *Above and left* A modern *kantha* sari, embroidered with mulberry-silk threads upon a *tasar* silk ground. *Kantha* is a running stitch embroidery used to make elaborately decorated quilts in the Bengal/Bihar area. This rural craft was in recession in the mid-twentieth century, until various government programmes (in both India and Bangladesh) started resuscitating it. It is now a cottage industry that produces many kinds of products, one of the more modern being the *kantha* sari. Although some *kantha* saris are embroidered with traditional nineteenth-century quilt motifs, many are created by professional designers for the mainstream urban market, such as this one, which was embroidered in the early 1990s.

72 *Below* Machine-embroidered saris have been available since at least the 1940s, when this sari was made. Despite their lack of glamour, many of the machine embroideries available in the region's market towns are well made, usually being created to the customer's specifications. This sari contains such regional characteristics as appliquéd braid. Patna, Bihar.

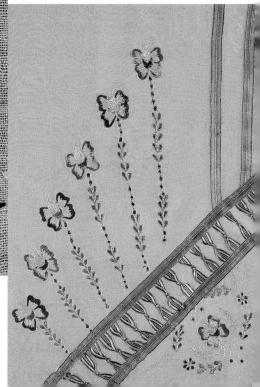

Banaras Brocades

Banaras is now the undisputed centre of India's silk brocade industry. The patterning is all supplementary-weft work, which results in a section of plain silk left at the end of the endpiece (see Pls. 75, 76). The silk and *zari* threads are usually the finest on the market, and the Mughal aesthetic dominates most patterns.

Banaras Saris: *Tanchoi* Brocades

73 A *tanchoi* sari worn as wedding sari in the mid-1970s (see Pl. 14). Many Indian weddings last several days, and different saris will be worn for different ceremonies. Although *tanchoi* textiles are traditionally *amru* brocades that originated in China, Banaras took over the market in the 1940s and 1950s, and began to incorporate *zari*.

74 *Right* A modern *tanchoi* brocade. *Tanchoi* brocades use at least three different colours woven so that the front surface has a (warp) satin ground between the (weft) pattern elements. The back of the textile is tightly woven, without floats, so the front pattern is usually not visible.

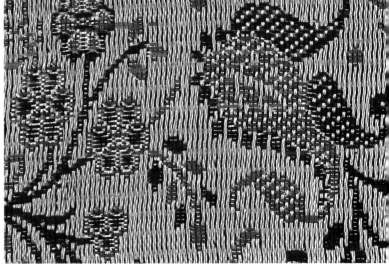

Banaras Saris: *Zari* Brocades

75, 76, 79 Typical Banaras brocade saris, with traditional Muslim colours of green and gold (*left*); with inlaid red and black silk work added as highlights to the *zari* brocading (*below*); and with traditional Hindu colours of orange and pale blue (*right*).

European Designs

During the 1890s, master-weavers from Banaras visited England, and returned with British wallpaper sample books. Because European designs were a novelty for traditional Indian weavers and their customers, the patterns in these books became a significant source of inspiration.

77 *Far left* This Art Deco pattern was woven into this sari in the 1940s, by which time many Banaras designers and master-weavers (often the same person) were familiar with European styles and could adapt them more easily to their own needs.

78 *Left* The *zari* patterning of this 1950s sari is reminiscent of both damask-style wallpapers (in the borders), and Arts and Crafts Movement floral patterns (in the endpiece).

Banaras Saris: *Amru* Brocades

Banaras has such a reputation for weaving *zari* brocades that its *amru* brocades, which do not use *zari* in the textile but only contrasting coloured silks, are often ignored. *Amru* saris appear to have been especially popular during the 1940s, perhaps because metal for *zari* was then scarce owing to the demand created by World War II and later economic dislocations in northern India caused by Partition.

80, 81 Both these examples were woven in the 1940s.

Banaras Saris: *Abrawans* and Tissue Saris

The transparent cloth of these saris, usually woven with the finest silk threads, has earned them the name *abrawan* ('flowing water'). The most luxurious, known as *tarbana* ('woven water') or 'tissue' saris, have a fine silk warp with a *zari* weft, giving them a metallic sheen. Different coloured *zari* threads are woven into supplementary-weft patterns upon the sheer ground.

82 *Above* A tissue brocade sari woven in the late 1970s.

83 *Above right* The back of a Banaras brocade sari. The supplementary threadwork of many Banaras brocades is woven as floats across the back. These are kept in place until the sari is bought, when the trader will have them cut away – hence the name 'cutwork sari'.

84 *Right* A tissue brocade sari woven in the early to mid-1950s.

85 *Bottom* A tissue brocade wedding sari woven in the 1940s. The dark brown of the silk warps was then a popular textile colour.

Banaras Saris: *Kincab* Brocades

Kincab brocades are largely covered by *zari* patterning, and in some cases the underlying silk cloth is hardly visible. They are commonly worn as wedding saris throughout South Asia, and families from all over India will travel to Banaras to buy a bride's trousseau and wedding clothes.

86 *Top left* A *kincab* wedding sari woven in the mid-1980s.

87 *Above* The *kincab* wedding sari of a Punjabi lady married in 1970. The black silk brocading in this sari is unusual, for among many northern- and eastern-region Indians black is regarded as an inauspicious colour.

88, 89 A *shikargah* brocade, originally part of the wedding trousseau of Shakuntala Singh, who was married in 1914 (see Pl. 67). Because of the complexity of the design, *shikargah* brocades cannot be easily reproduced on jacquard looms, and it takes a master-weaver between six months and a year to create such a sari.

71

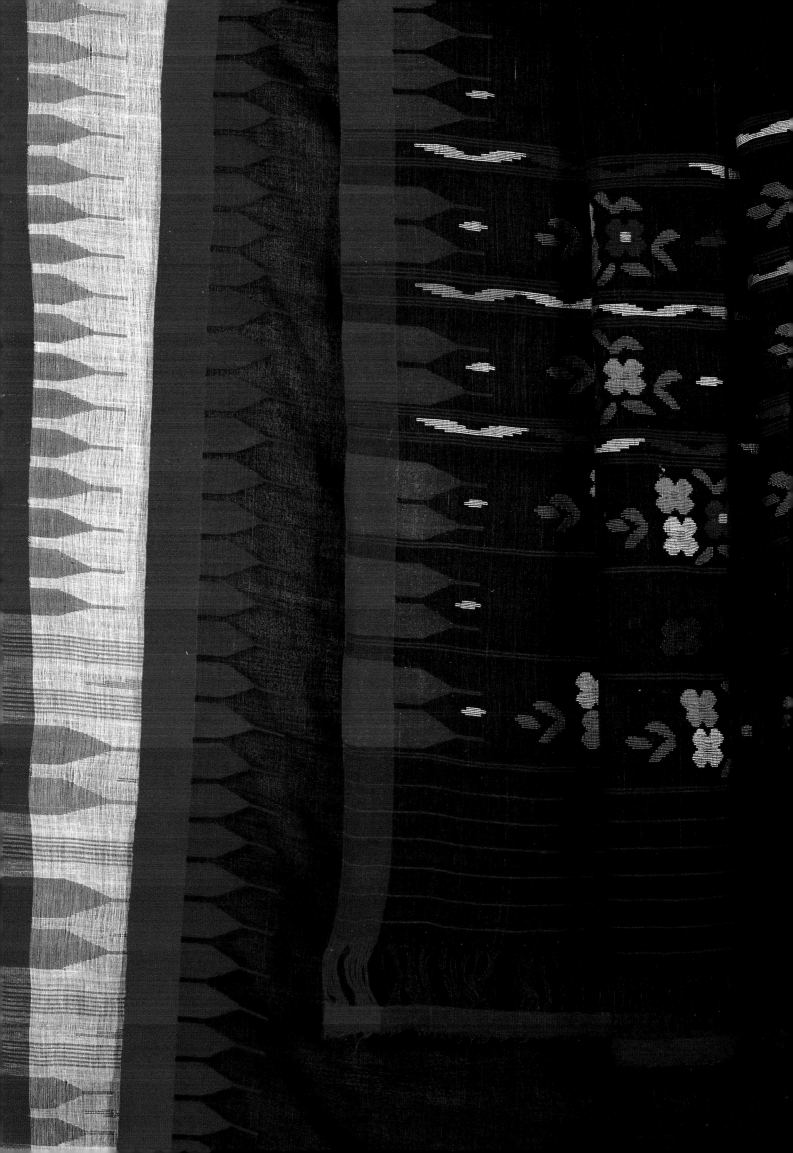

The North-East
and the Himalayas

North-east India consists of the states in the eastern Himalayas and mountains bordering Burma.[1] Of them, only Assam and Manipur have any significant history of weaving and wearing full-length saris, as does the central Himalayan nation of Nepal which lies north of Bihar and Uttar Pradesh, but such saris are now becoming increasingly popular throughout the region. Virtually all the tribes and ethnic groups that live in this region originated from China and South-East Asia,[2] and most of them speak Tibeto-Burman languages.[3] It was only within historical times that the Indo-Aryan languages began to spread in the major valleys of the Brahmaputra river (Assam), Kathmandu (Nepal) and Manipur.[4]

The region was not directly affected by the medieval Muslim conquests of the Ganga plain, but Nepal became the refuge for many Buddhists and Hindus who profoundly influenced the material culture of the Kathmandu valley.[5] Assam was affected by Bengali society as landowners of Bengali descent (Bhuyan) settled in the western Brahmaputra valley from about Pala times (AD 750–1200), while most of Manipur's contact with Bengalis and other Indians was through diplomatic exchanges and aristocratic marriages, as well as through the introduction of Tantric and then Vaishnavite Hinduism in the early sixteenth century.

Traditionally, full-body saris are not worn here. The Assamese of Ahom origin wear a *lungi* called a *mekhla* and an upper wrap or shawl (*chadar*); the Boro (Assam) and Garo (Meghalaya) wear large wraps that cover both legs and torso (*dokhna* and *dakmanda* respectively, the latter being fixed at the waist with a belt); the Khasi and Jaintia (Meghalaya) wear a one-metre wide cloth tied at the shoulder (*jainkyrshah* and *sempynwan* respectively) with the Khasi also wearing two cloths, one tied on each shoulder (*jainsem*) giving the appearance of a European dress; while the Meitei of Manipur and Tipperah of Tripura wear *lungis* (*phanek*, *pachera* respectively) and shawls (*enaphi* in Meitei). In Nepal, a tailored, tightly fitting, front-tying blouse of Tibeto-Chinese origin (*cholo*) is worn by many ethnic groups with a full-length sari (*fariya*) that is draped only around the lower body. Indian-style saris were often worn by the aristocracies of all these areas as well as by Indian women living in the valleys.[6]

MAJOR TRIBES

Opposite **90** The Moirangfee sari is woven as a fine cotton fabric, somewhat similar to Nepali *dhaka* cloth and Bengali *jamdani*. Named after the Moirangs, the valley tribe that is believed to have first woven this textile, the Moirangfee (literally, 'cloth of Moirang') probably originated in eastern India. Red borders with either dark blue or white grounds are the traditional colours for these saris. Imphal, Manipur, 1994.

Mughal designs and weaving techniques were never incorporated into local textile traditions and most weaving, textile and dress habits have more in common with those from China, South-East Asia and Tibet than mainland South Asia, although Bengali muslins had an impact on some upper-class textiles. Although traditional designs often differ from those of eastern India, the colour schemes and types of weaving found in the north-east are similar, with natural-coloured fabrics having patterns added through supplementary-thread weaving. Patterning is usually more elaborate, using a wider range of traditional supplementary colours and with motifs woven throughout the fabric, not just the borders [Pl. 93]. Cottons may be dyed red or black, especially among many tribal groups who have longstanding reputations for cotton dyeing, but wild silk is usually left its natural colour. Wild silk is abundant in this region and all three types – *tasar*, *eri* (*endi*) and *muga* – are cultivated.

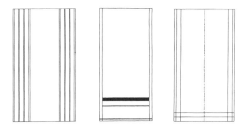

Above, from left to right A Garo *dakmanda*, Khasi *dhara*, and Tripura *pachera*.

Below A traditional Assamese sari border pattern often ascribed to the Boro tribe [Pl. 96].

Assam

Assam's complex ethnographic history is reflected in its saris (*xari*) even though they are not indigenous garments, most likely being introduced by the Bengalis who settled in the western Brahmaputra valley. The earliest record of a sari being worn in Assam is reportedly in a late seventeenth-century version of the *Bhagavata-purana*,[7] but it was probably not commonly found until the twentieth century, and even today most women ignore it.

Four natural fibres are indigenous to Assam: cotton, *muga*, *tasar* and *eri* silk. Of the three wild silks, *eri* silk is too heavy to be made into saris and is usually woven into *chadars*, but all four types of fibre are left their natural colours of off-white and shades of pale brown. Most weaving occurs in villages and towns surrounding Gauhati, with Sualkuchi to the north specializing in silk, and Nuagong, further east, specializing in cotton-weaving. Other smaller centres include Silchar, Karimganj and Uttar Gauhati.

Because the local government has been encouraging handloom-weaving cooperatives to create saris for the mainstream Indian market, this has become a significant local industry. Many commercial weavers are men, but the bulk of handloom weavers in the north-east are women. They traditionally weave textiles for personal and family use, and there is no history of caste specialization.[8] Backstrap and simple-framed looms are most often used for home and local commercial weaving, but in order to increase production, more cooperatives are using jacquard and powerlooms. The patterning falls into two types: tribal and mainstream pan-Indian – there is no significant difference in design between saris woven in cotton, wild silk or even mulberry silk.

Tribal Designs of Assam, Meghalaya and Tripura

Although Meghalaya, Tripura and Assam are all ethnically distinct, Assam often supplies the high-end textiles for neighbouring communities, such as the silk *dhara* worn by well-off Khasi women [Pl. 20]. In addition, the traditional textiles of different groups often show striking similarities, such as those of the Boro and Garo.

In general, tribal designs tend to be abstract and geometric with depictions of natural objects (flowers, leaves and animals) in highly stylized forms. The supplementary threads most commonly used are red, black, purple, white, yellow, green, and, today, turquoise [Pl. 96]. Many cotton textiles were traditionally dyed red or black, with supplementary work woven in contrasting colours, although in Assam natural-coloured grounds are still popular [Pl. 94]. Most textile designs were once tribe-specific, but constant social intermingling and trade, mill-woven fabrics, and an undiscriminating 'foreign' custom for 'tribal' textiles have caused many distinctions to disappear.[9]

Nevertheless, certain influences prevail, especially from the two major groups in the Brahmaputra valley: the Boros and Shan Ahoms.[10] The Boros are believed to be some of the earliest inhabitants of the Brahmaputra valley, as Boro language place names, such as 'Jonga' and 'Donga' are found in the *Arthashastra*, written in about 200 BC.[11] The Shan Ahoms were relatively late arrivals, originally migrating from Burma in the thirteenth century and slowly expanding eastwards until a series of wars in the fifteenth century made them the rulers of the entire valley region, after which they merged with the local population to form today's Assamese.[12]

It is believed that the Boros contributed densely woven diamond shapes and lozenges to the Assamese textile repertoire,[13] as well as a range of floral and animal forms, including a fish motif. Many Boro designs are small and repetitive, such as the *pareu megon* (pigeon's eye) [Pl. 100]; others are large, like the *pahar agat* (hill design) where each rounded triangle represents a hill [Pl. 102].[14] A motif that is regarded as peculiarly Assamese depicts birds and/or flowers on either side of a tree [Pl. 93]. It is called a 'sun-tree' design after Han Chinese (*c.* 200 BC–AD 200) patterns of the same type, or a 'Miri' design, after a Tibeto-Burman-speaking tribe from Arunachal Pradesh. Historical and cultural evidence, however, suggests that it is of Tai, and hence Ahom, origin, not Miri,[15] and even today, it is usually only woven on Assamese, not Boro or Khasi, textiles.

Garo *dakmanda* often contain elaborate, densely woven geometric designs in wide borders, such as diamond patterns and lozenges. Large floral sprays (even vases of flowers) are woven in a flowing (not angular) style in the fields of many *dakmanda*, and small *buti* are also common [Pl. 97]. The *pachera* worn by the women of Tripura tend to have simpler designs, with large angular floral forms and a border reminiscent of Manipuri *phanek* [Pl. 99]. The Khasi (and possibly Jaintia) appear to have no traditional textile designs, and the *jainsem* is made predominantly of mill-made fabrics [Pl. 22]. The much-coveted *dhara* are made in Sualkuchi, Assam, featuring essentially lowland Assamese/Boro designs [Pl. 98]. Today, the geometric 'Boro' design is common, although during the nineteenth century[16] animals such as lions and peacocks as well as foliate patterns were created.

Check patterns are common throughout this region. They come in all shapes and sizes on virtually all textiles, including saris [Pl. 107].

Above An Assamese sari with tribal patterns, and (*right*) an Assamese *chadar* and *mekhla*.

Top A traditional Assamese sari endpiece design.

Assam

Mainstream Indian Designs

Mainstream Indian designs in Assamese saris can be recognized both by their subject matter and by their flowing lines and curves. In terms of subject, the Mughal-derived *kalga* is the most obvious introduction [Pl. 103], with some expensive silk saris also woven to imitate Banaras and Dharmavaram brocades. Yet most are usually still recognizably Assamese from an angularity in many of the motifs, as well as colour schemes that include the natural colour of the silk ground upon which dyed supplementary threads are woven, especially black, red, yellow and turquoise. (Outside Assam, black is not a commonly used colour in Indian figured silk saris.) Not all Assamese designs are angular, however. Round-petalled *buti* and life-like depictions of animals and plants are common, although there is usually something in the mix that gives their origins away. For instance, Assam is the only area in South Asia where rhinoceros are woven into its saris as decorative motifs [Pl. 105]; also, *zari* was introduced into local textiles in the 1930s and even today it is only used in expensive silk saris mimicking mainstream pan-Indian designs [Pl. 104].

Manipur

Most of Manipur's population[17] live in the valley of Manipur, which, historically, was home to about seven different tribes that merged over time to form the clans of the Meitei community, the now-dominant group. The Meiteis have a literary and cultural tradition incorporating both Tibeto-Burman and Bengali-Indian elements,[18] and as in Assam, saris were only traditionally worn by women of Indian descent and the Indianized upper classes. Local women usually wear a densely woven warp-striped *phanek* [Pl. 91], a shawl (*enaphi*), a tailored top and sometimes a scarf tied around the waist.

Manipur has a centuries-old reputation for weaving fine textiles, and the complex *acheik* silk tapestry-woven fabrics, worn by Burmese royalty during the nineteenth century, are believed to have originated from the looms of Manipuri weavers brought into Burma in the late eighteenth century by King Alaungpaya (r. 1752–60) and his descendants.[19] Detailed interlocked-weft weaving is still found in Manipur's most famous, if not only, traditional sari, the Moirangfee [Pl. 90]. It contains interlocked-weft-woven triangular 'temple motifs' in single or multiple rows along the inner edge of the narrow border. These saris are made of Bengali cotton, woven as a fine muslin in the Bengali style with supplementary-weft designs created in the endpiece as a complex lattice of small geometric shapes or floral designs [Pl. 92]. The traditional colour scheme is usually grey, dark blue or white, with details woven in black, red, green, blue and/or white, although many bright colours are now found, such as an azure-blue for a ground with yellow borders.

Several different stories exist about this sari's history. One tradition describes a time when three tribes separately ruled the

Above A mainstream Indian-style Assamese design featuring white rhinoceros, deer and peacocks [Pl. 105].

Opposite Assamese-style patterning on a *muga* silk *chadar* [Pl. 94].

Below A Manipuri Moirangfee sari.

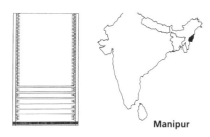

Manipur

Manipur valley, including the Moirang tribe located 43 kilometres (27 miles) south of Imphal.[20] ('Moirangfee' means 'cloth of Moirang'.) The rulers of Moirang paid homage to the king of Manipur, and in order to obtain the release of captives they had to give him handloomed textiles, including a fabric with a 'canine tooth' design which was later known as a 'temple motif'. Another legend describes a princess of Moirang marrying a Manipuri king and introducing the distinctive border design.[21] A third story tells how it was an Indian princess in the eighteenth century who introduced the design. Considering the strong Bengali appearance of these textiles, it seems likely that Indian or Bengali weavers were at some point involved in their creation.

Unlike Assam and Meghalaya, other Meitei tribal patterns, especially their embroideries [Pl. 91], have not been transferred to their saris, and most other handloom saris created here tend to have simple checks or stripes without further embellishment.

Wild Silk Saris

India has more indigenous species of wild silkworms than any other nation in the world, and consequently produces the largest range of wild silk fabrics – namely *tasar* (of which there are several kinds), *eri* (or *endi*) and *muga* silk – and the north-east produces most varieties. In fact, Assam accounts for 67 per cent of all the *eri* silk and 93 per cent of all the *muga* silk produced in India, while Assam and eastern India's Bihar together account for almost 70 per cent of India's total wild silk production.[22] Wild silk is produced in Kamrup and Nuagong districts in central and western Assam as well as in Lakhipu and Dibrugarh districts in the east.

Strictly speaking, wild silk is the product of silkworms living naturally in India's forests, although most are now actively cultivated by farmers, villagers and tribals. 'Wild silk' nowadays denotes any silk that is not produced by *Bombyx mori*, the Chinese silkworm which feeds on mulberry trees (hence the name 'mulberry silk') from which all varieties of commercial silkworm ultimately descend.[23] The product of *B. mori* (and its numerous subspecies) is different from that of all other silkworms because its silk filament (which its caterpillar produces to create the cocoon) is the only one that has a completely circular cross-section and that is easy to degum (that is, remove the binding 'glue' which holds the filament in place). The gum (called sericin) is what gives most wild silk its colour [Pls. 59, 94], for many silk filaments are naturally pure white. Unlike *B. mori*, however, the filaments of all other silkworm species are flat and tend to stick together, which, coupled with the sericin crystals adhering to them, makes fully automated mechanical reeling impossible.[24]

Raw silk is often misnamed 'wild silk'. In the silk industry, 'raw silk' refers to reeled, undegummed filaments of *B. mori*, but traders also call the spun silk fabric known as 'noil' raw silk. Noil consists of the broken ends and fluffy residue left after the long filament(s) from a *B. mori* cocoon have been reeled. Out of necessity these short ends are spun rather than reeled, just as the broken ends from wild silk cocoons are spun. These different uses of quite specific technical terms have

led to much confusion about wild silk nomenclature, especially as, by definition, wild silk retains most of the sericin on its filament.[25]

Tasar Silk

Tasar silk is produced in Assam and Manipur in addition to Bihar (see p. 51) and the eastern Deccan states.[26] It is created by several different species of caterpillar in the *Antheraea* family (*A. mylitta* and *A. pernyi* being the most common), with specific areas often cultivating different species, many of which produce different-coloured silks [Pls. 56, 119]. They feed on such forest trees as the arjuna (*Terminalia arjuna*), saja (*Toman tosa*) and sal (*Shorea robusta*), and were traditionally cultivated and collected by various tribal groups,[27] but there is now a significant cottage industry employing many non-tribal villagers throughout the north-east and eastern Deccan.[28]

Wild silk-rearing and -weaving is believed to date back to at least the first millennium BC, because phrases in the *Mahabharata* suggest that wild silk cloths were given to dominant kings. It states that rulers from a region 'shaded with bamboos whistling to the breath of the wind' gave cloth made of the fibres of insects, as well as boxloads of 'ant's gold' (*pipilika*), which is interpreted as being wild silk.[29] Some scholars argue that wild silk is mentioned in the *Arthashastra* of Kautilya (*c.* 200 BC);[30] and by AD 600, *tasar* was certainly worn in eastern India because Hsuen Tsang describes it as one of the two fabrics most commonly worn.[31]

Until the mid-twentieth century, *tasar* silk was regarded as a 'poor man's silk', as it was worn by well-off members of rural communities but not by the social elite who could afford mulberry silk. In 1900, the cheapest mulberry-silk sari recorded by Yusuf Ali in his survey of north Indian silk production was Rs 10, while a 5.5-metre (18-foot) *sania* sari cost Rs 4.5 and a mixed mulberry silk/*tasar* sari cost Rs 5. Today, however, *tasar* silk saris are usually more expensive than mulberry silk because the price of *tasar* jumped during World War II following escalating demand for parachutes and, afterwards, through various industrial uses.

Muga Silk

Virtually all the world's *muga* silk (93 per cent) is produced in Assam, as most attempts to cultivate it outside the state have failed, and the town of Sibsagar (Sibsagar district) is the centre of its *muga* sericulture industry. *Muga* silk naturally has a rich golden colour with a more lustrous sheen than the other wild silks, but is not as shiny as mulberry silk [Pls. 93, 94]. The *muga*-producing caterpillars (*Antheraea assama*) feed on a wide variety of local trees, including the adakuri (*Tetranthera quadrifolia*), chom (*Machilus rdoroatissima*) and champa (*Michelia*

pulnyensis), and like *tasar*, local tribal communities are the traditional sericulturalists, with the Boros being the earliest known.[32]

Muga silk production is probably at least two or three thousand years old: some scholars feel that the section in the *Mahabharata* quoted earlier refers to Assam and *muga* silk.[33] In addition to this, the fact that the Tibeto-Burman-speaking peoples of the region originated from China, where mulberry-silk cultivation developed in about 2500 BC, suggests that they, too, may have been cognizant of silk cultivation and weaving long before the rest of the subcontinent.[34] A section of the *Ramayana*, which was compiled during the first half of the first millennium BC, lists a kingdom with the enticing name of 'Country of the Cocoon Rearers' (Kosa-Karanam-Bhumih), lying to the east of today's Bihar (Magadha) and Bengal (Anga).[35] The first direct mention of 'Assamese silks' in the historical record comes in the seventh century AD, in Banabhatta's *Harshacharita*, in which King Harsha received gifts from the King of Assam, including elaborately woven silks, one of which had a jasmine pattern.[36]

From at least the sixteenth century, the Ahom kings were imposing strict sartorial rules on their subjects, with *muga* silk being restricted to the local aristocracy, although this did not prevent them from exporting it out of state. In the early seventeenth century, Baron Tavernier reported that *muga* silk was an article of trade in Bengal and on the Coromandel and Malabar coasts, which is corroborated by the Indo-Muslim historian Shihabuddin, writing a generation later.[37] By the mid-nineteenth century, *muga* silk was being woven into Dacca muslins,[38] and used as 'filler' thread on *chikankari* embroideries.[39] Forbes-Watson also includes samples of woven *muga* silk fabric in his collection; most, however, have bulky, crudely reeled or spun threads, which was probably not the quality worn by the aristocracy.[40]

There is no such thing as an inexpensive *muga* sari[41] and the majority are woven with a great deal of intricate supplementary threadwork (in silk, cotton, and/or *zari*). Such is the popularity of this fabric that many locally woven cotton and mulberry-silk saris are dyed the *muga* colour.

The Kingdom of Nepal

The kingdom of Nepal contains dozens of tribal and ethnic groups, most of whom have maintained their separate ethnic identities and languages, although the Indo-Aryan Nepali, the official language, is widely spoken in the valleys. The ethnic communities range from obviously Tibetan (in the high mountains) like the Sherpas, through to those of Indian origin, such as the Nepali Brahmins. Many peoples in the high mountains wear Tibetan clothes but most major groups traditionally living in the middle hills (below 7000 feet)[42] where the large valleys are located wear saris (*fariya*, also colloquially called *dhoti*),[43] which are usually about 5.5 to 6 metres (18 to 20 feet) long, or occasionally *lungis* that are sewn to form a tube-like sarong. Traditionally the sari endpiece (*pallo*) is never draped across the torso but is wrapped round the hips and tucked into the waist of the heavily front-pleated skirt that is created [Pl. 23].[44] A voluminous cummerbund (*patuka*) is traditionally worn around the waist,[45] with a

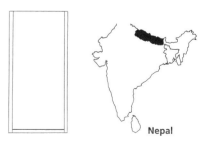

Nepal

Above A Nepali *patasi* sari.

Opposite, above A Boro/Garo-style endpiece pattern, Assam [Pl. 96].

Opposite, below An Assamese border pattern from a cotton sari, Nuagong, Assam.

Above A Moirangfee sari border, Manipur.

Manipuri Saris

The saris of Manipur are a mixture of hill tribal textiles and fabrics that probably originated in eastern India.

Opposite **91** The Manipuri *phanek*, woven on a backstrap loom with hundreds of densely packed cotton threads, is worn by many groups. The embroidery in the border is so tight and regular that it looks as if it were made by machine, but it is in fact created by hand.

92 *Below* The interlocked-weft 'temple design' and supplementary-weft floral and geometric patterning of a Moirangfee sari.

long-sleeved, front-tying tailored blouse (*cholo*),[46] and large shawl (*pachheura*). Even today, many Nepalese textiles are handwoven by women using backstrap and home-made bamboo-frame looms.

The distinctions between the dress of different ethnic groups who wear this ensemble usually relate to the types of textiles used. For instance, the Gurung, a widely scattered Tibeto-Burman-speaking group in western and central Nepal, usually wear saris (*gaun*) made of commercial fabrics draped in the usual Nepali style with a blouse of coloured cotton velvet[47] and a handwoven woollen shawl. On the other hand, many rural Newari, Rai and Limbu women in the Kathmandu valley and eastern Nepal still wear handwoven saris and a costly supplementary-weft-woven *dhaka* cloth shawl that is covered with fine white muslin to protect the fabric. *Dhaka* cloth looks like colourful, densely patterned coarse *jamdani* muslin or Manipuri Moirangfee muslin, but it is in fact an indigenous fabric woven on backstrap and bamboo-frame looms in eastern Nepal. It is virtually a national symbol today, and although saris were once made from it, it is now usually used only for sari borders.[48]

One of the most distinctive saris in Nepal is the homespun, handwoven sari of the Jyapu Newars, called a *parsi* or *patasi*, which is a heavy, twill-woven black cotton cloth with red borders (*ancala* or *kinara*) often with a fine yellow, orange or multicoloured line between border and field [Pl. 108]. Like all Nepalese saris, the *patasi* endpiece is almost non-existent, consisting of a narrow red stripe at each end of the cloth. The *patasi* is worn with the typical large cummerbund (*jani*) and front-tying tailored blouse and shawl (*ga*). The Newars are the original inhabitants of the Kathmandu valley with their own Tibeto-Burman language and literature.[49] Once the various mountain kingdoms were conquered and united by Prithvi Narayan Shah in the mid-eighteenth century, their language and literature was banned, and many now speak Nepali and use the Devangiri script.[50] They are not a single ethnic unit, however, rather a group of disparate communities that share the same culture.[51] Of them, the Jyapu are culturally one of the most independent, traditionally farmers but of much higher status (and wealth) than the Indian equivalent. Whereas most other Newars have either adopted Indian clothes outright or wear saris made of mill-printed fabrics, the Jyapu continue wearing their traditional dress.[52] Many women, however, now wear powerloom-woven versions which, although less expensive, are of much thinner cloth and have borders woven in a variety of different colours. A peculiar feature of these commercially made *patasis* is a jagged rather than straight edge to the border [Pl. 23].

Most other ethnic groups who wear saris tend to use mill-made printed cloth, often in various shades of red, although some women still wear homespun, handwoven fabrics.[53] Today even tribal women who have come down from the hills in search of work in Kathmandu and other major valley towns soon begin wearing Indian saris draped in the *nivi* style.[54] The only ethnic group which appears to wear *lungis* regularly is the Tharu of the Nepalese Terai[55], unlike the Tharu in eastern India, who wear mill-printed full-body saris draped in either the *sidha* or *ulta* (*nivi*) style.

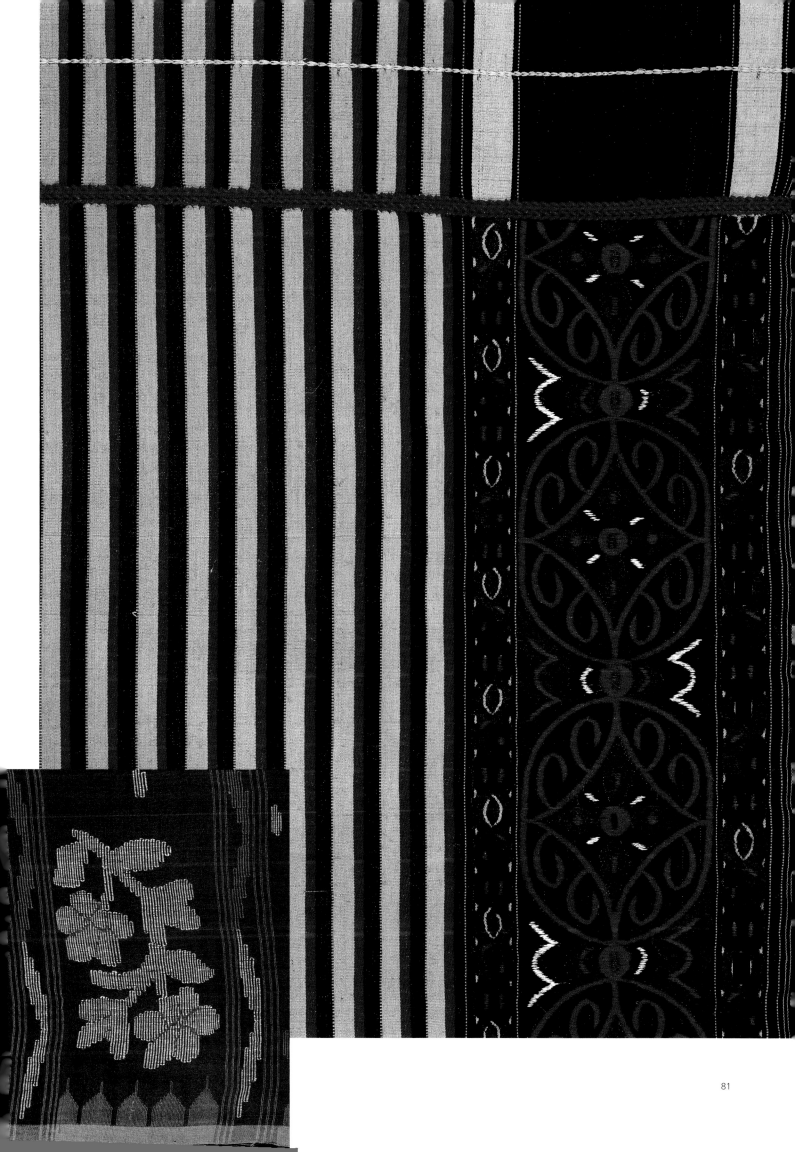

96 *Below* Such is the popularity of *muga* silk in Assam that even cotton saris are dyed the same colour. The geometric patterns woven into this sari are often associated with the Boro and Garo tribes of western Assam and Meghalaya, but they are now popularly used by many people in the region. Nuagong, Assam, 1993.

Assamese Tribal Sari Designs

Many traditional Assamese textile designs originate with the various Tibeto-Burman-speaking tribes living in the Brahmaputra valley and surrounding hills. Here, virtually all textile patterning is created through weaving contrasting coloured threads onto a single-coloured ground, usually as supplementary wefts or warps.

93, 95 *Opposite (top left) and above* A modern *muga* silk sari with traditional designs woven in coloured cotton. *Muga* silk is the rarest and most luxurious of all India's wild silks, being a natural deep gold colour (it is never dyed). The traditional red and black patterning on this sari, which was probably woven on a powerloom with jacquard attachments, is typically Assamese, with the distinctive sun-tree motif in the endpiece field. Sualkuchi, Assam, 1988.

94 *Opposite* A *chadar* of *muga* silk with dyed mulberry-silk supplementary-weft patterning. Woven on backstrap and simple frame looms, Assamese *chadars* of this type are coveted because of the quality of the silk and the traditional colours and designs. Sualkuchi, Assam, 1993.

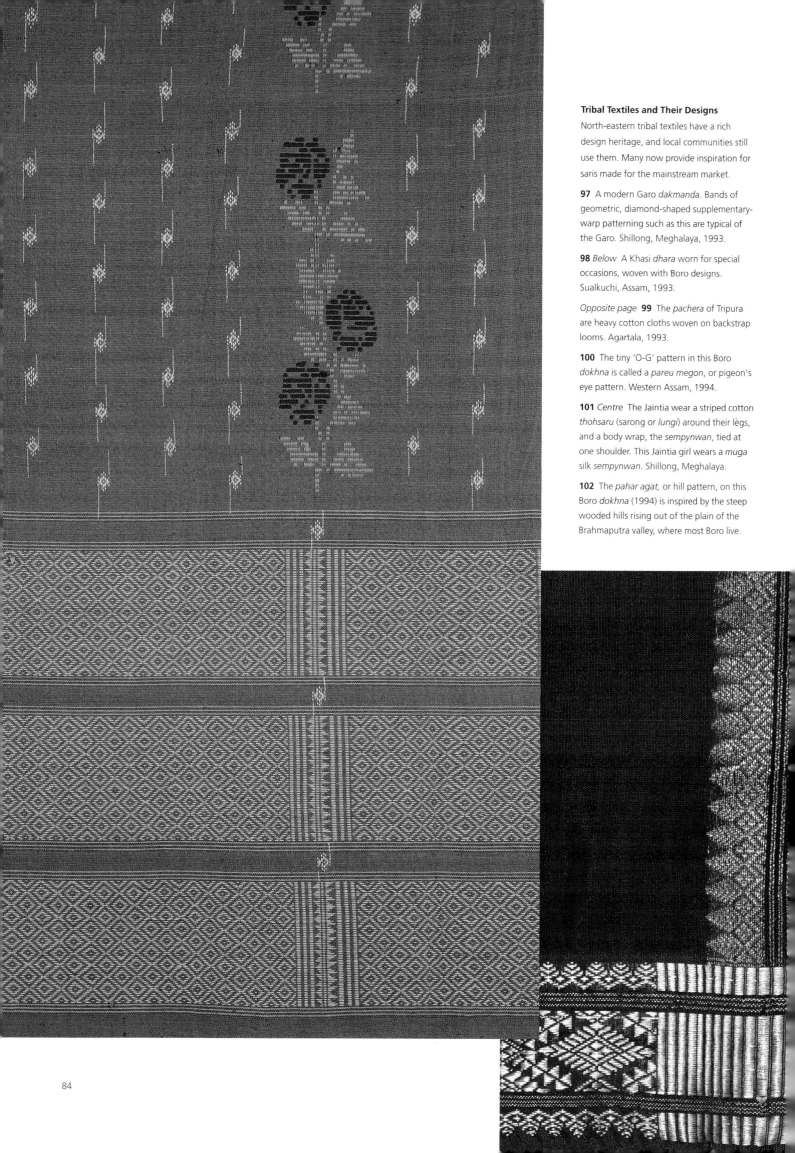

Tribal Textiles and Their Designs

North-eastern tribal textiles have a rich design heritage, and local communities still use them. Many now provide inspiration for saris made for the mainstream market.

97 A modern Garo *dakmanda*. Bands of geometric, diamond-shaped supplementary-warp patterning such as this are typical of the Garo. Shillong, Meghalaya, 1993.

98 *Below* A Khasi *dhara* worn for special occasions, woven with Boro designs. Sualkuchi, Assam, 1993.

Opposite page **99** The *pachera* of Tripura are heavy cotton cloths woven on backstrap looms. Agartala, 1993.

100 The tiny 'O-G' pattern in this Boro *dokhna* is called a *pareu megon*, or pigeon's eye pattern. Western Assam, 1994.

101 *Centre* The Jaintia wear a striped cotton *thohsaru* (sarong or *lungi*) around their legs, and a body wrap, the *sempynwan*, tied at one shoulder. This Jaintia girl wears a *muga* silk *sempynwan*. Shillong, Meghalaya.

102 The *pahar agat,* or hill pattern, on this Boro *dokhna* (1994) is inspired by the steep wooded hills rising out of the plain of the Brahmaputra valley, where most Boro live.

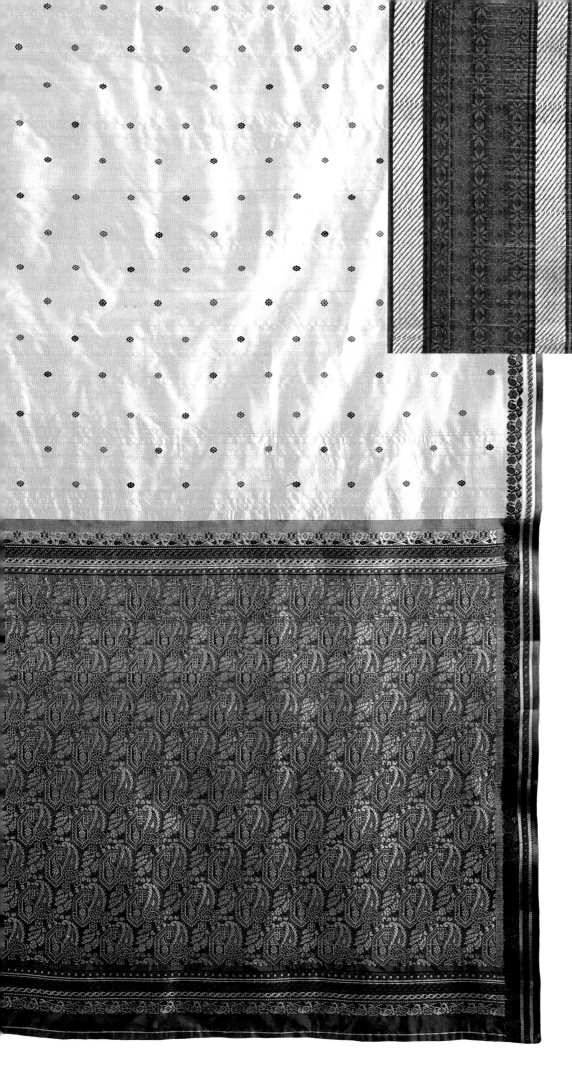

Mainstream Indian Designs

Mainstream Indian designs, in particular those from Bengal and northern India, are also found in Assamese saris, especially in modern ones.

103 *Left* A *muga* silk sari woven with mainstream designs, including the Mughal-derived *kalga*. Its large endpiece and narrow borders mark this as a fashion sari of the late 1980s/early 1990s. Sualkuchi, Assam.

104 *Above* A *muga* silk sari with *zari* patterning woven for the mainstream Indian market. *Zari* was only introduced into Assamese weaving in the 1930s and has yet to gain popularity. Sualkuchi, Assam.

105 A cotton sari from Kaziranga, Assam, where the one-horned rhino reserve is located. This style of sari, with its life-like depictions, has been popular in recent years.

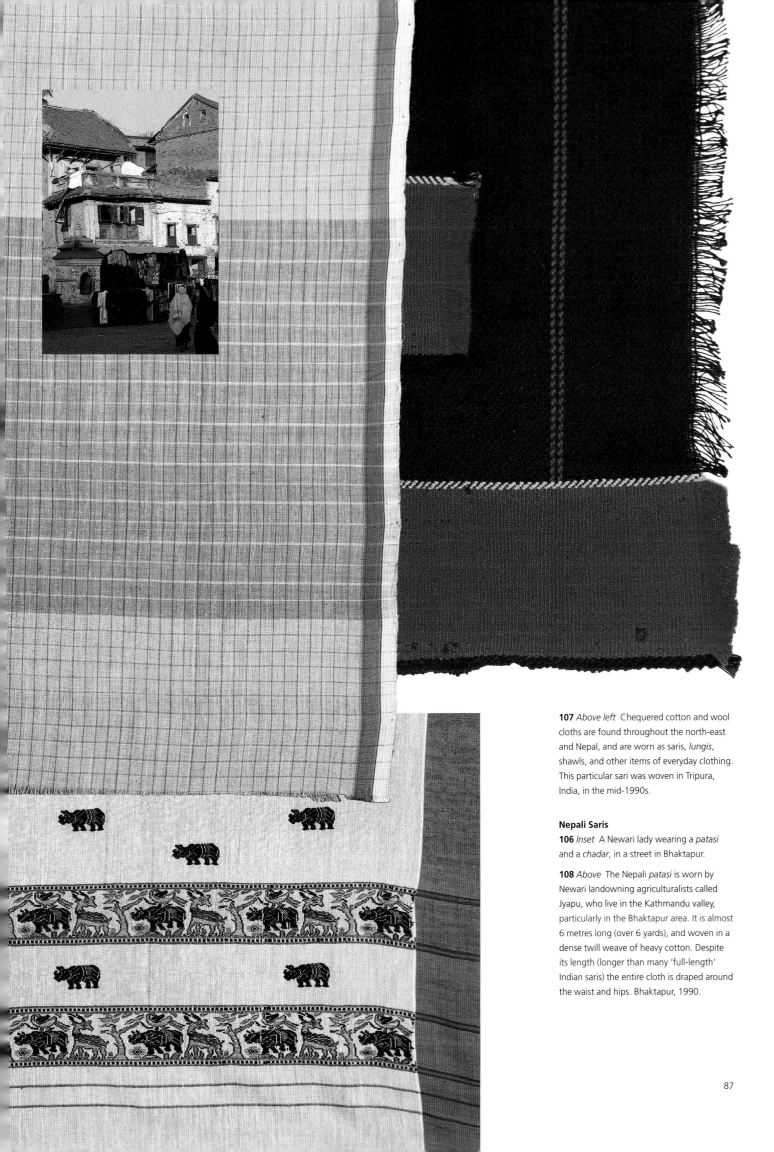

107 *Above left* Chequered cotton and wool cloths are found throughout the north-east and Nepal, and are worn as saris, *lungis*, shawls, and other items of everyday clothing. This particular sari was woven in Tripura, India, in the mid-1990s.

Nepali Saris

106 *Inset* A Newari lady wearing a *patasi* and a *chadar*, in a street in Bhaktapur.

108 *Above* The Nepali *patasi* is worn by Newari landowning agriculturalists called Jyapu, who live in the Kathmandu valley, particularly in the Bhaktapur area. It is almost 6 metres long (over 6 yards), and woven in a dense twill weave of heavy cotton. Despite its length (longer than many 'full-length' Indian saris) the entire cloth is draped around the waist and hips. Bhaktapur, 1990.

87

The Eastern Deccan

The eastern Deccan region consists of the eastern half of the Deccan plateau. This includes the rugged, forested mountains known as the Eastern Ghats that descend to the coastal plains facing the Bay of Bengal; the Chota Nagpur plateau of southern Bihar and south-western West Bengal; all of Orissa; eastern Madhya Pradesh; extreme eastern Maharashtra (Nagpur);[1] and the northern half of Andhra Pradesh. Because of the inaccessibility and relatively poor agricultural quality of much of the highland region, it was ignored by mainstream India, and it was not until British domination in the late eighteenth century that some tribal areas became seriously (usually negatively) affected by non-tribal populations. Prior to these incursions, much of the eastern Deccan was divided into large and often powerful tribal kingdoms that were socially, religiously and even economically completely outside surrounding Hindu and later Muslim societies.[2]

Historically, the only regions long-populated by Hindus were the fertile coastal plains and river deltas facing the Bay of Bengal, as well as the valleys of the major rivers.[3] Muslim dynasties eventually ruled many areas, but Islam had virtually no impact on the people and even less on the region's traditional textiles. Instead, most saris are influenced by tribal and Dravidian India, as well as the ikat textile traditions of Gujarat and the supplementary-warp weaving styles of the western Deccan. Although every state now caters to middle-class urban markets, northern Andhra Pradesh has the largest and most aggressive fashion sari industry. Today handloom saris made in the eastern Deccan range from some of India's most conservative and traditional to some of the most modern, with the latter often using local traditional forms as a springboard for contemporary styles.

The outstanding characteristic of most eastern Deccan saris is bright colour combined with sophisticated weaving techniques. Tribal saris tend to be white with coloured supplementary-warp and -weft woven embellishments, and before the spread of synthetic dyes during the past century many ethnic saris throughout the region had similar colour schemes. Today the use of colour has added new levels of

Opposite **109** A Dongaria Khond *gunderi*. Two of these wraps are used to create a two-piece drape. The patterns are created by the wearer, who buys heavy, low-count cotton cloth and embroiders it with brightly coloured, thick cotton yarn. Koraput district, Orissa, 1990.

89

sophistication to saris made for and worn by local women. In fact, in some areas[4] the range of rural ethnic saris, as opposed to fashion ones, has actually increased over the past fifty years.

Eastern Deccan saris often have patterns in their fields created through supplementary weaving, ikat resist-dyeing or, in the western areas merging into the western Deccan, fine woven checks. Even saris that have plain fields, such as the muslins worn by most Telugu-speaking Hindus of northern Andhra Pradesh, are still invariably coloured with supplementary-warp patterning in the border.

Tribal Saris of the Eastern Deccan

An estimated thirty-seven million tribal peoples live in the eastern Deccan,[5] comprising more than eighty different tribes.[6] Such large tribal communities as the Santhal (Bihar, West Bengal), Munda (Bihar), Oraon (Bihar, Madhya Pradesh) and Gond (Orissa, Madhya Pradesh, Andhra Pradesh), as well as smaller groups like the Khond, Bondo and Gadaba[7] of Orissa and Ho, Bhumij and Paharia of Bihar, live here. As in the north-east, many of these peoples are named after the group of languages they speak rather than their specific tribal communities,[8] and their languages range from Dravidian (Gond, Oraon) and Indo-Aryan (Chikbaraik), to Austro-Asiatic (Santhal, Munda, Ho).

Although tribal communities in some areas grow cotton, albeit in small amounts and of poor quality,[9] and even spin and dye it,[10] most refuse to weave textiles because they do not wish to be associated with the low-caste status that weavers have in Hindu society. In Chota Nagpur, only one semi-tribal group weaves and sells its products to other tribes, the Chikbaraik of Ranchi district,[11] who are also known by such names as Swansi and even Tanti (which reflect their mixed tribal-Hindu status). Most Hindu weaving groups in the tribal areas are known as Panr or Pank (literally, 'weaver'). There are Hindu Panka groups weaving Oraon saris in northern Madhya Pradesh; Daspanika weaving Gond saris in Bastar; and Mirgana weavers in Koraput who belong to the same community. The few tribal people who do weave their own clothes live in Koraput, which is still one of the more inaccessible areas of peninsular India.

MAJOR TRIBES

Traditional tribal saris are short and narrow, being made of heavy, thick, unbleached cotton with single-colour patterning woven in red, purple or brown [Pl. 111]. In some areas, particularly Koraput, natural dyes are still used, coming primarily from the roots of the aal (*Morinda citrifolia*) tree which produces a range of reds from a bright pink through to deep brown, depending on the age of the root bark and the proportion of dye.[12]

Both sari designs and draping styles vary as much by location as by tribal affiliation. For instance, in the eastern parts of Chota Nagpur, which extends into West Bengal, tribal women (Santhal, Munda, Ho) traditionally wear plain white saris with a red border and simple striped endpiece [Pl. 115]. They are draped in a version of the Bengali style, with its Dravidian elements coming to the fore (see pp. 14, 16). Such saris have no special name among the Santhalis, although the Munda call them *khanda* saris. A similar sari with purple borders is regarded as specifically Santhali. It is worn as a bridal sari (called a *khandi*) and is about 3.5 to 4 metres (11 to 13 feet) long. A longer, 6-metre (20-foot) version (*khanda*) is worn by the mother-in-law. Another Santhali wedding sari is the *sindur lugri*, which we have not seen but have been told is a tan-coloured textile, suggesting it may have originally, if not now, been made of *tasar*.[13] It is worn by the bride at the climax of the ceremony when the groom adds *sindur* to the bride's head, signifying that she is now a married woman.[14] Another Hindu custom that the Santhals have adopted is the wearing of a yellow sari after the birth of a child, so indicating motherhood [Pl. 24]; while the Santhal *pashan* sari, or festival sari, is a cotton sari usually containing three colours, with a contrasting border and large check design in the field.[15]

Most of the Munda live in the central and eastern parts of Chota Nagpur and are more likely to drape their saris (*paria*) in the Bihari *sidha* style [Pl. 18]. In addition to the *khanda* sari, there is the *sangol paria*, a heavy, elaborately woven textile with striped, interlocked-weft (*kumbha*) borders, and a large endpiece with densely woven, weft-faced, continuous supplementary weft-woven designs, most of which are geometric lozenges, diamonds and grids [Pl. 110].[16]

The Dravidian-speaking Oraon live mainly to the south and west of Chota Nagpur (southern Bihar, north-eastern Madhya Pradesh). They traditionally wear saris (*kichri*) draped in a Dravidian style[17] that are similar to the *sangol paria* with striped borders, which sometimes contain *kumbha*, and large striped endpieces. The elaborate weft-faced supplementary work of the Munda saris is missing, but various discontinuous supplementary-weft designs are found. For instance, a square-shaped object often called (in Hindi)[18] a *chauki* is woven into wedding saris. The *chauki* is a low square seat often used on special occasions such as the Hindu wedding ceremony, when the bride and groom would be seated. Another motif is called the *singhaulia* among Hindus [Pl. 19], after the box of *sindur* containing the red powder married north Indian Hindu women apply to their heads, although it is also called a *maachee phool* or 'fly flower' by weavers for and by, apparently, the Oraon.[19] In the past, long, intricately woven ceremonial cloths called *turra* were made to be used in ritual dances,

Above A Munda *sangol paria*.

Top A *chauk* pattern from a Chota Nagpur sari, Bihar.

Opposite A fish design on a Gadaba *kerong*, from Koraput, Orissa [Pl. 113].

and they contained continuous supplementary-weft patterning similar to the Munda textiles.[20]

Further south (Koraput, Bastar and Adilabad districts), the saris (*ganda*, *gisir*)[21] of the group of dominant tribes collectively known as the Gond[22] are shorter than those now worn by the tribes further north,[23] and are often knotted at the shoulder. They have borders and endpieces with bands of solid colour varying from bright red to dark brown, with discontinuous supplementary-weft designs in the endpieces. One distinctive motif is a stacked pyramidal pattern called by Hindu weavers the *phool cheeta chauk*, which translates as 'flower leopard seat' and is reportedly a marriage motif [Pl. 111].[24]

The weavers in both Koraput and Bastar also produce a variety of heavy white cotton tribal sari with many discontinuous supplementary-weft motifs placed in rows in the field, such as geese, leaves, snakes, axes, *chauka* and even such untraditional items as umbrellas and aeroplanes.[25] In addition to this, in Bastar a long ceremonial sari used by the Dhurua tribe incorporates ikat-dyed chequered bands as well as the above-mentioned motifs. In this sari, the weavers also change the warp threads in the two endpieces for threads of different colours, and weave the borders in the interlocked-weft technique.[26] These methods of textile creation are also found in the Orissan Bomokoi sari, discussed on page 98.

One type of motif commonly found in almost all east Deccan tribal textiles, from the northerly Munda through to the southerly Gonds, is the so-called 'temple motif', which varies in size from a row of small triangles to single, large stepped pyramids. They are created through the same weaving technique that produces interlocked weft-woven borders. Called *kumbha* by Oriya-speakers, these motifs have many different names among weavers of tribal saris.[27]

Koraput is also home to some of the few tribes who still weave and embellish their own textiles: the Gadaba, Dongaria Khond and Bondo. The first two wear short two-piece drapes. The Gadaba weave their cloths (*kerong* or *cila*) on backstrap looms with multicoloured stripes or checks [Pl. 113],[28] while the Khond,[29] who call them *gunderi* and *garnda*, embroider geometric patterns onto heavy cotton trade cloths with brightly coloured cotton threads [Pl. 109].[30] Bondo women wear only a single cloth forming a simple wrap like a short apron, which is woven by its wearer from local bark and bast fibres [Pl. 112].[31]

Ethnic Saris of the Eastern Ghats

Apart from the Nagpur area, the eastern Deccan was not affected by mill-woven textiles as early as most other parts of the subcontinent, and there are many more traditional saris still being worn and woven here than in most other regions. For the sake of simplicity, they are divided geographically into: (1) the plateau land and western part of the Eastern Ghats, comprising eastern Madhya Pradesh and Nagpur; (2) the western

Above A Gond *ganda*, shown (*right*) worn in the traditional manner, knotted at the shoulder.

Below A *kumbha* design on a Gond *ganda*, from Koraput, Orissa [Pl. 111].

Opposite, above Ikat elephants in the endpiece of a Sambalpur sari, Orissa [Pl. 121].

Opposite, below *Kachhua* (turtle) and *rui phool* (cotton flower) designs woven into the border of a sari from Madhya Pradesh [Pls. 117, 118].

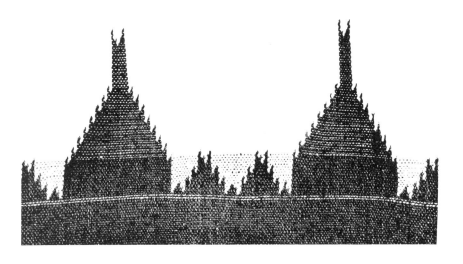

hills of Orissa; and (3) Orissa's eastern coastal plains. Because the saris of northern Andhra Pradesh show stronger ties with both high-caste Dravidian and Muslim cultures, they are considered in later sections (see p. 100).

The ethnic saris of the Eastern Ghats tend to be short and narrow, reflecting the local preference for saris that will not impede movement [Pl. 115]. The cotton saris are woven from coarse, heavy threads with low thread counts, although the *tasar* silk saris, as well as those made for special occasions, have more generous dimensions and finer threads. Today, many weavers create replicas of these ethnic saris for the middle-class urban markets, often in *tasar* or fine count cotton, but these saris are distinguishable by their larger dimensions (550 by 120 centimetres, or 18 by 4 feet) and fine-quality fabrics, and by the fact they have only one endpiece instead of two. Many ethnic saris are also more colourful than in the past as synthetic dyes have broadened the range of possibilities and many once-white saris are now created in rich dark reds, blues, greens and purples with supplementary-thread embellishments in colours such as bright yellow.

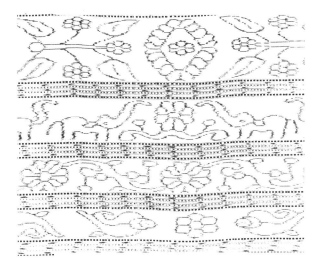

Like the saris of the western Deccan, the borders usually carry significant amounts of fine, repetitive supplementary-warp patterning, woven as narrow 0.5- to 2.5-centimetre (one-inch) bands [Pls. 122, 123]. Traditionally, local designs vary, with the most complex being woven in the hills away from the coastal belt. In the westernmost areas, the endpieces often have the western-Deccan style of a few simple broad bands (*patta*) of plain colour [Pl. 119], yet the commonest type of endpiece design throughout the eastern Deccan is what could be called the 'Orissan style' (also prevalent, however, in eastern Madhya Pradesh, Nagpur and northern Andhra Pradesh). The endpiece is usually long, often over a metre, and frequently contains dozens of bands of supplementary-weft and/or ikat patterning [Pl. 116]. In eastern Madhya Pradesh these bands are called *khapa* work after the wooden spatula used to beat down the supplementary-weft threads on the loom. Most ethnic saris also traditionally have endpieces at both ends, a feature that is called *do-muha* or 'two-faced' in Orissa [Pl. 114]. Some local draping styles show both endpieces, but they are primarily created to extend the life of the sari as it can be reversed when it has worn out on one side.[32] Double-endpiece saris are traditional throughout the Deccan plateau and are still common.[33]

Ethnic Saris of Eastern Madhya Pradesh and Nagpur

Most of the ethnic saris of eastern Madhya Pradesh and Nagpur show strong links with their tribal counterparts, being traditionally made of heavy unbleached or white cotton with plain (usually red) borders (*dhadi*) and striped endpieces (*anchra* or *jhela*), with or without supplementary-warp and -weft embellishments, and a plain field. Those worn by wealthier women or for special occasions either had dyed *tasar* borders or were completely of *tasar* silk, which is locally called *potia* or *kosa* [Pl. 119]. The more ornate saris (cotton or *tasar*) have borders containing narrow bands of supplementary-warp patterning with designs ranging from tiny *phool* (flower) and *rudraksha* (wrinkled seed) motifs to larger flowers (*rui phool*) as much as

2.5 centimetres wide [Pl. 117]. Repetitive geometric designs such as the herringbone-like *gom*, serrated *karvat* or net-like *jala* patterns are also created. The saris are woven by a variety of different castes, including the Mehers, Koshtas, Devangan, Panka and Mahar.

Endpiece decoration varies from the plain *patta* creating the five-striped western Deccan style to multiple bands of supplementary-weft (*khapa*) stripes. The latter are usually woven as either weft-faced ribbed bands or thin lines of 'dashes' which go by various names including *jeera*, meaning cumin seed. In the most elaborate saris, such as the *bhanwarai* wedding sari[34] of the Durg district north of Bastar, supplementary-weft designs of peacocks (*mor*), *chauka* and *singhaulia* are added. Today only wealthier members of the Lodhi (agricultural) community use it. Because of the accessibility of synthetic dyes, these and most other local saris now come in bright colours (such as red, green), with equally bright (often yellow) supplementary threadwork. As is also seen in Andhra Pradesh and Tamil Nadu, many wedding saris were dyed yellow (with turmeric) for the marriage ceremony, and these were called *pitamber* saris.[35]

Typical of this area's saris is the Goyal sari, traditionally worn by agricultural castes (Sauras) of Orissan origin in eastern Madhya Pradesh [Pl. 118]. It is a *do-muha* sari with long endpieces containing multiple bands of supplementary-weft patterning – usually geometric and *phool* motifs interspersed with many *jeera*. Traditional borders were plain bands of colour but today supplementary-warp patterning, including *phool* and turtle (*kachhua*) designs, is common.

Many saris with interlocked-weft borders are also found, and most are associated with the more costly *tasar* varieties. The resulting *kumbha* border patterns are called *phera* in Madhya Pradesh, after the three-shuttle weaving technique used to create them.[36] Like other saris of this area, most *phera* saris, whether of cotton or *tasar*, have supplementary-warp and -weft bands in the borders and large endpieces with multiple *khapa* bands. A red or dark-blue cotton sari of this style, with *phool* and fish (*maachh*) supplementary motifs in the borders and endpiece, and endpiece 'khadam tree' motifs,[37] is used as a *bhanwarai* wedding sari among local agricultural communities. Various saris of the Nagpur area died out during the early to mid-twentieth century, but are being resuscitated by local *tasar* weavers in the 1990s for sale in national urban markets [Pl. 119].

Most *tasar* saris were traditionally woven for weddings and special occasions, and only wealthier, high-caste women were able to afford them, but one distinctive type was woven as a wedding sari for poorer groups. It had wide red *tasar* borders containing narrow yellow and green stripes with the body of self-striped unbleached cotton. Its endpiece had multiple narrow bands of red, yellow and green, and the sari was dyed yellow for the wedding. Sadly, it has rarely been made, or worn, since the mid-1960s.[38]

However, high-caste, all-*tasar* wedding saris are still being woven for wealthier local communities. The silk is often dyed (red, yellow, purple), and today the range of colours has broadened considerably. Embellishments could include *phera* borders with supplementary-warp *phool* and fish bands, geometric *buti* in the field, and endpieces

Above A turtle (*kechu*) border from an Orissan landscape sari [Pl. 133].

Top A *das phoolia* sari border from Sambalpur, Orissa.

ranging from the broad *patta* to elaborate *khapa* striped varieties. In addition to Nagpur's Umrer sari (see p. 148), one of the more exclusive traditional *tasar* saris was probably the *dariyai*, which had dip-dyed borders and endpieces with a plain, natural-coloured field. The borders contain bands of supplementary-warp patterning, as does the *khapa*-woven endpiece.[39]

Saris of Orissa's Western Hills

Orissa's western hills consist of Sundargarh, Sambalpur, Balangir, Kalahandi and Phulbani districts, with Sambalpur and Balangir being the primary handloom-weaving areas, especially in such towns as Sambalpur, Sonepur, Bargarh, Butapali and Barpali. The saris from this area are often called 'Sambalpur saris', as many of the major weavers' cooperatives are in this district.[40] Traditional handloom saris were woven in heavy, low-count cotton and *tasar* silk, for both tribal and Hindu rural groups [Pls. 122, 123]. Since the mid-1970s, increasing numbers of *tasar* and mulberry-silk saris have been created, as the state government encourages sericulture, and introduces mulberry trees (and worms) to the area.[41] In addition, local women are now wearing lighter-weight cottons than in the past, which is changing the types of textiles being created [Pl. 114].[42] Most of western Orissa's traditional saris were woven by Mehers, with the Bhulia Mehers specializing in ikat work and the Costa Mehers in non-ikat *tasar* silk and cotton saris.

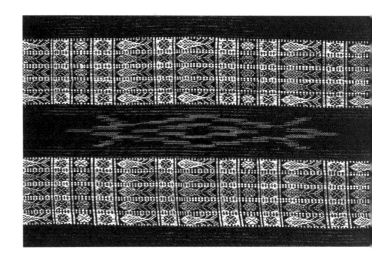

Today, Orissan saris are famous for their ikat work, called *bandha* [Pl. 206], yet it is unclear how widespread *bandha* was even a century ago. Scholars disagree as to whether ikat weaving in Orissa was a relatively recent introduction (about two centuries ago) or is much older (since the early Middle Ages), for there is evidence in favour of both theories.[43] Whatever its origins, ikat weaving now dominates Orissa's handloom sari industry, which constantly creates new designs and styles for the national market. Most ethnic saris, including daily-wear ones, contain *bandha*, usually as warp ikat in the borders (*dhadi*) and weft ikat in the endpieces (*muha*). These *bandha* saris also contain supplementary-warp and -weft work in addition to the ikat. In recent years saris combining *bandha* and supplementary threadwork have been called *kapta jala*, which refers to the dobby mechanism (*jala*) now used to create the supplementary-warp designs instead of the groups of sticks previously used on traditional looms.[44]

All Sambalpur saris are traditionally *do-muha*, with the most elaborate worn for special occasions, having wide borders with many bands of supplementary figuring and very long endpieces [Pls. 122, 123]. Everyday saris have narrower borders and sometimes, but not always, shorter endpieces. They also invariably have plain fields, a few supplementary-warp bands in the borders, and sometimes *kumbha* woven in the three-shuttle technique, as well as endpieces with simple supplementary-weft brocading and some relatively simple ikat designs. They sometimes also contain warp-ikat patterning in the borders, which may be a recent introduction.

Traditionally, the value of a sari in this area was assessed according to the amount of supplementary patterning in the borders and two

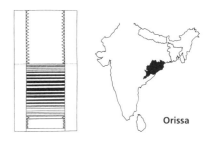

Above An Orissan ethnic *do-muha* (two-piece) *hansabali kapta* sari.

Top A *das phoolia* sari border with fish (*maachha*), Sambalpur, Orissa [Pl. 122].

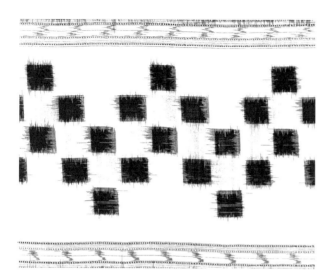

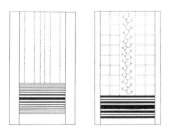

Above A *bichchitrapuri (left)* and *khandua* sari.

Top Part of an ikat field of a modern *saktapar* sari from Orissa.

endpieces, not the ikat work [Pl. 122]. The most highly valued saris had ten bands in each border, giving rise to the name *das phoolia* sari, literally 'with ten flowers', although other motifs were included. (*Phoola* is Oriya both for 'flower' and for these supplementary-warp bands themselves.) Geometric patterns are less common, but fish (*maachha* in Oriya), turtles (*kechu*) and the *rudraksha* are found. Sometimes sari borders consist of supplementary-warp bands woven 2.5 to 5 centimetres (one to 2 inches) wide in repetitive geometric patterns, usually with a small diamond-shaped design. In the Bomokoi sari, discussed on page 98, these panels are called *mukta panji*, which one researcher translates as 'panel of diamond beads'.[45] They have no *bandha* in the borders at all and show strong design links with eastern Madhya Pradesh figured saris. However, traditional Sambalpur saris without ikat work are now extremely rare, and some textile scholars feel that various types of non-ikat saris may have completely disappeared over the past fifty years.[46] The bands of border *phoola* are divided by a central band of warp *bandha* which can contain any of the traditional ikat designs of the region, including lotus flowers (*padma*), creeping vines (*lata*), geese (*hansa*), deer (*harini*), elephants (*haathi*), conch shells (*shankha*) or fish.

In the traditional Orissan style, the endpieces contain many, often dozens, of ikat-patterned bands of differing sizes with various levels of patterning complexity, ranging from elephants and lions standing by trees to simple triangles (*denti*) and dashes. Discontinuous supplementary-weft *buti* in the form of fish or *phoola* may also embellish the endpiece, as well as the body of the sari. They are traditionally made of coloured cotton or silk (mulberry or *tasar*), but now synthetic fibres are common [Pls. 122, 206].

The most elaborate saris are those made for weddings, with two well-known types having large central panels of supplementary-warp and warp-ikat patterning extending the entire length of the sari field in the warp direction. Yet it is the design in the blank spaces between this central panel and the two borders that gives these saris their names. The *bichchitrapuri* (or *vichchitrapuri*) sari contains a fine check, mesh or stripe in this area, with most older saris having these checks and stripes woven in, whereas modern saris often have the check created through ikat dyeing [Pl. 121]. The other, the *saktapar* sari, contains rows of squares with red and white chequerboard designs [Pl. 120]. The *saktapar* pattern mimics the board game of the same name which is traditionally played by the just-married couple when they retire to their nuptial chamber for the first time. The *saktapar* design is the only traditional motif in this region where the warp and weft are each separately tie-dyed and then woven together to form a combined ikat pattern in the manner of Gujarati *patolu* weaving.

Saris of the Orissan Coastal Plains
There is also a wide variety of traditional saris still being woven in Orissa's coastal plains, including: ikat saris woven in mulberry silk, *tasar* and cotton; figured mulberry silks; and a variety of figured saris with supplementary-weft and -warp designs as well as the interlocked-weft *kumbha* border.

The best known saris of this area are the mulberry silk and *tasar* silk ikats[47] that were once woven for local royal courts,[48] as well as for donation to temples and for weddings. Today such saris are still created for temple donations and weddings, but most are now woven for India's urban middle classes, their bright colouring being a popular feature [Pls. 125, 127].

Although they share many of the characteristics of the saris of the western hills, they are usually much more colourful, with fields of bright red or purple being a common choice, along with 'shot' fabrics, especially red and green [Pl. 125]. The borders of these saris contain fewer supplementary-warp bands than the Sambalpur varieties (usually only one along each edge), and have a relatively wide area of warp *bandha* between the bands, often created in cotton even when the rest of the sari is silk [Pls. 124, 126]. Most of the silk ikats are woven in the Cuttack, Puri and Dhenkanal districts by the Patras, a different caste from those of the hill region.

No one knows when silk ikat-weaving began here, although the weavers traditionally keep samples of their forebears' work for up to eight generations, and the samples studied by scholars all contain *bandha*.[49] In addition, a reference in the records of the Jagannath Temple in Puri dated to 1719 indicates that lines from the *Geetagovinda*, a twelfth-century devotional Vaishnavite poem, were worked onto cloths donated to the temple.[50] As saris with ikat renderings of stanzas (*shloka*) from this poem are known to have been made since at least the late nineteenth century, some scholars feel that the eighteenth-century document may have been referring to an ikat sari.[51] The script used in these inscribed textiles was traditionally Sanskrit, although today Oriya is more common. The stanzas vary. One master weaver, Sadam Guin of Nuapatna, makes a 'batch' of such textiles every few months, each with a different stanza [Pl. 128].[52]

Unlike the Sambalpur ikats, the mulberry silk and *tasar bandha* of this area always contain numerous weft-ikat patterns in the field. These patterns often dominate the sari, obscuring the detailed borders and endpieces. The local wedding sari, called a *khandua*,[53] is a typical example [Pl. 127]. It traditionally has lotus flowers, elephants,

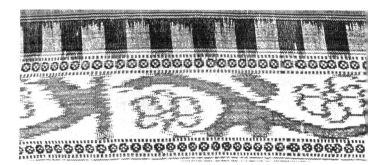

Above An ikat border from a sari made in Cuttack, Orissa, in 1950 [Pl. 126].

Below left An ikat conch design in a sari worn by local weaving communities, Cuttack district, 1992.

'fantastic beasts' and creeping lotus vines depicted in the field and borders containing two small, somewhat insignificant-looking supplementary-warp bands with a warp-ikat vine design between. Ikat-dyed *kumbha* are often created along the inner edge of the border, sometimes with flower buds in between [Pls. 124, 126]. All these motifs are regarded as highly auspicious, and were used in the older, nineteenth-century *khandua*, which were worn as a wedding veil over the sari. Today, the range of motifs found within the field of the coastal plains saris is much wider than in the past, and repeated designs based on stars (*tara*), lotus flowers, vines, and auspicious animals such as the elephant and peacock (*maira*) are common.

Less well known, but possibly much older, are the non-ikat saris of the area. Weavers in Berhampur, southern Orissa, specialize in figured mulberry-silk saris and still use natural dyes, in particular lac, a red dye produced from the secretions of the lac insect (*Lacifer lacca*), an indigenous pest on many local trees.[54] Although there are a few jacquard looms recently introduced into some weavers' cooperatives[55] that are creating 'modern' saris, most of the figured saris produced in the coastal plains follow the basic designs of east Deccan ethnic saris [Pl. 116]. They tend to have large endpieces with numerous (often dozens) of bands of supplementary-weft work, usually in geometric and *phoola* forms with bands of supplementary-warp patterning along the borders. In addition, interlocked-weft weaving is common in saris containing the *kumbha* motif [Pl. 130]. Unlike the saris of eastern Madhya Pradesh, however, the motifs within the supplementary bands tend to be of the *rudraksha* and small *phoola* type, along with depictions of fish and turtles. These saris are woven primarily by the Rangani caste who trace their ancestry from southern West Bengal.

Another traditional figured sari from the southern Orissan coastal plains is the Bomokoi sari, so named after the village where it was 'discovered' in the early 1980s [Pl. 131].[56] Only a few weavers were

Below Motifs from a *khandua* sari from Orissa: an ikat lotus flower, and an ikat elephant [Pl. 127].

still creating it at that time, but it was originally made for the local maharaja, aristocracy and Brahmins of the Chikiti *tahsil* in the Ganjam district a few kilometres from the Andhra Pradesh border. Although woven in heavy, often coarse, low-count cotton, these saris were always dyed bright colours, usually with black, red or white grounds and multicoloured supplementary-weft and -warp endpieces and borders. The field warp threads were cut and retied to different-coloured warps for the endpiece. This creates a dense layer of colour for the usually large endpiece. Such a time-consuming technique, which is known locally as *muhajorhi* (literally, 'endpiece with joined threads') was once much more common throughout India. Today it is only found in a few traditional saris in Tamil Nadu, Bastar and in the expensive Paithani sari of the western Deccan [Pls. 153, 154, 202].

The endpiece also contains angular discontinuous supplementary-weft patterns woven in contrasting colours. They have such names as *rukha* (pestle, stick), *dombaru* (small hourglass-shaped drum), *kanthi phoola* (small flower) and *kalera* (bitter gourd), peacock and fish [Pl. 131]. Unlike many eastern Deccan saris, the supplementary bands are not woven in progressive order from large to small, or vice versa, but are woven as the weaver sees fit. Yet despite all the work in the endpiece, it is the supplementary-warp patterns of the borders that give these saris their names. A broad band of supplementary-warp patterning (the *mukta panji* mentioned earlier) forming a latticework of small diamond shapes is the usual design. The size and shape of the lozenges determine its name, such as *dalimba* (literally, 'pomegranate seed'; the design has a dot inside the diamond shape).

Orissan Pictorial Saris

One distinctive type of twentieth-century ethnic sari is the multicoloured pictorial sari. When such textiles are seen in pan-Indian big-city emporia, it is tempting to assume they were created for the urban market, but they appear to be primarily made for Orissans, including rural women. Unlike the bright, Modernist saris of Andhra Pradesh, many of the Orissan designs are less popular out of state than locally, possibly because the colour combinations, which range from sombre to garish, do not fit comfortably with the aesthetics of the other regions.[57]

Their designs fall into three types: (1) architectural; (2) religious; and (3) landscape (although all three themes can be found in a single sari). Similarly, the endpiece, field and borders may all contain these patterns. Architectural designs usually consist of depictions of architectural embellishments found in temple walls, gateways, etc., while religious themes include depictions of various deities and motifs associated with them. For instance, an ethnic wedding sari [Pl. 132] made for the local Sambalpuri market features depictions of the 'real' *kumbha*: a clay pot with mango leaves and coconut on top, which is placed outside house doors as a gift to domestic deities during wedding ceremonies;[58] while another ethnic *do-muha* sari contains depictions of the ten incarnations or *avatars* of Vishnu [Pls. 134, 135]. The third group – the landscape saris – is perhaps the largest,

Above An Orissan landscape sari.

Top Das abatar patterning on an Orissan sari depicting incarnations of Vishnu [Pl. 134].

incorporating depictions of various local scenes from trees and butterflies to fully fledged views of locally familiar sites, with elephants, aeroplanes and sometimes even place names included [Pl. 133]. Orissa does not have a significant tourist industry – what it has is concentrated on the eastern coast in the Puri–Bhubaneshwar area, where the Jagannath Temple attracts pilgrims and the Konarak ruins foreigners – and these saris are made primarily for local consumption.

Most of these saris are used for *puja* and religious festivals,[59] and there seem to be trends for particular designs. Fewer saris with full landscapes in the endpieces are made today than in the 1970s and early 1980s, but the depictions of gods and goddesses, and wedding saris replete with symbolism (such as a man's and woman's hands clasped together to show their union) are currently popular [Pl. 132]. They are woven in both the western hills and the northern coastal plains, and often include the written names of gods, auspicious phrases as well as lines of poetry (religious and secular). Today English transliterations of Oriya phrases and words are commonly created in addition to Oriya and, more rarely, Sanskrit scripts; this probably reflects the increasing use of English among Oriya speakers.

Khans or Siddipet Saris

Throughout much of the central and western Deccan, the word *khan* is used to describe figured textiles with supplementary-weft and/or -warp patterning, usually created in narrow bands, which were made primarily for blouses. In northern Andhra Pradesh it also refers to a particular type of sari (*seera*, *koka*, in Telugu) containing a mix of central Deccan, Orissan and Mughal-style designs, which is woven in Siddipet, Jangaon and Cheryala (Medak and Hyderabad districts).[60] These fine unbleached muslins had unembellished fields, high thread counts, and finely woven, complex bands of supplementary-warp

patterning in the borders (*acu, aca, kammi*) and supplementary-weft in the endpieces (*kongu, ceragu, painta*). The supplementary threads were originally of many different vibrantly coloured silks, such as bright blue, red, yellow, green and orange, in one design; but today the threads are usually cotton, in only one or two colours.

The endpieces (there were traditionally two) are long, consisting of bands of supplementary-weft weaving featuring both geometric (such as the *gom* and *karvat*) and representational forms; the latter are *kalgas*, floral vines and leaves, animals, birds (swans, peacocks) and even women carrying water pots [Pl. 136]. Inanimate objects like shrines, the sun, moon and stars are also woven in. There is usually a large mix of motifs within the bands, which tend to decrease in width on either side of a large central one.

Different varieties of these saris had different names. For instance, a sari with a fine black check woven into the field was called a *jamindar* sari, presumably because it was popular among local landowning groups (Zamindars), while one with just floral patterning was called a *gollabhana* sari [Pl. 137].[61] Some even had interlocked-weft *kumbham* (Telugu for *kumbha*) woven into the borders.[62]

Pochampalli Ikats

Pochampalli, in Nalgonda district, lies close by, and is famous for its ikat saris. It is not the only town where ikat saris are woven, however, as many towns in Nalgonda, Hyderabad and Guntur districts, such as Chirala, Golgonda and Jalna, weave them. Here, ikat weaving is called *chit-ku* and *pagdu-bandhu*, while the tie-dyed yarn is *katak-buti*.

Unlike the Orissan industry, it appears to be a modern development without strong indigenous roots. Most evidence suggests ikat weaving began in the late nineteenth century,[63] when most of the original textiles were large scarves (*rumal*) made for export to Arabia. Only poor local fishermen ever wore these cloths, as *lungis*, although larger versions were also made as *dupattas* for the area's Muslim women. Although nowadays weavers are primarily Dravidian (Telugu-speaking) Hindus, namely Padmasalis and Devangs, these textiles did not impinge on the traditional sari-wearing habits of local women, and all older examples of Andhra ikats are of the *rumal* type. There are some intriguing exceptions to this theory of recent origins, however. For instance, an 8-metre (26-foot) sari called a *janani*, which had ikat bands in the endpiece, was once woven here,[64] while to the north in Bastar, the Dhurua tribal sari mentioned on page 92 also incorporated ikat checks in its body. Unfortunately, little is known about the history of either sari.

Overall, ikat saris do not appear to have been made in the Pochampalli area until the 1950s, and the earliest we have seen, bought in 1955,[65] show designs closer to the Siddipet *khans* rather than the ikat *rumals*. Like the *khans*, the borders of these early Pochampalli ikats were only embellished with supplementary-warp patterns, not ikat, while the endpiece consisted of a series of bands of different widths descending in size from the large central band. Unlike the *khans*, these bands were only embellished with weft-ikat dyed threads; that no supplementary-weft weaving is present in the

Above Motifs from a Pochampalli imitation *patolu*, Andhra Pradesh.

Opposite, above The ikat field design of a 'ten *avatars*' sari from Orissa [Pls. 134, 135].

Opposite, below Endpiece patterning from a Siddipet *khan*, Andhra Pradesh [Pl. 137].

Below Pochampalli saris: a *khan* ikat (*left*) and a *patolu*.

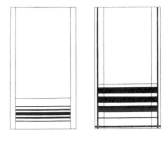

endpiece is suggestive of the *janani* sari documented by an anthropologist in the 1970s. Today, ikat silk saris with design layouts similar to the old *khan* style are made [Pl. 143], which indicates a possible link between the much older supplementary-thread Siddipet *khan* saris woven in this area and today's ikat industry.

By the 1970s, Pochampalli's ikat sari industry had mushroomed, and the rather timid patterns of the earlier pieces had evolved into what are now recognized as the characteristic saris of this area.

Patterning is big, bold and very bright [Pl. 140]. Motifs are modern – abstract, Modernist and geometric – with plenty of brilliant colours. Only a small group of saris is woven in the *khan* layout; most modern Pochampalli ikat designs have origins in the *rumals* traditionally made further east. *Rumals* have wide plain borders surrounding a field consisting of a lattice or network of small squares created in ikat, each of which contains a single motif. The motifs range from floral and foliate through to depictions of such everyday objects as clocks, gramophone records and aeroplanes. *Rumals* were always woven in dark red and black on white, and some *rumal* saris follow this aesthetic. This rather muted and conservative colour scheme gives them a classic appearance, even though they are a completely modern textile. The majority of Pochampalli ikats are vibrantly coloured, however, and although there is a wide range of modern designs, most still follow the *rumal* layout with wide plain borders, one or two plain bands marking the endpiece, and a field covered with ikat-created designs [Pl. 144].

Historically, Andhra Pradesh's ikat saris appear to have closer ties with Gujarat than Orissa. Two brothers from one of the original *rumal*-weaving families in Chirala are believed to have trained in Gujarat in the early years of the twentieth century,[66] and today the Pochampalli and Chirala areas specialize in creating imitation *patolu* saris [Pl. 141]. Some of these imitations are very close to the originals although the weaving is often less fine. The characteristic *patolu* motifs are often interspersed within the *rumal* format, leading to the typical *patolu* elephants (*enuga*), parrots (*ciluka*), dancing girls (*annu*) and flowers (*poovu*) being placed within the geometric grid of the *rumal*-style field [Pl. 140]. Other imitation *patola* have purely geometric forms within

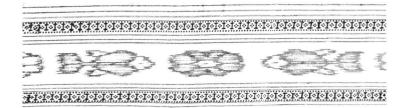

the field, something not seen in the traditional Gujarati versions [Pl. 142]. Most of these imitation *patola* also have ikat borders and endpieces which are usually less complex than the multiple bands found in the originals. They are woven in silk, cotton and silk-cotton mixes, and, as might be expected, are very popular in Gujarat because they are so much cheaper than the real thing.[67] All Andhra Pradesh ikats are sold in major urban centres; and like the older *rumal* trade goods, its ikat saris are primarily made for export out of state rather than for local markets.

Batik and *Kalamkari* Saris

Northern Andhra Pradesh is also known for its *kalamkari* saris [Pls. 138, 139], so named for the pen-like instrument that is used to apply dye or wax to create freehand dyed or resist-dyed patterns onto the cloth. In terms of saris, the most important centre for this work is Machilipatnam, located at one of the mouths of the Krishna river, although several other centres creating similar saris have sprung up in nearby towns such as Balyalagudam (Krishna district).[68]

Most of the work on Machilipatnam saris is not hand-drawn, however, as the black outlines and red-dyed patterning are usually block-printed on.[69] As these saris are typically red, red-brown and black, there may be little obvious *kalamkari* work. Most freehand work is employed in painting on other colours, such as green or yellow, or else in creating the wax-resists. Large areas of wax resist may be applied to the cloth, especially when it is dyed in indigo, as the fabric is dipped into the indigo bath after the wax has hardened.[70] Consequently, many of the saris created today are what are commonly called batik,[71] and the fine penwork associated with *kalamkari* is usually missing. The batiks usually have Mughal-style or abstract Modernist designs.

A class of *kalamkari* sari called a *multan* was once created here, with each type named after the colour of its ground. A white *multan* had a white ground with red and black designs, a red *multan* a red ground with black and white patterns, while a black *multan* had red and white patterns. The patterning showed strong Mughal influences and tended to be created from static-looking block-printed motifs. It is not known whether these saris were in any way connected with the Pakistani town of Multan. Another type of sari, the *sangadi*, had white and red dots upon a black ground, and it is likely that it was a descendant of the old Saurashtran *bandhani* work that used to be carried out in Andhra Pradesh in the nineteenth century.[72] Much of Machilipatnam's dyed-cloth industry probably has historical roots in the chintz industry that was based here after the British set up their port and then factories in 1611.

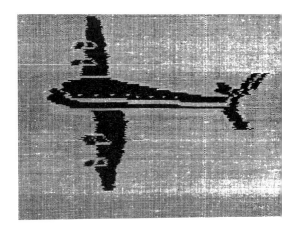

Andhra Pradesh

Above An ikat aeroplane from an Orissan landscape sari [Pl. 133].

Above left An ikat border from an Orissan 'ten *avatars*' sari [Pls. 134, 135].

Opposite A *Vohra bhat* design from a Pochampalli imitation *patolu*, Andhra Pradesh, 1992 [Pl. 141].

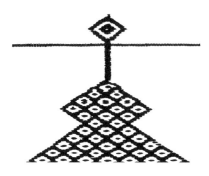

Above A *phool cheeta chauk* design from a Gond *ganda*, Koraput, Orissa [Pl. 111].

Opposite **110** The Munda *sangol paria*, or festival sari. Woven in heavy cotton, this is a rare sari intended exclusively for Munda use. The endpiece is created in a weft-faced weave that hides the red warps of the border, upon which are woven bands of geometric patterning in both continuous and discontinuous supplementary weft, usually in red and (occasionally) yellow yarn. Beyond the endpiece, the weaving changes to a plain weave with interlocked-weft red borders and the triangular *kumbha*. Woven by Kalwar Hans, Chondor village, Ranchi district, southern Bihar, 1994.

Cotton Muslins of Northern Andhra Pradesh

Cotton muslins are created in the eastern lowlands throughout Andhra Pradesh, especially in the coastal areas such as Krishna (Bezwada, Vijayawada) and Srikakulam (Uppada and Kathiawad) districts. They have many structural and design similarities to those of southern Andhra Pradesh and Tamil Nadu, and their weavers supply local markets as well as eastern India. Their output includes *jamdanis* and other fine muslins for the Bengali market.

Traditionally, muslins are preferred in Andhra Pradesh's lowland areas to the heavy cotton ethnic saris of the Indo-Aryan-speaking and tribal areas further north, but they have some common features. For instance, borders often consist of supplementary-warp patterning, usually a one- to 2.5-centimetre (one-inch) band with floral or geometric designs. However, the patterning is not usually of the Deccani type, being broader in width with a different repertoire of motifs. Unusually, for ethnic or tribal saris, the endpiece is generally extremely simple, with one or two unembellished warp stripes. Sometimes the field of these saris has a fine check, as in Maharashtran saris, although most have a plain coloured field.

Gadwal Saris

Gadwal saris show strong design links to the Kornad saris of south India (see p. 122) and the silk border-cotton field saris of the eastern central Deccan [Pl. 145]. They were traditionally woven in the interlocked-weft technique (called *kupadam* or *tippadamu* here), often with *kumbham* (also called *kotakomma*) in the borders, and were known as a *kupadam* or *kumbham* saris. The silk border was either *tasar* or mulberry, and the field was often of unbleached cotton, although it may have also contained coloured cotton or silk checks. A pure silk version of this sari also existed, usually woven in bright contrasting colours such as canary yellow and lime green. Gadwal saris usually carry a large, distinctive inverse temple motif in their endpiece known as a *reku*.[73] They are often regarded as *puja* saris by local women who wear them for religious and festive occasions.

Today Gadwal makes many saris for the mainstream south Indian market. Most still are woven with interlocked-weft borders of contrasting colours, and have designs of the Kornad or south Indian-Tamil brocade type discussed in Chapter Six. It is believed that the brocading abilities of many of the weavers in Gadwal originate from Banaras, where a local maharaja sent their ancestors to learn brocade-weaving skills;[74] the designs, however, do not show any Banaras influences but are strongly south-east Indian in structure and aesthetic quality.

Narayanpet Saris

The village of Narayanpet is so close to the northern Karnataka border that it may come as no surprise to find that its saris have more in common with those of northern Karnataka, called Ilkal saris, than most Andhra textiles. Because they are primarily worn by women in eastern Maharashtra in the west Deccan region, I have discussed this town's saris in Chapter Seven.

Tribal Saris

111 *Right* A Gond wedding sari (*ganda*) woven by L.T. Palti. Many tribal women traditionally bleach and dye their own cotton yarn, which they then give to the weaver to make the sari. A mixture containing cow-dung is used as the bleach, while the brown-to-red colour of the pattern yarn is created from dye obtained from the aal tree. Kotpad (Koraput district), Orissa, 1990.

112 *Below* A Bondo hip wrapper, 1970. Even today many Bondo women still wear their traditional hip wrapper, over which much jewelry is worn. Like the Gadaba, many Bondo women weave. The warp threads are spun from local bast fibres and the weft from coloured cottons the Bondo either dye themselves or buy in local markets. Padaiguda village, Koraput.

113 *Below right* A Gadaba *kerong*. This supplementary-weft design is similar to that found in ethnic (non-tribal) Orissan saris. Koraput district, Orissa, 1990.

115 *Below left* A Santhal woman wearing a *khanda* sari, in a village south of Jamshedpur (Singhbhum district) on the Chota Nagpur plateau, a remote, agriculturally poor area. Although the larger tribes, such as the Santhal, Munda, Gond and Oraon, are maintaining their cultural identity, many smaller tribal groups are becoming almost fully incorporated into mainstream Indian society, usually at the bottom.

Ethnic Saris of the Eastern Ghats

114 *Left* A typical *do-muha* sari worn by rural women in the eastern Deccan region. Like most indigenous Deccan saris, this has two endpieces, hence its name (*do-muha* means 'two-faced'). Sagarpalli (Sambalpur district), Orissa, 1991.

116 *Below* Although this is a mulberry-silk sari, it is otherwise typical of all eastern Deccan saris. It has interlocked-weft borders featuring the triangular *kumbha* design (the *kumbha* is a clay pot, a fertility symbol), in addition to supplementary-warp bands of patterning along the borders. The endpiece is large, featuring supplementary-weft bands in stripes of different widths. Berhampur (Ganjam district), Orissa, 1990.

Opposite page **119** *Bottom* A *tasar* silk sari of the Umrer type, from eastern Maharashtra. The supplementary warp border pattern of large flowers (*rui phool*) is a typical local design.

Ethnic Saris of Orissa: The Western Hills
This page **120** *Left* This *saktapar* wedding sari is so named because of the red, white and black 'chequerboard' pattern created through warp and weft ikat dyeing. The board game of the same name is traditionally played by the bride and groom after the wedding, when they are alone together for the first time. It is considered an auspicious symbol. Sambalpur, Orissa, 1980.

121 *Above* The *bichchitrapuri* sari is one of the traditional wedding saris worn in Orissa's western hills. Similar to the *hansabali kapta* (Pl. 122), it has warp-wise bands of ikat patterning and numerous supplementary-warp stripes in the field. The central chequered bands were once woven, but today they are usually created through ikat-dyeing. Sambalpur, Orissa, 1990.

Ethnic Saris of Eastern Madhya Pradesh and Nagpur
Opposite page **117, 118** *Left and top right* A *tasar* silk sari of the Goyal type. The border contains the typical eastern Madhya Pradesh *rui phool* design, as well as rows of turtles (*kachhua*).

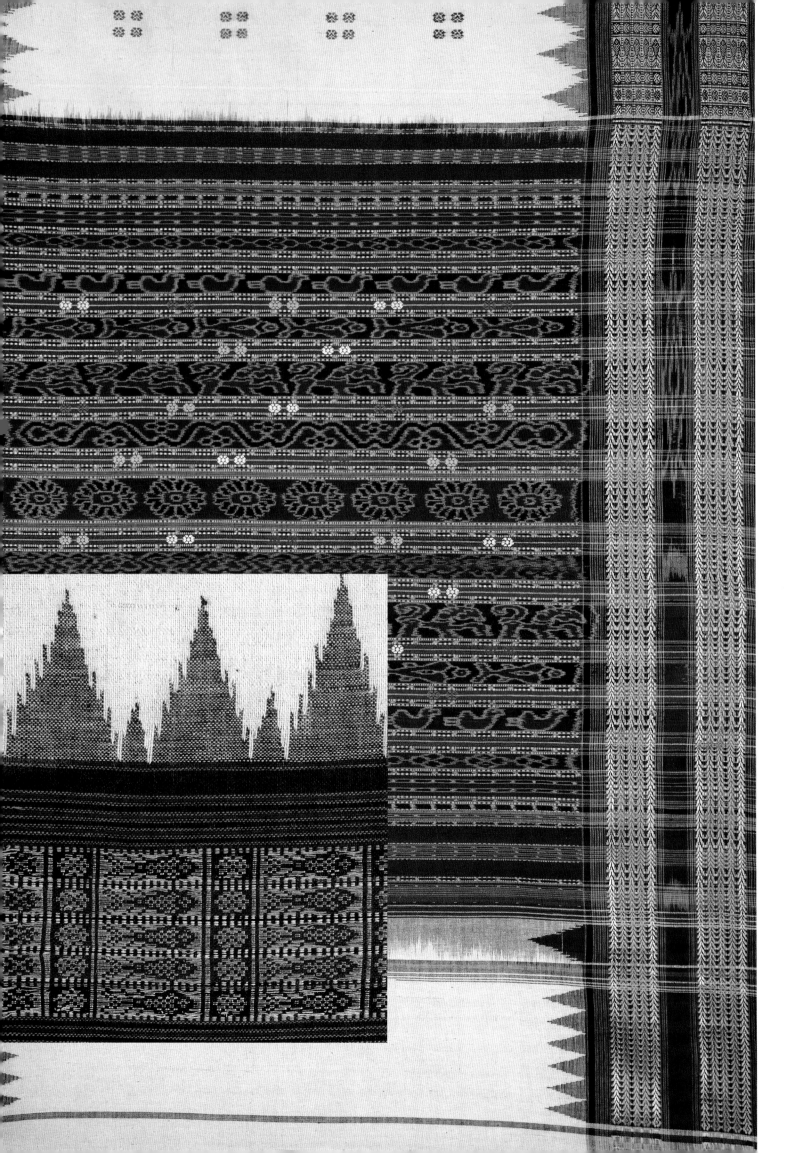

122, 123 *Opposite* A *do-muha* ikat sari. Often called a *hansabali kapta* ('cloth with geese and vines'), this sari is valued by local people for the number of supplementary-warp bands in its borders (*phoola*) rather than for its intricate ikat-work. There are ten bands (the maximum number possible), making this a *das phoolia* ('ten-flower') sari. Sambalpur district, Orissa, mid-1980s.

Ethnic Saris of Orissa: The Eastern Plains

124 *Top* The border of a mulberry-silk sari from Cuttack district, Orissa, created in the late 1980s. Today the *phoola* bands and warp-ikat border threads are usually cotton rather than silk.

125, 126 *Left and above* A mulberry-silk sari from Cuttack district, woven in the 1950s. This is a typical Cuttack sari, with weft-ikat patterning in the field, warp-ikat borders with only a small band of *phoola* along either edge, and ikat-created *kumbha* designs.

127 *Right* A *khandua* wedding sari from Nuapatna, Cuttack district, woven by master-weaver Sadam Guin in 1990. This is Orissa's best-known wedding sari. The cloth contains much traditional religious symbolism, including the lotus, elephant, vines and mythical beasts. During the nineteenth century, *khandua* were donated to temple deities, as well as worn as a veil during the wedding ceremony.

128 *Below* A mulberry-silk sari made for the Jagannath Temple in Puri, with a *shloka* (verse) from a twelfth-century religious poem that reads: 'Radhika's friend spoke to Krishna waiting helplessly in the bower, lost in the burden of his love.' (*Jayadeva, Gitagovinda,* 4.1 b-d, trans. John Cort). The ikat threads were tied by Madanath Naha, and woven by Harihar Kunda, in Nuapatna, in 1991. Although the script is Oriya, the words are actually Sanskrit.

129 *Below right* Part of the endpiece of a *khaṅdua* sari woven in the 1950s. Like the borders, the endpieces of most Cuttack saris have large bands of ikat weft-work with elaborate and colourful designs.

130 *Top left* This *tasar* silk sari has a plain (undyed) field and interlocked weft-woven borders with the typical two *phoola* bands and cotton warp-ikat patterning. Cuttack district, Orissa, mid-1980s.

131 *Above* The Bomokoi sari, so named after the village in southern Orissa where it is still woven for local women, is an ethnic Orissan sari without ikat work. The endpiece bands pictured here have numerous geometric discontinuous supplementary-weft motifs, and the supplementary-warp borders are woven with small repeat patterns. This sari was woven by Bapta Weavers' Cooperative Society, in Balangir district, Orissa.

Orissan Pictorial Saris

More styles of ikat-patterned ethnic saris are now created for the local Orissan market than in the past, and many of the new designs reveal the growing virtuosity of Orissa's already skilled textile artisans.

132 *Left* A modern ethnic wedding sari from the Sambalpur area. This sari features ikat representations of the *kumbha*, the clay pot that is traditionally filled with rice or water, covered with mango leaves and topped with a coconut, and left outside the house where a wedding is taking place. It expresses the wish for the marriage union to be fertile and materially comfortable. At the top of the endpiece is a pair of clasped hands, which indicate the willing union of man and wife. The sari is embellished with plastic gilt thread. Sambalpur, 1990.

133 *Below* Orissan 'landscape' saris were woven during the late 1970s and early 1980s, and bore depictions of local scenic views. This sari, created by P. Meher in 1977, is a view of Mina, a local lake in the Sambalpur area.

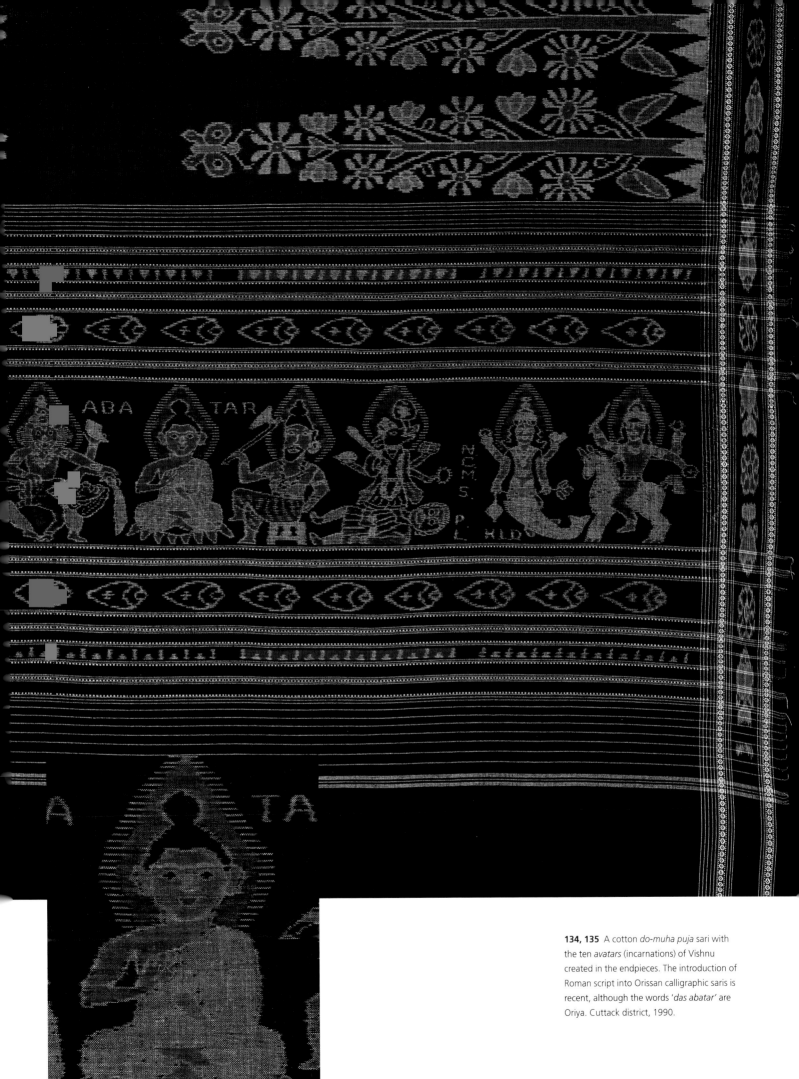

134, 135 A cotton *do-muha puja* sari with the ten *avatars* (incarnations) of Vishnu created in the endpieces. The introduction of Roman script into Orissan calligraphic saris is recent, although the words '*das abatar*' are Oriya. Cuttack district, 1990.

115

Siddipet *Khans*

Siddipet *khans* are traditionally made of unbleached cotton muslin with supplementary-warp and -weft designs created in multicoloured silks. Today the supplementary work is usually woven in monochromatic coloured cotton.

136 *Opposite* The endpieces of Siddipet *khans* often have one or more weft-wise bands with a pictorial subject, such as these women carrying water pots on their heads. Siddipet, Medak district, Andhra Pradesh, 1994.

137 *Above* A scrolling floral band in the endpiece of a *gollabhana khan* sari.

Kalamkari Saris

Although these saris are called *kalamkari* ('penwork'), most of the patterning is created through handblock-printing, and only a few areas of colour are painted by hand. These saris are descendants of the hand-painted fabrics once created in Machilipatnam for the seventeenth- and eighteenth-century European market.

138, 139 *Right* Cotton muslin saris with *kalamkari* designs, made in Machilipatnam, Andhra Pradesh, in 1994.

117

Andhra Pradesh Ikat Saris

The ikat saris of Andhra Pradesh are characterized by large, bold designs created in bright colours. Although many saris take their inspiration from Gujarati *patola*, their patterns have evolved into a distinctive Andhra style.

140 *Inset*, *above left* A sari made in the Pochampalli area, Nalgonda district, in 1975. Today Pochampalli is a major ikat-dyeing and -weaving centre.

141 *Above* A copy of a *patolu* sari in the *Vohra bhat* style, Pochampalli, 1992. Made of a silk and cotton mix, these saris cost about twenty times less than the 'real' *patola* saris of Gujarat.

Opposite **142** *Bottom* Not all Andhra *patola* saris are direct copies of traditional designs. Although identifiably a *patolu*, with its ikat warp and weft patterning, this sari has geometric patterns and colour schemes not seen in traditional *patola*. Pochampalli, late 1970s.

Gadwal Saris

145 *Below* Gadwal saris have many design features in common with south Indian saris, such as wide borders containing large bands of supplementary-warp *zari*, and graphic, two-dimensional patterning, but they have cotton bodies, with silk borders and endpieces. Gadwal (Mahbubnagar district), Andhra Pradesh, 1975.

144 *Above* The wide borders of this sari evolved from those of the *telia rumals* made for the Arabian market in the first half of the twentieth century. This is an ikat *khadi* sari created in Pochampalli in 1990.

143 *Above right* Some of the ikat saris created in Pochampalli are structurally similar to the Siddipet *khan* saris.

The South

The southern region covers the tropical lands of India's southern Karnataka, southern Andhra Pradesh, Tamil Nadu, Kerala and the island nation of Sri Lanka. Most languages spoken here are Dravidian, not Indo-Aryan,[1] and there are many distinctive cultural features that set this region apart from northern India, such as the way family and clan groups traditionally marry.[2] In addition, several markedly different cultures exist here, with the Tamil, Kerala and Sinhalese societies standing out most strongly.[3] During the first and early second millennia AD south India suffered from extensive regional warfare which gave rise to several communities with martial histories, including the matriarchal Nayars of Kerala, the Coorgs of southern Karnataka, and members of the Tamil Devanga weaving caste.[4] Although the last great Hindu empire, the Vijaynagar, centred near Hampi in eastern Karnataka, was destroyed by the Muslims in 1564, the culture of the south was almost completely unaffected by Islam and much of south India continued under the rule of Hindu kings, including several Maratha clans from the western Deccan. The coastal regions have been involved with international trade since at least Roman times,[5] and the people on both the western (Malabar) and eastern (Coromandel) coasts were involved with precolonial European traders, such as the Portuguese and French, although, again, most traditional south Indian textiles were not influenced by this contact.

Today the south is one of India's major sari-weaving regions, producing considerable quantities of rural, peasant and urban middle-class saris in silk, cotton, rayon and polyester. Its handloom cooperatives, such as Tamil Nadu's Co-op Tex, India's oldest handloom weavers' cooperative (founded in 1935), sell saris throughout India creating whatever the market demands.[6] Because of this, many traditional designs from different south Indian localities have become incorporated into the repertoire of other areas, which makes tracking down the origins of some textiles quite difficult; but many sari designs typical of particular areas are still distinguishable.

South India is also responsible for about 90 per cent of all the mulberry silk produced in India, with Karnataka alone accounting for about 60 per cent.[7] There, sericulture is practised mainly in the

Narrow-bordered saris
The narrow-bordered, coloured saris of southern Tamil Nadu are structurally very like the unbleached gold and white muslins of Kerala, suggesting some historical connection.

Opposite **146** *Top* These two narrow-bordered saris are traditionallly worn by rural and tribal women in southern Tamil Nadu. One is a brown rayon sari from Tirunelveli, with plastic gilt and synthetic supplementary embellishments; the other is a blue cotton muslin with cotton and rayon supplementary patterning, from Kanchipuram. Both were woven in the late 1980s. The weft-faced supplementary-weft bands of the endpieces (**147**, **148**, *centre and bottom*) are otherwise only found in Kerala and Tamil muslins and Munda saris.

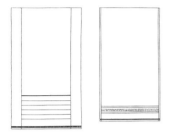

Above A wide-bordered cotton Kornad sari typically worn in Karnataka villages *(left)* and a narrow-bordered 8-metre sari from southern Tamil Nadu.

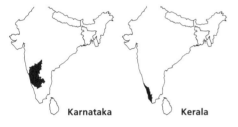

Karnataka   Kerala

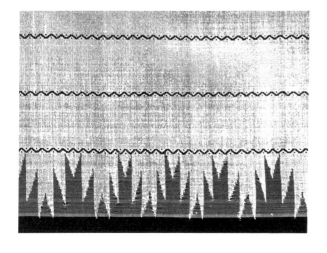

southern part of the state, in Bangalore, Kolar, Tumkar, Mysore and Mandya districts, although it is now expanding northwards. Virtually all the silk is mechanically reeled and much is exported to other states including Tamil Nadu, which itself accounts for over 10 per cent of India's raw silk production.[8]

Most Tamil and southern Andhra Pradesh weavers belong to either the Devanga (weaver)[9] or Saalikan (Saliyar) castes, the latter being the descendants of Saurashtran (Gujarati) weavers who migrated here between the tenth and eighteenth centuries. The Saaliya, Jaada (Lingayat) and Neekaara weaving communities are most often involved in Karnataka and Kerala, although there are fewer caste restrictions there, and both men and women from many non-traditional communities are also involved. In Kerala this is a consequence of the profound social changes that have occurred since Independence,[10] while in Karnataka the sericulture industry is only a century old, so there was no well-established local base of silk-weaving caste weavers to draw from.[11]

Traditional south-Indian sari designs fall into two basic types that are distinguished by their borders: (1) those with noticeably wide borders of contrasting colour to the field, which are created through a variety of different weaving and dyeing techniques [Pl. 152]; and (2) those with very narrow borders, often less than 2.5 centimetres (one inch) wide, which are created solely through supplementary-warp patterning [Pl. 146]. In both styles the border extends the full warp length of the sari and forms part of the endpiece, which is usually long. The earliest depictions of south Indian saris, in wall-hangings dating to the early seventeenth century (see p. 12), show women draped in distinctly narrow-bordered saris, and what little evidence there is suggests that this sari type is older than the wide-bordered varieties that have now become emblematic of the region.

The Kornad Sari

The Kornad sari[12] is now one of south India's most well-known saris. It has wide borders (*karai*, in Tamil)[13] approximately 10 to 40 centimetres (about 4 to 16 inches) across, woven in a plain colour, with two narrow bands of supplementary-warp patterning, known as *kampi* or *pettu* (stripe), positioned within 3 centimetres of each border edge [Pl. 159]. The body of the sari traditionally contains a woven pattern, usually checks (*kattam*) [Pl. 158] or stripes (*saarai, adyar*) [Pl. 160] reminiscent of, but larger and visually stronger than, those of western Deccan saris (p. 145). The endpiece (*mundhu, tholai*) contains either a series of widely spaced *zari* stripes (*adyar mundhu*) [Pl. 155] or, in more expensive and elaborate versions, supplementary-weft figuring [Pl. 152]. A wide (usually *zari*) band with weft-wise triangular points woven in the interlocked-weft technique is also commonly found in the endpiece, and is called a *reku*. In the more elaborate (and expensive) silk Kornads, the borders are also woven in the interlocked-weft technique, either with a straight edge [Pl. 149] or with various styles of triangular motifs called *mokku* (flower bud) ranging from simple triangles (*pogudi*) [Pls. 153, 154] to serrated mounds (*pillaiyar mokku*) [Pl. 150]. Such serrated borders are also known as *karavai* (sawtooth). Many Kornad saris are named after the colour of their borders.[14] For instance, an *arakku* sari has a lac-dyed (red) border, and a *pudapayalam karavai* a yellow serrated border.

Traditional Kornad saris used to be 7 to 9 metres (23 to nearly 30 feet) long, but today mostly 4.5- to 5.5-metre (15- to 18-foot) varieties are made, and are worn by virtually all Tamil women. They are mostly woven in eastern Tamil Nadu, in Kanchipuram, Salem, Arni, Madras, Kumbakonam and Thanjavore (Tanjore). In the nineteenth century, Arni was a major centre for these saris,[15] but today Kanchipuram is regarded as the most important Tamil silk-weaving town. The village of Kornad, near Kumbakonam, no longer weaves them.

Kanchipuram has only been weaving silk saris for the past 150 years,[16] and specializes in the *murukku pattu*, a heavy silk sari woven with tightly twisted three-ply, high-denier threads, using thick *zari* threads for supplementary-warp and -weft patterning. Interlocked-weft borders are common, as well as an endpiece created in the time-consuming *petni* technique. This requires each individual warp thread in the field to be twisted around a new set of warp threads the same colour as the border for about 2 to 5 centimetres (2 inches). Then the field warps are cut off. At the back of the sari the join is identified by two parallel warp fringes with the fringe facing the field the same colour as the endpiece, and vice versa [Pls. 153, 154]. This technique is still practised in various parts of the Deccan plateau, such as Aurangabad (Maharashtra) and Bomokoi (Orissa); while Dharmavaram (Andhra Pradesh) used this technique in the early twentieth century. Many of today's established Kanchipuram silk weavers trained in the cultural centre of Kalakshetra[17] during the 1970s, producing saris with designs that are somewhat 'heavy' in both style and fabric weight, with very wide borders [Pls. 152, 159].

Further south in the Kumbakonam/Thanjavur area, silk fabrics have been woven since at least the fourteenth century,[18] and today it creates heavy- to medium-weight Kornad silks similar in style and technique to Kanchipuram's, although the endpiece warps are attached differently. The technique used here, called *porai*, requires the threads to be dip-dyed before being set on the loom. When fixed, the weavers pull the warp threads at the 'join' of the two colours into two parallel rows of loops to even out the colour line. At the back of the cloth, the excess thread forms two parallel rows of loops that are cut to form parallel fringes containing threads of both colours rather than one [Pl. 150]. This method of creating the endpiece is traditional to Kumbakonam,[19] but is now also used in Dharmavaram and Arni.

Arni lies to the west of Kanchipuram, and along with Salem about 100 kilometres further south-west, it once created the more expensive Kornad saris.[20] Today these towns, as well as Kollegal in southern Karnataka, produce lightweight (single-ply) silk saris for everyday wear, which are usually single-colour textiles with borders and endpieces delineated through supplementary-warp and -weft bands (usually of *zari*) [Pl. 166], as well as imitation Kanchipuram saris with interlocked-weft borders and *porai* endpieces.

A more traditional variation of the Kornad sari is the so-called 'temple' sari. Technically, a temple sari is any sari woven for and

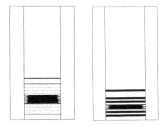

Above Two Tamil Kornad saris with different sized *reku* in elaborate endpieces.

Opposite, below A *pillaiyar mokku* border in a Kornad sari from Arni, Tamil Nadu [Pl. 150].

Below A Kornad sari draped in the Coorg style (*left*), in which it is pinned at the shoulder (Coorg women traditionally also wear long-sleeved blouses), and a narrow-bordered Tamil sari draped in the traditional Dravidian manner (*right*).

Tamil Nadu

donated to a temple deity in any part of South Asia [Pl. 161]. Originally it had to be perfectly executed, although it has always reflected what the donor could afford. Today, however, all wide-bordered Kornad saris have become popularly known as temple saris. One type of traditional Kornad sari often called a temple sari is the interlocked weft-woven *mubbhagam* sari that has its two borders and field of equal widths (each about 40 centimetres, or 16 inches, wide) [Pl. 6]. The borders are in the usual unembellished style with the two *pettu*, but in the type most often called a temple sari, the entire length of the narrow field is covered with fine-quality supplementary-weft *zari* patterning woven as a series of weft-wise rows, which include such motifs as elephants (*anai*), peacocks (*naviram*, *mayil*), double-headed eagles (*eruvai*) and foliate floral vines (*valli*) [Pl. 156]. The motifs are typical of Tamil Nadu/southern Andhra Pradesh – graphic two-dimensional representations quite unlike the more three-dimensional appearance of the northern Indian patterning typical of Banaras.

South Indian Figured Silks

Technically the Kornad sari is a figured silk, but its distinctive appearance sets it apart from the others, which can be divided into wide-bordered and narrow-bordered types.

Wide-bordered saris may be as technically complex as a Kornad, with interlocked-weft borders, and endpieces created in either the *petni* or *porai* techniques. Superimposed upon this ground would be, at the least, a relatively wide supplementary-warp woven border design often in *zari*. The endpiece and field may also have extensive supplementary-weft patterning. A traditional high-caste figured sari woven in this manner was locally known among Madrasi Tamils as a *pukai Madrasi* sari because it was considered very proper, conservative apparel in the early twentieth century.[21] It had a plain dark body (dark blue, dark green, purple) with bright red borders and endpiece. Supplementary-warp patterning in a band 3 to 8 centimetres (one to 3 inches) wide was woven in *zari* in the border, and there was additional silk supplementary-weft work in the endpiece [Pl. 168]. This sari was commonly woven in Dharmavaram and Madras, and Dharmavaram still weaves versions of it, albeit in a much broader range of colours and with dip-dyed endpieces.[22]

Today, wide-bordered saris containing very wide bands of supplementary-warp patterning are created in most major silk sari weaving centres, especially Kanchipuram, Dharmavaram, and such southern Karnataka towns as Kollegal, Mysore, Anekal and Molkalmuru. Many southern Karnataka saris, collectively known as Bangalore saris,[23] mimic interlocked-weft Tamil saris by having the warp and weft threads dip-dyed before weaving in order to give both warp and weft colouring to the borders and endpieces. The resulting irregular area of colour between the field and border is obscured by a band of supplementary-warp threads 2 to 5 centimetres (2 inches)

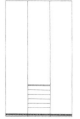

Above A *mubbhagam* sari.

Top Patterning in a wide-bordered sari from Dharmavaram, Andhra Pradesh.

wide woven across it in a satin weave. The dense colouring of the supplementary satin-woven threads hides the irregularities and gives the impression of a straight line [Pl. 164]. Sometimes, in the endpiece, the irregularities of dip-dyed threads are hidden by a band containing many fine supplementary *zari* threads forming thin stripes [Pl. 168].

Among the more inexpensive wide-bordered figured-silk saris woven in Kollegal, Arni and Salem is the skirt sari. This sari has a single wide border along only one side, which is often densely woven with supplementary-warp patterning, and an *adyar* endpiece [Pl. 165]. When worn, it has the wide-border look, and it is now sold throughout India in rural areas as a low-cost silk sari that poorer women can use for special occasions.[24] Polyester, rayon and mixed silk/synthetic versions are also made [Pl. 162].

Most narrow-bordered figured-silk saris are created in southern Karnataka. Woven in supplementary-warp *zari*, the border designs reflect Banaras influences rather than Tamil, although endpieces are usually of the *adyar* type. The finest of these saris is the Mysore crepe, which originated when Mysore began hand-weaving chiffons and georgettes in the 1930s and 1940s in an attempt to capture part of the growing market for French chiffon saris.[25] The Mysore crepe is a thin, opaque crepe silk with fine supplementary *zari* borders (*aca, ancu,* in Kannada) and an *adyar* endpiece (*seragu, sarangu*)[26] that is dip-dyed a contrasting colour after the cloth has been woven [Pls. 169, 170]. Today floral and abstract designs are often added to the field and endpiece through silk-screen printing.[27]

Above A skirt sari *(left)*, and a Mysore crepe sari from Karnataka.

Below A floral design from Bangalore, Karnataka, showing Banaras influence.

Kosara Pudava: White and Gold Muslins

Finely woven sheer muslins created in unbleached or white cotton, often with extremely fine *zari* and other supplementary threadwork in narrow borders, were traditionally worn in Tamil Nadu and Sri Lanka, and in Kerala, where they were called *kosara pudava* ('gold cloth'). These textiles have lost rather than gained popularity since Independence and, except for Kerala, are rarely woven today. Associated with high-caste Hindus such as the Nayars and Nambudiri Brahmins of Kerala, such white saris may have been more extensively worn in the past. Duarte Barbosa, who visited the Vijaynagar Empire between 1502 and 1508, described women as wearing '...white garments of very thin cotton, or silk with bright colours, 5 yards [4.6 metres] long...', apparently draped in the *nivi* style.[28] The muslins have high thread counts, plain fields and finely woven supplementary-warp borders, often no more than half a centimetre wide, containing several rows of tiny patterns such as peepal tree (*aracu*) leaves and zig-zags (*matanku*).[29]

The endpieces (Malayalam *tumpu*) of the Kerala muslins (*kavani, pudava*) usually have a band of ribbed, weft-faced supplementary-weft weaving with an elongated spike (*reku*) on either side, woven in interlocked weft [Pl. 172]. The borders (*kara, vilimpu*) were always created in

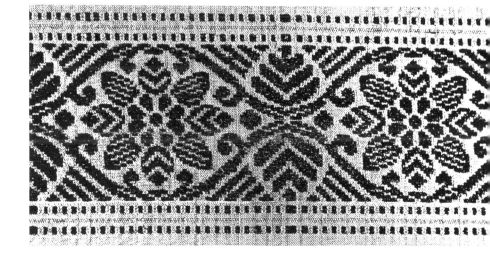

Above A scene from the Buddhist *Telapatta Jataka* depicting the king of Taxila with a *yakshi* in human form (Pahala Vihara, Malgiragala, Hambantola district, Sri Lanka, c. 1850). Both the king and the *yakshi* are wearing *lungis* that look as though they have been created through printing or batik. A triangular *tumpal* design is visible along the warp-wise edge of their garments.

Sri Lanka

either supplementary or ground warp threads; they were never interlocked [Pl. 171]. Although the *mundu veshti* worn on special occasions has all these embellishments in *zari*, daily-wear textiles have them in coloured cotton threads.[30] Other ethnic and religious groups in Kerala traditionally wore the same style of clothing with similar patterning but in different colours. Muslims, for instance, tended to wear black or dark-coloured cotton with the same patterning,[31] while Kerala's ancient Jewish community chose coloured, often chequered, fabrics.

In Tamil Nadu such saris were created in Madurai, Coimbatore, Tanjore and Arni,[32] by weavers of the Devanga caste. Like the Kerala textiles, they had supplementary-warp woven borders in *zari*, but also a few supplementary-warp stripes woven in the field, sometimes as blocks of geometric designs with floats cut away at the back. One traditional design is of a wavy line with a dot inside each curve, known as a *neli* (wiggly line), or, if a double stripe, a *rattai neli*, a pattern also used in Tamil floor paintings. Coimbatore specialized in adding wads of coloured cotton in the weft, producing long, tapering slivers known as *malli mokku* (jasmine bud), while Madurai muslins often had narrow, brightly coloured silk satin-weave borders woven in. The endpieces of the Tamil muslins were usually short versions of the *adyar* type [Pl. 174].[33]

Tamil and Telugu non-Brahmin caste groups, such as the Naidu, traditionally wear an 8-metre (26-foot) white muslin sari, dyed yellow with turmeric, during the climax of the wedding ceremony (hence the name, *muhurtham pudavai*), when the groom places the *thali* (wedding necklace) around the bride's neck.[34] *Muhurtham* saris are now also woven in 5.5-metre (18-foot) lengths, but their design structure remains the same with a narrow (2-centimetre) supplementary-warp border woven in red, and more recently green, cotton threads, with a simple two-band endpiece in the same colour [Pl. 173].[35]

The Saris of Sri Lanka

Sri Lanka's dress is closer to that of Kerala than Tamil Nadu, with a white *lungi* and veil (*tiraya*) traditionally of white cotton with a narrow border, and sometimes a belt or sash (*pattiya*). These clothes were worn by most of the population, including those who were not Buddhist Sinhalese (who make up about 70 per cent of its people). Sri Lanka's minority population consists of a mix of Ceylonese and Indian Tamils (22 per cent),[36] various Muslim communities (7 per cent) and a mix of Eurasians, Malays and Veddas (*adivasis*).[37]

Few handloom textiles are woven in Sri Lanka today, but nineteenth-century paintings and photographs show that prior to British domination, the aristocracy (male and female) wore white *lungis* with floral and geometric designs in black, blue and red, similar to Indonesian prints and batiks, and often including a row of *tumpals* along the weft end.[38] However, although the depictions of these cloths make them look like printed textiles – batik dyeing is traditionally carried out here – they may have also been embroidered because the mountain kingdom of Kandy had a cotton-upon-cotton embroidery tradition using blue, red and white threads on white or blue grounds.[39]

Upper-class women wore coloured warp-striped veils over their heads and upper bodies.[40] Kandy weavers also created cotton cloths, including sashes, with extensive continuous and discontinuous supplementary-weft designs that were very similar in style to the figured cloths of mainland South-East Asia, with many motifs almost identical to those woven by Tai-speaking groups.[41]

Today most Sinhalese women wear commercially printed *lungis* in a wide range of colours and typically floral designs, while many urban and upper-class women wear saris (*sariya*) draped in the *nivi* style.

Coloured Muslins

South India's coloured muslins are usually very fine and transparent although their rich colours often obscure this fact [Pl. 178]. Such centres as Venkatagiri (Andhra Pradesh) create high-quality muslins [Pl. 175], including cotton *jamdanis* for the Bengali market,[42] but many Tamil towns weave sheer muslin saris for local use that are of good technical quality with high thread counts [Pl. 176].[43] Although transparent, their most striking effect is saturated colour with yarn-dyed threads in such hues as purple, olive green, orange, bright red or bright green. Often different-coloured threads are woven in to create fine checks or stripes, and some are area-specific: for instance, a deep red muslin with thin white silk lines forming a 2.5-centimetre (one-inch) mesh check was typical of Madurai in the nineteenth century.[44]

Today, standard-length (4.5 to 5.5 metre, or 15 to 18 foot) saris are made for the middle-class market and heavier, but not necessarily coarser, 7 to 9 metre (23 to 30 foot) varieties are made for rural Dravidian women. Many of the coloured muslins are woven in the Andhra Pradesh style with two relatively wide, plain, weft-wise bands in the endpiece [Pl. 177]. However, many of the saris woven for the low-caste rural market have very narrow borders woven in intricate supplementary-warp designs no more than 2.5 centimetres (one inch) wide [Pl. 146]. They also have endpieces consisting of two ribbed, supplementary weft-faced bands, as found in the Kerala muslins, suggesting a possible historical link between these saris and the old upper-caste white muslin versions [Pls. 147, 148].

Resist-Dyed Saris

Today, Madurai is best known for its inexpensive, hard-wearing, medium-weight cotton saris that are printed and/or resist dyed. These saris are popular throughout southern India among both the rural and urban poor (8-metre) and the urban middle classes (5-metre), and are becoming increasingly common in the north as the range of designs and colours is expanding to suit north Indian tastes. These are not luxury saris. They are made of a tough opaque cloth that washes well, and usually contains narrow supplementary-warp bands of low- to high-quality *zari* woven in the border with an *adyar* endpiece [Pl. 179]. After weaving, the sari is dyed one shade for the field and a contrasting colour for the border and endpiece, the latter being added through either silk-screening or by resist dip-dyeing (placing the cloth between two long wooden blocks).[45] Various methods are used to embellish the cloth further, such as block-printing or silk-screen

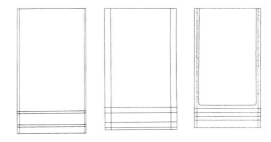

Above A Venkatagiri muslin sari (*left*), a Tamil coloured muslin daily-wear sari (*centre*), and a Madurai resist-print sari.

Below A *nili* pattern screen-printed on a Madurai resist-print sari [Pl. 179].

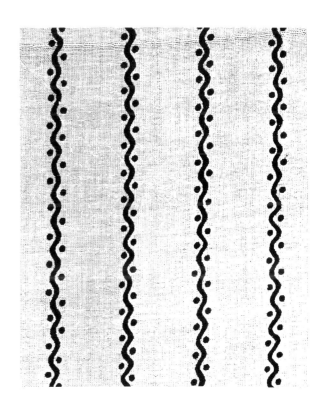

Above A fashion sari, Dharmavaram, Andhra Pradesh.

Below A border design from a Dharmavaram fashion sari, Andhra Pradesh [Pl. 2].

Opposite **149** *Top* A wide-bordered silk sari made in Kanchipuram, Tamil Nadu, in 1985, with the distinctive interlocked-weft border. One of the supplementary-warp *zari* threads has been inadvertently pulled into the border line where the weaver must have caught his shuttle. The woven *zari* pattern is called *mayilkan*, meaning 'peackock's eyes'.

150 *Below left Porai* is a time-consuming method of joining different coloured warp threads where the field and endpiece meet. The warp threads are dip-dyed prior to being set on the loom and are then pulled to form a straight line during weaving. The resulting double fringe formed at the join has a mix of different coloured threads along both sides. Arni, Tamil Nadu, 1992.

printing simple repetitive geometric patterns in the border or, more commonly, the field, with either resist pastes or a coloured dye [Pl. 180]. Until recently, most Madurai resist prints mimicked the nineteenth-century *bandhani* saris made for the region's expatriate Saurashtran community [Pl. 181]. They are known by a variety of names, such as *sungudi*, *chungudi* and *junnadi* (all based on the north Indian *chunari*) after the evenly distributed spots covering the field. The nineteenth-century *sungudis* (no longer made) had simple geometric patterns in different colours (usually red and black).[46]

At the opposite end of the social scale are *kalamkari* resist-dyed saris that were exclusively made for the Maratha *ranis* of Thanjavore until the end of the nineteenth century. Often known as Kodalikarupur or Karupur saris, after the village of manufacture, they consisted of a fine cotton muslin in which discontinuous supplementary *zari* patterns were woven in the *jamdani* technique. The muslins were then resist-painted by hand and dyed in various natural colours, giving a rich but sombre variety of red tones to the fabric.[47] In many ways the designs are reminiscent of the hand-drawn nineteenth-century Gujarati *saudagiri* prints made for the Thai market (see p. 25). In the early and mid-nineteenth century, 'fine cotton chintzes' (*kalamkari* saris) were also made in Madurai and Kalahat (north Arcot) as well as Machilipatnam.

Fashion Saris

It is impossible to ignore 'fashion saris' when talking about south Indian handlooms, for today the majority of its saris fit this category, although many traditional elements have been incorporated into them. For instance, the styles, techniques and designs of the fine white *kosara pudava* muslins are now commonly found in the popular 'Coimbatore' sari woven in the Coimbatore/Erode/Salem area [Pl. 183]. The cotton yarn is dyed before weaving and the *zari* replaced by coloured silks, but the traditional basic design structure of these saris is still visible in the form of narrow bands of supplementary-warp patterning and satin-weave borders. Today, most of the field patterning is woven in the weft rather than the warp, probably because powerlooms rather than handlooms are used.

Southern Karnataka also creates saris for specific regional markets, such as silk *bandhanis* for western India and silk *jamdanis* for Bengal. Although they are technically skilful, their colours are often atypical of the regional saris they mimic and their designs distinctly modern.[48]

151 *Above* Girls in the south do not wear saris until they have married or have reached marriable age; instead they wear a skirt (*paavadi*) and half-sari (*dhavani*). The women in this picture are all wearing saris draped in the *nivi* style, as well as the traditional flower garlands in their hair. Madapuram, southern Tamil Nadu.

152 *Opposite* A Kornad wedding sari traditionally worn by Brahmins or other wealthy high-caste women. It is woven from heavy *murukku pattu* (twisted, three-ply silk). Kanchipuram, Tamil Nadu, 1980.

153, 154 *Above left* The face and reverse side of the wedding sari in Pl. 152, showing the interlocked-weft 'join' of the border and field, resulting here in triangular *mokku* (flower buds). On the reverse, a fresh (red) warp thread is twisted around each (green) field warp, and then the green warp is cut off after the two threads have been woven together. This time-consuming technique called *petni*, more costly than *porai*, creates a fringe of red warp threads on one side and green warp threads on the other.

155 *Above* Rural women in southern Karnataka wear cotton Kornad saris, usually in more subdued colours than those of Tamil Nadu. Udipi, western Karnataka, 1994.

156 *Left* A brocaded silk endpiece whose graphic, two-dimensional style is typical of the Tamil area. Kalakshetra, mid-1970s.

157, 158 *Right and below* A Brahmin 8-metre (9-yard) sari typical of those worn by Tamil and southern Karnataka Brahmins. Although Brahmin saris were traditionally always made of silk, this sari also contains rayon. Note that the fine check ends at the 'join' with the wide, contrasting border – the threads do not pass all the way down to the selvage. This feature is time-consuming for the handweavers who create these saris. Kanchipuram, Tamil Nadu, mid-1980s.

159, 160 *Opposite* A typical Kornad sari, with wide borders containing narrow supplementary-warp bands (*pettu*), and both borders and endpiece in contrasting coloured threads to the central field. This heavy *murukku pattu* sari was woven in Kalakshetra, in the mid-1970s.

கர்க்கை

163 *Inset, right* Women cooking inside the temple compound, Mahakaliamman Temple, Madapuram, southern Tamil Nadu. The two ladies here are wearing traditional Tamil saris: on the left, a Madurai resist-print sari designed with a wide-bordered pattern; and on the right, a narrow-bordered sari typical of southern Tamil Nadu.

164 *Opposite* Relatively inexpensive, wide-bordered, brocaded silk saris made in southern Karnataka emulate the interlocked-weft look of traditional Kornad saris by using dip-dyed weft border threads. A band of warp-faced satin weave warp threads the same colour as the border is woven to hide the fuzzy line that occurs between the border and the field. Kollegal, southern Karnataka.

Wide-bordered Saris and Variations on the Kornad Design

161 *Above* A true temple sari such as this is donated to the temple deity and draped on its statue or else worn by temple dancers. Many Kornad saris are erroneously called 'temple saris' because some of them were once woven by weavers associated with major temple complexes. Here, the Tamil goddess Thirumaniamman, in her temple in Annanagar West, Madras, is draped in a silk Kornad sari.

162 *Right* This skirt sari, made of pink polyester with plastic gilt thread in the border, was woven for women at the lower end of the social scale. Its colour suggests that it was intended as a wedding sari for a poor woman who could not afford silk. Bangalore area, Karnataka, 1992.

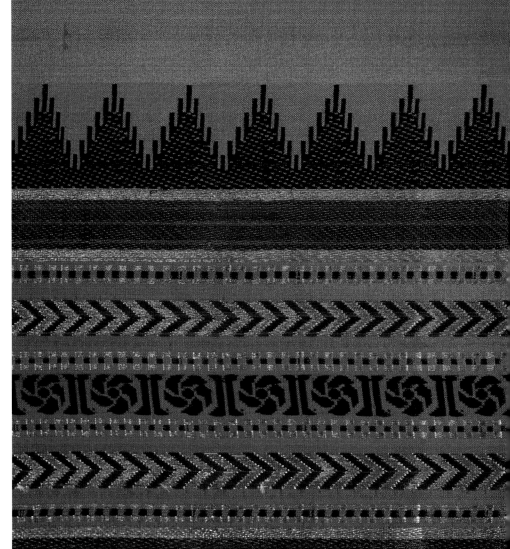

165 *Above* This skirt sari of medium-weight silk with a *zari* border was probably woven in Arni or Salem, as both towns specialize in lighter weight silks than those of Kanchipuram. Early 1970s.

166 *Right* Until the breakdown of the caste system, all Tamil Brahmin women had to wear silk saris, not cotton. Many would probably have worn daily-wear saris similar to that depicted here, which is woven in thin silk, with supplementary *zari* stripes framing the wide border and endpiece. The patterning in the stripe indicates that this sari is likely to have been woven in Kollegal, southern Karnataka, a town that specializes in weaving low-cost silk saris.

167 *Inset, right* Ladies wearing traditional Kornad saris of southern Karnataka, which usually come in earth tones such as green. Indwal village, Mandya district.

168 *Opposite, top* A *pukai Madrasi* sari, the traditional sari favoured by northern Tamil women in the early twentieth century. The red border and endpiece, deep blue ground and ample *zari* supplementary-warp work in the borders make it similar to other traditional saris woven in the central and western Deccan. This is a modern sari with an endpiece created through dip-dyeing the warp threads. The line where the two dye colours meet is hidden by a band of fine gold *zari* stripes. Dharmavaram, Andhra Pradesh, 1991.

Narrow-bordered Silk Saris

169 *Below left* A Mysore crepe sari. Crepe silk has only been woven in India (in Mysore, southern Karnataka) since the early to mid-twentieth century. The dye is added after the saris are woven, the endpiece usually being dip-dyed a different colour to the field. Fine-grade *zari* is used to create the supplementary-warp borders, which are woven on powerlooms using dobbies or jacquard attachments.

170 *Below* A lady wearing a Mysore crepe sari, with her grandchild, at the Meenakshi Temple, Madurai, southern Tamil Nadu. Little girls rarely wear saris today, but instead, tailored Western dresses.

White Muslin Saris

This page **171, 172** *Left* Traditional Kerala costume, whether a sari (*pudava*) or two-piece drape (*mundu veshti*), tends to be of fine white or unbleached cotton muslin. The fine *zari* borders and double-striped endpieces are often given a 'wash' of gold colour before being sold in order to make the gold look even brighter, and Kerala ladies will purposefully buy their *kosara pudava* ('gold cloth') before it has been so dyed. In addition to the *zari* bands, extra cotton stripes in thicker white, red or black yarns are also added. These textiles are always finely made, and stress understated weaving virtuosity. Kerala, 1990.

Opposite page **173** High-caste Hindu communities in Tamil Nadu and southern Andhra Pradesh traditionally wear cotton wedding saris. Even today, most Naidu women wear the 7.5-metre white cotton *muhurtham* sari. It is dyed yellow with turmeric and worn during the climax of the wedding ceremony when the groom puts the *thali* (wedding necklace, equivalent to the European wedding ring) around the bride's neck. Tiruchirapalli, Tamil Nadu, 1994.

174 Similar unbleached cotton saris, called *pudavai*, with gold *zari* embellishments, were also created in western Tamil Nadu, especially in the Coimbatore, Salem and Madurai areas, although today they have all but disappeared. They may be the saris the Portuguese traveller Duarte Barbosa described in 1511 when he visited the Vijaynagar Empire, for he talked of women wearing white cotton saris.

Coloured Muslin Saris

175 *Opposite* Venkatagiri cotton muslins are traditionally fine, sheer muslins that were often woven for 'foreign' markets such as Bengal and Chanderi. This particular muslin sari is made to traditional Andhra design specifications, with an unembellished field, a simple, fine *zari* border with extra black cotton stripe, and a two-striped endpiece. A fine quality, handwoven sari of this kind is always expensive, and such saris often cost more money than silk ones. Venkatagiri, Andhra Pradesh, 1989.

176, 177 *Right* Handwoven muslin saris, yarn-dyed in saturated colours, are commonly worn by most south Indian women. These two saris, at the opposite end of the social scale to the Venkatagiri muslins, have relatively wide borders, with the typical Andhra 'double band' in the endpiece. The white threads in both saris are synthetic, but the coloured threads are cotton. Coimbatore/Salem area, Tamil Nadu, 1990.

178 *Below* A Venkatagiri muslin woven for the Andhra Pradesh market. Its endpiece, however, is more typical of some Maheshwar and eastern Maharashtra saris, which its creator may have been emulating, although the saturated colour suggests that it was aimed at the local south Indian market. Venkatagiri, Andhra Pradesh, 1989.

Resist-Printed Saris

179, 180 *Above* The hard-wearing, resist-
printed saris of Madurai have now become
a significant industry. The three saris here
were created in the early 1990s. On the right
is an 8-metre sari that would typically be
worn in a *kachchha* drape by a low-status
working woman such as a sweeper (detail,
above right); in the centre, a 5-metre sari for
the middle-class Tamil market featuring
typical Tamil patterns; and on the left a sari
printed to look like an Orissan sari with large
temple designs, made for the same middle-
class market.

181 *Right* Two Madurai saris resist-dyed
with traditional *chungudi* patterns. Madurai
resist-dyeing developed in the early
twentieth century in an effort to produce
bandhani spots without actually tying them.
The turquoise sari featured here shows the
wax still in place after dyeing, while the
green and orange sari is the finished
garment, after the wax has been washed out
and the fabric ironed and starched, ready for
sale. Madurai, 1994

Fashion Saris

Both Madurai and the Coimbatore/Salem area, the major cotton-weaving regions of Tamil Nadu, produce large quantities of low-cost cotton saris aimed at the general, pan-Indian market. Their designs usually follow the current trends, although they also help establish fashions.

182 *Right* A lady wearing a typical fashion sari woven in Madurai. She is visiting the Hanuman shrine in the Meenakshi Temple, Madurai, southern Tamil Nadu.

183 *Below* Fashion saris woven in the Coimbatore/Erode/Salem area of western Tamil Nadu. Although most of these saris are woven on powerlooms, their supplementary-warp and -weft embellishments are often reminiscent of the older, white-and-gold, narrow-bordered saris depicted in Pl. 174. 1989–92.

The Western Deccan

The western Deccan region consists of Maharashtra,[1] central and southern Madhya Pradesh and northern Karnataka. It comprises India's heartland: the central and western Deccan plateau, with its broad, dry grasslands and hills traversed by wide river valleys;[2] the precipitous Western Ghats running parallel to the narrow coastal plains called the Konkan; and on the northern coast, Bombay, one of Asia's major commercial centres.

Although most of this region's history has followed the same general pattern as eastern India's, Islamic culture did not take such a thoroughly strong hold as in the north, with the Hindu Maratha kingdoms playing a significant role in the fall of the Mughal empire in the eighteenth century.[3]

The region's traditional saris (Marathi *sadi*, *lugade*)[4] are also very different in style from those of the north. Characterized by borders (*dhari*, *katha*, *kanth*) containing numerous narrow supplementary-warp stripes of repetitive patterning, and short endpieces (*padara*) with five alternating red and white bands, they show no Mughal influences. The only exceptions are a few of the aristocratic textiles once created for the royal courts. The classification of many of this region's indigenous saris poses problems because their differences can be very subtle, and almost identical motifs, colours and even fineness of weaving may be used on saris that only vary by the quality and type of fibres used. For instance, *zari* may replace the white cotton or silk thread used to create the supplementary-warp border bands in the more upscale versions. Those saris that are markedly different include, firstly, the once-aristocratic luxury textiles that are collectively known as *shallu*, which usually have fine muslin fields with *zari* woven into the borders and endpieces;[5] secondly, Bombay's Zoroastrian Parsi saris; and thirdly, the mass-market mill products that have been produced by the textile mills in and around Bombay since the mid-nineteenth century.

The Deccan Sari

The Deccan sari is the archetypal sari of this region. It is usually associated with Maharashtra and is often called a Maharashtran sari, but versions exist throughout the western Deccan [Pl. 189].

Opposite **184** This Ilkal cotton sari was woven in a pitloom in the Dharwar district in 1991, and was embroidered with cotton threads in designs traditional to the region. The Ilkal sari is worn and woven throughout northern Karnataka and southern Maharashtra.

Traditionally about 8 metres (26 feet) long, it was commonly woven in a thin cotton dyed typically dark colours (red, green, purple, blue, brown), with a field containing a fine check (generically known as *kothi* or *chaukdi*); a warp stripe (*rasta* or *selari*); or else a weft woven a different colour to the warp (*dhoop chhaon*, 'sun and shadow'). The threads creating the check were woven in a two-shuttle technique so the weft stripe ends at the border edge instead of the selvage, although today this technique is only used in the more expensive saris [Pl. 194]. The mesh of checks is often extremely fine, created by only one or two threads of contrasting colour on a ground that may contain four or six threads per square [Pl. 190].[6] Every tiny variation on the check design traditionally had a different name. The five broad endpiece stripes were originally woven in cotton or silk, but synthetic threads are now used, and like the ethnic saris of the eastern Deccan, most saris are still woven with two endpieces so they are reversible.

The border designs give most Deccan saris their names,[7] and borders are created as either a separate colour from the field (through contrasting-coloured warp threads) onto which the supplementary-warp bands are woven [Pl. 192], or simply a supplementary-warp band woven on a single-colour ground [Pl. 11]. Most western Maharashtran sari borders are narrow, but they are wider in the eastern (Nagpur) and southern (northern Karnataka) areas. The supplementary-warp bands are usually no more than 3 to 6 millimetres wide and several are woven side by side to form a collection of warp stripes.

The same supplementary-warp pattern often has many different names, only a few of which are given here. The most commonly found designs are: (1) a herringbone pattern generally called *gom* (centipede) or *katari* (dagger) [Pl. 190]; (2) a row of tiny sawtooth serrations called *karvat* (saw, sawtooth) or *bugdi* (ear ornament) [Pl. 190]; (3) various *phool* patterns, with the larger *rui phool* (cotton flower) and small *jai phool* (jasmine flower) being the most common [Pl. 193]; (4) the circular *rudraksha* motif; (5) a dense net-like design called *jaal* (net) or *chatai* (mat) which is usually woven in wider bands about 1.2 to 2.5 centimetres (one inch) across [Pl. 192]; (6) edge patterns looking like simpler versions of the Banaras *jhaalar*, usually named after pieces of jewelry, such as *chhada*, *kangora* (respectively, twisted cord, ornamental cord to hang jewelry) or simply called an 'edge' (*kanaa*) design [Pls. 185, 192]; (7) larger and more elaborate border patterns, ranging from one to 5 centimetres (2 inches) across, woven on looms with dobby attachments, such as a fan (*pankha*) or almond (*badaam*) [Pl. 185]; and

Above A Deccan sari, from Maharashtra.

Top A dobby-woven border from a modern Deccan sari, Malegaon, Maharashtra.

(8) red borders with white supplementary-warp bands traditionally called *gujroo*, a name also given to ankle ornaments [Pl. 184].

The Ilkal Sari

A sari with designs combining elements of the Deccan sari and the Tamil Kornad is common in northern Karnataka (Dharwar, Bijapur and Belgaum districts) and southern Maharashtra (Sholapur). Known by a variety of names,[8] it is generally called an Ilkal sari today, after a village in Dharwar district. It is worn throughout much of southern and western Maharashtra as well as northern Karnataka [Pl. 184].

Its field is usually dark (blue, purple, green) and plain, although the Maharashtran versions may contain a fine check. Both borders and endpiece are bright red with supplementary-warp bands (*kambi*) in white, commonly in herringbone, sawtooth and *phool* designs. The endpiece contains two large white supplementary-weft *reku*, here called *teni*, woven in the interlocked-weft technique.

Many Ilkal saris are also embroidered with a form of running-stitch work called *kasuti* ('embroidery'). The stitches create straight and zig-zag lines, as well as angular, often snowflake-like floral, geometric and representational forms, including elephants and shrines. The stitching has different names, such as *negi* for running stitch, *gavanti* for a double running stitch creating an unbroken line and *murgi* for a zig-zag line.[9]

There are several types of sari similar to the Ilkal in other parts of the western Deccan that were traditionally associated with higher-caste and wealthier women, and in Maharashtra many of these saris were called *lugade* to differentiate them from the more ordinary *sadi*.[10] One sari of this type is now becoming increasingly popular among lower-caste Maharashtrans. It has a silk (now often synthetic) warp with a cotton weft,[11] and a checked or *doop chhaon* field. In southern Maharashtra today, the endpiece warps are tie-dyed red and the white *teni* of the Ilkal sari are woven in, but elsewhere the endpiece matches the colours of the field (such as a darker shade of olive green with an olive-green field). Unlike the Ilkal sari, the borders are almost always the same colour as the field, being distinguished by a wide band of supplementary-warp threads usually woven in a mat-weave design, in addition to stripes of herringbone and small sawtooth patterns.[12]

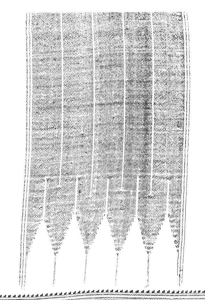

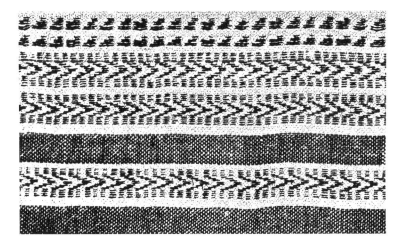

Above An Ilkal sari, Karnataka.

Top A *panja teni* ('five toed') band in the endpiece of an Ilkal sari from northern Karnataka [Pl. 184].

Left A Deccan sari border with *gom* and *karvat* supplementary-warp bands, Maharashtra [Pl. 190].

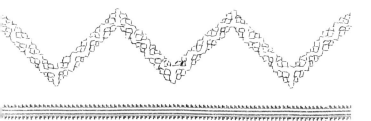

Western Deccan Silks

Finer versions of both Deccan and Ilkal saris were also created in silk, often with *zari* supplementary patterning instead of cotton or silk. One of the few towns still making traditional silk saris for the central Deccan market is Narayanpet in Andhra Pradesh, located very close to the northern Karnataka border. Its weavers create saris with opaque but lightweight silk fields and heavier borders woven with two-ply warp threads of contrasting colours. Like the Ilkal saris, the endpiece contains the interlocked-weft *teni*, woven in *zari*, and borders with small *zari phool* and sawtooth bands [Pl. 191]. Most other traditional weaving centres producing these saris have disappeared. In the nineteenth century, Poona was reported to have been a major centre although the industry had gone by 1900, while other towns (Yeola, Aurangabad) mentioned by Watt in 1903 no longer make them.

One type of traditional silk sari that was created until the1970s in south-central Madhya Pradesh and the neighbouring Nagpur area was called the *jot* or *jote*, which literally means 'yoked together', a reference to an aspect of its manufacture. From the available information, it is unclear what this 'yoke' was, but it may have been the name of the interlocked-weft border weaving technique commonly used here before the rise of the textile mills, or it could have signified the exchange of warp threads for those of another colour at the beginning of the endpiece, as found in the Kanchipuram *petni* technique. Low-cost Ilkal saris made of manmade fibres on handlooms or powerlooms still have such 'joined' endpieces today. If the latter was the case, this sari would have made a geographical 'link' between the *muhajorhi* of Orissa's Bomokoi, Bastar's Duhua, and the Paithani sari further west, which is also created with this technique. The *jote* traditionally had the familiar red borders and endpiece surrounding a dark blue field.

Another traditional silk sari of the Nagpur area was the Umrer, named after a nearby village.[13] This was similar to the Gadwal sari of Andhra Pradesh, with a cotton field, *tasar* or mulberry-silk borders and endpiece woven in the interlocked-weft technique, as well as rows of *kumbham* along the border edge. Like the Gadwal, it was used for *puja*, weddings and other ritually important occasions.

Sheer Muslins and *Shallu* Saris

The most famous of the fine *shallu* muslins were woven for the local aristocracy and the Mughal court during the eighteenth century, where they competed with Bengal's *jamdanis*. Chanderi (Madhya Pradesh) was the most well-known centre, although many other towns further south, such as Berhanpur and Maheshwar (close to the Maharashtra border), also produced them. Like the aristocratic *jamdanis* of eastern India, their manufacture ceased at the collapse of the Mughal Empire and the spread of mill-spun thread from Manchester in the early nineteenth century.[14] Nevertheless, fine transparent muslins continued to be woven in these towns for such royal patrons as the *maharanis* of Baroda, Gwalior, Nagpur and Indore, although once their patronage ended in the early- to mid-twentieth century these saris rapidly declined in quality.

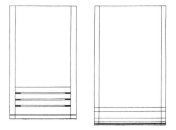

A Narayanpet sari, Andhra Pradesh (*left*) and a Chanderi sari, Madhya Pradesh.

Above A basket-weave pattern on a Dharwar sari, northern Karnataka.

Top A woven border design with *kasuti* cotton embroidery from an Ilkal sari, northern Karnataka [Pl. 184].

Since the 1940s silk warps have been used in Chanderi muslins instead of cotton;[15] the silk is of an undyed, still-gummed, low-denier variety that gives the cloth a crisp sheen while maintaining the off-white colouring typical of Chanderi fabrics [Pl. 204]. Although the traditional unbleached colouring is still popular, many Chanderi muslins are now in pastel and even bright colours. Despite their transparency, these saris often had two endpieces, the inner being white silk stripes and the outer (called a *tarz* in Chanderi) using *zari* and coloured threads. One characteristic of today's Chanderi muslins is that they have many *buti* in the field and endpiece, although these were only introduced in the late nineteenth century [Pl. 205].

Three types of Chanderi saris were traditionally woven: (1) The lightest muslins, which were almost completely plain, had a very narrow border of complementary-warp *zari* and an endpiece containing a few narrow *zari* bands, or one single, wider band. (2) Saris with broader borders woven in supplementary-warp *zari* with coloured supplementary-warp silk embellishments, woven into small repeat geometric or floral designs. The endpiece consisted of the border elements repeated twice (as two parallel bands), often with narrow woven lines and many *buti* woven between them. *Buti* would also appear in the field. Many of the patterns woven into the borders are influenced by Banaras styles, with creeping vines, *jhaalar* and *minakari* (coloured 'inlay' against gold) being common [Pl. 205]. (3) The third type of sari, called *do-chashmee* ('two streams'), is no longer made, but had wide borders with brightly coloured supplementary-warp silk in a satin weave upon which were supplementary bands of white geometric patterns. In some saris, the borders were reversible. The endpieces were always relatively insignificant, with either two narrow or one wider band of *zari* or coloured silk woven in.

The designs of Maheshwar saris are less influenced by Banaras and have more traditional Deccani elements, although like the Chanderi muslins they were traditionally woven by Muslim (Momin, Ansari, Julaha) rather than Hindu weavers. Silk warps did not appear in these saris until the 1970s, yet today 'muslins' with silk wefts as well as warps (separately or together) are now commonly woven.[16] The colours are usually understated, although green and pomegranate pink are popular for weddings. The borders traditionally had narrow bands of supplementary-warp patterning in fine *zari* or coloured silk, using all of the customary Deccan sari designs as well as a distinctive chain-link edge pattern (*aankh*) and lines of dashes (*muthda*).[17] Today, Maheshwar sari borders are often broader, containing various types of small edge patterns along the inner side, with the main band consisting of floral or mat designs. Unlike the Chanderis, Maheshwar saris traditionally had a very fine check or stripe in the field, and even today, when plain fields are most common, they never contain *butis* [Pl. 185].[18] The endpiece was traditionally either the five-band Maharashtran type or a series of stripes of different sizes [Pl. 187]. There has been a significant revival of Maheshwar saris in recent years,[19] although a large number are woven completely in silk with many *zari* embellishments. Nevertheless, the high standards of weaving and fine designs are maintained.

Above *Ankh*, *rui phool* and *kanaa* patterns on a Deccan sari from Sholapur, Maharashtra.

Madhya Pradesh

Above A Paithani sari, from Maharashtra.

Top A Paithani sari worn by an aristocratic lady of the Vaidya family of the Bombay Presidency (today the Gujarat and western Deccan region) in 1880. Note that the sari is draped in the *kachchha* style. The field was probably cotton muslin and the wide borders and endpiece of *zari* (gold thread) with inlaid coloured silk patterns. This was one of the most expensive saris produced in India during the nineteenth century.

Paithani Saris

The richest and most creatively time-consuming of all the *shallu* saris is the Paithani, named after a village near Aurangabad (Maharashtra), although it was once made in many parts of western Maharashtra and southern Madhya Pradesh in the nineteenth and possibly eighteenth centuries, including Aurangabad, Poona, Nasik and Malegaon. Traditionally it has a coloured cotton muslin field that often contains considerable supplementary *zari* patterning,[20] although even in the nineteenth century silk fields were also woven [Pl. 201].

The borders are created with the interlocked-weft technique, either with coloured silks or *zari*. A wide band of supplementary-warp *zari* (in a mat pattern) is woven upon the coloured silk border. In borders woven with a *zari* ground, coloured silk patterns are added as a supplementary-weft 'inlay' against the *zari*, usually in the form of flowers or creeping vines. The endpiece has fine silk warp threads that are cut and retied to a different colour, as in the *petni* technique of Kanchipuram [Pl. 202]. The weft threads are only of *zari*, forming a 'golden' ground upon which angular, brightly coloured silk designs are woven in the interlocked-weft technique, producing a tapestry effect [Pl. 203]. These patterns usually consist of intertwining vines, branches, leaves and flowers, as well as parrots, peacocks and even horses and riders.

The enormous amount of labour, skill and sheer expense of materials used to create the best of these saris rivalled the other luxury fabrics of the Mughal courts, and even into the twentieth century, these saris had royal associations.[21]

Parsi Saris

The Parsis originally came from Persia, being Zoroastrians who fled from Muslim persecution and forced conversions during the early eighth century. For the next thousand years they lived in Gujarat, adopting the local clothes and language but maintaining their separate religious and ethnic identity. It wasn't until the arrival of the British and the growth of the Gujarati ports and then Bombay in the eighteenth century that their social status changed. Boat builders and traders by profession, they developed good relationships with the British who used their services, and many Parsi families amassed huge fortunes in the nineteenth century.

Although they never lost their ethnic identity, the Parsis began to emulate British manners during colonial rule.[22] Throughout the nineteenth century, Parsi women continued wearing saris draped in the Gujarati style, but instead of the traditional bright reds and yellows of Gujarati textiles, they changed to sober blacks and whites. Originally, the Parsi wedding sari was of the usual red Gujarati type (presumably one of the various *bandhani* saris seen in Gujarat today), but this became a white sari made of either broderie anglais or lace from one of the Christian convents in Goa and other areas.[23] Although broderie anglais is usually cotton with embroidered floral motifs and buttonhole stitching, giving a lace-like effect, the Parsi versions were invariably of silk [Pl. 197]. In addition, coloured gauze or satin saris woven and embroidered with white silk from China were also worn on special occasions, and a red silk sari with white Chinese embroidery was often worn by the bride during the wedding festival, although not during the actual ceremony itself [Pl. 198]. When Indian upper-class fashions changed in the early twentieth century, wealthy Parsi ladies adopted embroidered chiffon saris in place of the traditional heavier fabrics.

Because much Parsi trade was traditionally with China, most nineteenth- and early twentieth-century Parsi saris had Chinese origins. Saris were made of a thin silk woven in a gauze weave (producing a ribbed effect), a heavier crepe-de-chine called *ghara*, or the Chinese-derived silk satin called *gaj* that was commonly worn in Gujarat (see p. 30).[24] Originally made in China on narrow looms, these fabrics were later woven in Surat on the wider Indian machines.[25] Because Chinese looms were only two-thirds the width of Indian ones, the Parsi saris made of Chinese-woven fabrics had a lengthwise seam adding the extra half-width of fabric, and were called *do-patti* (two-strip) saris.

All of these silks were embroidered in China using motifs that were often a mix of eighteenth-century 'trade' patterns once found in embroidered textiles exported to Europe[26] and Chinese versions of Indian motifs that often look very much like seventeenth-century chintz designs. These included depictions of flowers, leaves, birds, animals, people (in Chinese dress) and even such scenes as bridges spanning rivers. The embroideries were always elaborate, detailed and full, giving a very rich effect, and were invariably created in white silk with coloured highlights [Pl. 199]. Although black and violet were the commonest colours for the ground, many wedding-related *gharas* were brilliant red or orange-red [Pls. 198, 200].[27]

Other traditional Parsi saris include satin *bandhanis* from Kutch, usually dyed dark colours such as deep red and black. In the early to mid-twentieth century, gold *badla* embroidered onto navy and other dark chiffons was popular, as well as embroidered borders appliquéd onto plain fabrics; the borders are either Chinese embroideries on satin bands [Pls. 195, 196] or sequins embroidered onto net. Today the appliquéd borders are often removed from old saris and resewn onto newer ones, because the Chinese embroideries are no longer made.

Until about 1950, Chinese peddlars would annually visit wealthy Parsi families in Bombay to sell such embroideries (borders, blouses and saris) and *ghara* and *gajji* fabrics, which were sold by the *mon*, a Chinese weight.[28] In recent decades, those Parsis who still wear Indian clothes[29] favour pastel-coloured chiffons embroidered with sequins and gold for special occasions, although the old Chinese textiles have again become fashionable.

These Chinese embroideries were never adopted by mainstream India, but one Parsi fabric, the *tanchoi* (see p. 56), has become a popular, if exclusive, Indian textile. *Tanchois* were originally imported from China until the Chhoi brothers learned the weaving techniques and set up shops in Surat (Gujarat), but these Parsi-owned weaving concerns were pushed out of business by Banaras weavers who undercut their prices in the early 1950s [Pls. 14, 73].

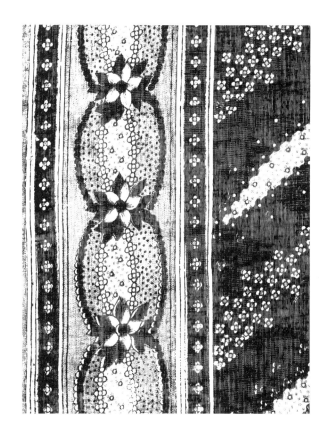

Maharashtra

Top A silk-screened design on an inexpensive Bombay mill sari made for the rural market.

Textile Mills and Sari Factories

The Parsis were some of India's first, and most important, industrialists, with one family, the Tatas, almost singlehandedly initiating much of India's basic industrial infrastructure during the early and mid-twentieth century.[30] Yet in terms of India's textile mills the family's founder, Jamsetji Tata, was a latecomer, opening his cotton mill at Nagpur in 1877.[31] More than twenty years earlier, in the 1850s, textile mills were appearing in Bombay and Ahmedabad and by the mid-1860s were booming.[32] However, the Indian mills were constrained by the self-protective trade laws of the ruling British, and the Swadeshi movement began as an effort to promote Indian mill cloth rather than village-made textiles.

Yet just as British mill cloth destroyed indigenous handweaving industries, leaving thousands of skilled craftsmen unemployed, so have the Indian mills, and without government support the handloom situation today would be much worse than it is.[33] Ironically, in industrial terms the physical layout of the sari actually prevents complete automation[34] because most women will only wear saris with a recognizable endpiece. Most 'mill saris' are screen-printed, and it is the quality of the materials, including the base fabric (often mill-woven in bulk) and dyes, as well as the quality of the design and the standard of the screen-printing, that determines a sari's market [Pls. 8, 25, 186].[35]

Manufacturers of India's most modern fabric, polyester, have broken the rule about endpieces and are producing roller-printed saris without them. Although the volume of polyester saris produced during the 1980s rose quickly (factory volumes of polyester production rose from 28,600 tonnes in 1980 to 100,800 tonnes in 1990) they still make up only a tiny proportion of all the saris made (total mill consumption of all fibres was over 2 million tonnes in 1990, which produced 2 billion metres of fabric).[36] Even many ethnic saris are now a mixture of traditional hand-processing (such as dip-dyeing or hand-reeling) and screen-printing, as can be seen not only in the *bandhani* of western India, but also in many of the *khadi* prints and the Madurai prints of Tamil Nadu.

Yet even with the cheapest screen-printed saris made for poor rural and urban women, regional differences abound. In Orissa, for example, most low-priced prints are decorated with Orissan colours, motifs and layouts; in northern and eastern India white saris with coloured printed embellishments are common; while in Andhra Pradesh most of these saris are still 8 metres (26 feet) long with two endpieces.

One has only to travel across an international border to see this regional variation in full force. Passing into Nepal from Bihar in the early 1990s, we found that rural women on the Bihar side were wearing brightly coloured, predominantly orange prints with large, almost florid designs [Pl. 188]. Over the border, Nepali women sported bright red saris (draped in the Nepali manner) with only a scattering of small black and white motifs. It seems that even the mass market is bending to the will of local demands, and expressions of ethnic and regional pride continue to evolve.

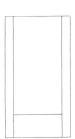

Above A low-cost mill-print sari, from Bombay.

Top A nineteenth-century mill-print cotton, probably from Bombay. It features a so-called 'Indianized' western-European pattern.

Social Extremes
Opposite The western Deccan region produces some of the most exclusive, individually crafted aristocratic saris, such as the Maheshwari sari shown here, as well as mass-market, industrial mill-made saris created for the urban and rural poor.

Maheshwari Saris

185 *Left* The borders of two Maheshwari saris: on the left, a cotton sari with *selari* (warp-wise field stripes), and on the right (the silk sari in Pl. 187), the border stripe of ikat 'dashes' is a modern innovation.

187 *Bottom left* A silk Maheshwari sari made to traditional specifications. Dye-master and designer Radeshyam Bhile of the Rehwa Society created this sari in the late 1980s.

Mill-Print Saris

186 *Inset* Maharashtran women wearing 8-metre, screen-printed mill saris draped in the *kachchha* style.

188 *Below* This screen-printed mill sari is probably the cheapest sari on the Indian market, and is worn by poor rural and urban women. Yet even at this economic level strong regional tastes affect colours and styles. Bold colours and naturalistic patterns (seen here) are favoured by rural women in eastern Uttar Pradesh and northern Bihar. Bombay, 1990.

153

Deccan Saris

The traditional Deccan sari is a fine, soft
cotton cloth whose transparency is hidden by
its rich, often dark colours. The borders have
numerous narrow supplementary-warp
bands, while the endpiece consists of five
(sometimes seven) broad stripes of
alternating red and white.

189 *Above* Three traditional Deccan saris.
On the left is an 8-metre cotton sari from
Ahmadnagar (detail, **190**); in the centre is a
sari from Belgaum, woven in polyester with a
'window-pane' check in orange, and gold-
coloured plastic *zari* along the borders; and
on the right (detail, **192**) is a *dhoop chhaon*
'sun and shadow' sari from Sholapur.

191 *Right* The dark blue field with bright red borders and endpiece is typical of a style found throughout the southern and eastern parts of the region. The supplementary-warp bands in the borders and weft endpiece stripes are woven in *zari*. These saris were traditionally worn by Brahmins and other wealthy women. Narayanpet, 1990

192 *Below* The border design of the *dhoop chhaon* sari opposite. The bands of yellow supplementary-warp threads are of synthetic yarn. The fine diamond-shaped pattern is called *chatai* (mat weave), and the border edging *kangora* (ornamental cord). Sholapur, Maharashtra, 1990.

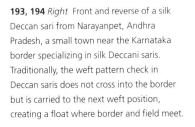

193, 194 *Right* Front and reverse of a silk Deccan sari from Narayanpet, Andhra Pradesh, a small town near the Karnataka border specializing in silk Deccani saris. Traditionally, the weft pattern check in Deccan saris does not cross into the border but is carried to the next weft position, creating a float where border and field meet.

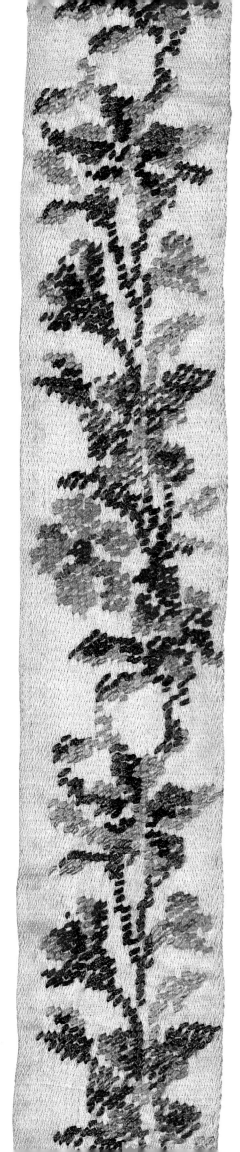

Parsi Saris

195, 196 *Left* Embroidered sari borders were created in China and brought to Bombay by itinerant Chinese traders who sold them directly to Parsi women in their homes. The women then sewed them onto crepe and later chiffon silk saris. This trade disappeared in the late 1940s/early 1950s when China's borders closed, but older Parsi women can still vividly recall individual traders, as they would visit the same family every year.

197 *Below* An early twentieth-century Parsi wedding sari. Although they continued wearing Indian clothes, nineteenth-century Parsis changed the colours of many of their formal garments to emulate British tastes. Wedding saris became white instead of red, and were woven in silk fabrics mimicking broderie anglais.

198 *Left* A Parsi *ghara* made in the 1920s. Elaborately embroidered saris were made in China for Parsi clients. Their designs were a mixture of Chinese and older European export patterns, such as those found on eighteenth-century Chinese export embroideries and Indian chintzes.

199, 200 *Below and bottom* This Parsi *ghara* is from the same period (1920s), but its embroidery is more elaborate.

Shallu Saris

Chanderi and Paithani saris, together with
Maheshwari saris, are the luxury saris of the
western Deccan that used to be made
exclusively for royal and aristocratic use.
Usually of fine cotton muslin, which until this
century was always more expensive than silk,
they also contained a lot of *zari* work, and
zari brocade saris in the region are still called
shallu.

Paithani Saris

201, 202 *Left, and below left* Paithani saris
were always associated with royalty because
of their cost, which resulted from the large
amounts of *zari* present, as well as their
detailed workmanship. The coloured silk
patterns in the *zari* endpiece are created
using the time-consuming interlocked-weft
tapestry weave, and the endpiece is joined to
the field by the demanding *petni* technique.
Aurangabad, Maharashtra, 1980.

203 *Below right* Intricate tapestry-woven
inlay in the endpiece of an eighteenth-
century Paithani sari (reverse side). This floral
spray is actually 18 centimetres high.

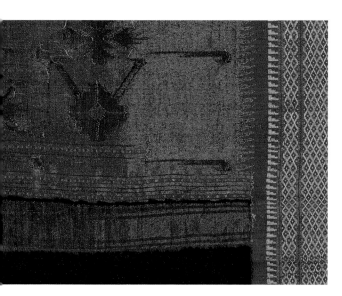

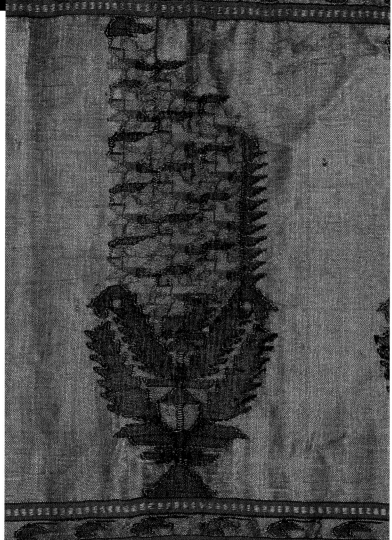

Chanderi Saris

204, 205 Traditional Chanderi saris were woven as fine translucent cotton muslins, with coloured silk and *zari* embellishments, for the local aristocracy. Today the warp is more likely to be of silk, as it is easier and faster to weave. *Buti*, which feature on the endpiece (*above*) of this sari made in the early 1970s, are regarded as a hallmark of Chanderi muslins, although they were only introduced in the late nineteenth century.

Iconography

In traditional rural India almost every aspect of life has special significance and that significance is translated into symbolic expression in clothing and other forms of personal adornment. Even the sari's colour can have meaning. For instance, in northern India a woman will wear a yellow sari for seven days after she has given birth to a child, while in Rajasthan, rural women still have red designs tie-dyed onto a yellow veil (*pido*) to indicate they are pregnant and hope to bear a son.

Although there are many striking differences between sari designs in different areas, certain motifs reappear throughout the subcontinent, or else in such numbers in one region that they must be part of long-standing traditions. Their original significance may have been lost years, if not centuries, ago, but they are often still regarded as important elements in particular saris.

A motif's past meanings and history are usually discovered from sources that have nothing directly to do with textiles; and the evidence based on archaeological finds, architecture, sculpture, painting and literature suggests that many traditional motifs are ancient. The peacock, for instance, is painted on Indus Valley burial pottery dating back to the third millennium BC, and its depiction in a wide variety of tribal art today suggests its origins may even predate Indus Valley use. Peacocks are found in Mauryan Buddhist sculpture, Gupta-period artefacts, Mughal miniatures, and in present-day wall-paintings, carvings and textiles. They are also used as metaphors in Sanskrit, Indo-Muslim and modern literature. That peacocks are found in the art of most post-Indus Valley cultures indicates that they remained a potent symbol up to the present day, for they are now India's national bird.

Although it is difficult, if not impossible, to ascribe the same symbolism and meaning to, say, an illustration of a peacock on a Indus vase, a Mauryan relief, and a modern rural wall-painting, it is possible to find continuities of meaning. Sometimes, as in the case of the peacock, there is even evidence that its symbolic significance evolved over time.

Most traditional sari motifs fall into one or both of two categories: first, they may serve a protective function, guarding their wearer against the evil eye and other misfortunes; and second, they may relate to fertility (in the broadest sense of the word). In agricultural communities (about 75 per cent of India's population is rural) fertility

Above A peacock design on a Baluchar sari from West Bengal [Pl. 62].

Opposite **206** Part of the endpiece (*muha*) of a traditional ethnic sari (*hansabali kapta*) from Orissa. It contains numerous iconographic elements, including geese (*hansa*), fish (*maachha*), *buti*, supplementary weft (*khapa*) stripes, bands and dashes (*jeera*). Sambalpur district, Orissa, *c.* 1980.

and wealth are closely linked, as the harvest is directly responsible for the level of a community's material well-being; and as might be expected, these elements can have religious connotations and connections.

In order to avoid the repetition of historical dates at each reference, a brief table outlining major historical periods and their dates is given in the Chronology (p. 200). Also, the Sanskrit, Prakrit and local modern names of motifs (where they appear in traditional saris) are listed at the beginning of each section. The abbreviations of the languages follow those of the Glossary of Indian Terms (p. 190).

Colour Symbolism

The symbolic use of colour has played a part in Indian life at least since Vedic times. The Sanskrit word for caste, *varna*, literally means colour, and certain colours are traditionally associated with different castes. This caste-colour association has also been reflected in traditional clothes, something which is still adhered to today, even though it is now much more diluted.[1]

The four *varnas* consist of the Brahmins (priestly caste), Kshatriyas (warrior caste, including most kings), Vaisyas (traders, merchants, scribes), and Sudras (farmers, serfs, artisans, including weavers, manual labourers), as well as the ritually impure groups (manual labourers, tanners, indigo dyers) who were completely outside (and below) the Hindu caste system. The tribals (*adivasis*), Muslims and foreigners were also outside the caste system but generally had better status than the untouchables, even though technically they were also ritually impure.

White: (Sk) *gaura*; (Pk) *goora*; (Per) *saped*; (U) *safed, safaid*; (H) *goraa, safed*; (G) *goruu*; (M, O) *goraa*; (B) *gora*; (N) *goro*; (Si) *gora*; (Ta) *vel, ven*; (Ma) *velukka, velaru*; (Ka) *belu, bile*; (Te) *veli, velidi*; (Mu) *pund, pundi*; (Kh) *ronglieh*.

In terms of clothing colours, Brahmins were traditionally associated with white, as any form of dyeing was regarded as impure, although in the 'colour belt' of the west and south, traditional Brahmin saris were often dyed bright colours. The Jain sect, the Svetambaras (literally, 'white cloth') also always wore white clothing. Today, colour has become a more dominant factor in women's clothing, and white is often only worn on ritual occasions, such as special *pujas*. In most regions it is never worn during weddings because white is also regarded as the colour of mourning, which is why widows in north India traditionally wear white saris without any coloured embellishments.

Red: (Sk) *rakt, raaga*; (Pk) *ramga*; (Per, U, H) *laal*; (B) *raanaa*; (O, S) *ranga*; (Ta) *kaavi, tukir, kuruti, tukku, toompu, pooval, ceyya, ceetakam, ceettu*, suffixes *ce- cevv-*; (Ta/Te) *arakku*; (Ma) *kaavi, pooval, ceeya*, suffixes *ce- cem-*; (Ka) *kaavi, togaru, ere, kurudi, jaaju, jaadu*, suffixes *ke- kem-*; (Te) *erupa, erra, erranu, errani, togaru, kaavi*, suffix *cem-, toopu* (red cloth); (Go) *erra*; (Ko) *era, erani*; (Or) *xenso*; (Mu) *aragh, purai*; (Kh) *rongsaw*.

The colour red was associated with the Kshatriyas, although today it is commonly worn by brides of all castes during weddings in the

Above The river goddess Ganga standing on a *makara* (half elephant, half fish), from a lintel of the temple at Beshnagar, Madhya Pradesh, *c.* AD 500. Ganga herself, the *makara* and the blooming mango tree above the goddess are images that relate to fertility, and all are found in the iconography of many traditional saris.

Opposite, above Celestial elephants showering the goddess Gaja-Lakshmi with water, Namunja, Bogra district, Bangladesh, *c.* AD 700–800. Lakshmi, the goddess of good luck, wealth and fertility, is surrounded by three important symbols often associated with her: the lotus (surrounding her, in her hand and beneath her feet), elephants, and the *kumbh*, or water pot, which is used here to pour water (by elephants) and coins (by attendants).

Opposite, below A lotus flower and vine ikat border from a silk Sambalpur sari, Orissa.

north and by Brahmin brides in the south. Red is regarded as auspicious because it has several emotional, sexual and fertility-related qualities, making it a suitable colour for brides and young married women [Pls. 15, 127]. Even today, most older married women eschew the wearing of bright red.

Green: (Sk) *hari, harita, haarita*; (Pk) *hari, hariya*; (H) *haraa, harin, hariyaa*; (G) *haryu, haru*; (N) *hariyo*; (O) *haraa*; (Ta) *paca, pacu, pacappu*; (Ma) *pacu*; (Ka) *pasi, pasu*; (Te) *paccana, pacca*; (Go) *pahna*; (Ko) *pasi, puc*; (Mu) *hariyar*.

The Vaisyas were traditionally associated with the colour green but today it usually has Islamic connotations, being popular among Muslim groups [Pl. 75]. (It is no coincidence that the flag of Pakistan, a Muslim state, is green.) In some areas of the central Deccan and the south, a green wedding sari is sometimes worn, often in place of the yellow sari worn during certain marriage rituals (see below). The name for green is often the same for the colour yellow, such as *pitambara* (H, yellow cloth) or *pacu* (Ta).

Blue: (Sk, Pk) *neela*; (H) *neelaa, leelaa*; (G) *neeluu, leeluu*; (M) *neel, nilaa*; (B) *nila*; (A, S) *nil*; (N) *nilo*; (O) *nila*; (Ta) *asidai, avuri, nili, nalakkali, toli*; (Ma) *amari, nilam, nili*; (Ka) *ajara, nili*; (Te) *aviri, nili, syama*; (Ko) *puc*; (Mu) *leel*.

Black: (Sk) *kaala*; (Pk) *kaala, kaalaya*; (H) *kaalaa, kaaliyaa*; (G) *kaalu, kaaliyu*; (M) *kaalaa*; (B) *kaala*; (A) *kola*; (N) *kaalo*; (O) *kalaa*; (S) *kalu*; (Ta) *karu*; (Ma) *karu, kari*; (Ka) *karidu*; (Te) *karan, kaaru, karen, kareyan*; (Go) *kaarial, kaariyal*; (Ko) *kari* (Mu) *hendey, hendy*; (Kh) *rongiong*.

Blue is the colour relegated to the Sudras, and high-caste Hindus avoided this colour because the fermentation process used to create indigo was regarded as ritually impure. Among caste Hindus, blue and black were both considered inauspicious colours, reflecting sorrow and ill omen, but since at least the mid-nineteenth century, blue and black embellishments to white saris have been worn by older married women, especially in the east [Pl. 54]. In the west, blue was commonly worn by many tribal and low-caste groups [Pl. 29], as it was seen as protection against the evil eye (see p. 26). Today, blue is a widely worn colour, and many older women and widows tend to wear modern saris with muted tones of blue, black and even green, rather than the more traditional pure white sari.

Yellow: (Sk) *Peeta, peetala, harina, harita*; (Pk) *peea, peeala, halidda*; (H) *peelaa*; (G) *peelu, peeyal, peel*; (B) *pilaa, haladiaa*; (Ta) *mancal, pul, paca*; (Ma) *manna*; (Ka) *pasu*; (Te) *paccana, pacca*; (Go) *puvraali*; (Mu) *sasang*; (Kh) *rongstem*.

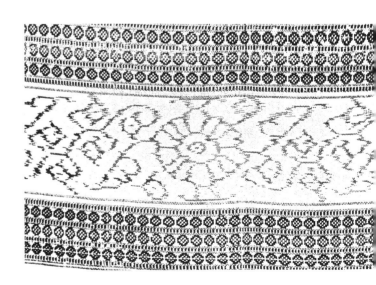

The colour yellow is traditionally regarded as the colour of religion and asceticism, as saffron yellow or orange is the colour of Saddhus and other individuals who have relinquished their caste and family to lead a spiritual life aimed at releasing themselves from the endless round of rebirths. On the first day of the Hindu wedding ceremony in the eastern region, the bride is washed in *haldi* (turmeric) to ritually purify her, during and after which she wears a yellow sari. Yellow saris are also commonly worn during the climax of the Tamil and Telegu wedding ceremony among non-Brahmin communities,

Above Part of a south Indian gold necklace with beads fashioned as jasmine buds, *c.* 1900. Many traditional necklaces in southern and eastern India use bud-shaped beads of the type shown here as the main decorative element, which are often called 'jasmine-flower buds'.

Top A border and field of a screen-printed Gujarati sari showing *bel phool* (floral vines) and *jhaalar* (ornamental border frills) [Pl. 32].

and a yellow sari is traditionally worn for seven days after the birth of a child, when the mother conducts various *pujas* [Pl. 24].[2] In general, yellow is seen as an auspicious colour that still has religious connotations [Pl. 25]. (The orange robes of East Asian Buddhist monks are derived from the same tradition.)

The use of colour to represent spiritual and emotional states is also found in painting of the classical period,[3] and traditional drama,[4] although the symbolic roles of different colours do not necessarily follow the patterns outlined above.

Yet, whatever its function, colour has a long history in India. Madder is believed to have been used in Mohenjo-daro in about 2000 BC, while the dye plants used for yellow and orange in Mesopotamia (*c.* 2000 BC) and Egypt (*c.* 1500 BC) (pomegranate rind and turmeric) are indigenous to India, suggesting such technology may have been available at an equally early date.[5] Although the higher castes rejected blue, indigo dyeing is believed to have been known as early as Vedic times, along with dyeing techniques using safflower (*mahaaranjana*), madder (*manjisthaa*), turmeric (*haridraa*) and possibly lac. After this period, increasing numbers of dye types and colours continued to be added to the written repertoire in later Sanskrit and other literature.[6]

Small Geometric Shapes

Stripes: (H) *dhari, phita, patti*; (M) *mugta, raastaa, selari, shalaicha*; (Ta) *saarai, pattai, kampi*; (Ka) *saara, patti, kambi*; (Te) *saara, saarika, patte.*

Dashes: (H) *jeera, chaas, thikri, oncha*; (M) *sokha, chaasa*; (G) *chaas*; (Ta) *muthai*; (Ta/Te) *muthu.*

Checks, squares: (H) *charkhana, chaukdi, moong, goonji, chand tara, gunji, khan*; (M) *chaukdi, khan, kothi, moongi, mungi*; (Ta) *valai*; (Ka) *bale*; (Te) *vala.*

Edges, 'frills': (H) *jhaalar, kanni, kangra, kannat*; (M) *jaal, kanaa, kangora, kagani, got, chhada, gujroo*; (Ta/Te) *pannu sambu.*

Serrated bands: (M) *karvat, bugdi.*

Herringbone bands: (M) *katar, gom*; (Ta) *vanku, vanki, venki, venku*; (Ka) *baagu*; (Te) *vaannuka.*

Diamond/basket-weave bands: (H) *chatai, jali, badaam, pankha, aankh*; (M) *chatai, jaal, jaalli, chaudhari*; (O) *saara, dalimba*; (Ta) *kan, kuyilkan, mayilkan*; (Ka) *kan*; (Te) *kannu.*

Small geometric shapes include a wide range of different motifs, from dense basket-weave and interlocking diamond-shaped designs to checks, serrated patterns and chevrons. Most are woven in supplementary-warp or -weft threads, creating bands of patterning in sari borders. Because of the nature of their weaving, which traditionally involved the use of several sticks to lift the supplementary-warp threads on the loom, the designs are not only very small but also repetitive.[7] In addition, checks and other net-like patterns are woven into sari fields using ground-warp and -weft threads of contrasting colour.

The names of most of these small repeat patterns are usually descriptive, taken from nature, items of jewelry or everyday objects.

Jewelry-related names. The flower-bud like *jhaalar* (H, frill) found along the inner edge of many sari borders and endpieces is often given names in other languages that translate into either 'edge' (M, *kanaa*) or items of jewelry (M, *kangora*). Much Indian jewelry features rows of elongated beads called 'jasmine flower buds', a pattern that is similar to the *jhaalar* pattern itself.

In the western Deccan, very fine checks with 1/1 or 2/4 coloured/ground thread sequences are often called *goonji* or *gunji* (H, M). The *goonj* is a very thin wire used in women's earrings and the name refers to the fine line of the check (Pl. 185 has a 4/4 check).

Names from nature: seeds. Names of seeds are frequently found even when there is no clear visual connection. A common name for a slightly larger, but still fine, check in western Deccan sari fields is *moongi* or *mungi* (H, M, lentil seed). The thread sequence of these checks is usually about 6/6 contrast/ground. Many repetitive supplementary-warp and -weft designs in Deccan saris are also named after seeds. For instance, small dashes created in eastern Madhya Pradesh saris are called *jeera* (H, cumin seed) [Pl. 206], while the repetitive diamond or mat-like bands in some Pochampalli and Bomokoi saris are called *dalimba* (O, pomegranate seed) or *saara* (O, seed) depending on the size and shape of the fine-woven pattern [Pl. 142]. The Tamil/Telugu word for the *jhaalar*-like edging along sari borders is *pannu sambu*, spikes of rice or paddy [Pl. 160].

Names from nature: eyes. The supplementary warp-woven bands typical of the Bomokoi saris are usually quite wide (one to 5 centimetres), and are woven in saris throughout the Deccan and the south. Slight variations in the repeat design usually result in totally different names. For instance, a diamond-mesh design similar to the Bomokoi *dalimba* in Tamil *puja* sari borders is called *kuyilkan* (cuckoo's eyes), but if there is a small central dot within each tiny lozenge, it is called *mayilkan* (peacock's eyes) [Pl. 149]. In Maharashtra, such designs usually have more down-to-earth names such as *chatai* (basket or mat weave) and *jali* (net), although the 'eye' (*aankh*) appellation is also found in the narrow chain-like bands of Maheshwari saris [Pl. 192]. These references to eyes may have once had a connection with concepts relating to the evil eye, widespread throughout India.[8]

Names from nature: centipede. The name 'centipede' is commonly given to a variety of different geometric motifs. It denotes a herringbone-like Sri Lankan embroidery used to join two seams; part of the *Vohra bhat* design found in Gujarati *patola* (G, *kaankhalushi*); and the tiny herringbone-weave bands created in Maharashtran and other west Deccan saris (M, *gom*). In the early nineteenth century, Marathi speakers also used this word to describe the natural partings found in horses' hair around the neck, which, depending on the direction of the parting, were considered either auspicious or inauspicious.[9] Such attitudes suggest that the *gom* may have once been woven into local sari borders for symbolic, auspicious reasons [Pls. 185, 190].

Protection: weapons and other devices. An alternative Marathi name for the herringbone motif is *katari*, a dagger, which again suggests possible past symbolic connections, perhaps with keeping

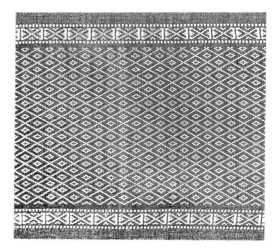

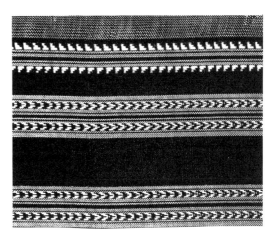

Above *Gom* and *karvat* border bands from an Ilkal sari, Gulegudd, northern Karnataka.

Top The reverse side of a *mayilkan* pattern on a Kanchipuram sari, Tamil Nadu [Pl. 149].

165

away the evil eye. It is also possible that the tiny supplementary-warp bands woven as a serrated 'ribbon' in west Deccan sari borders may also have had a protective function. It is often called a *karvat*, literally, a saw [Pls. 185, 190].

The 'Temple Motif'
(B) *daant*; (O) *kumbha*; (H) *kumbh*, *phera*; (G) *kungri*; (Ta) *mokku*, *mottu*, *reku*, *karavai*; (Ma) *reku*; (Ka) *teni*; (Te) *muggu*, *mogga*, *kumbham*, *kotakomma*, *kupadam*.

The temple motif consists of rows of large triangles found along ethnic and tribal sari borders, as well as in the endpieces of Dravidian and some central Deccan saris. They are usually woven into the ground fabric of the sari in the interlocked-weft technique, so making the triangles point in the weft direction of the fabric, never the warp.

They should not be confused with the Indonesian *tumpal* design,[10] which consists of large warp-wise triangles found in the endpieces of trade textiles made for the South-East Asian market. This design is never found in Indian textiles, except for two extraordinary occurrences, namely in the wedding *patola* of Vohra Muslims who exported *tumpal-patola* cloths to Indonesia, and in the *lungis* worn by some eighteenth- and nineteenth-century Kandy (Sri Lankan) aristocrats, many of whose textiles showed strong stylistic connections with Indonesia (see illustrations on pp. 9, 30 and 126).

The temple motif has different traditional names in different parts of India, none of which translate into 'temple'. In the north-east, West Bengal and Bangladesh it was commonly called *daant* (teeth). In West Bengal and eastern Deccan, especially Orissa and northern Andhra Pradesh, it is called a *kumbh* (B), *kumbha* (O) or *kumbham* (Te), a reference to the round clay storage pot and its contents (usually rice or water). Although the *daant*, like the *kungri* of Gujarat, may have originally been added for protection against the evil eye, the *kumbha* is a fertility symbol. The round clay pot is explicitly involved in this capacity in weddings, religious rituals involving female goddesses (especially Lakshmi and Durga), and on domestic wall-paintings that welcome Lakshmi into the house or keep out evil influences.[11]

In Dravidian India this border design usually refers to flower buds (*mottu* or *mokku* in Tamil), while the endpiece design is called a *reku* (bundle of grass). The *reku* is a large design that looks like a reverse temple design because visually the central panel dominates instead of the border edge [Pl. 184]. However, flowers themselves are fertility symbols, a fact which reinforces the relation of this design with fecundity. In northern Karnataka five pointed spikes are embroidered and woven into local saris in an effort to keep away the evil eye.[12] Kanchipuram weavers who speak the northern Tamil/Telugu dialect use the term *karavai* (saw) for serrated borders, which also suggests a protective association. Current evidence indicates that the temple motif is of pre-Islamic, possibly tribal, origin adopted by caste Hindus.

Floating Geometric Motifs
Squares: (H) *chauk, chauki*
Triangles and Pagodas: (H) *singhaulia, singarna, singhara*

A separate subgroup of geometric motifs are those woven as discontinuous supplementary-weft figures free-floating against a plain ground. They are usually larger than the supplementary-warp and -weft motifs discussed earlier, although not necessarily any larger than temple motifs, and are often found in tribal and ethnic saris of the eastern Deccan. Most of these motifs fall into two types: patterns based on the square (H, *chauk*), and on the triangle (H, *trikon*).

The triangular shapes are usually depicted with an additional small diamond or triangle placed on top of the main triangle peak [Pl. 19]. They are known by a variety of names taken from daily life, none of which refers to triangles. According to some scholars,[13] the commonest name for this motif is *singhaulia*, but this is a Hindi word and many of the motifs are found on the saris of Dravidian-speaking Gond, Baiga and Oraon tribal women. *Singhaulia* may simply mean 'embellishment' or 'decoration', being derived from *singar* (to embellish); or it may be derived from *singhara*, the water chestnut (*Trapaceae bispinosa*), which has an edible, triangular fruit with a spine on each side.

An alternative name is *maachhee* (H, fly), but given the numerous different local pronunciations of the word *maachhlee* (H, fish), it may be a misinterpretation of the latter. The tribal words for fly, such as Gondi *veesi* and Oraon *tinglee*, have no connection with this name, while fish are regarded by all groups as a potent fertility and wealth-related symbol.

The *singhaulia* has the distinction of being one of the oldest patterns found in the archaeological record, being depicted in early Neolithic pottery in a site on the western edge of the Afghani plateau (Mundigak, level I), dating from 4500 to 3500 BC.[14] However, it never appeared in depictions of upper-class textiles in later classical, medieval or Islamic-period art.

Double triangular motifs created in an hourglass-shape are also found in tribal saris. In Oraon saris they are known as butterflies (H, *titlee*, which is reminiscent of the Oraon *tinglee*); and in Orissan Bomokoi saris as *dombaru*, the small double-faced drum (also called *damru*) [Pl. 131].

Unfortunately, little is known about the origins and symbolism of a distinctive pagoda-like motif, *phool cheeta chauk* (H, flower leopard seat) found in Gond saris [Pl. 111]. It has been translated as a 'marriage motif', which it is, but so far there has been no serious study of this uniquely Gond design.

Square motifs are also commonly found in the tribal and ethnic saris of the eastern Deccan [Pl. 110]. The patterns are rarely simple squares, however, and they usually have several internal concentric squares inside the main one, with embellishments on the outer sides of each corner. They are generally known as *chauk* (H, square) by non-tribals, but the tribal names have not been researched. They have a variety of Hindi names in addition to *chauk*, although most refer to a low wooden seat (*chauki*), bedstead (*khatiya*) or bed raised on a

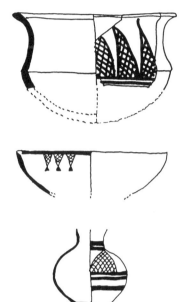

Above Painted potsherds: a leaf-blade pattern, and a triangular pattern (*top*, from Navdatoli, Madhya Pradesh, period I, *c.* 2000 BC, *and bottom*, from Mitathal, Haryana, period I, *c.* 2000–1750 BC) reminiscent of the temple design in many central, southern and eastern Indian ethnic and tribal saris; and a triangular pattern (*centre*, from Mundigak, Afghanistan, period I, *c.* 4500–3500 BC) similar to the *singhaulia* pattern in some east Deccan saris.

Opposite, above A *kumbha* border on an Orissan landscape sari [Pl. 133].

Opposite, below A *kumbha* design on a Gond sari from Koraput, Orissa [Pl. 111].

Below Painted pottery from Mundigak, Afghanistan, period III, *c.* 3000–2500 BC. These angular, geometric designs are very similar to those found on Munda and north-east Indian tribal saris.

Above The *lungi* that this figure (Vrikshaka, Gyaraspur, Madhya Pradesh, c. AD 900) is wearing is believed by many scholars to represent a brocaded fabric. Note the floral *buti* in a style suggestive of a woven design, in addition to the vine-like pattern in the borders.

Top The creeping vine (*kapalata*) is depicted twice in this temple door pillar (Orissa, c. AD 800), as a foliate scroll and as an undulating vine upon which people climb. The latter is a graphic symbol of the vine representing the interconnectedness of all life.

Right Bel patterning from a Rajasthani block-printed sari, Sanganer, 1990.

pedestal (*machela*, derived from *maachaa*). These are all caste Hindu references to the raised stage or pedestal often used to seat the bridegroom and/or bride during the Hindu wedding ceremony.

As with the *singhaulia*, these square motifs are not in evidence in the sculpted, cast or painted textiles worn by the elite in ancient, classical, medieval or Islamic art. Nevertheless, the square is an ancient and potent motif, being regarded as a symbol for cosmic order,[15] which is traditionally used as the framework for designing temples and shrines.[16] It is also commonly used in ritual floor- and wall-paintings – for instance, in west India, village priests draw a square altar design for fire ceremonies to protect children born under inauspicious astrological signs.[17]

The Creeping Vine
(Sk) *lataa, velli, vallri*; (Pk) *veelli*; (S) *bela, beli*; (M) *vel*; (H) *belii, bel, lataa, vallri*; (O) *lataa, lati*; (G) *vel, velii*; (B) *bel, lata*; (Ta) *valli*; (Ka) *balli, biru*.

Today, the creeping vine motif is primarily associated with expensive figured textiles that have Islamic connections [Pl. 13]. Muslim religious rules against depicting animals encouraged such a motif in the textiles of Mughal and other Muslim elite. Yet although it became an 'establishment' design on expensive fabrics from at least Mughal times, the creeping vine has a longer and more psychologically subtle history.

It first appears in Shunga-period stone railings at the Stupa of the Saints at Sanchi[18] as a stylized and somewhat angular representation of a lotus rhizome. From then on it becomes an important Hindu architectural and sculptural device to be known as 'the vine of wish fulfilment' (Sk, *kalapalata, lata*, or *kalpavalli*), which is said to denote the life force that is shared by all living things – so linking the gods with men, animals and plants. It was believed to grant the wishes of all those who revere it, which makes it a highly auspicious symbol.[19] Linguistically, this close connection between the vine and the life force is seen in the fact that the Indo-Aryan word *lata*[20] means both 'creeper' (the plant) and 'entanglement' (the action or resulting situation). The alternative name for this motif, *bel*, refers to both a floral vine in general and a fruit-bearing tree (*Aegle marmelos*).

The creeping vine was commonly carved around the doorways of temples and other important buildings throughout the first millennium AD.[21] The gateway, or threshold, is still a significant Indian symbol, as temporary gateways are often made to welcome visiting dignitaries to a town or even a household, and many rural women still paint their thresholds and doorframes with designs aimed

at welcoming auspicious elements (such as Lakshmi, the goddess of wealth and good luck) and keeping out the inauspicious (such as malignant spirits and the evil eye). The fact that vines often graced the gateways of ancient, classical and medieval Hindu temples, symbolically leading the worshipper to the spiritual realm, is an indication of their iconographic importance. Even as late as the nineteenth century, objects made as wedding gifts often depicted the vine design as a symbol for health and prosperity [Pl. 127].[22]

Vines are depicted on the clothing of medieval north Indian sculptures from about AD 1000, such as on the border of the *lungi* worn by a tree goddess (Vrikshaka) from the Deccan.[23] Vines were also printed onto fabrics excavated at al-Fustat, Egypt.[24]

So much time has elapsed since the rise of this motif around classical temple doorways that its symbolic significance in traditional north Indian saris has probably been lost. Yet in Central Asia and eastern Europe, people traditionally embroidered red vegetal and floral designs onto the cuffs and collars of their shirts and blouses to keep out evil spirits, and the Ancient Greeks are known to have woven roses into their garments for the same reason.[25] Could a similar motivation have been behind the introduction of this design into India's garments? And was the vine in the edges of the tenth-century Vrikshaka's *lungi* more than just a pretty embellishment?

Flowers

(Sk) *phoolu*; (Pk) *phulla*; (H) *phool*; (O) *phoola*; (M) *aral*; (Ta) *pu, bu, aral, alari*; (Ka) *alar, aral, puvu*; (Te) *alaru, nana, puvu*.

Various types of floral forms abound in Indian saris. Flowers have played a major role in Hindu and early Buddhist iconography, and many designs were then used by the Muslims. Although the Islamic depictions seem to have been purely decorative, various Hindu representations were often symbolic of good luck, health and prosperity. It is in this aspect that, even today, garlands of flowers are still so extensively used in South Asia, being given to honoured guests and deities (during *puja* and festivals), as well as to the bride and groom during the marriage ceremony.

As a group, flowers also represent the female principle. In some Indo-Aryan languages, the usual name for flower, *phool*, additionally refers to aspects of female anatomy,[26] so their common depiction in saris is probably no coincidence. According to some students of Indian iconography,[27] they are also explicitly used in rural domestic art as fertility symbols, especially the chrysanthemum, lotus, jasmine and plantain. The jasmine flower (Ta, *malli*; H, *chameli, jai*)[28] has long been a popular floral motif, known to have embellished textiles given to the seventh-century north-Indian king Harsha,[29] as well as being commonly found on traditional Tamil and north-Indian jewelry datable to the nineteenth century.

But flowers are not always linked with the feminine. The Tamil warrior-god Maruka is associated with a large number of different flowers, most of which are red.[30] Vishnu is also often depicted with a garland of five rows of flowers, each row representing one of the five senses. In the domestic art of Dravidian India, the lemon flower is

Above A stupa railing with a *yakshi* (an auspicious tree deity relating to fertility) standing on an elephant, with lotus rondels carved on the side railings. Bharhut, Madhya Pradesh, c. 150 BC.

Below Pottery sherds with six-petalled flowers painted on them, from Kot Diji (southern Pakistan), period I, c. 2750–2500 BC (*left*), and from Surkotada (Lothal), Gujarat, period IA, c. 3000–2200 BC.

Above The designs on these seals from Baluchistani Neolithic sites are reminiscent of several different traditional patterns, including the woven *rudraksha* motif (*top*, from Mundigak, Afghanistan, period III, *c.* 3000–2500 BC) and the combined ikat *patolu* and block-printed *ajrak* (*centre and bottom*, from Damb Sadaat, Pakistan, period II, *c.* 3150–2630 BC, and period III, *c.* 2500 BC).

Below Ikat lotus flowers in the endpiece of a modern silk Sambalpur sari, Orissa.

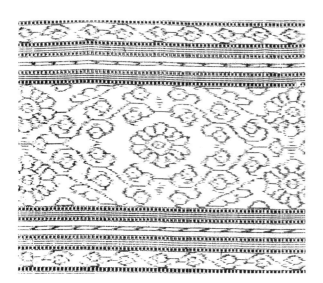

used as protection from the evil eye, as is the pointed-petalled pumpkin flower, which is a symbol of protection and good luck during harvest time (mid-January).[31]

Apart from the lotus, which is considered separately (see below), flowers are not as commonly depicted in the historical and archaeolgical record as might be expected. Early Indus Valley pottery from Kot Diji and Kalibangan[32] explicitly depicts large six-petalled floral forms, but few other representations are found until Shunga times, when six-petalled flowers appear in the headdresses of women portrayed in terracotta plaques.[33] Flowers are infrequently painted in the Ajanta murals; there, most textile motifs are geometric.[34] When they do appear in classical Indian art, such as on the north gate at Sanchi (Andhra, late first century BC) or in Gupta-period sculpture, they appear to be purely decorative.

Various types of flowers are depicted in traditional saris. In many Deccan saris, narrow bands of repeat supplementary-warp figuring are generically called *phool(a)*, even if the design is not strictly floral. The patterns in these bands tend to range from small circular geometric motifs (0.3 to one centimetre) called *jai-phoola* (jasmine flower) in Orissa [Pl. 126], to large (1.5 to 2.5 centimetre) four- to eight-petalled flowers often called *rui phool* (cotton flower) [Pl. 119]. Although these supplementary-warp bands appear never to have been depicted in India's art, some of their geometric shapes are found in seals as early as the Indus Valley period.[35]

Related to the *phool* design is the *rudraksha*, a circular geometric motif consisting of V-shaped radiating lines from an unmarked centre [Pls. 122, 123]. Typical of south-eastern Deccan and Orissan saris, this motif is believed to have Shaivite associations because the wrinkled *rudraksha* seed is made into rosaries for counting and repeating mantras by Shaivite devotees, in particular the Shaiva Sidhanta school. The name *rudraksha* literally means 'eye of Shiva'. Larger versions of this design in Tamil Nadu saris are called *pavun* (Ta/Te, the sun) [Pl. 160].

The Lotus
(Sk) *padma*; (Pk) *padama, paiima, poomma, pomma*; (H) *kamal, padma*; (O) *padma*; (G) *kamal*; (Rajasthani) *pomcha*; (Ta) *aampal, taamarai, tammi*.

One of the most complex and enduring symbols of both Buddhism and Hinduism has been the lotus. The lotus flower is used in religious iconography as the seat upon which members of the Hindu and Buddhist pantheons rest, representing their spiritual power and authority. It also symbolizes the material world in all of its many forms, with its multi-petalled depiction in *mandalas* representing the multiplicity of the universe.

Gupta-period and later sculptures of Vishnu asleep upon the serpent Ananta drifting on the eternal sea of milk, where he dreams the universe into existence, feature a lotus blossom issuing from Vishnu's navel, upon which Brahma sits. This is a symbol of the creation of the material universe, with Brahma as the creator and the universe represented by the lotus flower. Leading on from such symbolism are concepts of fertility and fecundity. The concept is emphasized by both the multi-petalled flowers and depictions of the lotus pod, which contains hundreds of seeds that scatter to the wind. Consequently, the lotus symbolizes prosperity and material wealth, which is why it is so intimately associated with the goddess Sri Lakshmi, who is often just called Padma or Kamala (both meaning 'lotus').

It is likely that the fecund aspect of the lotus, not the spiritual, is emphasized when it is depicted on traditional saris, in particular wedding saris. For instance, some of the ethnic printed saris in the western region feature stylized lotus pods; the *chhaabi bhat* pattern in *patola* are, according to one source,[36] depictions of an eight-petalled lotus flower with tendrils spreading out to form a basket (see p. 31); as well as the Orissan *khandua* wedding saris [Pl. 127].

The lotus symbol appears to be of Indo-Aryan origin, for although many water-related motifs are found in Indus Valley artefacts, the lotus is conspicuous by its absence. Sri Lakshmi, with whom the lotus is so intimately connected, is believed to have early proto-Indo-European beginnings (that is, to come from the tribes from which the Indo-Aryans descended). A goddess (Sri) associated with regal power and wealth was worshipped by these pre-Indo-Aryan (and, later, Indo-Aryan) tribes.[37] This association with royalty and wealth is later seen in many Gupta-period coins that feature Lakshmi with a lotus flower on one side and the reigning monarch on the other.[38]

Today most rural domestic art created throughout the subcontinent is expressly made in order to welcome Lakshmi into the house. Whether it is a Tamil *kolam*, Orissan *kumbha* or Bengali *alpona*, the fundamental message is the same: let good fortune enter; and both the *kolam* and *alpona* can be depicted as multi-petalled lotus blossoms.

Buta and Buti

(Persian) *boota*; (Parachi/Iranian) *buta*; (Kashmiri) *buuta*; (U, H) *buta*, *buti*; (A, B, O) *buthaa*; (G) *butto, buttii*.

Another group of floral motifs found in saris is the small *buti* and large *buta*, which are depicted as flowers, sprigs or bushes. As with the *phool*, however, these names are also given to geometric and zoomorphic motifs. They are always created as floating design elements placed against a plain background [Pl. 94]. The smaller *buti* are usually woven in repeated rows across the sari field, while the *buta* are usually created in rows along the endpiece [Pl. 32]. Floral *buti* first appear in the artistic record in the *lungis* worn by figures depicted in classical north- and east-Indian bronzes dating from the seventh to the ninth centuries.[39] The rows of geese (*hansa*) depicted on the textile worn by a fifth-century Ajanta figure could also be classified as *buti*, but that design was probably printed, not woven. The appearance of the floral patterns depicted on the bronzes, however, suggests that the *buti* of these early medieval textiles may have been woven in discontinuous supplementary-weft, for such woven *buti* have remained a common element in eastern, north-eastern and south-eastern Indian saris ever since. The depictions of free-floating textile design elements at Ajanta suggest block-printing and dyeing techniques rather than weaving.

Above A *kolam* design called the 'lotus pattern'. The *kolam* is a floor painting traditional to Tamil Nadu that is created by using rice powder. It is an auspicious diagram consisting of interconnecting lines based on a gridwork of 'points'.

Below A bronze Balarama, Kurkihar, Gaya district, Bihar, c. AD 800. Bronze and stone statues from about the eighth and ninth centuries begin to show deities and their attendants wearing *lungis* and *dhotis* containing *buti* (small patterns scattered throughout the field of the fabric). Some patterns have the appearance of being printed or dyed, while others look more like the designs seen in woven *buti*, such as single floral or vegetal motifs.

Although it is highly likely that *buti* and *buta* are indigenous north-Indian designs, the words used to describe them are of Persian origin. In fact, the Persian/Turkish carpet motif similar to the Indian *kalga* is called a *boteh* or *bota*. Many large *kalga* depicted in Indian saris have been called *buta* in northern India. The use of a Persian rather than Indian name for this motif may reflect the fact that *buti/a* were commonly created on expensive figured textiles worn by the old Muslim elites. (Persian was the court language of the early Mughals, which developed into Urdu, a Perso-Arabic language.)

The Kalga

Mango: (Sk) *aamra*; (Pk) *amba, ambaya*; (H, G, B) *aam, amb*; (M, O) *aambaa*; (A) *aam*; (Ta) *maanti, maatti*; (Ma) *maanna*; (Ka) *maam, maavu*; (Te) *mangayu*.

Corner Motif: (H) *konia, kon, konaa*; (G, B) *kon; konaa*; (M) *konya, kon*.

Kalga: (U) *qalb, qulqula, qaalika*; (H) *kalga, kalka*.

The *kalga* motif is now so ubiquitous in Indian sari and other textile designs that it is hard to imagine it is only about 250 years old [Pl. 37]. It evolved from seventeenth-century floral and tree-of-life designs that were created in expensive, tapestry-woven Mughal textiles, primarily *patkas* (sashes) made for the Mughal court.[40] The early designs depicted single plants with large flowers and thin wavy stems, small leaves and roots. In the course of time the design became denser, with more flowers and leaves, giving rise to tree-of-life and mixed floral patterns issuing from vases or a pair of leaves. By the late eighteenth century the archetypal curved point at the top of an elliptical outline had evolved [Pl. 203]. The *kalgas* created on Kashmir shawls, which became a fashion item in Europe for over a century, were certainly the most imaginative and intricate; and it was from the imitations of these shawls woven in factories at Paisley, Scotland, that the name 'paisley' was derived, still commonly used in Europe and the United States.

During the late eighteenth and nineteenth centuries, the *kalga* became an important motif in a wide range of Indian textiles, perhaps because it was associated with the Mughal court. A double-sided block-printed cotton *dupatta* created in 1795[41] contains large *kalga* at either end, while many nineteenth-century saris in museums carry this motif, especially saris from the north. It rarely appears in nineteenth-century south-Indian textiles, and is only found on traditional tribal and low-caste textiles in the western region, which suggests it has a

Above A block-printed *kalga buta* motif in the border of a Kashmiri silk sari.

Right The evolution of the *kalga* motif: (*from left to right*) a poppy design in a Mughal shawl, Kashmir, *c.* 1680; an early *kalga* pattern in a Mughal shawl, Kashmir, *c.* 1700; and *kalga* patterns in Kashmiri shawls, *c.* 1770 and *c.* 1850.

longer history in the west than elsewhere, indicating a possible western Indian, if not Persian, origin.

In addition, the name *kalga* appears to come from the Urdu. The word *qalb* literally means 'hook', and this word and its variants describe a range of curvilinear objects with hook-like ends, such as a goad, fishhook, or a hood covering a hawk's head. Another, possibly ancillary meaning may also be related to a series of Urdu words relating to Turkish and Persian carpets, such as *qalika* (small rug), which presumably carried *buteh* designs (see section on *buta* and *buti*, p. 171).

The motif probably caught the attention of poorer and non-Muslim Indians because of its similarity in shape to the mango fruit, and even today the *kalga* is often called a mango (H, *aam*) by many rural Indians. The mango was a potent fertility symbol from at least Shunga times, and sculptures of Ganga, *yakshis* and *shalabhanijka*, which are symbols of fertility and fecundity, are often depicted under the boughs of mango trees, which are usually in flower or fruit.[42] In addition, north-Indian folk traditions indicate that treading on mango fruits will induce fertility,[43] while in wedding rituals, a pot full of rice with mango leaves and a coconut on top is an explicit wish for prosperity and fertility within the union.[44]

The Peepal Leaf

(Sk) *Pippala*; (Pk) *pippala*; (H) *peepal*; (G) *peepal, piplo*; (Ta) *arasu, cuvalai*; (Ma) *arasu, arasaal, arayal*; (Te) *raavi, raagi*.

Depictions of the heart-shaped leaves of the peepal tree (*Ficus religiosa*) are one of the earliest and most common motifs found in Early and Mature Indus Valley pottery and seals,[45] usually portrayed as if issuing from the heads of horned cows or bulls. This association with cattle is probably significant because within historical times orthodox Hindus have venerated the peepal tree as much as the cow. It is constantly grown near Hindu temples and villages for shade, and planting such a tree is regarded as auspicious.[46] The Buddha attained enlightenment under this tree (it is also known as the bo tree), which suggests this event had symbolic associations with older beliefs of the time that incorporated this tree.

Yet, subsequent to the Indus Valley period, few depictions of the peepal or its leaves have survived in Indian art. Most ancient and classical Indian art does not contain this motif, and it is absent from the majority of the artwork of the second millennium AD. It mainly appears in traditional textiles worn by high-caste Hindus, in particular Gujarati *patola* made for Nagar Brahmin and Jain communities

Above, left to right A painted pottery sherd, Lewan, Pakistan, *c.* 3000–2500 BC; painted pottery, Mundigak, Afghanistan, period IV, *c.* 2500–2000 BC, and a seal, Mohenjo-daro, Pakistan, *c.* 2500–2000 BC. Depictions of the peepal tree and its leaves appear in early Indus Valley art, indicating that the importance of this tree was well established at a very early date. Peepal-leaf designs have been commonly found in many traditional saris, including those worn for *puja* (worship) and weddings.

Below A *paan bhat* or *peepal patra bhat* motif on a nineteenth-century Gujarati *patolu* [Pl. 28].

[Pl. 28], and in Dravidian unbleached cotton and *zari* muslins (*kosara pudava*). In the *patola* the design is traditionally called *peepal patra bhat*, although today it is increasingly called *paan bhat*, the paan bush also having heart-shaped leaves. Paan leaves are used as part of the betel-nut concoction that is passed around and chewed by participants in weddings and other social events; and this name change indicates that the past, longstanding religious significance of the peepal tree may be fading from popular memory.

The Tree of Life
(Sk, Pk, H) *Jeevan vriksh.*
Tree: (Sk) *Vriksha, patri*; (Pk) *patti, vriksh*; (H) *per, vriksh*; (Ta) *maram*; (Te) *mraanu, mranku.*

Throughout rural India the tree has been a symbol of fertility and protection for both tribals and caste Hindus. Both groups traditionally have rituals that revere and protect trees, which were (and still are) a significant source of livelihood for the community,[47] although this is now being lost because of the severe shortage of wood in India caused by drastic deforestation.

Trees in general, as opposed to specific species like the peepal, are depicted in some Mature Indus Valley seals, although they are not so commonly found in pottery artwork. The concept of the tree of life, which is used as a symbol for the interconnectedness of all life, appears to have been in existence by the Gupta period. Cave 17 at Ajanta uses a tree and its branches to link different scenes from the Buddhist *Mahakapi Jataka* painted on the walls, with the branches interconnecting smaller, collateral scenes.[48]

The tree of life is a metaphysical extrapolation of the basic concepts of fertility and protection. Specific trees supplied pre-industrial India with food, medicines, timber, utensils and even cloth.[49] Many of the rural rituals (and concepts) still being practised reflect this heritage.

Sanskrit literature talks about the mythical Forest of Bliss (Anandavana) from which Varanasi developed,[50] while the depiction of *yakshis* and *yakshas* (female and male tree spirits) was common in much sculpture from Shunga times onward. Even today, many Orissan tribal groups still protect specific areas of forest for important religious and social ritual occasions, and the trees in these areas are not allowed to be destroyed.[51]

Different tribal groups living in the same geographical area often revere different species of trees. For instance, in Koraput (Orissa) the Hill Sora regard the sahanda (*Tropis aspera*) as most sacred, as its products saved the tribe from starvation after the Deluge, while the Gonds regard the bel (*Aegele marmalos*) and other plants as sacred elements that helped create the original tribe.[52] Species-specific focus in local religious life is also found in caste Hindu society. For instance, temples in Tamil Nadu are often associated with specific trees: the punnai tree (*Calophyllum inophyllum*) is the sacred tree at the main temple of Mylapore; the kadamba (*Adina cordifolia*) at Madurai; the mango (*Manifera indica*) at Kanchipuram; and the bamboo (*Bambusa* spp., *Dendrocalamus* spp.) at Tirunelvelli (see Pl. 25).

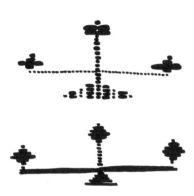

Above A woven *kadam* motif found in some east Deccan ethnic saris in Raigarh district, eastern Madhya Pradesh. The kadam tree is a local fertility symbol.

Below A supplementary-weft woven Assamese sun-tree design from an Assamese *mekhla, c.* 1950. Although Ahom, the Tai language, is no longer spoken in Assam, the fact that motifs of the sun-tree type are found exclusively in traditional textiles created by Austro-Tai-speaking peoples suggests that the Assamese sun-tree design is of Tai (Shan Ahom) origin.

Although tribal peoples traditionally revere and protect specific species for a wide variety of reasons, today most caste Hindus maintain rituals associated with fertility. The most well-known example is the 'marriage' of two important trees (often the peepal and margosa) in the village to ensure fertility. Various myths also hint at past rituals and beliefs, such as the ashoka tree (*Polyalthia longifolia*) bursting into bloom after it has been touched by a mythical virgin[54] called a *shalabhanjika* (Sk), a term which has been used at least since Mauryan times.[55]

Such symbolism adds greater potency to the depiction of various trees, or their parts, on traditional saris. Specific types of trees are usually delineated in textiles, as has been outlined above with the peepal and mango. For example, an abstracted symbol showing a tree with three branches is found in east Deccan ethnic saris, and is specifically called a *kadam* or *kadamba* motif. The kadam tree (*Adina cordifolia*) forms part of an Oraon agricultural festival involving marriageable girls, where marriage agreements are often made. At this festival, called the festival of the *karam luga* or *karam kichri*, the parents of a boy give the hoped-for daughter-in-law a sari as a gift. If the girl is in favour of the wedding she wears it.[56]

The Sun-Tree Motif

(A) Miri; (Tai) *Hong* ('swan').

The Assamese sun-tree motif is now such an archetypal pattern of the north-eastern region that many Assamese textiles are recognized as such just on the basis of this design [Pl. 93]. It depicts two birds, animals or flowers, facing each other on either side of a tree whose branches spread above them. The motif is rigidly symmetrical, highly stylized and angular, with a pointed roof-like top to the tree, and its sides are often straight.

It is often called a Miri design, after a Tibeto-Burman-speaking tribe living in Arunachal Pradesh and the northern part of Assam's Brahmaputra valley, but none of the Tibeto-Burman groups in the Brahmaputra valley or surrounding hills creates this design in their traditional textiles. In fact, the design is of Austro-Tai origin.[57] The once-ruling Shan Ahoms of Assam, who arrived there in the early thirteenth century from Burma, were originally Tai-speaking people,[58] and today this type of design is only found in the traditional textiles of Tai-speaking groups living in South-East Asia. In addition to this, the Austro-Tai-speaking Miao and Yao tribes of southern China and northern South-East Asia create sun-tree-like motifs in their traditional textiles. Among the Thailand Tai, the motif is known as a *hong* or swan design, after the birds portrayed at either side of the tree.

All of the Austro-Tai-speaking peoples are known to have migrated from central China (the Tarim basin) about two thousand years ago. It may be significant that several Han dynasty (*c.* 200 BC–AD 200) silks also contain versions of this design, although it is not depicted in later Chinese textiles. The Chinese sun-tree is an important feature of several early Chinese cosmological myths, and it is depicted in much Han-dynasty art in addition to textiles.

Above The Assamese sun-tree motif in a cotton sari from Nuagong, Assam, 1992.

Top A warp-faced Han dynasty brocade from Lou-lan, China. The origins of the sun-tree design can be traced to the Tarim basin, central China. Han silks excavated from various sites, such as the example illustrated here, show versions of this distinctive design.

Yet whether early Austro-Tai groups picked up the sun-tree motif from the Han, or the Han from the Austro-Tai, is open to debate. But whatever the sun tree's origins, the motif obviously resonated with local Austro-Tai, and, later, Assamese sensibilities. It was probably wholeheartedly adopted by the Assamese population because the Ahoms ruled eastern Assam for eight hundred years, and the entire area for three hundred. Its association with the ruling elite was probably sufficient incentive for many groups to adopt it.[59]

Above This sculpture depicts Karttikeya, the god of war, astride his mount, the peacock, which reinforces the older Mature Indus Valley associations linking the peacock with death and immortality. AD 700–800, provenance unknown.

Above, right Painted pottery, from Harappa, Pakistan, c. 2000–1700 BC (*left*), and from Rangpur, Gujarat, period II B, c. 2100 BC. From many of the funerary pottery paintings found in Harappa, it can be surmised that peacocks were believed to carry souls into the afterlife (note the tiny human bodies depicted inside the peacock).

Below A peacock embroidered on a *kantha* sari from West Bengal [Pl. 70].

The Peacock

(Sk) *mayuura*; (Pk) *maura, maaula, moora*; (H) *mor, mhor, murhaa*; (M, G) *mor*; (O) *maira*; (A) *mairaa*; (S) *mayura, miyuraa*; (Ta) *mayil, tukai*; (Ka) *navil, maylu*; (Te) *nemali, nammi*; (Go) *mal, puurmal*.

The peacock [Pls. 144, 156] has had several associations that at first glance appear to be unrelated: immortality, love, courtship, fertility, regal pomp, war and protection. Its traditional significance is probably lost, but nevertheless its depiction and symbolism has a long and complex history.

Peacocks were painted on Mature and Post-Indus Valley burial pottery dated about 2000–1500 BC.[60] That some of these birds have horns and vegetation issuing from their bodies suggests that they might signify fertility or rebirth, while others carrying tiny human beings inside their stomachs suggest that they are the bearers of the spirits of the dead to the other world.[61] (In fact, the peacock's association with death and rebirth appears throughout Sanskrit literature.) Peacocks reappeared in Buddhist architecture and by the first century AD were incorporated into the developing Brahmanic Hindu pantheon. Shiva's son, Karttikeya (Kumara), was the god of war and lord of immortality and was depicted riding a peacock mount,[62] suggesting that its associations of death and rebirth were still viable at that date.

By the late first millennium AD, Karttikeya and his peacock were associated with the worship of Maha Devi, the Great Goddess, and the group of violent goddesses known as the Matrikas. Like Shiva, these goddesses were part of the pre-Aryan religion which became incorporated into Hinduism, and their attributes became concerned with life, death, rebirth and fertility.[63]

The peacock's association with fertility may also partly derive simply from the fact that it has a reputation for producing many young, and that it heralds the coming of the rains by dancing to attract a mate. The sudden regeneration of plant life brought on by the monsoon must seem like rebirth to farmers who go through the 'death' of the summer drought. It is probably the bird's courtship- and fertility-related attributes that made it a symbol for courtship and love in both classical and folk literature. The peacock's association with royalty and regal pomp is almost equally old, however. It had regal associations in western Asia in about 1000 BC, as it is referred to in the Bible's Old Testament (the Hebrew name *thukkiyyum* is believed to have been derived from the Tamil word *tukai*).[64] Today the peacock is still an important symbol; it is India's national bird, and is a protected species.

The Goose and Other Water Birds

(Sk) *hamsa*; (Pk) *hamsa*; (H) *hansa, hans*; (O, G) *hans*; (Ta) *ooti, ceeval, ootiman*.

Depictions of the goose [Pl. 206] in Indian art prior to the Mughal period were common, but since then it has virtually disappeared. It was often found in Hindu sculpture, painting and textiles, having connotations that were completely opposite to Western Europe's negative associations. The earliest depictions of these and other water-related birds appear in Mature Indus Valley pottery,[65] and over a millennium later they became an important symbol in Buddhist iconography, representing not only spiritual purity, but also the travelling monks who spread Buddha's teachings: the image of the goose flying from the water to the sky made it an apt symbol for spiritual knowledge and dissemination, as well as for intellectual learning, knowledge in general and creativity.[66] In Vedic literature it was associated with the sun and the male principle of fertility and divine knowledge.[67]

It commonly appeared in Gandharan and Kushan sculpture, and later became incorporated into Brahmanic Hindu iconography (it can often be seen in temple sculpture). Sarasvati, the goddess representing learning, culture and the arts, as well as sound – literally, 'the word', language – has the goose as her vehicle. In addition, Brahman, with whom she is intimately associated as both his daughter and his wife, also has the goose vehicle.[68]

The goose and water birds in general have additional connotations of fidelity, and were known in ancient literature as *cakravaka*,[69] which were believed to mate for life and die if their mate expired. It was probably in this context that geese were described as being a feature in the decoration of the heroine's wedding sari in the fourth-century *Kumaarasabhava*.[70] A repeat design of geese is painted on the clothes of one of the Ajanta Cave One figures, while some resist-printed medieval cotton fragments from western India excavated at al-Fustat also show them.

With so much evidence of this motif's popularity in the past, it may seem strange that it virtually disappeared after Muslim rule solidified throughout India. Presumably this was because most elite groups adopted Islamic styles in their decorative arts, which avoid zoomorphic representations. In the early years of the twentieth

Above A character in the crowd watching a procession, in a mural of the *Mahajanaka Jataka*, Part 1, Ajanta, left corridor, Cave One, c. AD 475–500. He wears a tailored top decorated with rows of geese. Although it is impossible to say how the geese were created on this garment, they have the appearance of a block-printed design. As most of the textiles depicted in Ajanta seem to be of western Indian origin, it is likely that the technique used to make this pattern also came from this region.

Below A painted pot from Lothal, Gujarat, c. 2300–1750 BC, depicting water birds.

Above A fish pattern in the endpiece of a Bangalore sari, Karnataka.

Top A block-printed fish motif from a West Bengali sari.

Opposite A seal from Mohenjo-daro, Pakistan, c. 2500–2000 BC. Elephants are consistently depicted in Indian art from the Indus Valley period.

Opposite, below A sculpture of Ganesh on Mundesvari Hill, Shahabad district, Bihar, c. AD 400–500.

century the only evidence of geese and water birds in traditional textiles is found in some Tamil saris and ethnic Orissan ikats.

The Parrot

(Per) *tota*; (U, H) *tota, totaa*; (G) *popat*; (Ta) *kili, killai, tattai*; (Ka) *gili, gini*; (Te) *ciluka*.

Representations of the parrot do not have the historical and iconographic depth of those of the goose. It is not depicted in ancient, classical or even medieval Indian architecture, nor does it appear in the illustrations found in Jain manuscripts. This dearth of historical representation suggests that it is a relatively recent addition to the traditional Indian textile repertoire, although it appears to be common in north-Indian folk songs and art – for instance, the eastern-region Madhubani wall-paintings that William Archer 'discovered' in the Maithili-speaking areas of northern Bihar, which he photographed in 1939–40, feature parrots in nuptial-chamber wall-paintings.[71] This location has a direct link with the parrot's symbolic function as a messenger for lovers and its associations with courtship, love and passion. These functions are often mentioned in west- and north-Indian folk art and literature.[72] They are also seen in some later east-Indian temple sculptures, such as a five-towered Bengali temple with terracotta reliefs built in 1643. There, parrots are depicted with Krishna and Radha, Hinduism's most famous pair of lovers. The parrot is also associated with Kama, the god of physical desire and love, as well as with Sarasvati, presumably in her cultural, artistic or musical aspect rather than her more intellectual expression.

Despite its iconographic spread across north India, depictions of the parrot in Indian textiles are almost exclusively western (mostly Gujarati). Over the past two hundred years it has been depicted in elaborate coloured-silk embroideries created for Rajput courts, for nomadic ethnic groups such as the Rabari, and in the more expensive types of Gujarati wedding sari: both the *patolu* and the *gharcholu* often depict parrots, as occasionally do other *bandhani* fabrics [Pl. 27].

The Fish

(Sk) *Meena, matsya*; (Pk) *machchha*; (H) *maachh, machhli*; (O) *maachha*; (B) *maachh*; (A) *maas*; (Ta) *meen*; (Te) *meenu, meenga*; (Ka) *meen*; (Ko) *meen*.

Fish are potent fertility symbols throughout tribal and caste Hindu India, indicating abundance of food, wealth and children, as well as the generative powers of the supernatural [Pl. 113]. The fish is also an *avatar* of Vishnu who, as the Preserver, is associated with prosperity and material comforts. Matsya, the fish, is regarded as his first incarnation. Matsya was saved by Manu (the first man) when a tiny fish, and because he cared for it until it became large enough to return safely to the sea, Matsya warned him of the coming Deluge, advising him to build a boat in which to house many different plants and animals.[73] Matsya is also one of the eight iconographic symbols of good luck found in Hindu iconography.[74]

The fish appears early in the archaeological record, and is painted onto Early Indus Valley pottery at Kalibagan as well as carved into

Mohenjo-daro seals and plaques of the Mature Indus Valley civilization. It is also one of India's earliest numismatic motifs, and is found on punch-marked coins (*karhapana*) from both western and eastern India dating from at least 550–350 BC.[75] Yet it was rarely depicted in the sculptures and architecture of later historical periods and was never a vehicle for any deity. Nevertheless, its relationship with Indian folk and tribal art remains strong, and it is often depicted in textiles where fish form a major part of the diet, as in Orissa, or where Vaishnavism is important [Pl. 206].

The Elephant

(Sk) *Gajar, hastin*; (Pk) *gajar, gaja, gaya, haati*; (H) *haathi, gaiyar*; (G) *kunjar, haathi*; (O) *haati*; (B) *haati*; (Ta) *anai, veeram, yanai*; (Te) *eenugu, eenika*.

The symbol of the elephant has appeared throughout Indian history since Mature Indus Valley times when it was depicted on seals and as terracotta figurines excavated from Mohenjo-daro.[76] Since then it has appeared on early Indian coins,[77] and on Buddhist and Hindu architecture through to the present day. During the classical and medieval periods its head was part of a mythical beast called a Makara, which had a fish's body and elephant's trunk and was commonly found in depictions of river goddesses, especially Ganga.

Today terracotta elephants are created in rural India as gifts to local-community deities in return for such things as a blessing, the recovery of an ill child, a good harvest, or for a happy union when the bride and groom are going through the marriage ceremony.[78]

The elephant is considered an auspicious animal, traditionally associated with water and fertility, and with royalty and regal power. In addition to their temporal power, the kings of ancient India were linked with the natural fecundity of the earth, and they had to perform various spring rituals in order to ensure the success of the following year's crops. An aspect of these rituals associated elephants with rain and fertility,[79] and even today they are often depicted with Lakshmi, shown standing between two elephants who are showering her with water.[80] In addition, the sheer physical power of elephants has traditionally been harnessed during war, natural disasters and for major construction projects, all of which, again, have regal (central government) associations.

The elephant is also one of the few animals that is actually a god within the Hindu pantheon, namely the elephant-headed Ganesha, the remover of obstacles and maker of good beginnings. Another of Ganesha's attributes is perspicacity, learning and memory, traits traditionally valued by traders and merchants. He is also regarded as a protector, which is why his form is often found over or by doorways.

Elephants have been depicted on the more expensive traditional saris of Tamil Nadu, Gujarat and Banaras, such as the Tamil *mubbhagam*, Gujarati *gharchola* and *patola*, and Banaras *kincabs* [Pls. 27, 89], as well as elephant-headed beasts (*gajasinha*) being depicted in the clothes of women painted in late medieval Gujarati Jain manuscripts.[81]

Above An ikat elephant from an Orissan landscape sari [Pl. 133].

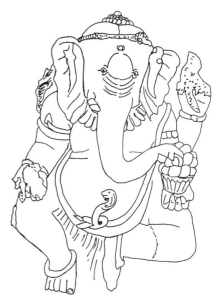

179

Above A *kachhua* (turtle) design on a painted sari from Madhubani, Bihar, 1992.

Bottom A cotton fragment depicting the *shikar* (hunting scene), with stamped and painted mordants, dyed brick red and dark brown, *c.* 1400–1600. There are many versions of the *shikar* design in Indian textiles. This one was created on low-cost cotton cloth that was found in the rubbish dumps of al-Fustat, near Cairo, Egypt. It depicts the Gujarati mother-goddess Khodiar hunting or chasing a wild boar, with other characters either fighting her or else also in pursuit of the animal.

Below A conch in an ikat endpiece, from a Cuttack weavers' sari, Orissa, 1992.

The Tortoise

(Sk) *Kachchhapa*; (Pk) *kachchhava*; (H) *kachhua*; (O) *kechhu*, *kachhima*, *kechho*.

The tortoise (Koorma) is the second incarnation of Vishnu, who was both the Cosmic Tortoise upon which the universe rests, and the foundation of the churning stick with which Vishnu stirred the Cosmic Ocean that created the universe.[82] Koorma's association with the birth of the universe and Vishnu lead to Lakshmi, who issued out of the churning waters and became Vishnu's consort. Consequently, the tortoise has associations with prosperity and the creation of wealth. Tortoises are known to have been part of the late, Upper Palaeolithic diet,[83] and they were depicted on Early Indus Valley pottery from Kalibagan,[84] which suggests they were already a noticeable part of local life. During the Gupta period, when Vaishnavism began to take recognizable shape, tortoise amulets were made in the north-west.[85] Today, tortoises are traditionally woven in the supplementary-warp bands of east Deccan saris [Pl. 117].

The Conch

(Sk) *Shankh*; (Pk) *shamkha*; (H) *shankh*; (O) *shankhaa*.

The conch shell is both a symbol of Vishnu and of Nada Brahma, god in the form of sound. It is one of the eight auspicious symbols, representing temporal power, and as such was used in ancient India as a war bugle. One of its first known depictions is in the Vaishnavite caves at Udayagiri near Bhopal (Madhya Pradesh, *c.* AD 401), and has been found in Vaishnavite art from then on. In terms of textiles, the conch only appears to have been depicted on twentieth-century saris, primarily on ikat-patterned Orissan ethnic saris made in the last fifty years [Pls. 132, 134].

The Hunting Scene

(U) *Shikaar*; (H) *Shikar*.

The hunting scene usually features men, horses, elephants, tigers, rabbits, deer, peacocks, parrots, and other animals, cavorting between entangling branches and leaves. This might seem an unusual design for a sari or any other textile made for personal use, but it was found in eighteenth- and nineteenth-century Banaras brocades [Pl. 89] and Gujarati *bandhani* [Pl. 40], late sixteenth- and early seventeenth-century Bengali embroidered quilts made for the Portuguese market, and in some fifteenth-century resist prints excavated at al-Fustat.

The origins of the hunting-scene design are obscure. It is easy to assume that these textiles were inspired by the elaborately figured seventeenth-century Safavid lampas textiles whose designs are conceptually similar because they also depict hunts and war, but the style of representation is completely different. The hunting scene prints excavated at al-Fustat suggest that the roots of this design are much older. For instance, a print dated to the early fifteenth century depicts a horsewoman, dog and mythological beast (*gajasinha* or elephant-lion) in conflict with a boar[86] and are believed to represent a Gujarati myth concerning the mother-goddess Khodiar, a warrior-goddess similar in type to Durga.

Notes on the Text

Chapter One ~ Lifting the Veil

1 *Adivasi* is an abbreviation of the Hindi *adi* (first, initial) and *nivasi* (inhabitant). The *adivasis* are the peoples listed as Scheduled Tribes in the Constitution of India and they were never part of the Hindu caste system. Nor were they originally involved with the complex of beliefs that is generically called Hinduism. Many *adivasis* speak Tibeto-Burman or Austro-Asiatic languages as well as Dravidian and Indo-Aryan tongues, although scholars debate whether the latter two replaced older languages.

2 Throughout this book we use 'ethnic' to refer to rural and sometimes urban communities which have maintained strong cultural identities even though they are usually socially, economically and religiously within mainstream India, often being part of the Hindu caste system or converted to Islam, Buddhism or Christianity. Many of the Scheduled Castes listed in the Constitution of India, as well as other groups, fall into this category. Nomadic pastoralists, such as the Rabari of Gujarat, Dhangar of Maharashtra and Lingayat of the southern Deccan plateau, as well as more settled communities, such as the Kols (fishermen) of Bombay, are included.

3 These may include descendants of India's ruling elite whose ancestors were involved with various regional or imperial courts; intellectual and artistic elite; and various groups whose primary occupations have traditionally been business or trade, such as the Parsis, Jains and Marwars. Although many are now highly Westernized, most still maintain their communities' traditions, some of which are reflected in their saris.

4 This makes it about the same size as Western Europe and one-third the size of the continental United States.

5 The mass migrations of people caused by the creation of India and Pakistan in 1947 are a poignant example.

6 For instance, the Buhlia Meher caste of weavers in Orissa trace their ancestry back to twelfth-century Rajasthan when local Rajput princes and their courts and artisans were forced into exile by Muslim invaders.

7 Allchin, 1988, pp. 33–62.

8 Ibid., p. 351. A Neolithic site at Chirand, Bihar.

9 Dyeing cotton with natural dyes is no mean feat. Like all plant fibres, cotton does not take dyes well and needs colourless metallic oxides called mordants to act as a catalyst and 'glue', binding the dye onto the cotton fibre. Mordants are used to dye cotton in many colours, most commonly red and black, and the textile fragment at Mohenjo-daro was believed to have been dyed with madder (red).

10 Allchin, 1988, pp. 298–308, 354–58; also Mallory, 1991, pp. 24–67.

11 Ibid., p. 351.

12 Austro-Asiatic languages are spoken by a few tribes in the north-east Deccan (Santhal, Munda, Ho) and the hills of Meghalaya (Khasi). Believed to be the language of the oldest inhabitants of the subcontinent, it is also spoken by the Khmer of Cambodia and the Mon of Burma.

13 Dravidian languages are indigenous to South Asia and are believed to have had a wider distribution in the past, perhaps as far west as Persia, but were 'pushed' east and south by encroaching Indo-Aryan languages.

14 The latest breakdown of India's languages occurred in the 1971 census, which listed the fifteen 'official' languages recognized by the Constitution of India and eighty-nine other 'non-scheduled' languages. Even these lists are not definitive, however, as the various dialects found in the states of Rajasthan and Bihar were collectively grouped together as 'Hindi' while many local dialects and minority languages were completely ignored.

15 Craven, 1977, pp. 81–3, 195–200.

16 Chishti and Sanyal, 1989, pp. 223–31.

17 In the collection at the Ashmolean Museum, Oxford, acc. no. X201.

18 The need for modesty in dancers' clothes is indicated in Kalidasa's poem *Malavikagnimitra* (*c.* AD 300–400), where two dancers compete. The characters discuss what the dancers should wear so the dancing is visible but decorum is maintained (Ch. 1, before v. 20).

19 For example, women in a Gandharan frieze depicting Buddha's birth (*c.* AD 100) in the Freer Gallery of Art, Smithsonian Institution, Washington, acc. no. 49.9.

20 Brooklyn Museum, acc. no. 1990.226, gift of Dr Bertram H. Schaffner.

21 According to Amy Poster, an authority on Gupta-period terracottas, who brought this particular piece to our attention.

22 Ajanta is a complex of rock-carved temples near Ellora, Maharashtra, many of which are painted with highly detailed, naturalistic murals.

23 Not everyone agrees that this figure is that of a woman. Ajanta scholar Leela Wood believes that it is a man, partly because of the pose in which the character sits, with legs akimbo. Although this obvious lack of modesty is not seen in other women depicted in the Ajanta scenes, we feel that because there is a comic element to the depiction of this provincial pair, such a pose might be part of the comedy.

24 Based on photographs of the cave murals published by The Archaeological Survey of India.

25 Seventeenth-century wall-hanging, Brooklyn Museum, acc. no. 14.719.7.

26 Very few saris found in museum collections can be confidently dated to even the early nineteenth – let alone eighteenth – century, and the few that are known to be older than about 1850 are usually the more expensive textiles worn by India's royalty. Such saris usually followed Mughal court fashions and therefore tell little about the traditional styles of the local people.

27 For instance, the *Viddhashalabhanjika* of Rajashenkhara (*c.* AD 900) mentions that when the love-sick heroine loses weight, her bodice (*kanchuka*) 'sits loosely on her' (2:18). Quoted in Ghurye, 1951, p. 243.

28 Two important public collections are: (1) A collection of saris worn by H.R.H. Princess Niloufer of Hyderabad, a gift to the Museum at the Fashion Institute of Technology. They consist predominantly of silk chiffon, hand-beaded and embroidered with European motifs, possibly made in France, late 1930s–40s. (2) A similar collection of the saris of H.R.H. Princess Barrar (sister-in-law of the above) at the Musée du Louvre, Paris, one of which has a Lanvin label.

29 As does the sari. See p. 198 for different regional names of full-body saris and allied clothes.

30 Note that the name of the female wrap in Burma, on the South-East Asian side of the Bay of Bengal, is similar to *lungi*, being *lon-gyi*.

31 *Census of Handlooms*, 1987–8, pp. xi–xiii.

32 According to C.V. Radhakrishnan, secretary-general of the Indian Cotton Mills' Federation.

33 Ghurye, 1951, p. 71. He notes that passages in the *Mahabharata* indicate that only high-born ladies could wear a veil or upper wrap, a practice continued in Kerala until the nineteenth century.

34 The veil may have Indo-Aryan and proto-Indo-European origins. The archaeological evidence from Ukrainian *kurgan* (mound or tumulus) burials (*c.* 500 BC) indicates that important women were interred wearing a large veil decorated with gold foil 'sequins', while earlier evidence from ancient Greek burials (*c.* 1500 BC) also suggests that veils may have been worn. See Barber, 1975, p. 318.

35 Today, only older ladies wear these styles regularly, otherwise they are usually only worn for special ritual occasions and weddings.

36 For instance, the supplementary-weft borders of Banaras saris, with their Mughal-style designs, are instantly distinguishable from the supplementary-warp borders of Assamese saris which usually contain highly detailed tribal designs.

37 A draping style that tucks in the endpiece usually results in a traditional sari with an insignificant-looking end, whereas the endpiece of a sari traditionally draped (that is, with it on show) is often highly embellished.

38 There is no consistent all-Indian name for this style of sari drape. Dongerkerry, in her monograph on the Indian sari (1959) called this the *nivi* style, and we have adopted it for ease and convenience. However, *nivi* actually refers to the knot made in the front of the sari where pleats may or may not fall, something that does not even appear in modern saris as petticoats are used. In Sanskrit, *nivi* means either an ornamental tasselled border or a knot which holds a garment in place. Saris draped in this manner have different names depending on the region – for instance, they are called a *gola nesana* (round-wrapped sari) in Maharashtra and *nerege* (frill) in Karnataka.

39 Chantal Boulanger, who has made a special study of south Indian and Deccan sari draping styles, supplied much of the information in this section, and spurred considerable discussion on the subject.

40 According to Archana Sinha from north Bihar. She is one of the many people who use this terminology but only wear the *nivi*-style sari. (Told to the author December 1993.)

41 *Kachchha* comes from the Sanskrit, where the word has exactly the same meaning as today, referring to the hem of a lower garment being gathered up behind and tucked into the waistband. A similar Sanskrit word, *kacha*, means a binding, band, or hem of a garment, while the word *kaksha* has the same meaning as *kachchha*. Sometimes *kachchha* saris are called *sakachchha* saris – the prefix *sa* means 'with' in Hindi, and *sakachchha* therefore means 'with a *kachchha* drape'. The Bhil tribes of eastern Gujarat used to wear this drape and called it *kachchhota*.

42 The Coorgs, a wealthy community in south-western Karnataka, have recognizable tribal origins, although today they are strongly Hinduized, seeing themselves as members of the warrior caste because of their strong military heritage.

43 This is not the only name by which this outfit is known in Kerala – it is also called an *onnariyum mundu* and *angavastram mundu*.

44 Gujarati Jain paintings from the eleventh to the fifteenth centuries always show women wearing a *lungi* wrapped around their lower half and a large veil covering the upper body. Sewn clothes are never in evidence and were probably introduced by later Muslim and Central Asian nomadic groups. Today, the Gujarati female *lungi* is also called a *ghaghra* by some ethnic groups. The cotton *lungi* worn by Rabari women is called a *pathernu*, with the older woollen version called a *pachhedo*. The Rabari are a major group of nomadic pastoralists who have many clans extending through Kutch and Saurashtra (Gujarat) and southern Rajasthan.

45 Today even poor rural women are fashion-conscious. Anthropologist Doreanne Jacobson, in her extended study of a village in central Madhya Pradesh, told us how in the late 1960s most women were wearing the *ghaghra* and *odhni*. By 1979 she had difficulty persuading a woman to model such clothes for a photograph because it was regarded as 'unfashionable'. By the early 1990s, only very old ladies wore the *ghaghra* and all other women wore *nivi*-style saris.

CHAPTER TWO ~ The Western Region

1 Such as Srinagar in Kashmir.

2 The Bhils, including the Bhilala and Bhil Garasia subgroups, are the largest tribal group in India. Consisting of about 5.2 million people, they live in the eastern Gujarat/western Madhya Pradesh area, a region they once ruled until conquered by Rajput forces in the seventeenth century. The name Bhil is believed to be of Dravidian origin (*bheel*, meaning 'arrow') relating to their prowess in archery; but they now speak dialects of Hindi. Although the Mina of western Rajasthan are also a major tribe (about 1.5 million people) their social and ethnic autonomy was destroyed in the nineteenth century by combined British/Rajput efforts which concentrated on successfully stealing their old land and kingdom. They, too, speak a dialect of Hindi.

3 For instance, a mural in Cave One depicts a man wearing a shirt with what appears to be a printed *hansa* (goose) design (the *Mahajanaka Jataka*, left corridor, Cave One).

4 Barnes, 1990, pp. 178–91.

5 That is, about 500 x 116 centimetres (16 feet x 45 inches), the average size of the urban, middle-class sari draped in the *nivi* style. The coarse fabrics once worn by poor women are no longer used, nor are the long 7- to 8-metre (23- to 26-foot) saris once worn by the Bhil tribes. The *kachchha* mode of drape is rarely, if ever, worn by the Bhils today, and is believed to have died out in the early 1960s.

6 According to textile designer Roshan Lala, who has worked extensively among weavers and printers in northern India for the past twenty years. (Interviewed January 1994.)

7 The Bhilala are traditionally of mixed Rajput/Bhil marriages, with whom the Bhils refuse to intermarry even though this group is often better off and more integrated into mainstream local culture.

8 Chishti and Sanyal, 1989, p. 228.

9 The emphasis is on small. The suffix 'i' in Hindi and other north Indian languages is a diminutive, referring to something being small or of lesser value.

10 The suffix 'a' which is often used in words with masculine associations refers to an object that is large in size rather than small. Hence *buta* are always large, while *buti* are always small.

11 Among collectors of Oriental rugs and Kashmir shawls these designs are often called *buteh*.

12 American Museum of Natural History, New York, acc. no: 72.2/8281, collected in the early 1970s.

13 Watt, 1903, pp. 240–50. Watt's catalogue, *Indian Art at Delhi*, is one of the most important documents giving details about the saris and other textiles of late nineteenth-century India, and is the only comprehensive source of information about many types of regional saris during that period.

14 Watt, pp. 247–9.

15 Watt, pp. 240–1.

16 Outside India, this technique is better known as *plangi*, an Indonesian term. Within India itself, tie-dyed saris and other textiles have a variety of names, usually referring to the method of creation, such as *bandhani* and *bandhana* (tied) or the final spotted appearance, such as *chunari*, *chundadi*, *chundari*, *chunri* and *chunni*. The latter names are also given to veils which may or may not have tie-dye spots on them.

17 Dancers and other women depicted in Cave One, Ajanta.

18 In particular, to Multan, Pakistan. One major traditional *bandhani* centre, Jamnagar (Gujarat), was founded in 1540 by Jadeja Rajputs from Sind, and it is believed they may have introduced the craft there.

19 Traditional silk weavers as well as *bandhej*, the Khatri community is divided into Hindu and Muslim groups.

20 Fitzgerald, 1992, pp. 217–24.

21 Such a sari exists in the collection at the Victoria and Albert Museum, London, dated to *c.* 1867 (IS 0584).

22 Victoria and Albert Museum, London, acc. nos. IS 142-1953, IS 200-1960, IS 202-1960.

23 Frater, 1993, p. 115.

24 The name 'Khoja' comes from *kwaaja*, which means 'honourable convert', for the ancestors of these people are believed to have been Hindus who converted to Islam in the eleventh century. See Majmudar, 1966, p. 253.

25 Buhler, Fischer and Nabholz, 1980, pp. 105–6.

26 When a double *lahariya* is created, forming a chequered pattern, it is called *mothra*.

27 Murphy and Crill, 1991, pp. 80–1.

28 The brother-sister relationship is one of the pivotal relationships within the Hindu family. Jokes about brother-in-laws interfering in family affairs and brothers' attachment to their sisters are common. The very term *sala* (brother-in-law) is often given between men as a friendly insult.

29 According to Roshan Lala.

30 Buhler, Fischer and Nabholz, 1980, p. 20.

31 Buhler and Fischer, 1979, p. 304.

32 Some Brahmin groups traditionally used it for weddings and to cover the corpse before the last rites.

33 The *tumpal* pattern consists of a row of isosceles triangles created at the short end of the fabric in the warp direction.

34 Recently, some printed saris with designs based on these embroideries have been appearing on the market.

35 For instance, in 1907, H.R.H. Princess Prem Kaur of Kapurthala (Punjab) was married in a densely embroidered *zardozi* sari which contained intricate diagonal patterning of vines and bees. It is in the collection of the Metropolitan Museum of Art, New York, 1977.237.

36 Irwin, 1973, pp. 65–8.

37 Gillow and Barnard, 1991, p. 92.

38 Watt, 1903, pp. 267–9.

39 A figured textile is any fabric with a woven pattern. This includes such weaves known as brocades, samitas, and lampas. We are using the technical meanings of these names in this book. See the Glossary of Textile Terms (p. 196) for the technical definitions of these terms.

40 Based on samples collected by Elizabeth Bayley Willis in the mid-1950s, in the Henry Art Gallery, Seattle.

41 Watt, 1903, p. 326.

CHAPTER THREE ~ The Eastern Region

1 He was born in a small kingdom in the Terai of Nepal close to the Uttar Pradesh border, and spent the rest of his life in the area we now call Bihar and eastern Uttar Pradesh.

2 Craven, 1977, pp. 35–65.

3 Mathur, 1966, p. 6; Stockley, 1988, p. 14.

4 Fine muslins were used during Mauryan times and were exported to Rome at the turn of the first millennium AD. See Ghuznavi, 1988, p. 51.

5 They were either encouraged or ignored by the region's local rulers.

6 Prior to the entrenchment of the East India Company in the mid-eighteenth century, eastern India exported silk brocades to Persia and cotton fabrics to the Middle East, South-East Asia, Europe and North America. See Sinha, 1984, pp. 10–13.

7 Stockley, ibid.

8 Emery, 1980, pp. 78–84.

9 Forbes-Watson, 1873, samples 647–60.

10 Quoted in Dar, note no. 39, p. 187.

11 According to several wealthy women of eastern Indian origin living in New Delhi and the USA.

12 Such as in the Shantiniketan area.

13 Thapar, *JITH*, 1 (1955).

14 Casson, *Periplus* 63:21.5–6. The line actually reads 'cotton garments of the very finest quality, the so-called Gangetic'.

15 Naturally coloured wild silks, such as *tasar* or *muga* silk, may also be used. For instance, in the American Museum of Natural History, New York, a Bengali sari (acc. no. 1-6931) dated to 1900 is woven with alternating warp stripes of unbleached cotton and *muga* silk. Forbes-Watson also gives samples of muslin textiles with woven *muga* silk designs (nos. 647–52).

16 Notes, Elizabeth Bayley Willis, Henry Art Gallery, Seattle (58.1, nos. 1–6).

17 *Neel* means blue or indigo, while *ambara* may indicate a cloth that often has ritualistic associations with the Maha Devi (Great Goddess).

18 Even today, many widows and older women in the region prefer to wear black or dark blue saris in addition to the white saris usually associated with widowhood.

19 Dacca is the old British name for Dhaka, but to avoid confusion we have kept to Dacca.

20 Watt, 1903, p. 287. He confuses the issue by calling the weaving *jamdani* work, but from the overall description of the saris, it is unlikely to have been *jamdani* weaving as that would have been too expensive.

21 Two such saris are in the Henry Art Gallery, acc. nos. 58.1-6, 58.1-367.

22 See note 14. The *Periplus* is believed to have been written between AD 40 and 70 by an Egyptian Greek merchant. See Casson, pp. 6–7.

23 Ghurye's description given in *Indian Costume*, p. 238; the reference is for p. 168 of A.A. Fuhrer's translation of the *Harshacharita* (1909).

24 Crill, 1988, p. 33.

25 Some scholars feel that the word *jamdani* is of Persian origin because the term is used there to describe a fine cotton cloth with spots and flowers woven on the loom. *Jam-dar* means flowered or embossed, and *jamewar* refers to a brocade weave. See Ghuznavi, p. 51.

26 The drawloom is believed to have been developed in the early centuries of the first millennium AD, either in China or Persia. Current evidence suggests that the Indian drawloom was a Sassanian or post-Sassanian introduction, and most written historical evidence, mainly dating from the first half of the second millennium AD, associates the drawloom with Muslim weavers.

27 Ali, 1900, p. 75.

28 Alternative spellings include *gorod*, *garud*, *garad*.

29 For instance, the wedding robes in Bhavabhutti's *Malati-Madhava* (*c.* AD 650–700) consist of a long gown (*cholaka*) of fine white silk and an upper garment (*uttariya*) of fine red cloth. See Ghurye, *Indian Costume*, pp. 240, 299.

30 Ostor, 1980, pp. 50–71.

31 A good example of such differences is seen in two saris in the Smithsonian Museum, Washington, DC: No. E399478 is of a fine silk with a high thread count, with a white field and red interlocked-weft border. Where the border joins the field, a fine line (6 millimetres wide) of warp *zari* threads is woven in a small serrated edge pattern. No. E399451, labelled a *puja* sari (a gift from the Government of India, 1962) is of a coarse whitish silk/cotton mix with a plain red border. According to local traders, poorer women would wear cotton saris of the same type instead of silk. (Bengali sari trader Ashish Sharma, interviewed April 1994.)

32 Mohanty, 1979, pp. 247–8.

33 Watt, p. 306.

34 Irwin, 1952, pp. 65–73.

35 Watt, p. 286.

36 Forbes-Watson, 1873, samples 647–52.

37 Singh, pp. 32–3; Dharmija, 1966, p. 35. Appliqués are traditionally created in the Saran, West Champaran, Muzaffarpur, Darbhanga and Madhubani districts, including such towns as Bettiah, Dighwara and Revelganj in the north-western part of the state.

38 Based on the memories of local people, none of which extend beyond the early twentieth century (conversations held in 1989, 1990–1).

39 Grierson, 1885, p. 150, para. 749.

40 That the wearing of cotton wedding saris had nothing to do with the wearer's wealth, or lack of it, is reflected in the fact that during the first half of the twentieth century, when they were regularly worn, most Bhumihar Brahmins owned huge stretches of land and were usually the wealthiest people in their community. Changing land laws during the 1960s and 1970s have caused them to

lose much, if not most, of their land-based wealth, and this group is arguably less well off today than in the past, even though the women now wear silk saris instead of cotton at their weddings.

41 *Gota* comes in different widths, from about 3 millimetres to as much as 20 centimetres, but is usually less than 8 centimetres wide.

42 When Bhumihar Brahmin bride Nandita Singh of Patna was married in the late 1980s, her family did not have time to order the making of a *gota* sari, so they had to rely on what was available in local stores. They found that the choice was very limited and that the Marwari saris with their sequins, tinsel and plastic gilt threads were much more common. Also, to their chagrin, they found that these were often being sold as *gota* saris. (Told to the author December 1991.)

43 Singh, B.N., 1974, p. 33.

44 Payne, 1989, pp. 18–31.

45 Grierson, p. 150, para. 749.

46 Ibid.

47 *Tasar* is the Hindi name for this silk, derived from the Sanskrit *dasuria*, as is *kosa*, a southern Hindi term. Many other local names, such as *pokol* (Or) and *potia* (H) may be of tribal origin.

48 *Atlas*, 1987, p. 184.

49 According to Gulshan Nanda, buyer from Cottage Industries for thirty years before she retired in 1990. (Interviewed by the author February 1991.)

50 *Atlas*, p. 184; also Singh, p. 37. In the early 1970s, Singhbhum had 25,800 silk rearers, Santhal Parganas 12,000, and Ranchi 6,178. The other districts had considerably fewer.

51 It is mentioned by the sixteenth-century British visitor, Ralph Fitch, and seventeenth-century reports indicate it was a thriving *tasar*-producing centre at the time. See Sinha, ibid., pp. 34, 44, 50–2.

52 Sinha, 1984, pp. 34, 44, 50–2.

53 Ali, 1900, pp. 22–5, 35.

54 *Atlas*, pp. 182–4.

55 Sinha, p. 37.

56 Ali, p. 76.

57 Ibid., pp. 75–6.

58 The fabric samples collected by J. Forbes-Watson in the 1860s were extremely fine. See Forbes-Watson, 1873, sample numbers 613–45. In addition, *tasar* saris in the private collections of Indian women in Bihar, dated to about 1960, also show finer quality fibres and workmanship.

59 According to Gulshan Nanda.

60 In Patna, 1991, the cheapest *tasar* saris cost about Rs 700, whereas mulberry-silk saris were

being sold for Rs 480 and up, and synthetics were selling for about Rs 300.

61 Bihar accounts for about 15 per cent, West Bengal about 3 per cent. About 1.4 million people were employed in the industry nationwide in 1990. See *Census of India*, 1991, and *Atlas*, 1987.

62 Cohn, 1989, pp. 343–5; Bean, 1989, pp. 355–76.

63 To complicate matters further, technically, a *tanchoi* with several layers of weft threads and only one warp is known as a samitas.

64 Krishna and Krishna, 1966, pp. 11–24.

65 Kumar, 1988, pp. 49–52.

66 Ibid., pp. 14–25.

67 Ibid., p. 50.

68 Watt, p. 336; Krishna and Krishna, 1966, p. 44; Lynton, 1993, pp. 18-21, 1994, pp. 207-16.

69 Many brides in the Middle East and North Africa also wear Banaras saris, a result of the popularity of Indian motion pictures in Islamic countries.

70 Mohanty, 1979, p. 27.

71 For example, the collection at the Museum of Art at the Rhode Island School of Design, Providence, Rhode Island, nos: 55.298, 55.297, collected by Lucy Truman Aldridge during a visit to India in 1922.

72 According to Roshan Kalapesi, an authority on Parsi culture and dress. (Interviewed in June 1993.)

CHAPTER FOUR ~ The North-East and the Himalayas

1 They are: Arunachal Pradesh, Assam, Manipur, Meghalaya, Nagaland, Sikkim, Tripura, Mizoram.

2 Allchin, 1988, p. 351.

3 Choudhury, 1966, p. 83.

4 Nepalese is spoken in the Kathmandu valley, while Assamese is the most common language of the Brahmaputra valley.

5 Such as the sixteenth- and seventeenth-century temple complexes of Kathmandu, Patan and Bhaktapur.

6 For instance, the family of Geetanjali Bora, who let us photograph some of her saris (see Pl. 21), is based in Gauhati, Assam, and traces its ancestry back to the Punjab. Four hundred years ago an ancestor was sent by a local king to be ambassador at the Ahom court. The Assamese king of the time granted him land so his family could live there. Her family remained highly Indianized even though, over time, many members married into local Assamese families.

7 Neog, 1981, p. 98.

8 An estimated one million households in Assam weave textiles for domestic use, according to the *Census of Handlooms*, 1987–8.

9 Almost immediately after Partition, Assam's government encouraged the weaving of tribal textiles with the mainstream Indian market in mind, and this may have also influenced the 'merging' of various local and ethnic textile designs.

10 Most of these names are based on groups of tribes speaking a certain family of languages, not individual tribes.

11 Choudhury, p. 344.

12 Baruah, 1985, pp. 220–4.

13 Mohanty, 1979, vol. II, pl. 209, pp. 213, 330, 328.

14 We thank Runrekha Mushahary, Odlaguri village, Kokrajhar district, for information about Boro textiles.

15 Lynton, 1993, pp. 73–132.

16 Based on the collection of the joint family of Davina M. Lyngwa and Mrs M. Daly, Shillong. The *dhara* featured in Pl. 20 belonged to Sarah Diengdoh, an ancestor who lived in the late nineteenth century.

17 *Census of India*, 1991, 1.8 million people lived there, consisting of twenty-nine different tribes, each of which speaks a different language.

18 The Meitei speak one of the Kuki-chin group of Tibeto-Burman languages, which also contains numerous Bengali and Hindi words.

19 Fraser-Lu, 1988, p. 88.

20 Although they are believed to have been a significant political force in the valley in the early second millennium AD, the Moirang are today divided into two groups: one of the seven endogamous clans of the Meitei, and a separate, low-status tribe (called Loi or Chakpa) living in the less fertile areas of the valley.

21 *Designs of Manipur Handlooms*, also Mohanty, ibid.

22 *Atlas*, 1987, p. 184. Manipur also has a small wild-silk-producing industry, but there is very little information on it.

23 In other words, all the varieties of commercial silk, such as the naturally yellow Thai silk or white Japanese silk, are produced by silk worms of the same species, only different (specially bred) varieties.

24 Barber, 1991, pp. 30–3.

25 Many manufacturers have also encouraged this confusion, calling noil fabric made from waste *Bombyx mori* fibres 'tasar silk' in the hope of giving it greater status, and hence saleability.

26 Assam and Manipur only produce small amounts of *tasar*, and after Bihar, Madhya Pradesh is the second largest *tasar*-producing state.

27 Ali, 1901, pp. 22–5, 35.

28 *Atlas*, 1987, pp. 182–4.

29 Choudhury, 1966, pp. 330, 341.

30 Ibid.

31 Quoted in Dar, 1969, p. 187: 'Their garments are made of *kauseya* and of cotton. *Kauseya* is the product of the wild silk worm.'

32 *Census of India*, 1981. Part X-D, Series 3. Handicraft Survey Report. *Endi Silk Industry of Assam*, p. 9.

33 Choudhury, 1966, pp. 330, 341.

34 Xia, 1983, *Jade and Silk of Han China*, p. 51.

35 Choudhury, pp. 339–40.

36 Ibid., pp. 343–4.

37 Baruah, 1985, p. 437.

38 Forbes-Watson, 1873, samples 647–52.

39 Paine, 1989, cover picture.

40 Forbes-Watson, samples 625–8.

41 To give an idea of *muga* silk's expense, in 1994 plain-woven *muga* (without embellishments) cost Rs 550 a metre, while mulberry-silk *tanchoi* brocade began as low as Rs 350 a metre.

42 Such as the Tamang, Gurung, Limbu, Magar and Brahmins.

43 Other groups, who usually speak Tibeto-Burman languages and dialects, give it other names. For instance, the Tamang call it *gunyu* and the Gurung *gaun*.

44 The dictionary definition of *pallo* actually describes it as the end portion of the *fariya* that is turned back to form a purse.

45 This garment is probably of Tibetan origin as many Tibetan groups wear it. Although bulky, the voluminous cloth gives extra warmth against the extreme mountain temperatures as well as acting as a useful storage place for personal items.

46 Anthropologists do not report Tibeto-Burman groups using different names for this particular garment.

47 Although the Gurung have maintained their own strongly Tibetan dialect, calling the *fariya* a *gaun*, their blouses are known by the Nepali term *cholo*.

48 Women in government service wear white saris with *dhaka* cloth borders containing rhododendron designs (the Nepali national flower) for formal occasions. See Dunsmore, 1993, pp. 93–132.

49 Scholars debate their origin and history, because although it is clear they once ruled the Kathmandu valley, they show many linguistic, cultural and social characteristics similar to the Nayars of Kerala. Indeed, the traditional architecture of both cultures is very similar, built of brick with carved wooden beams and windows, and sharply sloping roofs.

50 Bistra, 1971, pp. 16–30; Shreshtra and Singh, 1972, pp. 29–38.

51 They are divided into twenty-six different castes; yet although they are now Hindu, the Hindu caste system was probably only introduced between seven and four hundred years ago. Prior to that they were probably Buddhist.

52 The drape of the *patasi* is such that the lower legs are often exposed at the back, which may explain why many older Jyapu ladies have intricate scroll-like tattoos on the backs of their ankles and lower legs, once also the practice of other groups such as the Tharu.

53 Dunsmore, p. 118.

54 In December 1990, when we asked the Tamang servants of a wealthy friend in Kathmandu to pose for us in their local dress, the wife insisted on appearing in a bright pink polyester sari draped in the *nivi* style. She could not understand that her daily-wear clothes – inexpensive mill prints draped in the typical *fariya* manner – were of more interest to us.

55 Bista, p. 126; Shreshtra & Singh, pp. 24–8.

CHAPTER FIVE ~ The Eastern Deccan

1 Although the Maharashtran districts of Bhandara, Godchiroli and Chandrapur make up this area, with Nagpur district in the western part, we have used the name 'Nagpur' as a convenient shorthand to describe this entire area.

2 Throughout history, most tribal groups have resisted incorporation into mainstream Hindu and Muslim society. For instance, the incursions of Hindu and Muslim squatters, farmers and moneylenders, followed by East India Company officialdom, led to the Chota Nagpur riots of 1831–2. This struggle against mainstream Indian domination continues today in the form of the Jharkhand Party (aiming at the secession of the north-eastern Deccan from the Republic of India) and other tribal political movements.

3 Such as the rivers Mahanadi (Orissa), Godavari and Krishna (Andhra Pradesh).

4 Primarily Orissa.

5 Based on population figures given for Scheduled Tribes in the 1991 *Census of India:* Madhya Pradesh (15.4 million), Orissa (7.0 million), Bihar (6.6 million), Andhra Pradesh (4.2 million) and West Bengal (3.8 million).

6 Counting tribes is complicated because there are many 'sub-tribes' in addition to separate tribes having been considered single units in the past because they spoke the same language. According to the *Census of India*, in 1981, Orissa alone contained sixty-two different tribes.

7 The Gadaba is a name given to several different tribes that speak a wide range of different languages.

8 For instance, the Gonds all speak the Dravidian tongue Gondi, but are divided into such distinct groups as the Koya, Raj, Maria, Naik and Bisonhorn Gonds, among others.

9 Ahmad, 1965, p. 172.

10 Chishti and Sanyal, pp. 79–83.

11 Prasad, 1961, p. 172; Minz, 1982, pp. 1, 20–1, 27–8.

12 Mohanty, Chandramouli and Naik, 1987, pp. 67–75.

13 The Santhal and other tribal people on the Chota Nagpur plateau have traditionally been involved with *tasar* sericulture, so a *tasar* sari may not have been out of place.

14 Overall, the Santhals are the most Hinduized all of the peninsular Indian tribes, but more members of the northerly tribes, such as the Munda, Oraon, Ho, have entered mainstream Indian (Hindu) society than those further south.

15 We thank Mr Chhote Hembram, public relations dept., Tata Steel, and Mr C.R. Hembram, for their information and help on Santhal dress and society.

16 We thank Messrs C.R. Hembram and S. Bhengra of the Tribal Cultural Centre, Kagalnagar, Singhbhum district, for their information and help on Munda dress and society, in addition to Mrs Nimi Oria and Mrs Jolen Kanduna of Muingutu, Singhbhum district.

17 Campion, 1980, p. 84; Tirkey, 1989, pp. 77, 52–3; Chishti and Sanyal, pp. 70–5. Also, we thank Mr Murari Oraon, Gorwantar, Palamu district, for his information about Oraon dress and culture.

18 This is probably because most weavers are caste Hindus, not tribals, and most researchers have talked with the weavers rather than with the tribals themselves.

19 Chishti and Sanyal, p. 7. However, the names that Chishti and Sanyal attribute to the Oraon saris they feature are all Hindi words, not the tribal languages. This makes tribal identification of the motifs difficult.

20 Chishti and Sanyal, pp. 71, 75.

21 The word *gisir* is linguistically related to *kichri* which is used in several tribal languages, including the Austro-Asiatic Mundari and Dravidian Oraon. Among the Gonds it means garment or cloth. The Gondi word *ganda* – note the similarity to the Mundari *khanda* – refers to cloth that women wear.

22 Furer-Haimendorf, 1982, pp. 14–21. Among some of the Gond tribes are the Raj Gonds, Hill Marias, Bisonhorn Gonds and the Koyas.

23 It is unclear what tribals wore in the past, but it is likely that one or two centuries ago most tribal women were wearing considerably less clothing than today (and possibly more jewelry). The written evidence over the twentieth century is contradictory. For instance, Ghurye (1951) talks of Santhal and Munda women wearing *kachchha* drapes while Minz (1982) describes Munda women in remote areas wearing very short *paria*.

24 An alternative translation is 'coloured flower seat'. Like the *chauk* mentioned earlier, this appears to refer to the Hindu wedding ceremony – something no tribal would be involved with. The low seat where the bride and groom sit is often decked with sweet-smelling flowers.

25 Mohanty, Chandramouli and Naik, 1987, pp. 67–75.

26 Chishti and Sanyal, p. 86.

27 For instance, weavers of Gond saris call small border triangles *bundki;* medium (serrated) triangles *tikki;* and the largest ones *kumbh*.

28 Gadaba cloth stripes are not necessarily multicoloured, although Huylerj's photograph and text, p. 177, indicates this. Photographs taken by Furer-Haimendorf, *c.* 1941 (F-H, 1990, photos after p. 86) show many upper and lower cloths woven with warp (and occasionally weft) bands which appear to be of a single colour.

29 Their name is spelt differently in different regions, with 'Kond' and 'Kandh' being the most common variations. Although about 93 per cent of all Khonds live in Orissa, they also live in Bihar, Madhya Pradesh, West Bengal, Maharashtra and Andhra Pradesh.

30 Huyler, 1985, p. 181.

31 When fibre artist Jon Eric Riis visited Bondo villages in Koraput in 1970, the women used

home-spun local bast fibres in the warp, and coloured cotton threads bought from itinerant traders in the weft. Also see Furer-Haimendorf, 1990, pp. 50–1.

32 Even today most rural women only have one sari which they wear every day. Under these conditions, a heavy-count cotton handloom of good quality can last for as long as two years.

33 Even the extremely expensive aristocratic Paithani sari of western Maharashtra often has a *patta* endpiece woven into the opposite end of the sari to the intricate *zari*-woven endpiece that is displayed.

34 *Bhanwarai* saris are those worn for the final part of the wedding ceremony where the bride and groom follow each other seven times around the sacred fire.

35 The word *pitamber*, which means 'yellow cloth' (*pit*, yellow; *amber*, cloth) is commonly used in the Deccan to describe many yellow saris, most of which are used during weddings or for other ritual occasions.

36 Chishti and Sanyal, 1987, p. 87.

37 A fertility symbol.

38 Saris with cotton fields and *tasar* borders appear to have once been commonly made throughout most of the *tasar*-growing regions of India. Historical records indicate that such saris were once made in Bihar to the north, and the aristocratic Gadwal saris of Andhra Pradesh further south also reflect such a tradition.

39 Chishti and Sanyal, p. 130, no. 64/268.

40 In the nineteenth century they were also known as *hansabali kapta* and *hansabali datapur*, according to Watt, 1903, p. 276.

41 The encouragement of mulberry sericulture in Orissa has become an important state priority as it is a good means of creating out-of-state revenue while employing rural people. See, for instance, *Indian Express, Orissan Edition, Vizianagaram*, Feb. 20, 1991, p. 3. transcript of Governor's address. Also, Virginia Davis notes, February 15, 1991.

42 See collection at Calico Museum of Textiles, Ahmedabad; also, Virginia Davis notes, Feb. 15, 1991.

43 Early fourteenth-century Maithili (north Bihar) documents use the term *vandha* to describe several types of textile, such as *Surya vandha* and *Gaja vandha* as well as other names similar to Oriya terms, such as *vichitrangada*. Some scholars take these to refer to ikat textiles, possibly of the Orissan type. In addition, the Buhlia Meher caste trace their ancestry to the court of twelfth-century Rajput kings who lost their kingdoms to Muslim conquerors and whose courts were forced into exile. (See Mehta, 1961, pp. 62–70.) However, because there is no direct visual proof (illustrations or extant textiles) until the mid-nineteenth century,

other scholars refuse to accept such early possible references. See, for instance, Mohanty and Krishna, 1974, pp. 15–22.

44 Virginia Davis notes, Feb. 20, 1991.

45 Rebanta Goswami, 'Bomokoi', in *The India Magazine*, vol. 5, no. 4, March 1985, pp. 44–51.

46 Ibid.

47 Nuapatna is well known for its *tasar* silk saris, both ikat and non-ikat.

48 Such local courts as that at Puri, Tigiria, Baramba and Athagarh. See Nayak, pp. 47–56.

49 Mohanty and Krishna, 1974, p. 19.

50 Such cloths, including saris, were used in various aspects of religious worship, from draping the sacred log used in annual rites, to being worn by priests and worshippers.

51 Mohanty and Krishna, pp. 20–1.

52 Virginia Davis notes, Feb. 26, 1991.

53 The word *khandua* appears to be of Dravidian or Austro-Asiatic tribal origin. *Khanduva* refers to an upper garment in Telugu – most nineteenth-century *khanduas* in museum collections appear to have been shawls rather than saris – while the linguistically related Gondi *ganda* means 'woman's cloth', Kondh *garnda* refers to a garment or cloth, and the Mundari *khanda* refers to particular saris.

54 Mohanty, Chandramouli and Naik, 1987, pp. 75–83.

55 Virginia Davis notes, Feb. 20, 1991.

56 Research by Rebanta Goswami (1985, pp. 44–51) and others indicates that it was once much more widespread in the plains and even hill regions.

57 De Bone, 1984, p. 37.

58 Virginia Davis notes, Feb. 20, 1991.

59 De Bone, pp. 36–40.

60 The name *khan* probably comes from the group of tribal words such as *khanda* that have been discussed earlier.

61 The name used here, *gollabhana*, may be a corruption of *gulbadan*, which was a floral (*gul*) sari containing light ikat-work in the form of ikat 'dashes' dyed into the warp or weft threads. Such saris were commonly made throughout much of northern and southern India during the nineteenth century. (See Watt, 1903, pp. 275, 298.)

62 Elizabeth Bayley Willis Collection, Henry Art Gallery, Seattle (58.1-104, 105, 106).

63 See Mohanty, pp. 21–3. He also notes, however, that *patola* cloths from Gujarat were exported to South-East Asia via Masulipatnam in the seventeenth century, which suggests that ikat dyeing and weaving techniques may have been introduced as a result of this export trade. However, all the 'early' cloths were primarily made for export to Islamic countries; they did not impinge on local sari-wearing habits. They go by various names, such as *Asia rumal, telia rumal*, and *chauka*, all referring either to the place of export (Arabia) or the square lattice-like design.

64 Hacker and Turnbull, 1982, pp. 55–9.

65 Elizabeth Bayley Willis Collection (58.1-383, 384).

66 Jayakar, 1955, pp. 55–9.

67 The difference in prices is considerable. In 1993, a silk *patolu* woven by the Salvi family in Patan, Gujarat, cost about Rs 63,000, while a silk/cotton mix *patolu* from a merchant in Hyderabad only cost about Rs 3,000.

68 See Elizabeth Bayley Willis Collection, 58.1-550.

69 To be more exact, the mordants for the red dye are block-printed on and then the sari is dipped into the alizarin dye.

70 For more details, see Mohanty, Chandramouli and Naik, pp. 100–30.

71 The word 'batik' is Indonesian; it was adopted into the English language to describe the painted wax-resist process and so became incorporated into Indian speech as English is so widely spoken.

72 Murphy and Crill, 1991, pp. 112–17.

73 Like the *kumbha* border motifs, the *reku* is woven in the interlocked-weft technique, but the field weft threads are usually more visually outstanding than the border threads, so creating a central motif with 'jagged' sides. (In some Dravidian languages, *reku* means blades or bunches of grass.)

74 Mohanty, 1979, p. 180.

CHAPTER SIX ~ The South

1 The major Dravidian languages are Tamil, Telugu, Kannada and Malayalam, although the Indo-Aryan Sinhalese is spoken in Sri Lanka.

2 For instance, many Dravidians traditionally allow first cousins to marry, whereas this is banned in Indo-Aryan society.

3 Kerala is home to many different religious groups including Christian and Jewish communities who trace their ancestry to ancient times. Its Brahmins spoke Sanskrit until the late eighteenth century, and many elements of Kerala's traditional material culture have pre-Islamic north Indian elements. Tamil Nadu has distinct Jain and Lingayat communities and several of its Hindu deities, such as the warrior-god Muruka, are not found elsewhere in the subcontinent.

4 The 'warrior' Devangas are a community within the Devanga caste. During the tenth to fourteenth centuries when they were known as the Kaikkolar, they were professional warriors and royal bodyguards who took up weaving as a peace-time occupation. The memory of their warrior heritage is still strong, and notes made by Elizabeth Bayley Willis in 1955 (HAG 58.1–31) indicate that she was told how 'warrior' Devangas lived and worked in certain towns.

5 Several different ports and cotton cloth-exporting areas are mentioned in the *Periplus of the Erythrean Sea* (Casson, trans.). See 59:20.2, 61:20.19, 62:20.22.

6 The market need not be a fashionable one. In January 1990, Gulshan Nanda told us that in the mid-1980s, when she was still a buyer for Cottage Industries, she visited a market in Bastar (Madhya Pradesh) and bought what she thought were locally made Gond saris. It was not until she returned to her hotel room that she discovered that the heavy-count cotton saris with the typical traditional Gond designs had a label stating they were made in Kerala.

7 In the 1983–4 season, Karnataka accounted for 59 per cent of India's silk 'crop', Andhra Pradesh 16 per cent, Tamil Nadu 11 per cent and West Bengal 12 per cent.

8 In Tamil Nadu the following districts are involved with sericulture, in descending order: Dharmapuri, North Arcot, Salem, Tirunelveli, Periyar, Madurai, Thanjavore, Coimbatore, and South Arcot.

9 The Devangas are believed to have emigrated to Tamil Nadu from Karnataka and Andhra Pradesh between AD 1000 and 1400.

10 Kerala has been governed by various Communist Party administrations for much of the time since India's Independence, and the state has probably gone through the most sweeping social changes of any in the subcontinent. Not only was the caste system outlawed, but also one of the dominant groups, the Nayars, have given up their legal matrilineal inheritance rights in order to fit in with mainstream India's legal system.

11 Karnataka's modern silk industry began under the encouragement of industrialist Jamsetji Tata. In 1893 he brought Japanese sericulturists to Mysore and southern Karnataka to help set up the industry there. In the course of their work they discovered that centuries earlier the region had a flourishing sericulture industry which was presumably destroyed by one of the invading powers of the previous few hundred years.

12 The name 'Kornad' is one of many names given to this sari, but we have chosen it because (1) it is short and simple, and (2) Kamala Dongerkerry (1959), who wrote one of the first books on the sari and is herself from southern India, uses this name. Most of the other names given to this sari usually refer to the town of manufacture or some salient element in its design.

13 Most of the terms used in this chapter are Tamil, but please note: (1) Kornad saris are worn throughout southern Karnataka as well as Tamil Nadu, with the Karnataka colour schemes usually being more subdued (dark greens, browns, greys) than the Tamil versions. (2) Many different Tamil dialects and words regularly used in one area are completely unknown in another; consequently, the words used here were either told to the author during field research or were written in one of the publications listed in the Bibliography.

14 It is known by such names as *pavun pettu* (*rudraksha* motif stripe) or *vanki pettu* (herringbone motif stripe).

15 Watt, 1903, pp. 313–16.

16 Ramnarain, 1991 (a), p. 2.

17 Kalakshetra was founded in 1936 by Rukmini Arundale, who began it as a school focusing on traditional Tamil dance; it now also houses a textile museum.

18 Ramaswamy, 1985, p. 65.

19 Mohanty, 1979, pp. 156–63.

20 During the nineteenth century Arni was famous for producing a classic Kornad sari called *pattu sarigai pudavai*. Watt, in 1903, described one example as being 'woven in checks outlined by gold threads and black, the meshes being orange, dark brick red, or green, orange and red. The borders are broad, of deep maroon with double rows of gold geometric scroll' (pp. 313–16). Nearby Salem also created interlocked weft-bordered saris which presumably were of the Kornad type. All we know of them are their names: *mayilkan* and *kuyilkan* (Mohanty, p. 169).

21 Elizabeth Bayley Willis notes, Henry Art Gallery, acc. no. 61.1-28.

22 Note the similarity of the *pukai Madrasi* sari to the Ilkal (p. 147) and *jote* (p. 148) saris of the south-west Deccan.

23 Bangalore is a distribution centre for Karnataka's silk industry, not a weaving centre.

24 Today, with the rising cost of silk, even well-off middle-class women buy the inexpensive skirt saris.

25 As they are woven by hand, only the very rich could afford Karnataka chiffons, for they were much more expensive than imported fabrics.

26 We thank M. Sridhara, Govt. India Tourist Office, Narasimha Iyengar and Rajalaxmi Iyengar of Amruthur village, Kunigal Taluk, for their help and advice with the Kannada language and sari terms. (Interviewed May 1994.)

27 The design structure of the Mysore crepe and other southern Karnataka saris is similar to the thin-bordered white muslins found in surrounding states, which suggests they may have once been worn here.

28 Barbosa (ed. Dames), 1: 205, quoted in Chandra, 1973, p. 177. The quote continues, '...one part of which is girt round their below, and the other part on their shoulder and across their breasts in such a way that one arm and shoulder remains uncovered, as with a scarf'. That this is a description of the *nivi* style is not, perhaps, surprising as it is in the Karnataka (Mysore) and western Maharashtran area that the *nivi* style is believed to have originated.

29 The names are Tamil, although they are also found in Malayalam, which uses many Tamil-derived words. An extensive public collection of these saris is found in the Elizabeth Bayley Willis Collection, Henry Art Gallery, Seattle, nos: 58.1-57, 78, 79, 80.

30 See collection, American Museum of Natural History, New York, acc. nos.: 70.2/4498, 4499, 4500, and 70.3/4371.

31 Known as Mappillas or Malabar Muslims, they are the descendants of seventh- and eighth-century Arab traders who settled permanently along the Kerala coast. Because they were involved in trade rather than conversion (as happened in the north), they became much more integrated into local society than many Muslim groups elsewhere in India.

32 Such muslins were also woven in Venkatagiri in the nineteenth century, and may have been woven in Kanchipuram as early as the fourteenth century because documents of that age indicate that 'gold embroidered' or 'gold woven' cloths were created there.

33 These gold and white muslins are rarely made in Tamil Nadu today, and although many Tamils we talked with recognized these saris as traditional, no one knew their original Tamil name.

34 The *thali* is the traditional symbol of wifehood throughout most of Dravidian south India. Characterized by two large dome-like or pronged pendants (each supplied by the bride's and groom's family) it is initially tied round the bride's neck with a yellow string. Ten to thirty days after the wedding, the string is replaced, with the correct rites, by a gold chain, and older women from both families contribute beads and pendants from their *thali* to the new bride's necklace, so making it a repository of family heirlooms and history.

35 Many thanks to V. Manimekalai, Madras, for her extensive help in the linguistic and cultural fields relating to southern Andhra and northern Tamil saris, jewelry and domestic art.

36 The ancestors of Ceylonese Tamils emigrated to Sri Lanka in medieval times, and they are usually fully integrated into Sri Lankan society; however Indian Tamils arrived during the nineteenth century as cheap labour for the British tea plantations, and were never integrated into the local culture.

37 Sharma, 1988, pp. 9–34.

38 It is not known whether these textiles were made locally or imported from either South-East Asia or the trading centres in Gujarat.

39 Coomaraswamy, 1913, p. 203.

40 UNESCO World Art Series, pl. xxx (Telvatta Shrine, Galle district); and p. xxxiii (Telepatta Jataka, Pahala Vihara, Mulgiragala, Hambantota district); both of which show murals painted in the early nineteenth century.

41 Coomaraswamy, 1913, pl. 150, p. 192.

42 Elizabeth Bayley Willis notes, Henry Art Gallery, acc. nos. 58.1-51, 52, 53, 54.

43 These muslins are woven in such towns as Madurai, Thanjavore, Arni, Tiruchirapalli, Chingleput and the entire Coimbatore/Erode/Salem area in Tamil Nadu, while in southern Andhra Pradesh there is Vavilla, Nellore, Pulivendla and Cuddapah.

44 Watt, 1903, p. 280.

45 Mohanty, 1979, pp. 166–8.

46 Murphy and Crill, 1991, p. 111.

47 Irwin and Hall, 1971, Ch. IX.

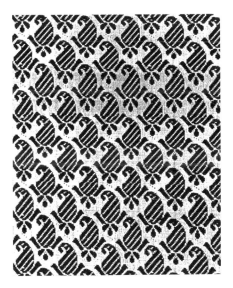

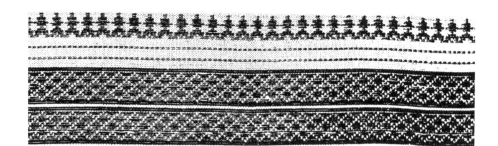

CHAPTER SEVEN ~ The Western Deccan

1 Except for the area east of Nagpur discussed in Chapter Five.

2 Such as the Narmada, Tapi, Godavari, Bhima and Krishna rivers.

3 The battle for independence from the Mughals began with Shivaji (1627–80) and continued through the mid-eighteenth century.

4 Even though several different major languages are spoken in this region, namely Hindi, Kannada and Marathi, only Marathi names are given here.

5 The word *shallu* appears to have regal associations as the Sanskrit *shallanga* refers to king or sovereign, which many such saris certainly had. In the nineteenth century, similar Marathi words, *sala* and *sela*, referred to veils worn by the elite during ritual occasions.

6 According to Sally Holkar (interviewed May 1994: see note 19), the fine checks and stripes evolved out of the weavers not wasting any of the coloured threads used in the weaving (wastage is more likely to occur in a single-colour sari). Also, the multiple use of many colours of often similar hues in a fine check or stripe sari ensured that if any one colour ran, it would not be noticeable.

7 For instance, a *gomi-katha* sari is one with a herringbone border, a *baavadhani* one with a wide border and *asaavarikaatha* one with depictions of a local plant (*asaavari*) woven into the border.

8 Such as the *hublidhardi* after the region where it is woven (Hubli district), and *baavadhani lugade* (wide-bordered sari).

9 Jain and Aggarwala, 1989, p. 136.

10 Most of these saris always have red borders and sometimes red endpieces as well.

11 Today, synthetic fibres often replace the silk.

12 Catalog *Visvakarma Ksetra*, no. 3.

13 Chishti and Sanyal, pp. 139–44; Watt, 1903, p. 276.

14 The machine-spun thread imported from England in the late eighteenth and nineteeth centuries was not fine enough to create these muslins, which required the fibres of a specially grown local variety of cotton to produce the fine threads.

15 Very fine silk threads are easier and faster to weave than the equivalent sized cotton threads.

16 This silk warp/cotton weft sari is called a *neem-reshmi* sari.

17 A typical motif of Maheshwari saris is the *aankhi-muthda*, where the chain motif is bounded by extra-warp dashes or lines.

18 The *garbh-reshmi* sari had a silk check upon a cotton ground and was popular in the nineteenth century.

19 This revival began when Richard and Sally Holkar founded the Rehwa Society in the 1970s, in an attempt to improve the lives of the by-then destitute weavers and local women. The Rehwa Society now produces some of the finest saris and other textiles of this type and its success has encouraged the formation of local (independent) weavers' cooperatives in the area.

20 Such as grids of *zari* squares with discontinuous supplementary weft motifs in each, or rows of circular *butis*.

21 Their high cost is revealed in a story Watt tells about a Paithani sari shown at the 1903 exhibition. It was ordered by the Maharaja Bhosla of Nagpur in 1853 at a cost of Rs 2,200 (compare this with the fact that fifty years later, in 1900, a silk sari could cost as little as Rs 5). Because the Maharaja was in financial difficulties, the sari was left with Baba Shetha of Paithan (status unclear, possibly a trader). When he became bankrupt it was offered for sale at Aurangabad, although the price was not mentioned. It was rare in India for textiles of any kind to be kept, let alone given a provenance, but the exceptional technical as well as financial value of this sari kept it in the public record. Its history since 1903, unfortunately, is not known. Most Indians traditionally burn old saris that contain *zari* in order to recycle the gold from the metallic thread.

22 This included such changes as wearing shoes and white stockings under the sari, instead of the ubiquitous Indian sandal. However, it is unclear where the Parsi tradition of wearing the hair bound by a white cloth, with the sari endpeice draped over it, originated.

23 Our thanks to crafts and Parsi costume and culture expert, Roshan Kalapesi, for the information about the development of Parsi dress and many other aspects of Parsi textile history mentioned here. (Interviewed June 1993, May 1994.)

24 The name *ghara* also referred to the heavily embroidered saris.

25 According to many Parsis (Kalapesi, Lala, Sabavala, Wood), a popularly held story that Chinese weavers and embroiderers lived in Surat during the late nineteenth century is a myth. Chinese goods were regularly exported to Bombay, and some Parsis had Gujarati Indian weavers, living in Surat, trained in Chinese textile techniques.

26 According to Pamela Parmal, assistant curator, Museum of Art at Rhode Island School of Design, an authority on eighteenth-century French and English costume and textiles. (Interviewed October 1993.)

27 Throughout much of the twentieth century, these Chinese embroidered saris were out of favour, being seen as old-fashioned, but since the 'ethnic revival' that has affected much of India's urban society, these saris are now extremely expensive. Prices in the Rs 30,000 to Rs 50,000 range were quoted in early 1993.

28 According to Leela Wood and Shirin Sabavala, who gave this information, the right length of fabric to make a sari cost about Rs 8 in the late 1940s/early 1950s.

29 Many Parsis now exclusively wear Western clothes.

30 The Tata organization was the first to open Indian-owned steel mills, chemical plants, soap factories and many other industries, and also founded Air India.

31 Lala, 1992, p. 6.

32 The boom of the 1860s was caused by the cotton shortage in the United States brought on by its civil war. Once that nation's cotton industry was reinstated, however, there was a severe recession in the Bombay mill industry.

33 In May 1994, the Indian Government announced it was cutting many subsidies to the handloom sector. How this will affect the handloom sari industry is as yet unknown, and in the long run it may be beneficial. Under the old system, many weavers were forced to weave low-end *janta* saris which compete with the cheaper mill products, yet most people involved in India's textile market agree that the place for handlooms is at the opposite, high end of the market where weaving and design virtuosity is at a premium.

34 Such as roller printing.

35 We thank textile designer Roshan Lala for much of the information in this section.

36 *The Handbook of Statistics on The Cotton Textiles Industry*, 1991.

CHAPTER EIGHT ~ Iconography

1 Turner, 1937. Until recently, low caste and ethnic women in western India wore saris dyed dark blue, a colour traditionally avoided by local higher castes. Today, tellingly, few dark blue saris are made in the region and women from these old communities wear brighter colours from the cotton mills and factories.

2 The practice of a new mother wearing a yellow sari is mentioned in the seventh-century *Kadambari* of Banabhatta (of *Harshacharita* fame). It is still continued among many groups today, such as the Santhal of Chota Nagpur. Middle-class women in Patna also wear a yellow sari when performing *puja* in their local temple seven days after the birth of their child.

3 Kramrisch, 1983, pp. 270, 287–90.

4 Dar, 1969, pp. 128, 131.

5 Barber, 1991, p. 233.

6 Mohanty, Chandramouli & Naik, 1987, pp. 1–3.

7 The supplementary warp bands of Deccan sari borders are usually woven with no more than five

or seven sticks. This restricts both the size and pattern style of these bands, and is the reason why so many of these traditional bands are very narrow, often being no more than 3 millimetres wide.

8 Maloney, 1976, pp. 102–48; Roberts, 1976, pp. 223–78.

9 Molesworth, 1975.

10 The now ubiquitous English term 'temple motif' is a recently introduced word that was probably a corruption of the Malaysian term *tumpal*, which is used interchangeably with 'temple motif' by some scholars of Indian textiles.

11 Nagaraja, 1993, pp. 197–201.

12 Archana, p. 66.

13 Chishti and Sanyal, 1989, p. 23.

14 Allchin, 1988, p. 103, pl. 5.20.

15 Kramrisch, 1946, vol. 1, pp. 22–8.

16 Ibid.

17 Freed and Freed, 1993, p. 224, fig. 10.

18 Kramrisch, 1954, p. 39.

19 Ibid.; Stutley, 1985.

20 The word *lata* occurs in most Indo-Aryan languages.

21 For instance, the stupa in Nagarjunakonda, Andhra Pradesh, third century BC; the fifth-century Vishnu temple, Deogarh, Uttar Pradesh; and the ninth-century temple gate from Orissa, now at the entrance to the Patna Museum, Bihar.

22 *Aditi*, p. 77.

23 Krishna and Krishna, 1966, p. 10, fig. 4.

24 For instance, sample 1990.1122 in the Newberry Collection at the Ashmolean Museum, see Barnes, 1990; Gittinger, 1982, figs. 14, 16, 17, 18, 20, 41, 42.

25 Barber, 1991, pp. 297, 372–73.

26 The other meanings of *phool* and similar words include the menses (P, N, O, G), and ovaries (M, N).

27 Archana, p. 72

28 The jasmine flower is commonly depicted in traditional jewelry throughout the subcontinent, and the flower is also strung together in long strands to decorate the low stage used in wedding ceremonies as a means of perfuming the air.

29 Chandra, 1973, p. 57.

30 Among the flowers and flowering trees used in Maruka rituals are: katampu (*Eugenia racemosa*), kantal (*Gloriosa superba*), asoka (*Uvaria longifonia*), and venkai (*Pterocarpus bilobus*).

31 Archana, pp. 72, 82.

32 Allchin, p. 146.

33 Poster, 1986, p. 101. A terracotta from Berachampa (West Bengal) in Asutosh Museum of Indian Art, Calcutta University.

34 Flowers in Ajanta murals are preponderantly depicted in the roof panels – for example, at Cave 17, *c.* 500 BC.

35 Stone and clay seals from Murdigak and Damb Sadaat, levels II and III. Allchin, p. 139, pls. 6.8, 6.9.

36 Dhamija and Sarabhai, 1988, p. 19.

37 Kinsley, 1986, pp. 19–22; n.3, p. 223.

38 Pal, 1986, pp. 93–110.

39 For instance, a Jain bronze shrine from western India dated to the seventh century, see Sotheby's catalogue, June 13, 1993, no. 97; and a bronze Balarama from Nalanda, dated Devapali period (818–56), Asher, pl. 177.

40 Irwin, 1973.

41 In the collection of the Rhode Island School of Design. The textile still contains the label of its manufacturer with the date of manufacture attached. Acc. no. 37.395.

42 Craven, 1977, pp. 136–7.

43 Archana, p. 10.

44 Archer, 1985, pp. 8–10.

45 Depictions of the peepal leaf are commonly found in the pottery of such early Indus Valley sites as Mundigak IV (western Afghanistan), Mehrgarh VI (Baluchistan) and Lewan (upper Indus valley), as well as on many seals found at Mohenjo-daro during the Mature phase. See Allchin, pp. 134–211.

46 Santapau, 1991, pp. 46–8.

47 Fernandez, Menon and Viegar, 1988, pp. 148–74.

48 Kramrisch, 1983, pp. 297–8.

49 Until at least 1970, Bondo tribal women in Koraput were weaving their simple hip wrappers out of bark and bast fibres from local plants.

50 Eck, 1982, p. 29.

51 Fernandez, Menon and Viegar, 1988, pp. 162–3.

52 Ibid. pp. 163–6.

53 Archana, p. 10.

54 Ibid.

55 Ibid.

56 Tirkey, 1989, p. 77.

57 Austro-Tai speakers are believed to have originated from the Tarim basin area of north-western China about two thousand years ago, after which they migated into southern China and South-East Asia, where most are still found today.

58 The original language of the Shan Ahoms, Ahom, is believed to be extinct.

59 All the points brought up in this section are discussed in depth in Lynton, 1993, pp. 73–132.

60 Allchin, 1988, pp. 246–9, pl. 9.15.

61 Mode and Chandra, p. 35; Bharathalyer, p. 82.

62 Bharathalyer, ibid.

63 Kinsley, 1988, pp. 130–60. Collectively they were associated with childbirth and childhood diseases and accidents.

64 Bharathalyer, ibid., p. 82.

65 Allchin, 1988, pp. 199–201, pl. 8.7.

66 Craven, 1977, p. 95.

67 Stutley, 1985.

68 Kinsley, 1986, pp. 57–64.

69 Stutley, ibid.

70 Kalidasa, in the *Kumaarasabhava*, V.67, calls the design *kalahamsalaksanam*, quoted in Ghurye, 1951, p. 298.

71 For instance, see the photographs of the bridal chamber in the house of Mohan Lal Das, Darema Village, Darbhanga, Archer took in 1940, and reproduced in Archer, 1985. Today there is a 'mass market' for these paintings, so modern versions cannot be considered truly indicative of local iconographic uses and symbolism. The paintings that Archer found, however, had never been seen, or even known of, by people outside of the villages where they were created.

72 Mode and Chandra, p. 174; *Aditi*, pp. 45–6.

73 Some scholars believe that the first three *avatars* of Vishnu (two of which are discussed in this chapter), the fish, turtle and boar, may have been tribal totems which became associated with Vishnu when the tribes became Hinduized.

74 The eight auspicious symbols in Hindu iconography vary according to time and place, and they do not always contain the fish. In later Hinduism the three following groups of auspicious symbols were common: (a) lion, bull, elephant, water jar, fan, flag, trumpet and lamp; (b) Brahmin, cow, fire, gold, ghee, sun, water and a king; (c) in south India, a fan, full vase, mirror, goad, drum, lamp and two fish.

75 Mode and Chandra, 1985, pp. 182–5.

76 Allchin, 1988, pls. 8.12, 8.15.

77 Mode and Chandra, ibid.

78 Huyler, 1993, pp. 206–10, 216.

79 Hindu myth states that elephants originally had wings and would fly around the sky pouring rain upon the earth. One day some elephants landed in a tree and disturbed the meditation of an ascetic who cursed them, causing them to lose their wings. Mythologically, rain clouds are still regarded as their closest cousins.

80 Kinsley, 1986, p. 22.

81 Gittinger, 1982, p. 30.

82 Kinsley, p. 27, Bharathalyer, p. 77.

83 Allchin, 1988, p. 77.

84 Ibid., p. 160, pl. 6.29.

85 Poster, 1986, p. 195, cat. no. 139.

86 Gittinger, 1982, pp. 46–56.

General Note
The maps in this book are based on various sources. They have not been authenticated by the Government of India.

Sanjay K. Singh took all photographs on Eastman Kodak film. For colour: Ektachrome 100 Plus in various formats (4 x 5", 120 and 35mm). For black-and-white high contrast: Kodalith Ortho film, type 3 in 4 x 5" sheets, developed in Kodalith Super RT and printed on Kodak Polycontrast III RC paper. Colour processing was done by Carol Professional Color Lab., Inc., New York. Black-and-white high contrast processing was done by the photographer.

Glossary of Indian Terms

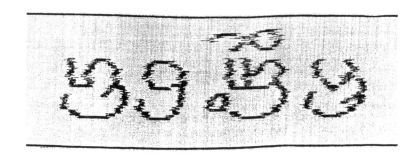

Most of the Indian words used in the text are listed here except for regional words for 'sari', 'border', and 'endpiece', although some names of particular types of saris are included. The name of the language to which the word belongs is given after the word, and the abbreviations for the languages that are represented in the book (and hence, this glossary) are listed below. With a few exceptions, all the words are dictionary transliterations (dictionaries used are listed in Bibliography) or what people told and spelt for us during our field research. Instead of using diacritical marks, I have used a double vowel to express long vowels. Where applicable, the literal meaning of a word is given before the textile/sari-related meaning.

The Indian languages represented:

Austro-Asiatic: (Ja) Jaintia; (Kh) Khasi; (Mu) Mundari (includes Munda, Santhal, Ho, Gadaba and Sora dialects).

Austro-Tai: Ahom, now a dead language, but influenced Assamese.

Dravidian: (Ta) Tamil; (Ta/Te) Tamil/Telugu dialect spoken in major weaving centres of northern Tamil Nadu; (Ma) Malayalam; (Ka) Kannada; (Te) Telugu; (Or) Oraon; (Go) Gondi; (Ko) Khondi; (Ga) Gadaba.

Indo-Aryan: (Sk) Sanskrit; (Pk) Prakrit; (H) Hindi; (G) Gujarati; (M) Maratha; (O) Oriya; (B) Bengali; (A) Assamese; (N) Nepali; (S) Sinhalese; (U) Urdu.

Tibeto-Burman: (Me) Meitei; (Ne) Newari; (Bo) Boro; (Gr) Garo.

Indian words used in the text:

Aal (H) Local name of the tree *Morinda citrifolia* from which red dye is derived.

Aankh (H) Eye. Small chain-link design in Maheshwari sari borders.

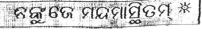

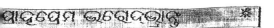

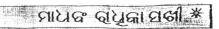

Abrawan (H) Flowing water. Very fine transparent fabrics of cotton or silk.

Acheik (Burmese) Intricate tapestry-woven silks worn by nineteenth-century Burmese royalty.

Adivasi (H) India's tribal peoples, believed to be the subcontinent's original inhabitants, who are neither Hindu nor part of the mainstream social system.

Adyar (Ta) Stripe. A series of thin supplementary-weft *zari* stripes woven to create the endpiece in many Tamil and Kannada saris, often about five to fifteen stripes approximately 7.5 centimetres (3 inches) apart. *Adyar mundhu* (Ta).

Agat (Bo) Pattern, often used as a suffix in name for a particular textile design.

Ahom The original Tai language spoken by Shan Ahom tribes of Assam.

Ajanta A series of elaborately carved and painted caves in western Maharashtra which were used as Buddhist temples, *c.* 100 BC to AD 500.

Ajrak (G) Detailed, geometric block-print designs in Muslim textiles of the Sind.

Alari (Ta) Flower. Formal (dictionary) word; the term *arali* is more commonly used. *Alar, aral* (Ka), *alaru* (Te), *aral* (M).

Alpona (B) Ritual domestic floor paintings.

Ambara (H, M) Name for both a goddess and for saris, the latter usually having ritualistic associations. Often used as a suffix, as in *pitambara* (yellow sari). *Ambar* (H), *ambari* (B).

Amru (H) Figured silk that only has coloured silks, not *zari*, in its construction.

Anai (Ta) Elephant. *Yanai* (Ta), *aane, yaane* (Ka).

Annu (Te) Woman. Motif in Pochampalli ikats imitating *patola*.

Ansari (H) Weaver. Common name of Muslim weavers in Banaras.

Arakku (Ta) Lac. Used to describe red saris dyed with lac.

Arasa (Ta, Ma) Peepal tree, usually called **arasamaram**. Peepal or paan leaf (both have heart-shaped outlines) pattern. **Arai, arasu** (Ta), **arasaal** (Ma).

Avatar (H) Incarnation of a deity, especially Vishnu.

Baavadhani (M) Wide-bordered saris of south-western and central Deccan, includes Ilkal and Nagpur saris.

Badaam (H) Almond. Name given to elliptical motif in dobby-woven borders of some west Deccan saris.

Badla (H) Flattened gilt wire used in embroidery.

Baft-hana (H, U) 'Woven air'. Banaras brocades where less than 50 per cent of the surface is woven

with supplementary-weft *zari* designs; also used to describe fine muslins.

Baluchar (B) *Amru* sari traditionally from Baluchar, West Bengal.

Ban (M) To dress, adorn. Typical sari of western Deccan with chequered field and narrow borders.

Bandha (O) Ikat cloths of Orissa.

Bandhani (H,G) Tie-dyed work. *Bandhana* (H).

Bandhej (H,G) Craftspeople who create *bandhani*.

Bel (B, H) Floral creeping vine design in printed and figured saris. The name *bel* refers to both a vine in general and a fruit-bearing tree (*Aegele marmelos*). See *Veelli*. **Belii** (H), **bela, beli** (S).

Bel buti (H) Tiny vine pattern in printed saris of western Madhya Pradesh.

Bel phool (H) Large floral vine patterns printed in the saris of western Madhya Pradesh.

Bel phool rekh (H) As above, printed using *rekh* or outline block.

Bhamiyo Agricultural caste of western Madhya Pradesh and eastern Gujarat.

Bhanwarai (H) Part of wedding ceremony where bride follows groom around a fire.

Bharat (G) Embroidery.

Bhat (G) Pattern. Used in describing *patolu* patterns, probably derived from *bharat*.

Bhatia Gujarati traders.

Bhil Indo-Aryan-speaking tribal group of eastern Gujarat, western Madhya Pradesh.

Bhilala Sub-group of Bhil tribe, descendants of mixed Rajput-Bhil marriages.

Bhumihar Landowning Brahmin caste in Bihar.

Bhumij Austro-Asiatic (Mundari)-speaking tribe of southern Bihar.

Bichchitrapuri (O) North-western Orissan wedding sari, fine checks in field.

Bile khaddi (M) Dark blue and white sari.

Bindi (G, H) Dot, drop. Small spots created in *bandhani* work without central dark spot. **Bindu** (G), **bundi** (H), **bund** (G, H).

Bomokoi High-caste ritual and wedding sari from southern Orissa, named after the village where it is still woven.

Bondo Austro-Asiatic (Mundari)-speaking tribe of Koraput district, southern Orissa.

Boro Tibeto-Burman-speaking tribes of Assam's Brahmaputra valley; language and dress are related to Garo. Also spelt **Bodo**.

Brahma Hindu god representing the power behind the creation of the universe. One of the three major Hindu deities.

Brahmin (H) Highest Hindu caste, traditionally priests.

Buddhism Religion founded by Gautam Sakyamuna b. 556 BC, based on release from cycle of rebirth.

Bugdi (M) Ear ornament. Sawtooth motif in central/west Deccan sari borders.

Buhlia Meher Orissan ikat-weaving caste in western hills.

Bund (G,H) Drop. See *Bindi*.

Bunda (H) Big spot or drop. See *Bindi*.

Buta (H) Large, usually floral or foliate motif created in corners and endpieces of saris. From Persian *buteh*.

Buti (H) Small, usually floral motif usually created as a repeat against a plain ground. See *Buta*.

Butidar (B) *Amru* sari from West Bengal with many *buti* in field.

Carika (Te) *Zari*. Sometimes used to describe a stripe.

Chaas (G, H) Furrow in ploughed field. Dark, chequered stripe in border patterns of west Deccan saris and Banaras brocades of the same style. **Chaasa** (M).

Chadar (H) Common north-Indian name for shawl or upper wrap, literally a sheet or cloth.

Chameli (H) Jasmine.

Chanderi Town in northern Madhya Pradesh, weaves fine *shallu* saris.

Chapati (H) Unleavened bread made of wheat, cooked without oil, in northern India.

Charkhana (H) Very fine check design. See *Chaukdi*.

Chaudhari (M) Diamond border design. From Sk. *chaturdhara*, having four edges.

Chatai (H, M) Mat-weave design found in east and west Deccan sari borders.

Chaukda (H) Plait or chequered pattern.

Chaukdi (M, H) Fine check pattern in west Deccan saris; derived from *chauk*, meaning four-cornered, four-sided, square.

Chauki (H) Low seat or platform, commonly used during ritual occasions; name derived from *chauk*.

Chhaabdi bhat (G) Basket design. Geometric floral design in some *patola* fields.

Chhada (M) Twisted cord used to hang jewelry. Border edge pattern like a simplified *jhaalar*, in west Deccan saris.

Chhipa Caste of textile printers and dyers, derived from Pk. *chivai* from which *chunari* also originates.

Chikankari (H) Whitework embroidery from Lucknow.

Chit-ku (Te) Ikat work.

Choli (H) Tight-fitting tailored blouse worn with most modern saris.

Cholo (N) Tibetan-style, front-tying, tailored blouse worn by many Nepali women.

Chunari (H) To crimp or fold cloth (which happens when tying *bandhani* knots). Alternative name for *bandhani*, also name given to a *bandhani* *odhni*, or *odhni* in general in Rajasthan. **Chundadi, chundari, chunni** (H); **Chinvu, chunvu** (G); **Chundadi, chungudi** (Ta).

Churi (H) *Bandhani* spot created with a dark central dot, related to *chunari*.

Ciluka (Te) Parrot.

Coorg High-caste warrior community of southern Karnataka.

Coromandel Name of south-eastern coastline of Dravidian peninsular India.

Daant (H) Teeth. **Danti** (O).

Dabbi (H) Small box. Name given to square or large circular *bandhani* spots containing concentric rings of colour. **Dabba** (H). In Ka, means fruit.

Dalimba (O) Pomegranate border motif in Bomokoi sari. **Darim** (H).

Dakmanda (Gr) Large full-body wrap worn by Garo women, finely woven with supplementary warp and weft designs, may be of silk.

Daksari (Gr) Simpler, everyday version of the *dakmanda*, plain or striped.

Dariyai (H) Type of *tasar* silk sari worn by Brahmins in eastern Madhya Pradesh. Name *daryai* mentioned in Mughal accounts of silk cloth, so may be an old name signifying good-quality silk cloth.

Das phoolia (O) Orissan saris with ten bands of supplementary-warp patterning in borders.

Deshi (H) Of the country, indigenous. **Desh** (B).

Devanga Weaving caste in Tamil Nadu and much of eastern peninsular India.

Dhaka (N) Figured cotton cloth indigenous to eastern Nepal, woven on narrow bamboo looms, visually similar to Bengali *jamdanis*.

Dhangar Nomadic pastoralists of western Maharashtra.

Dhara (Kh) Silk. Also name for two-piece silk *jainsem*.

Dhoop chhaon (H) Sun and shadow. Fabrics with different-coloured warp and weft threads.

Dhoti (H) Male lower garment wherein untailored cloth is draped and drawn between the legs.

Diwali Post-monsoon (October/November) festival of lights, a major South Asian festival involving worship of Lakshmi.

Dokhna (Bo) Large full-body wrap worn by Boro women, similar to Garo *dakmanda* but draped differently.

Dombaru (H) Small drum commonly carried by Shiva Nataraja (dancing to create new universe when old one is being destroyed). **Damru**.

Do-chashmee (H) Two streams. Reversible, silk satin borders in Chanderi saris.

Do-muha (O) Two faces. Sari with two endpieces, one at each end.

Do-patti (G) Parsi saris made of two strips of narrow Chinese fabrics sewn along selvage.

Dukula (Ka) Fine silk cloth.

Dupatta (H) Two cloths (referring to cloth being folded in two when worn). Veil worn with *salwar kameez*.

Durga Goddess of power, life, death. Sometimes seen as female incarnation of Shiva; also incarnation of the Maha Devi, the Great Goddess.

Duria (B) String, thread. Very fine striped pattern.

Dor (B, H) **doria, dor, dhari** (H).

Endi, Eri (H, B, A) Heavy wild silk produced in eastern and north-east India, usually makes *chadars* and other heavy textiles. From cocoons of *Philosamia ricini* which produces silk ranging from white to brick red.

Enuka (Te) Elephant. **Enuga** (Te).

Eruvai (Ta) Eagle.

Gad (H) Block used to create 'filler' design in block-printed textiles.

Gadaba Name given to several different tribes in Koraput, Orissa; speak either Dravidian or Austro-Asiatic languages.

Gaj (H, G) One yard. Parsi term for satin-weave silk cloth a yard wide, originally imported from China.

Gaja (Ka) One yard. Used as name for nine-yard sari (*ombathu gaja seerai*).

Gaja (Pk) Elephant; name found in most Indo-Aryan languages.

Gajji (G) One-yard wide satin-weave silk cloth once popular in Gujarat, now rarely made. See *Gaj*.

Ganda, gende (Go) Female cloth or garment. Word may be related to Mundari *khanda*.

Ganesha Elephant-headed son of Shiva and Parvati; god of good beginnings and perspicacity.

Ganga (Sk, H) Name of goddess who personifies River Ganga (Ganges) in pre-classical and medieval Hindu art.

Ganga-Jamuna (H) The two sacred rivers. Used to describe any pair of contrasting elements. In saris, usually refers to two borders and endpieces of different colours, so making the sari reversible.

Garbh-reshmi (H) Maheshwari sari with silk check on cotton ground.

Garnda (Ko) Garment. Possibly related to Mundari *khanda*.

Garo Tibeto-Burman-speaking tribe of eastern Meghalaya; dress and textiles similar to those of the Boro, with whom they are also linguistically related.

Gavanti (Ka, M) Double running stitch found in *kasuti* embroidery.

Geetagovinda Twelfth-century devotional poem to Krishna, written in Orissa.

Getla, gette (Go) Cloth. Various dialects mainly in Madhya Pradesh: **gatla, gete, gende**. See *Ganda*.

Ghaghra (H, G) Full-gathered sewn skirt worn by nomadic and other ethnic groups in western India; also used as name for *lungis* by some groups. **Ghaghara** (H).

Ghara (G) Parsi name for (i) opaque Chinese-woven silk gauze or crepe-de-chine, (ii) saris embroidered by Chinese artisans in China. No longer woven or embroidered, but popular during nineteenth and early twentieth century, now a fashionable antique. Singular **gharo**, but term rarely used.

Gharchola (G) House dress. *Bandhani* wedding sari worn by Jains and Hindus. *Ghar* (house) means more than just the building, but 'birthplace' or 'family', suggesting the name *gharchola* refers to the fact that the sari is from the 'home' or 'birthplace' of the bride. Consequently, 'family dress' might be a more accurate translation.

Ghatadi (G) Square tie-dye spot.

Gisir (Go) Garment, sari. Name related to Mundari *kichri*.

Godel (Go) Axe. Motif found in Gondi and other tribal saris of Koraput, Orissa. Similar to Kerala's *kootaali* (Ma, axe) where traditional saris are also woven for the Gond market.

Gola nesana (M) Round-wrapped sari. Sari draped in the *nivi* style.

Gollabhana (Te) *Khan* sari with floral patterning, from *gul* (flower), *bhana* (tie-dye design creating dashes in the warp).

Gom (M) Centipede. Narrow herringbone pattern woven in supplementary-warp border stripes of west Deccan saris.

Gomi-katha (M) Sari with herringbone border.

Gond Various Dravidian (Gondi)-speaking tribes in south-east Deccan.

Gorad (B) Undyed silk sari with simple border, often used as *puja* sari.

Gota (H) Ribbon with *badla* warp and silk thread weft.

Goyal (H) Sari from eastern Madhya Pradesh worn by groups of Orissan descent.

Gul (H) When used as a prefix often means flower, also is a shade of pink.

Gulabi (H) Pink, rose-coloured.

Gulkari (H) Flower work. Embroidery.

Gul-e-bachadar (H) *Kalamkari* cloth used for long coat.

Gulli (H) Standard length of yarn.

Gujroo (M) Name of red Maharashtran sari border containing white stripes.

Gurung Tibeto-Burman-speaking tribe of western Nepal.

Haathi (H) Elephant. Also G, M, O.

Hallak Gauda Southern Karnataka tribe.

Hansa (H) Goose, sometimes translated as swan, but the latter did not exist in India and tend to be called *rajhansa* (big goose). An auspicious and iconographically significant bird.

Hansabali kapta (O) Nineteenth-century name of Orissan ikat sari with goose and vine design. **Hansabali datapar**.

Harini (O) Deer. **Hananee** (O), **harin, hiran, hirnaa** (H).

Harshacharita Seventh-century biography of King Harsha of Kanauj (today's Uttar Pradesh), written by Banabhatta.

Harijan (H) God's child. Euphemism for Untouchable.

Ho Austro-Asiatic (Mundari)-speaking tribe of southern Bihar.

Holi (H) Spring festival where coloured water is thrown; associated with Krishna (March/April).

Hublidhardi (M) Sari border from Hubli (a town in northern Karnataka). Nineteenth-century name of Ilkal sari.

Ilkal (M) Sari from northern Karnataka, after village in Dharwar district.

Jaada, Jeeda Karnataka weavers belonging to Lingavanta (Shaivite) sect.

Jaal, jaala, jaali (H) Net, mesh. Any net-like design, large or small.

Jagannath A form of Krishna, one of the *avatars*

of Vishnu that is worshipped in Orissa; has tribal origins. Root of English 'juggernaut'.

Jai phool (M, O) Jasmine flower. *Phool* band in borders of west Deccan saris with tiny circular design. Word also may be a corruption of *jai-phal* (M), nutmeg. *Jabi, jae-phal* (H), *Jai-phala* (O).

Jain Religion of non-violence and asceticism, founded by Mahavira (*c.* 599–527 BC).

Jain (Kh) Cloth. Used as prefix describing various types of drapes.

Jainkyrshah (Kh) Chequered cloth. One-piece drape knotted at shoulder used for everyday wear.

Jainsem (Kh) Two-piece drape worn by Khasi women, each knotted separately on either shoulder.

Jaintia Austro-Asiatic-speaking tribe of western Meghalaya, culturally and linguistically related to the Khasis but with more Assamese and Hindu traits.

Jalebi (H) Bright orange sweets made into twisted strands. Name of multicoloured *dabbi* tie-dye spots created in Rajasthani textiles.

Jala (O) *Naksha* or dobby. Mechanism used to create supplementary weft or warp figuring. See *Naksha*.

Jamdani (H, B) Fine transparent cotton muslin with discontinuous supplementary-weft motifs woven in heavier cotton threads.

Jamindar Central Deccan term for landlord. **Zamindar**.

Jat Pastoralists of western Rajasthan, Haryana and southern Punjab.

Jeera (H) Cumin seed. Name given to supplementary-thread 'dashes'.

Jhaalar (H) Frill. Decorative, usually leaf-like, edging along inner border. **Jhul** (G).

Jowaria (H) Barley grain. Tiny printed motif.

Jot, Jote (M) Yoke, yoked together. Sari with red borders and endpiece worn by high-caste women in Nagpur area. Possibly refers to tying new warp threads onto the field warps to create the endpiece.

Junaagadi (Te) *Bandhani* sari of Machilipatnam, name probably derived from *sungadi*.

Junani (Te) Nine-yard ikat-dyed sari once made in Pochampalli area.

Junnadi (Ta) *Bandhani* sari made in nineteenth-century Madurai.

Jyapu Landowning agriculturalist caste of Newars of Kathmandu valley, Nepal.

Kachchhota (G) Bhil term for *kachchha* sari draping style.

Kachchha Sari drape where pleats of cloth are tucked in front and at the back to form 'trousers' (from Sk, used in many Indo-Aryan languages). (Sk) **Kachchha, kachchhati, kaksha**.

Kachhua (H) Turtle, tortoise. Motif in borders of east Deccan saris. **Kechhu, kachhima, kechho** (O).

Kala (H) Black.

Kalabattun (G, H) Old-fashioned term for gold-wrapped thread once commonly used in the western region. Alternative name for *kamdani* embroidery.

Kalamkari (H) Painted cloth. A special pen (*kalam*) is used to draw freehand designs in ink or resist medium (e.g. wax, resin).

Kaledar (H) Traditional Rajasthani *odhni* which extensively uses *kodi* and *laddu* work in geometric patterns.

Kalera (O) Bitter gourd. **Karaila** (H).

Kalga (H) Curvilinear *buta* with hook-like end, also called mango (*aam*), *konia*, paisley design. Name derived from Urdu *galb* (hook). **Kalka**.

Kamal (H) Lotus.

Kambi (Ka) Supplementary-warp bands in sari borders. **Kampi** (Ta, Ma).

Kamdani (H, G) Embroidery using fine *zari*, often created on fine sheer fabrics.

Kameez (H) Cut and sewn top traditionally worn by western Indian Muslim women.

Kampi (Ta, Ma) Narrow warp stripe running along the border of a cloth. **Kambi** (Ka).

Kan (Ta) Eye. Suffix of names given to supplementary-warp 'mat' and 'diamond' designs; for instance, *kuilkan* (peacock's eyes). **Kannu** (Te).

Kangora (M) Ornamental cord, niched battlement. Border edge pattern like simplified *jhaalar* in west Deccan saris.

Kanaa (M) Edge, ridge. Border edge pattern like simplified *jhaalar* in west Deccan saris. Also used as term for sari border.

Kantha (B) Embroidered quilt made from used clothing.

Kapta (O) Cloth. Also the name of some Orissan ethnic saris.

Kapta jala (O) Orissan saris with dobby-created supplementary warp designs.

Karaila (H) Bitter gourd. **Karela** (O).

Karanam (Sk) Workers, rearers, as in silk rearers, *kosa karanam*.

Karavai (Ta/Te) Sari border with tooth-like serrations. From *karukku* (Ta) tooth and *karagasamu* (Te) saw.

Karchopi (B) Embroidery.

Kari (H) Work, craft. Often used as a prefix or suffix in Indo-Aryan languages, denoting a certain kind of work or skill, such as *kalamkari* (work with a pen).

Karvat (M) Saw. A supplementary-warp 'sawtooth' serrated design in west Deccan saris.

Karvatikanth (M) Serrated edge.

Kasuti (Ka, M) Cottonwork. Embroidery based on running stitches, in northern Karnataka.

Katak-buti (Te) Tie-dyed yarn.

Katari (M) Dagger. Herringbone pattern in borders of west Deccan saris.

Katarkanth (M) A border with a *katar* design.

Kattam (Te/Ta) Check pattern in Kornad saris, from *kattadam* (Te), building. See *Kothi*.

Kadam (H) The tree *Adina cordifolia*. A fertility motif in east Deccan saris and among some tribal groups.

Kerong (Ga) Cloth or wrap.

Khaddar (H) Homespun cloth.

Khadi (H) Colloquial term for *khaddar*, now more commonly used than correct word.

Khan (M) Piece of cloth. Textile of central and western Deccan with supplementary-warp and -weft designs made for women's blouses. Possibly from same Sanskrit root (*khaksana*) as for division of house, compartment, *khan* (H); or of east Deccan tribal origin (see below).

Khan (Te) Name of northern Andhra Pradesh sari, probably derived from *khanduva* (Te) or *khanda* (Mu).

Khanda (Mu) Name of two tribal saris with white bodies and simple borders: (i) 6-metre sari with purple border worn by Santhali mother-in-law during wedding; (ii) red-bordered sari commonly worn by Munda women. When spoken, the 'd' is silent.

Khandi (Mu) Santhali bridal sari, white with purple border, 4–5 metres long.

Khandua (O) Traditional wedding veil, now sari, from Orissan coastal area.

Khanduva (Te) Veil from Andhra Pradesh. Word probably derived from *khanda* (Mu).

Khapa (H) Spatula used in beating down weft threads on eastern Madhya Pradesh looms; produces supplementary-weft bands in sari endpieces.

Khari (H, G, M) Thick, often coloured resin used in tinsel-work and inexpensive patterns. Literally 'chalk', but word is now used generically for tinsel saris.

Kharisari (H) Worker's cloth/silk. Eighteenth-century mixed cotton-*tasar* cloth made in Bhagalpur for local people.

Khasi Dominant tribe of Megalaya, Austro-Asiatic speakers with a matriarchal society.

Khatiya (H) *Chauk* motif in eastern Madhya Pradesh ethnic saris; may be related to *khatya* (small bedstead) or *khatal* (fruit).

Khatri(ya) Gujarati communities (Muslim and Hindu) specializing in weaving, dyeing and *bandhani* work.

Khond Dravidian-speaking tribe of southern Orissa.

Khoja Gujarati Muslim community whose ancestors converted to Islam in eleventh century.

Kichri (Mu, Or) Cloth. Oraon also use as word for sari.

Kincab (H) Figured silk with more *zari* than silk showing in the fabric surface.

Kodalikarupur Nineteenth-century resist-dyed sari made for Tanjore (Thanjavore) aristocracy; after village where it was made.

Kol Nineteenth-century term for tribal groups; still used for fisherpeople of Bombay.

Kolam (Ta) Ritual domestic floor paintings aimed at welcoming Lakshmi (good luck) into the home.

Konia, Kona (H, M, G) Corner. Name given to *kalga* design when placed in corner of sari between endpiece and border. **Konya** (M).

Kornad Typical wide-bordered Tamil and

southern Karnataka sari, plain borders and checked or striped field. Named after village where once created.

Kori (H, G) Cowrie shell. Teardrop-shaped *bandhani* tie-dye spot. **Kauri** (H).

Kosa (Sk) Silk-moth cocoon. Name for *tasar* in parts of eastern Deccan.

Kotakomma (Te) Cornices along a fort wall. *Kumbha* design in Gadwal saris.

Kothi (H, M) House, room. Fine check found in west Deccan saris. **Kothlaa** (H), **kothdi** (M).

Ksai dhara (Kh) Tasselled silk. Fringe of tassels along bottom of Khasi *dhara*.

Kumbha (H, O, B) Triangular motif found in sari borders, an auspicious symbol; also ritual domestic wall-paintings in Orissa. **Kumbham** (Te).

Kungri (H, G) Zig-zag or large serrated pattern; also a name given to small geometric/scroll block-printed bands. **Kangri** (H, G).

Kunjar (G) Elephant.

Kupadam (Te) Three-shuttle weaving technique producing interlocked-weft fabric.

Koorma (H) Tortoise incarnation of Vishnu.

Kuyilkan (Ta) Cuckoo's eyes. The Indian cuckoo, the *koel*, is an auspicious bird frequently referred to in poetry; name given to Tamil 'mat-weave' supplementary-warp border designs.

Kyrshah (Kh) Check design.

Lac (H) Red dye derived from secretions of insect *Lacifer lacca*, common in eastern Deccan.

Laddu (H) Ball-shaped yellow sweet. Multicoloured tie-dye spots in Rajasthani textiles.

Lahenga (H) Skirt or lower wrap, also used by Munda tribes to describe lower wrap.

Lahariya, Laheriya (H, G) Waves. Striped tie-dye pattern.

Lakshmi Goddess of good fortune, prosperity and fertility; Indo-Aryan origins.

Lata (H, B, O) Creeper, creeping vine; also used to mean 'entanglement', symbol of all life being interconnected.

Lingayat Shaivite sect founded on premise that all people are equal; includes merchants, farmers, priests, in south India and Deccan.

Lohana Hindu traders from the Sind.

Lungi (H) 2.7-metre (9-foot) wrap covering legs from waist down, commonly worn by men as well as some women in various ethnic groups. Name derived from *lunga* (Sk) cloth, rag, as is *lugda* (sari).

Maachee (B, O) Fly. Name given to motifs in some north-east Deccan saris. **Makkhi, maachhee** (H). In terms of sari designs, the name may be a variant of *machhli* (fish).

Maalaa (H) Garland, wreath of flowers. The Hindi prefix *maal* usually has associations with wealth and good quality.

Machela (H) *Chauk* motif. From either *machaan* (H), scaffold, raised platform, or *maachaa* (H), bed raised on a platform.

Machhlee (H) Fish. **Maachh, machchh, machchhee** (H), **maachha** (O), **maachh** (B), **maas** (A).

Maha Devi (H) Great Goddess. Name given to the generally earth-centred, omnipresent principle force in the mother-goddess cults of Hinduism, from which the various goddesses are derived.

Mahabharata Religious work orally compiled *c.* 800–700 BC, but written 500 BC– AD 500.

Maheshwar Town in southern Madhya Pradesh, weaves very fine muslin *shallu* saris.

Malabar Kerala coastline.

Malli mokku (Ta) Jasmine bud. Name for wad of coloured cotton added to muslin wefts during the weaving process. **Malli muggu** (Te).

Malmal (H) Fine cotton muslin.

Malmal khas (H) Special muslin. One of the finest Dacca muslins.

Mandala (H) Circular diagram which functions as a schematic map of the sacred universe in symbolic paintings.

Marwari Hindu traders from Rajasthan.

Masuria (H) 'Muslim cloth'. Fine muslin from Kota (Rajasthan) with alternating silk and cotton threads; name related to *mashru*, a heavy silk/cotton cloth worn by Muslims.

Matanku (Ta) Zig-zag.

Matichar (H) Mass of tie-dye spots created close together. **Matichur** (H).

Matsya (H) Fish incarnation of Vishnu. Matsya helped save the world from the Deluge by warning and advising Manu.

Mayil (Ta) Peacock.

Mayilkan (Ta) Peacock's eyes. Supplementary-warp borders woven in 'mat' design with central spot in each lozenge.

Mayura (Sk) Peacock. All Indo-Aryan names derive from this.

Meitei Tibeto-Burman-speaking tribe of Manipur valley.

Mekhla (A) *Lungi* worn by Assamese women.

Meher High-status weaving caste in Orissa and eastern Madhya Pradesh.

Meen (Ta, Bo, Ko) Fish. **Meenu** (Te), **meena** (Sk).

Mina Indo-Aryan-speaking tribe of western Rajasthan.

Minakari (H) Inlay or enamelling. Supplementary coloured silks woven onto a golden ground.

Miri Tibeto-Burman-speaking tribe in northern Assam.

Moirangfee (Me) Sari traditionally ascribed to Moirang community of Manipur but probably of Bengali origin.

Mokku, mottu (Ta) Flower bud, sprout. Name given to triangular border design woven in interlocked-weft technique. Variations of name for this motif occur in neighbouring languages and dialects, namely: **mukku, muggu** (Ta/Te); **muggu, mogga** (Te); **moggu, maggu, mukke** (Ka).

Mor (H, G, M) Peacock. **Mhor, murhaa** (H). See *Mayura*.

Mothra (H) Bundle, fist. Double *lahariya* forming a chequered design. **Mothara**.

Mubbhagam (Ta) Kornad sari with borders and field of equal width, usually about 38 centimetres (15 inches) each.

Muga (A) Light brown. Golden-coloured wild silk grown almost exclusively in Assam (*Antheraea assama*).

Muhajorhi (O) Literally 'joined *muha*', where weft threads are broken and changed at beginning of the endpiece. See *Do-muha*.

Muka (G) Embroidery using heavy metallic threads that are couched onto the ground fabric.

Mukta (H) Freedom. *Tasar* silk fabric made from

193

spun threads from cocoons where the moth had escaped; consequently the name 'freedom'.

Mukta panji Type of supplementary-weft border in Bomokoi saris, fine diamond pattern; name probably refers to use of five sticks in creating the pattern.

Multan (Te) Type of resist-printed or -painted sari with Mughal-style designs, from Machilipatnam.

Munda Austro-Asiatic-speaking tribe of southern Bihar.

Mundari Austro-Asiatic languages spoken by Munda and other tribes in peninsular India.

Mundu veshti One of the traditional names for the *lungi* (*mundu*) and upper wrap (*veshti*) worn by Kerala women.

Murgi (Ka, M) Zig-zag stitch found in *kasuti* embroidery.

Murukku pattu (Ta/Te) Twisted silk. Heavy silk sari woven with twisted three-ply threads, typical of Kanchipuram.

Muthda (H,M) Bundle, handful. Supplementary-warp 'dashes' woven as lines in Maheshwari saris. *Muthi* (H), *muth* (M).

Muthu (Ta/Te) As *muthda*; may be linguistically related to *muthai* (Ta), plait, braid, or *muttu* (Ta) pearl.

Nambudiri Brahmin caste of Kerala.

Naksha (H) Traditional drawloom of northern India which uses warp-lifting devices based upon threads tied to each warp thread. Called *adai* (Ta/Te) in the northern Tamil weaving belt, and *jala* (O) in eastern Deccan.

Nan (H) Bread baked in clay oven.

Nandana (H) Joy, happiness. Blue/black printed sari of west Madhya Pradesh. In the western region blue is seen as protection against the evil eye among the people who traditionally wear it.

Nari (G) Woman. Female figures depicted in *patolu* sari borders.

Navaratna (G) Nine jewels. A geometric *patolu* design.

Navaratri (H) Nine nights. Nine-day festival worshipping the Maha Devi, often in form of Durga, takes place twice a year.

Nayar Matriarchal warrior caste of Kerala.

Neela (H) Blue.

Neelambari (H, B) Dark blue sari (silk or cotton), from Bengal. *Nilambari* (B)

Neelgar (H) Indigo dyers of western India.

Neem reshmi (H) Maheshwari sari with silk warp and cotton weft.

Negi (Ka, M) Running stitch, in Kasuti embroidery.

Neli (Ta) Wiggly line. Tamil sari motif also found in domestic ritual wall paintings; a wavy line with dot within each curve.

Nerege (Ka) Frill, *nivi* drape. Refers to front 'frill' or pleats of sari.

Newar Tibeto-Burman-speaking peoples of Kathmandu valley, Nepal.

Nivi (H, Sk) Contemporary name of the sari draping style most commonly worn by urban middle-class women.

Odhni (G, M) Large 2.7 metre (9-foot) half-sari worn as veil in western India; name also means sheet. *Orhna, orhni* (H), *odhvu, odhnu, odhaavvu,*

odbo (G), *orna* (B), *orani, orona* (A).

Ombathu gaja (Ka) Nine yards. Name of local nine-yard sari.

Oncha (H) Supplementary-weft lines in endpiece of eastern Madhya Pradesh saris.

Onnariyum mundu (Ma) Alternative name for *mundu veshti*.

Oraon Dravidian-speaking tribe of east Deccan.

Paan bhat (G) Geometric design in field of *patola* saris depicting paan or peepal leaves.

Pachheura (N) Shawl.

Padma (H) Lotus. *Pomcha, pom* (H).

Pagdu-bandhu (Te) Ikat weaving.

Pahar agat (Bo) Hill pattern. Traditional Boro *dokhna* design, like a series of pointed mounds or large *jhaalar*, includes floral elements.

Pahari Austro-Asiatic (Mundari)-speaking tribe of south Bihar.

Panji (H) Five. *Panch*.

Paithani (M) Sari traditional to Paithan and Aurangabad, Maharashtra, gold borders and endpiece with interlocked-weft woven designs.

Panetar (G) Wedding, wife. White and red *bandhani* wedding sari. Word derived from *pan*, promise. *Parnetar, pantar, parnet* (G).

Pank, panr East Deccan weaving caste which traditionally supplied tribal communities.

Pankha (H) Fan-shaped designs in west Deccan sari borders.

Pareu megon (Bo) Pigeon's eye. Traditional Boro *dokhna* design, series of small circles and dashes.

Pashan (Mu) Santhali name for festival sari of three colours, with large checks in field.

Patadar (H, G) Broad stripes in sari borders created through dip-dyeing, in western-region saris. *Pattdar* (H).

Pathernu (G) Cotton *lungi* worn by Rabari women. Older type made of wool, called *pachhedo*.

Patolu (G) Combined (warp and weft) ikat silk saris once made for export to South-East Asia, now only made for home market. Pl. *Patola*.

Patta (Sk) Silk, upper garment, veil, cloth. *Paata* (Ko) cloth.

Patta (H) Broad bands that create the endpiece of central Deccan saris.

Pattai (Ta) Painted stripe. Sometimes used for supplementary-warp stripes in Kornad saris. *Pattu, pettu* (Ta/Te).

Pavun (Ta/Te) Sun. Large *rudraksha*-type motif in *pattai* bands of Kornad saris. *Paavu* (Ta).

Peela (H) Yellow.

Peepal (H) Tree (*Ficus religiosa*) holy to Hinduism and Buddhism; has heart-shaped leaves.

Peepal patra bhat (G) Older name for *paan bhat* above.

Petni (Ta/Te) Technique of replacing field warp threads with those of a different colour for the endpiece, commonly used in Kanchipuram.

Phera (H) Eastern Madhya Pradesh term to describe interlocked-weft weaving technique.

Pheta (H) Term used by Allahabad block printers for *bel* vine band. Variation of *phita*, stripe, band.

Phool (H) Flower and/or flower design depicted as narrow supplementary-warp band in sari borders. *Phoola* (O).

Phool cheeta chauk (H) Flower leopard seat. Pagoda-like motif in Gond saris.

Piari (H) Yellow sari worn by bride during early part of Hindu wedding ceremony.

Piliya (H) Yellow veil, usually with *bandhani* work, worn by Rajasthani and Haryana ethnic groups. See *Peela*.

Pillaiyar muggu (Ta/Te) Ganesha's flowers. Large 'temple motif' in Kornad sari borders.

Pitambar (H, M) Yellow cloth. Various saris woven in eastern Maharashtra area have this name, usually have ritualistic associations including marriage.

Pomcha (H, G) Lotus flower. Central medallion in western Indian *odhnis*. See *Padma*.

Pomia (H) Black or dark blue resist-printed Bhil sari.

Pogudi (Ta/Te) Triangular border design woven in interlocked-weft or supplementary-weft techniques.

Pokol (Or) Cocoon, wild silk.

Popat (G) Parrot.

Porai (Ta) Technique of replacing field warp threads with those of a different colour for the endpiece by dip-dyeing warps prior to weaving and pulling them into an even line once on the loom; commonly worked in Kumbakonam, Thanjavur, Arni, Dharmavaram. From *poru* (Ta), to join.

Potia (H) Eastern Madhya Pradesh word for *tasar* silk, possibly of tribal origin. See *Pokol*.

Pot-than (H) Fine silk cloth with supplementary-weft *zari* patterning, a typical Banaras brocade. Name *pot* a corruption of *pat* (silk)?

Pukai Madrasi (Ta) Praiseworthy Madrasi sari. Colloquial name for traditional sari with red borders and endpiece traditionally made in Dharmavaram and popular in Madras.

Puja (H) Worship.

Puvu, poovu (Ka, Te) Flower. *Pu, bu* (Ta).

Rabari Nomadic pastoralists of western Gujarat and western Rajasthan.

Rabet (H) Type of running stitch used in *chikankari* embroidery.

Raja (H) King.

Rajput Warrior caste traditionally from western desert region, many of whose ancestors created the kingdoms of Rajputana (Rajasthan).

Raksha bandhan (H) Tied protection. Festival held in August where sister gives brother a thread (*rakhi*) to tie round his wrist. Acceptance of this thread means a brother promises to protect and care for his sister's welfare.

Ramayana Major religious text based on life of Rama (*avatar* of Vishnu), compiled about 600 BC.

Rani (H) Queen.

Rangrez Western Indian caste of dyers. From *rang* (H) colour.

Rasta (H, M) Road, path, rope. Fine warp stripe in west Deccan saris. *Raas* (H), *rassi* (M).

Rattai neli (Ta) A *neli* consisting of two wavy lines.

Rekh (H) Block that creates the pattern outline in block-printed designs. From *rekha* (H) line.

Reku (Ta) Inverted *kumbh* or 'temple motif' woven in interlocked-weft technique.

Resham (H) Persian-derived word for silk. *Reshme* (Ka).

Roghan (G) Thick, often coloured resin used to print patterns, including imitation *bandhani odhni* for rural ethnic communities; also a name given to tinsel saris.

Rong (Kh) Colour. Used as suffix to describe colour, as in *ronglieh* (white), *rongsaw* (red).

Rui phool (H) Cotton flower. Repeated, large floral border motif woven into saris of Madhya Pradesh.

Rudraksha (H) Eye of Shiva. Wrinkled-looking seed of the tree *Eleaocarpus ganitrus*, a common design in supplementary-warp bands of Deccan and Tamil sari borders; the seed used as rosary among Shaivites.

Saaliga (Ka) Weaving caste. See Saaliyan. **Saaliya** (Ka), **Saale, Saalida, Saliyar** (Ta).

Saaliyan (Ma, Ta) Weaver caste from Kerala, related to Saliyar caste found throughout peninsular India, which is often associated with silk weaving. **Saalikan** (Ta).

Saaluva pora (H) Piece of fine cotton cloth.

Saarai (Ta) Stripe. **Saara** (Te, Ka), *saarika* (Te).

Saktapar (O) Board game, also feature of wedding sari in north-western Orissa.

Sakachchha (M) A sari 'with *kachchha* drape'.

Salvi Gujarati weaving caste.

Salwar (H) Baggy trousers usually worn with a *kameez*, traditionally by western Indian Muslims but now by many urban young women of all religions.

Sangadi (Te) Printed saris mimicking tie-dye technique. See *sungadi*.

Sania (H) *Tasar* silk saris made from reeled threads, worn by Brahmins and other orthodox Hindus during such ritually pure tasks as cooking.

Santhal Austro-Asiatic-speaking tribe of southern Bihar and West Bengal. Name also spelt Santal.

Saraswati Goddess of learning, culture and the arts, including speech, seen as both daughter and wife of Brahma.

Sarong English version of the Indonesian *sarung*, a *lungi*-like wrap worn by Indonesian women, warp ends are sewn together to form a tube.

Saudagiri (G) A trade textile; *sauda* means trade or trading.

Selari (H, M) Fine warp stripe in west Deccan saris.

Sempynwan (Ja) The Jaintia equivalent of the Khasi *jainkyrshah*, except it is usually warp-striped or plain, not chequered.

Shab-nam (H) Evening dew. Very fine transparent muslins from Bengal, and silks from Banaras.

Shaivite Worshipper of Shiva.

Shallu (M, H) Fine muslin and silk saris containing *zari*. Name also given to heavy *zari*-woven Banaras brocades now worn as wedding saris by many Maharashtrans (traditional Paithanis, etc., are too expensive for the average citizen). **Shalu**, *salu* (M).

Shan-Ahom Tribes that migrated from Burma to Assam and which ruled from the thirteenth to the nineteenth centuries.

Shankh (H) Conch. **Shankha** (O).

Shikar (H) Hunt. Hunting-scene textile design. From Urdu *shikaar* (hunt). **Shikargah** (H).

Shiva Major Hindu deity of pre-Vedic origin; god of destruction and re-creation.

Shloka (H) Stanza, couplet or hymn of praise.

Sidha (H) Correct, straight, good. Used by north Indian women to describe their traditional manner of draping the sari, with the endpiece falling in front.

Silhahra (H) Form of *chikankari* embroidery created in nineteenth-century Bihar.

Sindur (H) Red powder used in hair-parting by north Indian women to indicate married state.

Singhaulia (H) Triangular motif in ethnic and tribal saris of east Deccan. Name probably from either singhara, the spiny fruit of water chestnut (*Trapaceae bispinosa*) or *singarna*, to adorn, decorate.

Sodha Rajput Rajput pastoralists of western Gujarat and Sind.

Sorahi (H) Type of appliqué created in Bihar.

Sungadi (Ta) Tie-dyed fabric. From the Gujarati *sun*, emptiness, referring to the undyed spots created through tie-dyeing. **Sungudi** (Ta). See *chunari*.

Sujani (H) Bihari domestic embroidered quilts made from used clothing, similar to Bengali *kantha*.

Suti (H) Cotton cloth.

Swadeshi (H) Late-nineteenth/early-twentieth-century political movement against the British Raj favouring local rather than imported products.

Tahsil (H) Subdivision of a state district.

Tamang Tibeto-Burman-speaking tribe of central Nepal.

Tanchoi (H, G) Three Chhois (Parsi name). Warp-faced satin silk lampas originally woven in China, introduced to Surat and Bombay but now only woven in Banaras.

Tangalia (G) Woollen *lungi* worn by Bharwad caste, Saurashtra.

Tanti (B) Woven, weaver. Name given to caste of Hindu weavers and a low-priced woven sari with low thread counts and *jamdani* embellishments.

Tantra (H) Esoteric religious movement that developed in last half of first millennium AD emphasizing the union of opposites, male and female.

Tara (H, O) Star.

Tarbana (H) Woven water. Tissue sari with warp of silk singles and weft of fine *zari*.

Tarz (H) Outer endpiece in Chanderi muslins that has *zari* bands.

Tasar (H, M) Most widely produced type of wild silk, from cocoons of various *Antheraea* spp., such as *A. mylitta*, *A. pernyi*.

Tasi (H) Uninterrupted diagonal lines in Banaras brocades. From *tasma* (H) strap, ribbon.

Teej (H) Festival celebrating arrival of rainy season in western India taking place in July/August.

Teni (Ka) Three-shuttle interlocked-weft woven motif in northern Karnataka sari endpieces.

Than (H) Bolt of cloth usually 37–46 metres long.

Tharu Indo-Aryan-speaking tribes of Mongoloid descent in lowland south Nepal and Terai region of eastern India.

Thikri (H) Madhya Pradesh term for supplementary threads creating 'dashes'.

Tili (H) Straw. Sliver of bamboo used as a needle to weave in supplementary-weft patterns of *jamdani* muslins.

Teeni, Tinglee (Or) Fly.

Tippadamu (Te) Interlocked-weft weaving technique.

Tota (H) Parrot. From Persian *tota*.

Tumpal (Malay) Isosceles triangles found at the end of Indonesian sarongs and other textiles.

Turra (Or) Oraon ceremonial textile, very long with extensive supplementary-weft patterning.

Ulta (H) Reverse, opposite, bad. Used by north Indian women to describe the *nivi* style of draping the sari, which is a relatively recent introduction there.

Umrer Name of sari from village near Nagpur, Maharasthra, similar to the Gadwal sari.

Vaishnavite Worshipper of Vishnu and his many incarnations.

Valli (Ta) Foliate floral creeping vine design, from *veelli* (Pk).

Vanki pettu (Ta/Te) Bent stripe. Herringbone stripe in Tamil sari borders.

Veelli (Pk) Term from which creeping vine names *bel* and *vel* are derived. **Vel** (M), **vallri** (H), **vel, velee** (G).

Vichchitrapuri (O) See *Bichchitrapuri*.

Vishnu One of three major Hindu deities; god of preservation.

Veesi, Weesee (Go) Fly.

Vohra Gujarati Muslim trading community, traded *patola* to South-East Asia.

Vohra bhat (G) Foliate geometric design in field of *patola* saris traditionally worn by Vohra community.

Vrikshaka (Sk) Tree goddess.

Zardozi (H) Embroidery using *zari*, both *muka* and *kamdani*. **Zardoshi** (H).

Zari (H) Gold-wrapped thread, usually a core silk or cotton thread (*asara*) around which is wound fine, flattened gilded silver wire. **Jari**.

Zoroastrian Worshipper of a pre-Islamic religion founded by Zarathustra in Iran about 1000 BC and still practised by the Parsis of western India.

Glossary of Textile Terms

Alizarin A chemical that produces a red dye. It occurs naturally (as in the madder plant, *Rubia tinctorum*), and has also been synthesized since the mid-nineteenth century.

Art silk Early name for fabrics made from synthetic fibres, usually rayon. Term still used in India, but may now also refer to acrylic or polyester fabrics woven to create fine, smooth-surfaced textiles with a silk-like sheen.

Backstrap loom A body-tensioned loom where the warp tension is created by the weaver's body via a strap.

Batik An Indonesian word commonly used in Europe and English-speaking countries to describe resist dyeing where a resist medium (usually molten wax) is applied to a woven cloth by means of special metal tools, brushes or stamps.

Block-printing Printing dyes, mordants or a resist medium (such as gum) onto a textile by means of a relief-carved wooden block (a different block for each colour). In India, the blocks are usually 23 or 30 centimetres (9 or 12 inches) square in size.

Brocade Figured textiles with the patterning woven in supplementary, usually discontinuous, weft threads.

Broderie anglaise A form of whitework 'open work' embroidery where small holes are cut at regular intervals into the fabric and the raw edges overcast (bound) in buttonhole stitch (to preserve and decorate them). Satin stitch embroidery is often added.

Calico A plain weave, opaque cotton fabric.

Chiffon A plain weave, filmy, fine silk crepe woven with the finest silk singles. They are highly twisted with a thread count of about 43 warp/43 weft per centimetre. The threads are degummed after weaving.

Cocoon The hardened pupa-case of moths and butterflies, here referring to that created by silkworms. It consists of hundreds of metres of continuous filament (silk) which can be reeled from the cocoon after boiling.

Complementary threads/elements Threads usually of contrasting colours woven into a textile to create a pattern (*below*). Unlike supplementary threads, they are structurally integral parts of the weave, and their removal damages and weakens the fabric.

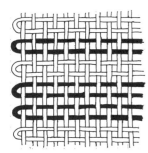

Continuous threads Those threads that extend the full length or width of the textile.

Count, thread The number of warp and weft threads found in a specified linear measurement, such as a centimetre or inch. A high thread count usually denotes fine, thin threads (or else medium-sized threads in a very dense weave). Thus a 200-count cotton has 100 warp and 100 wefts per inch (39 warp/39 weft per centimetre).

Crepe A textile wherein all or some warp and/or weft threads are given a high twist, in the same or alternating directions. Consequently, they 'retwist' onto themselves when not under tension, giving a crimped texture to the finished fabric.

Cutwork Warp or weft floats (at the back of the textile) cut away by hand, so that the pattern may appear as if woven in discontinuous supplementary-weft technique (a more time-consuming process).

Denier A measurement of weight originally created for synthetic filaments, now used for weighing silk thread. One denier equals 9000 metres per gramme, so a filament 9000 metres long weighing one gramme equals one denier, another weighing two grammes is two denier, and so on.

Discontinuous weft A weft thread that does not extend the full width of the textile (*below*). Usually of a contrasting colour to the ground threads (if supplementary) or to surrounding weft threads (if tapestry-woven).

Drawloom Believed to be of Sassanian Persian origin (*c.* AD 200). The fully developed drawloom uses a double harness set, one providing the weave structure, the other the figured patterning. Drawlooms developed differently in the Far East, Middle East and Europe. Until the early nineteenth century invention of the jacquard loom, most drawlooms required 'drawboys' who activated the pattern harness by lifting sets of threads. Today, Indian figured textiles woven commercially are usually created on jacquard looms.

Figured fabric A textile in which patterning is woven into the cloth, rather than painted, printed, dyed or embroidered. Figured textiles are popularly, but erroneously, called 'brocades' (see Brocade). They include those fabrics with continuous or discontinuous supplementary-warp and -weft patterning; samitas and lampas, velvets, etc. Historically, figured fabrics were woven using the traditional drawlooms (*naksha, jala*); today, jacquard attachments are generally used.

Filament A continuous fibre created by natural (e.g. silk) or man-made processes. In silk cocoons, one or two such filaments are created by the caterpillar to form the cocoon; in man-made fibres the filament is created by being extruded through a 'spinneret'.

Gauze In true gauze weaves the warps are crossed and uncrossed between wefts at intervals to create a transparent openwork fabric (*below*). The name is also given to plain-woven fabrics where the warps do not cross, but are often 'paired', creating uneven spacings in the weave between the series of warp threads. (This makes the textile look more transparent than it otherwise would be.)

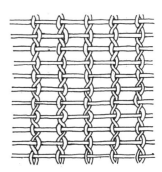

Georgette A fine, transparent plain-weave silk crepe with a lower thread count than chiffon, about 40 weft/40 warp per centimetre. Both warp and weft threads have a very hard twist, and threads are woven still gummed; the cloth is degummed after weaving.

Ikat Indonesian word commonly used in English-speaking and European countries to describe the process by which the warp and/or weft thread is selectively tied with dye-resistant materials to create a pattern prior to weaving. In Orissa, this work is known as *bandha*.

Indigo Blue dye extracted from a wide range of related plants, foremost the *Indigofera tinctoria* of India. Since the 1911 replication of this dye, synthetic indigo is usually used.

'Inlaid' A term used to describe discontinuous weft patterning, although in India it usually refers to silk or cotton discontinuous weft patterning against a *zari* background.

Interlocked weft Term used here to describe the technique which causes two or three 'interlocked' weft threads woven in the same shed. Technically, the sari field weft is shuttled across the entire span of the warp threads; it then catches the border weft thread, pulling it into place. The resulting look of the fabric is of a tapestry – discontinuous weave with interlocked wefts – but the process used to create it is different and less time-consuming.

Interlocked-weft weave in tribal and ethnic saris, Eastern Deccan (below).

Interlocked-weft weave in many south Indian and Paithani saris (above).

Jacquard A punch-card pattern-selecting device for handlooms or powerlooms, which was originally invented to replace the drawboy. It was refined and patented by J. M. Jacquard in 1804. Its speed and ease of use has made the older drawlooms obsolete throughout most of India.

Lampas A figured textile that has patterning created through at least two different warps and two different wefts in the weaving. Warp-faced and weft-faced integrated weave structures form the motifs, typically polychrome, using plain weaves and satins.

Man-made fibres Fibres created artificially, either reconstituted from cellulose (rayon) or completely synthetic (such as acrylic and polyester). Rayon was introduced into Indian saris in the 1950s, but in India, polyester did not become a major part of the textile repertoire until the 1980s.

Mordant A colourless chemical (metallic oxide) that is necessary to bind dye to a cellulose fibre such as cotton or linen. The two most common mordants in India are (1) aluminium sulphate (alum), which binds, for instance, alizarin dyes to cotton and produces bright colours; and (2) iron-based compounds which in alizarin create the darker hues.

Muslin Fine, sheer, often transparent cotton fabric. Usually has high thread counts, ranging from about 150 to 300.

Noil Spun silk, usually made up of the waste 'floss' and other short filaments from *Bombyx mori* cocoons.

Organdy Light, fine, transparent, plain-weave cotton muslin with a permanent crisp finish. Thread count usually 30 warp/30 weft per centimetre, with the weft threads being finer than the warp. See Organza.

Organza A fine, transparent, stiff plain-weave silk or rayon fabric. With silk organza, the threads are left undegummed, as is the cloth after weaving, and this produces the fabric's crisp stiffness. There is no standard thread count for this class of fabrics, although there are more weft threads per centimetre than there are warp threads. See Organzine.

Organzine Undegummed, twisted silk warp threads used to create organza. The silk filling yarn (wefts) used with organzine, called tram, is not so highly twisted.

Pitloom A horizontal, ground-staked handloom at which the weaver sits in a pit dug below floor level; this is a space- and lumber-saving loom-type typical of most village production in India today.

Plain weave An over-one, under-one weave structure. Also called tabby weave (*left*).

Powerloom A loom powered by steam or electricity, making it much faster to use than a handloom. Today, many urban Indian workshops use these looms.

Raw silk Undegummed silk; where the sericin has not been removed from the filaments.

Reel Process by which silk filaments, in groups of six or more, are unwound from their cocoons and wound onto a circular contraption, which is also called a reel.

Resist dyeing Any form of dyeing where the dyestuff is prevented from adhering to selected areas of the thread or woven textile. See ikat, batik, tie-dye.

Samitum(as) A figured textile that has only one warp but two or more wefts, providing weft-faced designs across the width of the fabric. Like lampas, these textiles are often called 'brocades' by the general public. Also called a compound twill.

Selvage The outer edge of a textile parallel to the warp. It is made by the weft threads wrapping round the outermost warp threads. Often the group of warp threads at the selvage is more densely set than the rest of the fabric, making the selvage stronger than the inner cloth.

Sericin The gum that binds the two filaments of a silk cocoon together and which is removed by boiling and washing in warm water.

Shuttle A boat-shaped device containing a supply of weft thread on a spool. It travels through the shed from one side of the loom to the other, propelled either by a weaver's hand or by a mechanical fly-arm.

Silk Natural fibre produced by silkworms. Originally cultivated by the Chinese about 2500 BC. Many filaments are used to create a single fine thread, which, when woven, creates a thin, lustrous fabric. See cocoon, denier, filament, noil, raw silk, sericin, silkworm, singles, wild silk.

Silk-screen printing A stencil-based printing technology using flat or rotary screens, introduced commercially for textile printing in the second quarter of the twentieth century. In India today, silk-screen printing is cheaper and faster than block printing. The screens for flatbed silk-screening Indian saris usually measure the width of the textile by 38–46 centimetres, producing a repeat pattern of the same width.

Silkworm The caterpillars of moths of *Bombidiceae* and *Saturnidae* families, from which silks are derived.

Single The finest silk thread that can be woven. Single silk filaments are too fine to see or to weave, and usually 3–10 pairs of silk filaments are combined and/or lightly twisted to form the 'single'.

Spin/spun Fibres of limited length (e.g. cotton, wool, linen) can be carded (aligned so the fibres lie parallel to each other) and then drawn out and twisted to form thread. The process is called spinning.

Supplementary warp or weft Supplementary threads are those added to a textile that already has one set of warp and weft threads. If supplementary threads are removed from a woven textile, the remaining fabric will still be complete.

Synthetic fibres Those fibres created from chemicals based on oil or coal residues, which are extruded through tiny dies (spinnerets) to create long continuous filaments. The most well known are nylon, acrylic and polyester.

Tapestry weaving Various weaves wherein the warp is continuous but the weft threads forming the design are not. Instead, they either interlock with other weft threads or wrap around a warp thread. This discontinuous weaving is very time-consuming, and is used to create polychrome, sometimes representational motifs.

Three-shuttle weaving Three shuttles used in a single shed to create an interlocked-weft design. Although this term is often used to describe saris with interlocked-weft borders, the weaving technique here is usually of the two-shuttle variety. See Interlocked weft.

Tie-dye Called *bandhani* (G) in western India. Resist patterning created on an already-woven textile by tying selected sections of cloth with thread, so preventing the dye from entering the tied areas.

Twill weave Warp threads interlace with the wefts in a progressive, stepped sequence producing diagonals in the fabric (*left*).

Two-shuttle technique See three-shuttle weaving, interlocked weft.

Warp Set of parallel threads mounted on a loom's frame, kept in supply on a warp beam. In India, handweavers make warps long enough to make three to six saris at one time. (The length of the warp determines the overall length of the woven cloth coming off the loom.)

Warp-faced weave A cloth wherein the warp threads predominate on the face of the fabric. In terms of fabric count, this can also result from there being either considerably more warp threads than weft, or else much thicker warp threads than weft.

Weft A set of threads that runs at right-angles to the warp, interworking with them to create various structures of weaves, such as plain or twill weave.

Weft-faced weave A cloth wherein the weft threads predominate on the face of the fabric. In terms of fabric count, this is produced by there being either more weft threads than warp, or else thicker weft threads than warp.

Whitework Embroidery using white threads upon a white fabric, which is usually fine and translucent so the embroidery stands out.

Wild silk Silk from the products of silkworms that are not varieties of *Bombyx mori*. Because their filaments are flat and spiral instead of circular or triangular, and their sericin is difficult to remove, they usually cannot be mechanically reeled or woven on powerlooms. Sometimes the spun threads from the broken ends and 'floss' from *B. mori* cocoons are also – erroneously – called wild silk instead of raw silk. Indian wild silks include *tasar*, *muga* and *eri* (*endi*).

Yarn-dyeing The yarn used to weave a textile is dyed before it is woven (as warp or weft).

'Sari' in Indian Languages

Although the word 'sari' now has general usage throughout India, it is a modern term that was not frequently used before the twentieth century. It is derived from the south-western Dravidian word *sari*, which was one pronunciation of the more general Kannada word *sire*.

Below are listed many of the indigenous words for saris, veils, two-piece outfits and their borders and endpieces. Dravidian and Austro-Asiatic words are given before Indo-Aryan. All the words are spelt as exact transliterations of the indigenous script, so, for example, the Hindi word for sari is spelt '*saari*' as that is the exact transliteration, even though in everyday language it is never written that way.

DRAVIDIAN

Tamil ~ Sari: *Pudavai, selai, silai, adai;* **Lungi:** *paavadi* (skirt), *veshti* (men); **Veil:** *dhavani;* **Sari border:** *karai, vatimpu, acu, aca, ansu;* **Endpiece:** *munti, mundhu, mundhi, mundani, mundhanai, tholai, talaippu, vitun talaippu, marapu* (drape across torso).

Malayalam ~ Sari: *Sela, seela, pudava, puta, putava, pudara, tuni;* **Lungi:** *mundu, kavani, kavini;* **Veil:** *veshti, angavastram, kaun;* **Sari border:** *kara, karal, vilimpu, vilumpu, tirukku;* **Endpiece:** *attam, munti, tumpu, tunpu.*

Kannada ~ Sari: *Sire, sari, seere, seerai, sela, cila, cela;* **Lungi:** *langa* (skirt); **Sari border:** *anchu, seerai anchu, aca;* **Endpiece:** *serugu, seragu, saraga, sarangu, serangu.*

Telugu ~ Sari: *Seera, Seere, koka;* **Lungi:** *dhoti;* **Veil:** *khanduva;* **Sari border:** *kongu, kammi, acu, aca, ancalam;* **Endpiece:** *kongu, painta, sengu, seragu, pamita, vallevatu* (drape across torso).

Gondi ~ Sari: *Ganda, gisir, gatla, getli, getla, gette, gete, gende.*

Khondi ~ Sari/body wrap: *Gunderi, garnda, paata.*

Gadaba ~ Sari/body wrap: *Kerong, sila.*

Oraon (Kurux) ~ Sari: *Kichri, luga;* **Upper wrap:** *turra.*

AUSTRO-ASIATIC

Mundari (Munda) ~ Sari: *Paria, sangol paria, khanda, kichri.*

Mundari (Santhal) ~ Sari: *Khanda, khandi, lugri, pashan, kichri.*

Khasi ~ Sari/body wrap: *Jain, jainsem* (two-piece outfit), *dhara* (*jainsem* of silk), *jainkyrshah* (one-piece outfit, usually chequered cloth).

Jaintia ~ Sari/body wrap: *Sempynwan* (one-piece outfit); **Lungi:** *Thohsaru.*

INDO-ARYAN

Gujarati ~ Sari: *Saadi, saari, saalu, lugadu, cira, salla;* **Lungi:** *lungi, ghaghra* (skirt), *tangalia, pathernu, pachhedo;* **Veil:** *odhni, odhvu, odhnu, odhaavvu, odho, chunni, chundadi, sadlo, ludi, abocchnai;* **Sari border:** *kora, laaka, gotha, patali;* **Endpiece:** *palava.*

Hindi (western Deccan and Rajasthani dialects) ~ Sari: *Salla, saari;* **Lungi:** *dhabli, ghaghara* (skirt); **Veil:** *chunni, chundadi, chundari, suhagadi, pido, orhna, orhni;* **Sari border:** *kora, kinara;* **Endpiece:** *pallaa.*

Hindi (Bihari, eastern Deccan dialects, Bhojpuri, Maithili) ~ Sari: *Saari, saadi, saadhi, lugra, lugad, lugi, lugda, patori, pata;* **Lungi:** *lungi, lahanga* (skirt); **Veil:** *odhni, odhna, chadar* (sheet, cover); **Sari border:** *kore, kora, kanni, kinari, hasiya, dadhi;* **Endpiece:** *anchala, anchra, jhela.*

Bengali ~ Sari: *Saari, lugi, lugda;* **Lungi:** *lungi, lahanga;* **Veil:** *odhni, chadar* (cover); **Sari border:** *kinara;* **Endpiece:** *anchala.*

Oriya ~ Sari: *Saadi, sardhi, luga, kapta;* **Veil:** *khandua;* **Sari border:** *dhadi, dhari;* **Endpiece:** *muha, muhan, anchala.*

Marathi ~ Sari: *Saadi, sardhi, shallu;* **Sari border:** *dhari, kanth, katha, kathi, hashaa, haashaa, dhadi, achal;* **Endpiece:** *padara, padar.*

Sinhalese ~ Sari: *Sariya;* **Veil:** *Tiraya.*

Assamese ~ Sari: *Xari;* **Lungi:** *mekhla, mekhala;* **Veil:** *rihi* (ritual scarf), *chadar* (upper wrap).

Nepali ~ Sari: *Fariya, dhoti;* **Lungi:** *lungi;* **Sari border:** *anchala, kinara;* **Endpiece:** *pallo.*

TIBETO-BURMAN

Meitei (Manipur) ~ Lungi: *Phanek;* **Veil/upper wrap:** *enaphi.*

Tripuri (Tripura) ~ Lungi: *Pachera;* **Veil/upper wrap:** *riha.*

Mizo (Mizoram) ~ Lungi: *Puanfen;* **Veil/upper wrap:** *riah.*

Boro (Assam) ~ Lungi/body wrap: *Dokhna;* **Veil/upper wrap:** *jumgra.*

Garo (Meghalaya) ~ Lungi/body wrap: *Dakmanda, daksari.*

Gurung (Nepal) ~ Sari: *Gaun*

Tamang (Nepal) ~ Sari: *Gunya*

Newari (Nepal) ~ Sari: *Parsi, patasi;* **Sari border:** *kinara.*

Table of Sari Measurements

Region/Sari Type	Dimensions (cm)		Thread Count (per cm)	
	L	W	Wp	Wf
All Regions				
Modern 'fashion' sari	500	114	varies	
	560	120		
The Western Region				
Bhil print saris	410	159	25	19
Ethnic *bandha* odhnis	196	158	18	15
Panetar gajji saris (silk)	389	117	25	24
19th-century *gajji* saris (silk)	377	121	47	54
Kota muslin (cotton/silk)	503	115	25	26
Kashmir silk print saris	508	112	39	37
19th-century *patola* saris	404	117	31	19
Mill prints (cotton/synthetic)	518	122	varies	
Korewali mill saris (cotton)	464	113	29	22
The Eastern Region				
Bengali *deshi* muslin, coarse	470	114	24	27
Bengali *deshi* muslin, fine	508	122	32	30
Jamdani, coarse	467	111	25	17
Jamdani, Tangail	533	119	30	25
Jamdani, 19th century	470	114	28	39
1914 muslin *gota* sari (Pl. 67)	426	108	28	19
Khadi cotton saris	511	117	22	19
Khadi silk saris	516	117	40	40
Gorad or *puja* saris (silk)	493	112	32	19
Tasar silk saris	538	117	31	31
19th-century Baluchar silks	447	112	43	32
Baluchar saris, modern (silk)	558	112	38	35
Banaras *amru* saris, 1940s	470	109	46	35
Banaras brocade, modern (silk)	548	117	47	32
Banaras 5-colour *tanchoi* (silk)	559	117	107	132
The North-East and the Himalayas				
Assam, cotton saris	500	111	28	23
Assam, *muga* silk saris	508	113	24	22
Manipur, Moirangfee saris	514	117	30	20
Boro *dokhna*	277	136	22	22
Garo *dakmanda*	170	115	22	19
Khasi *dhara* (silk)	188	97	44	28
Assamese *chadar*, *muga* silk	224	80	35	28
Assamese *mekhla*, cotton	170	109	25	19
Tripura *pachera*	152	108	28	10
Meitei *phanek*	178	112	95	32
Newar *patasi*	579	98	17	21

Region/Sari Type	Dimensions (cm)		Thread Count (per cm)	
	L	W	Wp	Wf
Eastern Deccan				
Santhal *khanda*	426	104	17	16
Munda *sangol paria*	664	96	25	25
Gond *ganda*	345	91	19	16
Khond *gunderi*	158	57	9	10
Eastern Ghats ethnic sari	382	100	19	16
Orissa Sambalpur fashion saris	531	119	31	30
Eastern Ghats *tasar* saris	525	117	32	21
Orissa Cuttack silk saris	521	119	34	25
Andhra Pradesh Siddipet *khans*	554	121	29	32
A.P. Pochampalli ikat *khans* (silk)	521	117	32	30
A.P. Pochampalli ikat silks	488	117	38	36
A.P. Gadwal saris (cotton/silk)	531	119	28	24
The South				
A.P. Dharmavaram silks	559	114	45	41
Tamil Nadu Kornad, silk	559	119	38	30
Karnataka Kornad, cotton	528	113	32	32
Skirt saris (silk, polyester)	475	109	37	31
Low-cost silk saris	483	109	35	35
Mysore crepe saris (silk)	508	117	50	57
A.P. Venkatagiri muslins	518	117	32	29
Coloured daily-wear muslins	554	112	31	35
T.N. *kosavu* saris	533	122	37	42
Kerala *kosavu mundu*	190	127	41	28
8-metre narrow-bordered saris	653	112	30	25
T.N., Madurai prints	523	117	30	29
T.N., Fashion saris (cotton/silk)	541	119	37	86
The Western Deccan				
8-metre Deccan saris	838	118	26	23
Modern Deccan saris	502	117	24	27
Ilkal saris (cotton, synthetic)	507	117	24	30
Narayanpet silks	526	122	41	33
Maheshwar saris (cotton, silk)	538	121	47	44
Chanderi saris (cotton/silk)	524	123	57	25
Paithani silks	547	120	35	22
Parsi *ghara*, silk crepe	513	116	41	41
Low-cost mill prints, rural	430	111	21	26

Note: All textiles mentioned are cotton, unless otherwise stated. 'Cotton/silk' denotes a cotton and silk mix but 'cotton, silk' denotes separate saris made of either cotton or silk. The average measurements were taken from samples between three and twenty-four pieces, in both public and private collections. Usually at least six saris were measured.

Chronology

Major Historical Periods and Events

'Ancient' *c.* 500 BC–0

'Classical' *c.* 0–AD 700

'Medieval' *c.* 700–1200

'Early Islamic ' *c.* 1100–1526

Late Palaeolithic   prior to *c.* 6000 BC

Early Indus Valley *c.* 3000–2500 BC

Mature Indus Valley *c.* 2500–1750 BC

Chalcolithic *c.* 1500–1000 BC

Iron Age   after 1000–800 BC

Buddha's Birth *c.* 556 BC

Mauryan   320–187 BC

Shunga 187–*c.* 50 BC

Gandhara *c.* 50 BC–AD 300

Kushan *c.* 50 BC–*c.* AD 320

Andhra *c.* 50 BC–*c.* AD 300

Gupta AD 320–*c.* 600

Painting of Ajanta Caves *c.* AD 475–500

King Harsha r. AD 606–647

Travels of Hsuen Tsang AD 630–643

Pala *c.* 750–1162

Sena (Bengal) 1097–1223

Marco Polo in India 1293

Vijaynagar Empire 1336–1564

Mughal Empire 1526–*c.* 1765

Arrival of first European traders Early 16th century

British domination *c.* 1765–1947

Domination of East India Company 1765–*c.* 1850

British Empire *c.* 1850–1947

Swadeshi Movement Began in late nineteenth century; adoption of *khadi* 1920

Independence and Partition 1947

Museum Collections

AUSTRALIA
Canberra Australian National Gallery, GPO Box 1150, Canberra, ACT

BANGLADESH
Dhaka National Museum, Junction of New Elephant Road and Mymensingh Road, Dhaka

BELGIUM
Brussels Musées Royaux d'Art et d'Historie, 10 Parc du Cinquantenaire, 1040 Brussels

CANADA
Montreal Museum of Fine Arts, 1379 Sherbrooke St West, Montreal
Toronto Royal Ontario Museum, 100 Queens Park, Toronto, Ontario M5S 2C6; The Museum for Textiles, 55 Centre Avenue, Toronto, Ontario, M5G 2H5

CZECHOSLOVAKIA
Prague Naprstek Museum, Betlemske Namesti 1, Stare Mesto 11000, Prague 1

FRANCE
Lyons Musée Historique des Tissus, 34 rue de Charite, 69001 Lyons
Mulhouse Musée de l'Impression sur Etoffes, 3 rue des Bonnes-Gens, 68100 Mulhouse
Paris Musée des Arts Decoratifs, Pavillon de Marsan, 107–109 rue de Rivoli, 75001 Paris; Musée Guimet, 6 place d'Iena, 75116 Paris; Musée de l'Homme, palais de Chaillot, 75116 Paris; Musée du Louvre, 34 quai du Louvre, 75058 Paris

GERMANY
Berlin Pergamon Museum fur Volkerkunde, Bode Strasse 1-3, 102 Berlin; Museum fur Indische Kunst, Takustrasse 40, 1000 Berlin
Hamburg Museum fur Volkerkunde, Binderstrasse 14, 2000 Hamburg 13
Heidelberg Museum fur Volkerkunde, Portheim Stiftung, Heidelberg
Stuttgart Linden Museum, Hegel Platz 1, 7000 Stuttgart, Baden Wurtemberg

INDIA
Ahmedabad Calico Museum of Textiles, Retreat, Shahibagh, Ahmedabad, Gujarat; Shreyas Folk Museum of Gujarat, Shreyas Hill, Ahmedabad 380015
Bhavnagar Arts and Crafts Museum, Gandhi Smriti, Bhavnagar, Gujarat
Bhopal Madhya Pradesh Tribal Research and Development Institute Museum, 35 Shimla Hills, Bhopal
Bhubaneshwar Orissa State Museum, Bhubaneshwar 750014

Bhuj The Kutch Museum, by Mahadev Gate, Bhuj, Kutch, Gujarat; Madan Singhji Museum, The Palace, Bhuj

Bombay Prince of Wales Museum, M.G. Road, Fort Bombay, Maharashtra

Calcutta Indian Museum, 27 Jawaharlal Nehru Road, Calcutta 13, West Bengal

Gauhati Assam State Museum, Gauhati 781001

Hyderabad Jagdish and Kamla Mittal Museum 1-2-214 Gagan Mahal Road, Hyderabad 500002

Imphal Manipur State Museum, Polo Ground, Imphal

Jaipur Maharajah Sawai Man Singh II Museum, City Palace, Jaipur, Rajasthan

Jamshedpur Tribal Cultural Centre Museum, Kagalnagar, Jamshedpur, Bihar

Lucknow Crafts Museum, Central Design Centre, 8 Cantonment Road, Lucknow, Uttar Pradesh; State Museum, Banarasibagh, Lucknow

New Delhi Crafts Museum, Bhairon Marg, Pragati Maidan, New Delhi 110001; Tribal Museum, Thakkar Baba Smarak Sadan, Dr Ambedkar Road, New Delhi 1100055

Panaji Museum of Goa, Daman and Diu, Directorate of Archives and Archaeology, Ashirvad Buildings, St Inez, Panaji, Goa

Pune Raja Dinkar Kelkar Museum, 1378 Shukrawar Peth Natu Bag, Pune 41002, Maharashtra

Rajkot Watson Museum, Jubilee Bagh, Rajkot, Gujarat

Ranchi Department of Anthropology Museum, University of Ranchi, 834001, Bihar

Shillong Central Museum, Lachumeria, Shillong 793001

Surat Sardar Vallabhbhai Patel Museum, Sonifalia, Surat 395003, Gujarat

Varanasi Bharat Kala Bhawan, Banaras Hindu University, Varanasi, Uttar Pradesh

INDONESIA
Jakarta Textile Museum of Jakarta, HKS Tubun No. 4, Jakarta

JAPAN
Osaka National Museum of Ethnology (Kokuristsu Minzokugaku Hakubutsukan), 23–17 Yamadaogawa, Suita-Shi, Osaka; Kanebo Museum of Textiles, 5–102 Tomobuchi-Cho, 1-Chome, Miyakojima-Ku, Osaka

NETHERLANDS
Amsterdam Museum of the Royal Tropical Institute, Linnaeusstraat 2, 1092AD, Amsterdam

Leiden National Museum of Ethnography, Steenstraat 1, 2300 A.E. Leiden

PAKISTAN
Karachi National Museum of Pakistan, Burns Garden, Karachi

Lahore Lahore Museum, Sharah-e-Quaid-e-Azam, Lahore; Museum of Folk Arts of Punjab, Lahore

POLAND
Warsaw Asia and Pacific Museum (Muzeum Asji I Pacyfiku), Galeria Nusantary ul. Nowogrodska 18a, Warsaw

PORTUGAL
Lisbon Museum of Overseas Ethnography, Rua das Portas de Santo Antao, Lisbon

RUSSIA
St Petersburg Peter the Great Museum of Anthropology and Ethnography, 3 Universitetshaya Naberezhnaya, St Petersburg

SWITZERLAND
Basle Museum fur Volkerhunde, Augustinergasse 2, 4001 Basle

St Gallen Volkerkundliche Sammlung, Museumstrasse 50, 9000 St Gallen

Zurich Volkerkunde Museum der Universitate, Pelikanstrasse 40, 8001 Zurich

UNITED KINGDOM
Bradford Cartwright Hall, Lister Park, Manningham, Bradford

Bristol Bristol City Museum, Queen's Road, Bristol BS8 1RL

Cambridge University Museum of Archaeology and Ethnology, Downing St., Cambridge

Durham Gulbenkian Museum of Oriental Art, University of Durham, Elvet Hill, Durham DH1 3TH

London British Museum, Department of Oriental Antiquities, Great Russell Street, London WC1B 3DG; Horniman Museum, Forest Hill, London SE23 8PQ; Museum of Mankind, 6 Burlington Gardens, London W1X 2EX; Victoria and Albert Museum, Cromwell Road, South Kensington, London SW7 2RI; Whitechapel Art Gallery, Whitechapel High Street, London E1

Manchester Manchester City Art Gallery, The Athenaeum, Princess Street, Manchester; The Whitworth Art Gallery, University of Manchester, Manchester M15 6ER

Nottingham Museum of Costume and Textiles, 51 Castle Gate, Nottingham NG1 6AT

Oxford Ashmolean Museum, Beaumont Street, Oxford OX1 2PH; Pitt-Rivers Museum, South Parks Road, Oxford 0X1 3PP

Powis Powis Castle, Welshpool, Powys SY21 8RF

UNITED STATES
Allentown Allentown Art Museum, 5th and Court Sts., P.O.B. 388, Allentown, PA 18105

Berkeley Lowie Museum of Anthropology, Kroebber Hall, Bancroft Way, University of California, Berkeley, CA

Boston Museum of Fine Arts, 465 Huntingdon Ave, Boston, MA; S.P.N.E.A., Harrison Gray Otis House, 141 Cambridge St., Boston, MA

Cambridge Peabody Museum of Archaeology and Ethnology, Harvard University, 11 Divinity Ave., Cambridge, MA

Chicago Art Institute of Chicago, Michigan Ave at Adams St., Chicago, IL; Field Museum of Natural History, Roosevelt Road at Lakeshore Drive, Chicago, IL

Cincinnati Cincinnati Museum of Fine Art, Eden Park, Cincinnati, OH

Cleveland Cleveland Museum of Art, 11150 East Boulevard, Cleveland, OH

Denver Denver Art Museum, 100 West 14th Ave., Parkway, Denver, CO

Detroit Detroit Institute of Arts, 5200 Woodward Ave., Detroit, MI

Hartford Wadsworth Atheneum, 600 Main St., Hartford, CT 06103

Houston Museum of Fine Arts, PO Box 6826, Houston, TX 77265

Indianapolis The Indianapolis Museum of Art, 1200 West 38 St., Indianapolis, IN

Los Angeles Los Angeles County Museum of Art, 5905 Wilshire Boulevard, Los Angeles, CA; Mingei International Museum of Folk Art, 4405 La Jolla, Village Drive, La Jolla, CA; Museum of Cultural History, University of California, 405 Hilgard Ave., Los Angeles, CA

Madison The Hellen Allen Collection, The Museum, University of Wisconsin, 1300 Linden Blvd, Madison, WI 53706

Minneapolis Minneapolis Institute of Arts, 2300 Third Ave. S, Minneapolis, MN 55404

Newark Newark Museum, 43–49 Washington Street, Newark, NJ

New York City American Museum of Natural History, 79th St & Central Park West, New York, NY; Brooklyn Museum, 188 Eastern Parkway, Brooklyn, NY; Cooper-Hewitt Museum of Design, Smithsonian Institution, Fifth Avenue at 91st St., New York, NY; Metropolitan Museum of Art, Fifth Avenue at 82nd St., New York, NY; The Museum at F.I.T., The Fashion Institute of Technology, 227 W27th St., New York, NY 10001

Philadelphia Philadelphia Museum of Art, Parkway at 26th St., Philadelphia, PA; The University Museum, University of Pennsylvania, 2304 Waverly St., Philadelphia, PA 19146;

Providence Museum of Art, Rhode Island School of Design, 2 College Street, Providence, RI 02903;

St Louis St Louis Art Museum, 1 Fine Art Drive, Forest Park, St Louis, MO 63110

Salem Peabody Museum of Salem, East India Square, Salem, MA

San Francisco M.H. de Young Memorial Museum, Golden Gate Park, San Francisco, CA

Santa Barbara Santa Barbara Museum of Art, 1130 State Street, Santa Barbara, CA 93013

Seattle Henry Art Gallery, University of Washington, Seattle, WA; Seattle Art Museum, Volunteer Park, Seattle, WA

Washington National Museum of Natural History, Smithsonian Institution, Washington, DC; Textile Museum, 2320 S Street NW, Washington, DC.

Bibliography

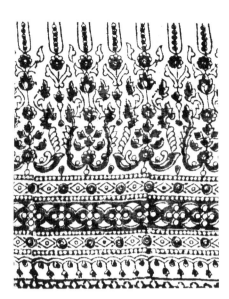

Abbreviations: *JITH: Journal of Indian Textile History*, Ahmedabad; *TMJ: Textile Museum Journal*, Washington; *Woven Air: Woven Air: The Muslin & Kantha Tradition of Bangladesh*, Whitechapel, 1988.

Ahmad E *Bihar: A Physical, Economic & Regional Geography*, Ranchi, 1965

Agrawala V S 'References to Textiles in Bana's *Harshacharita*', *JITH*, 4 (1959): 65–8

Ali Y *A Monogram on Silk Fabrics Produced in the N.W. Provinces and Oudh*, Ahmedabad, 1974, reprint of 1900 text

Allchin B and **R** *The Rise of Civilization in India & Pakistan*, Cambridge, 1988

Apte K V *The Practical Sanskrit Dictionary*, Delhi, 1989

Archer W G *Songs for the Bride: Wedding Rites of Rural India*, New York, 1985

Asher F *The Art of Eastern India 300 – 800 AD*, Minneapolis, 1980

Ayyar K V *A Short History of Kerala*, Ernakulam, 1966

Barber E *Prehistoric Textiles*, Princeton, 1991
'The Proto-Indo-European Notion of Cloth and Clothing', in *Journal of Indo-European Studies*, 3 (1975): 294–320.

Barnes R 'Indian Trade Cloth in Egypt: The Newberry Collection', in *Symposium of the Textile Society of America, 1990*: 178–91.

Baruah S L *A Comprehensive History of Assam*, Delhi, 1985

Basham A L *The Origins and Development of Classical Hinduism*, Oxford, 1989

Bean S 'Gandhi and Khadi, The Fabric of Independence', in Weiner, ed., 1989, pp. 355–76

Bennett L *Dangerous Wives and Sacred Sisters*, New York, 1983

Bharathalyer K *Animals in Indian Sculpture*, Bombay, 1977

Bhushan J B *Costumes & Textiles of India*, Bombay, 1958

Bilgrami N *Sindh Jo Ajrak*, Govt. Sind, Pakistan, 1990

Bista D B *People of Nepal*, Kathmandu, 1971

Brett K B 'The Flowering Tree in Indian Chintz', *JITH* 3 (1957): 45–57

Buhler A and **Fischer E** *The Patola of Gujarat*, Basel, 1979

Buhler A, Fischer E and **Nabholz M** *Indian Tie-Dyed Fabrics*, Ahmedabad, 1980

Burrow and **Emereau** *A Dravidian Etymological Dictionary*, Oxford, 1984

Campion E *My Oraon Culture*, Ranchi, 1980

Casson L *The Periplus Maris Erythraei: Text with introduction, translation and commentary*, Princeton, 1989

Chandra M 'Indian Costumes & Textiles: 8th to 12th Century' *JITH*, 5: 1–41
'Indian Costumes & Textiles: Sultanate Period', *JITH*, 6: 5–61
Costumes, Textiles, Cosmetics & Coiffure, Delhi, 1973

Chattapadhyay K *Indian Embroidery*, Delhi, 1977

Chishti and **Sanyal** *Saris of India: Madhya Pradesh*, Delhi, 1989

Choudhury P C *The History of the Civilization of the People of Assam to the 12th Century*, Gauhati, 1966

Cohn B S 'Cloth, Clothes and Colonialism in India', pp. 303–54, in Weiner, ed., 1989.

Coomaraswamy A K *The Arts and Crafts of India and Ceylon*, New York, 1964, reprint from 1913

Craven R *A Concise History of Indian Art*, London, 1976

Crill R 'Supplying the Mughal Court', in *Woven Air*, pp. 33–7

Crooke W *A Glossary of North Indian Peasant Life*, Oxford, 1989, reprint from 1879

Dar S N *Costume of India & Pakistan*, Bombay, 1969

Das J 'Textile Art of Assam', in *Assam: The Land of Sankaradeva*, ed. Pandey, V., Bombay, 1979

Dasgupta P *Temple Terracotta of Bengal*, New Delhi, 1971

De Bone M G *Patolu and its Techniques, TMJ*, 4 (1976): 49–62
'Woven Landscape Saris of Orissa', in *Landscape* (California), 28 (1984): 36–40

Desai C *Ikat Textiles of India*, London and San Francisco, 1987

Desai V and **Mason D** eds. *Gods, Guardians and Lovers: Temple Sculptures from North India, 700 – 1200 AD*, New York, 1993

Dhamija J 'Bihar Embroidery', in *Marg*, 20 (1966): 34–9
ed. *Crafts of Gujarat*, Ahmedabad, 1985

Dhamija and **Jain** eds. *Handwoven Fabrics of India*, Ahmedabad, 1989

Dhamija and **Sarabhai** *Patolas & Resist Dyed Fabrics of India*, Ahmedabad, 1989

Dongerkerry K S *The Indian Sari*, Delhi, 1959

Dunsmore S *Nepalese Textiles*, London, 1993

Eck D *Banaras: City of Light*, Princeton, 1982

Emery I *The Primary Structure of Fabrics*, Washington, 1980

Forbes-Watson J *Textile Manufactures & Costume of the People of India*, London, 1866
Collection of Specimens of the Textile Manufactures of India, Second Series, London, 1873

Fraser-Lu S *Handwoven Textiles of Southeast Asia*, Oxford, 1988

Frater J 'The Meaning of Folk Art in Rabari Life', *TMJ*, 4 (1975): 47–60
'Elements of Style: The Artisan Reflected in Embroideries of Western India', in *Mud, Mirror and Thread: Folk Traditions of Rural India*, Ahmedabad & Albuquerque, 1993
Rabari Dress: Adornment that Tells of Tradition, ibid.

Freed R & Freed S *Ghosts: Life and Death in North India*, New York, 1993

Furer-Haimendorf C von *Life Among Indian Tribals*, Oxford, 1990
Tribes of India: The Struggle for Survival, California, 1982

Garraty J and **Gay P** *The Columbia History of the World*, New York, 1988

Geijer A *A History of Textile Art*, Stockholm, 1979

Ghurye G S *Indian Costume*, Bombay, 1951

Ghuznavi S R 'Jamdani', in *Woven Air*, pp. 51–5

Gillow J & Barnard N *Traditional Indian Textiles*, London, 1991

Gittinger M *Master Dyers to the World*, Washington, 1982

Gittinger M & Lefferts L *Textiles & the Tai Experience*, Washington, 1992

Goswami R 'Bomokoi' in *The India Magazine*, 5 (4) (1985): 44–51

Grierson G *Bihar Peasant Life*, Delhi, 1975, reprinted from 1885

Hacker K & Turnbull K *Courtyard, Bazaar, Temple: Traditions of Textile Experience in India*, Seattle, 1982

Haque E 'The Textile Tradition of Bangladesh', in *Woven Air* as above, Whitechapel, 1988

Huyler S *Village India*, New York, 1985

Irwin J 'Indo-Portuguese Embroideries of Bengal', in *The Journal of the India, Pakistan and Ceylon Society*, 26 (2) (1952): 65–73
'Indian Textiles in Historical Perspective' in *Textiles and Ornaments of India*, New York, 1956
The Kashmir Shawl, London, 1973

Irwin J and **Hall S** *Indian Painted and Printed Fabrics*, Ahmedabad, 1971
Indian Embroideries, Ahmedabad, 1973

Jain J ed. *The Master Weavers*, Delhi, 1982

Jain J and **Aggarwala A** *National Handicrafts and Handlooms Museum*, Ahmedabad, 1989

Jayakar P 'A Neglected Group of Indian Ikat Fabrics', in *JITH*, 1 (1955): 55–9
'Indian Fabrics in Indian Life', in *Textiles & Ornaments of India*, New York, 1956
Naksha Bandhas of Banaras, JITH, 7 (1967): 21–44

Jeyechandrum A V 'Muruka in Iconography' pp. 491–521, in *Heritage of the Tamils: Temple Arts*, eds. Subramanian and Rajendran, Madras, 1985

Jhala U *Brocades of Ahmedabad*, Student Study, National Institute of Design, Ahmedabad, 1981

Kinsley D *Hindu Goddesses*, California, 1988

Kramrisch S *The Hindu Temple*, Vol.1., Delhi, 1946
The Art of India Through the Ages, New York, 1954
Exploring India's Sacred Art, Philadelphia, 1983

Krishna R and **V** *Banaras Brocades*, Delhi, 1966

Kumar N *The Artisans of Banaras*, Princeton, 1988

Lal L *The Tree in India, Myth & Symbol*, Delhi, 1988

Lala R M *The Creation of Wealth: The Tata Story*, Bombay, 1992

Lynton L 'The Wild Silk Saris of Eastern India', in *Arts of Asia*, 22 (5) (1992): 86–99

'Victorian & Edwardian Designs in East Indian Handloom Saris', in *Surface Design Journal*, 18 (1) (1993): 18–21

'The Origins and Significance of the Assamese Sun Tree Motif', in *Ars Textrina*, 20 (1993): 73–132

'Banaras Brocades' in *Arts of Asia*, 24, (3) (1994): 80–93

'The Assimilation of European Designs into Twentieth-Century Indian Saris', in *Contact, Crossover and Continuity: Proceedings of the Fourth Biennial Symposium of the Textile Society of America*, September 1994: 207–16

Majmudar M R *Cultural History of Gujarat*, Bombay, 1966

Mallory J P *In Search of the Indo-Europeans*, London, 1991

Maloney C ed. *The Evil Eye*, New York, 1976 *Don't Say Pretty Baby*, in ibid., pp. 102–48

Mathur J C 'Historical and Cultural Heritage of Bihar', *Marg*, 20 (1966): 4–12

Mehta R *The Story of Khadi*, Bombay, 1974

Mehta R J *Handicrafts & Industrial Arts of India*, Bombay, 1960

Mehta R N 'Bandhas of Orissa', *JITH* 6 (1961): 62–72

Minz B *Weaving Then and Now: A Tale of Declining Village Industry in Chotanagpur*, Ranchi, 1982

Mode H and **Chandra S** *Indian Folk Art*, New York, 1985

Mohanty B *Brocaded Fabrics of India*, Ahmedabad, 1979

Mohanty B Chandramouli, K. and Naik, H. *Natural Dyeing Processes of India*, Ahmedabad, 1987

Mohanty B and **Krishna K** *Ikat Fabrics of Orissa & Andhra Pradesh*, Ahmedabad, 1974

Mohanty B and **Mohanty J** *Block Printing and Dyeing of Bagru, Rajasthan*, Ahmedabad, 1983

Molesworth J *Molesworth's Marathi-English Dictionary*, 1831, Corrected Reprint, Poona, 1975

Mookerjee A *Designs in Indian Textiles*, Calcutta, no date

Munck V de *Seasonal Cycles: A Study of Social Change in a Sri Lankan Village*, Delhi, 1993

Murphy V and **Crill R** *The Tie-dyed Textiles of India*, London, 1991

Nabholz-Kartaschoff M L *Golden Sprays & Scarlet Flowers*, Kyoto, 1986

Nanavaty M *Silk: From Grub to Glamour*, Bombay, 1965

Narayanan N ed. *The Language of Symbols*, Delhi, no date

Nayak P K 'Woven-Craft, Economy and Religion of the Sarak of Orissa' pp. 47–56, in *Art and Artisans of Orissa*, ed. Sahoo, B., Bhubaneshwar, 1989

Neog M *Tradition and Style: A Few Studies in Assamese Culture*, Gauhati, 1981

Nilakanta Singh E *Manipur: History*, in *Marg*, 16 (2): 1–10

Ostor A 'The Play of the Gods: Locality, Ideology, Structure and Time', in *The Festival of a Bengali Town*, Chicago, 1980.

Paine S *Chikan Embroidery: The Floral Whitework of India*, Aylesbury, 1989

Pal P *The Ideal Image*, New York, 1978 *Indian Sculpture*, California, 1986

Parkin R *The Munda of Central India*, Oxford, 1992

Peebles M *Court & Village: India's Textile Tradition*, Santa Barbara, 1981

Platts J *Dictionary of Urdu, Classical Hindi and English*, Delhi, 1977, original 1884

Polo M *The Travels of Marco Polo*, New York, 1986

Poster A *From Indian Earth: 4,000 Years of Terracotta Art*, Brooklyn, 1986

Prasad N *Land and People of Tribal Bihar*, Ranchi, 1961

Ramaswamy V *Textiles and Weavers in Medieval South India*, Oxford, 1985

Ramnarain G (a) 'Heritage of the Loom', in *Homage to Rukmini Devi* (no page numbers) (b) 'A Story is Woven', ibid.

Roberts J 'Belief in the Evil Eye in World Perspective', in Maloney, ed., pp. 223–78, New York, 1976

Roy S and **Rizvi S** *Tribal Customary Laws of North East India*, Delhi, 1990

Santapau H *Common Trees*, Delhi, 1991

Sen S *Tribes and Castes of Manipur*, New Delhi, 1992

Sharma K L *Society and Polity in Modern Sri Lanka*, New Delhi, 1988

Shreshtra D & **Singh C** *Ethnic Groups of Nepal and Their Ways of Living*, Kathmandu, 1972

Simmons P *Chinese Patterned Silks*, New York, 1948

Singh B N *Trade & Industrial Markets of Bihar*, Patna, 1974

Singh C *Textiles and Costumes from the Maharaja Sawai Man Singh II Museum*, Jaipur, 1979

Singh E N 'Manipur: History', in *Marg*, 16 (2): 1–10

Sinha A K *Transition in the Textile Industry of Bihar*, Delhi, 1984

Smart E 'A Preliminary Report on a Group of Important Mughal Textiles', in *TMJ*, 25, 1986: 5–25

Sontheimer G-D *Pastoral Deities of Western India*, Oxford, 1989

Spear P *A History of India*, Vol. 2, London, 1970

Stockley M 'Woven Air: An Introduction' in *Woven Air*, pp. 13–20

Strip P and **O** *The Peoples of Bombay*, Bombay, 1944

Stutley M *The Illustrated Dictionary of Hindu Iconography*, London, 1985

Thapar R 'State Weaving Shops of the Mauryan Period', *JITH*, 1 (1955)

Thurgood G 'Benedict's Work: Past and Present', in *Linguistics of the Sino-Tibetan Area: The State of the Art*, Pacific Linguistic Series C, no. 87. Australia National University, 1985

Tirkey B *The Smiling Oraon*, Patna, 1989

Trivedi H R *Tribal Land Systems: Land Reform Measures and Developments of Tribals* (Gujarat), New Delhi, 1993

Turner C W 'India, Its Dyers and Its Colour Symbolism', in *CIBA Review*, 2, 1937

Turner R L *A Comparative Dictionary of the Indo-Aryan Languages*, Oxford, 1966

Verma R C *Indian Tribes Through the Ages*, New Delhi, 1990

Weiner A and **Schneider J** eds. *Cloth and the Human Experience*, Washington, 1989

Willis E B 'The Textile Arts of India's North East Borderlands', in *Arts of Asia*, 11, 1987: 211–22

Watt G *Indian Art at Delhi, 1903, Being the Official Catalogue of the Delhi Exhibition, 1902–1903*, Calcutta, 1903

Westfall C *The Web of India: A Diary*, Montclair State, N.J., 1983

Xia Nai trans. Chu-tsing *Jade and Silk of Han China*, Kansas, 1983

Anonymous/catalogues

Atlas *A Social and Economic Atlas of India*, Oxford, 1987

Catalogue *Arts of Bengal*, Whitechapel, 1979

Catalogue *Homage to Rukmini Devi*, Kalakshetra, 1991

Catalogue *Visvakarma Ksetra*, Delhi, 1987

Directorate of Industries *Designs in Manipur Handlooms*, Delhi, 1960

Govt. India *Census of India*, Delhi, 1981, 1991

Indian Cotton Mills' Federation The *Handbook of Statistics on Cotton Textile Industry*, Bombay, 1991

Ministry of Textiles *Census of Handlooms in India* 1987–88, Govt. India, Delhi

Ntl Crafts Inst. of Jaipur *Hand Printed Textiles*, 1986: '*Bandhej*-Craft of Rajasthan', pt. V

New York Graphics Soc. with UNESCO *Ceylon's Paintings from Temple, Shrine and Rock* (UNESCO World Art Series, no date)

Sotheby's North America *Indian, Himalayan & Southeast Asian Art*, New York, June 1993

Tata Industries *A Short History of the 'Empress Mills'*, Nagpur, Bombay, 1927, reprinted 1977

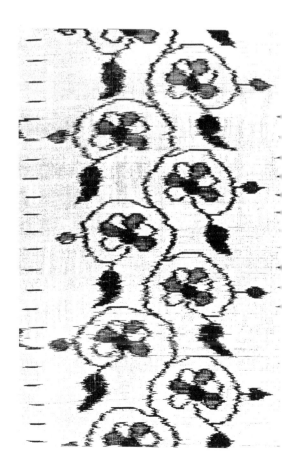

Acknowledgments

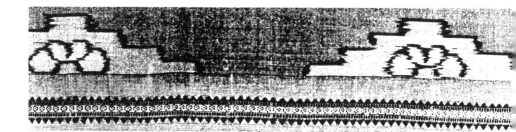

Many different people from a wide variety of backgrounds helped us create this book. Some were kind enough to conduct research for us or else openly shared their independent work, and we give special thanks to all of them, namely: Chantal Boulanger (Tours, France), Eliza Chakravarty (Baltimore, USA), Virginia Davis (New York, USA), Sabra Feldman (New York, USA), Desire Koslin (New York, USA), Roshan Kalapesi (Bombay, India), Roshan Lala (Bombay, India), Kranti Mitra (New Delhi, India) and Carol Westfall (New Jersey, USA).

Many individuals also openly shared their personal experiences and family histories and although most are listed below, we wish to emphasize the help that V. Manimekalai (Madras, Tamil Nadu), Sanjay and Renuka Singh (Jamshedpur, Bihar), and the families of Mrs M. Daly (Shillong, Meghalaya), Emanuel Oria (Muingutu, Bihar) and Narasimha Iyengar (Amruthur, Karnataka) gave us, for they all made enormous efforts on our behalf despite almost no notice at all.

Also, we wholeheartedly thank the staff of the Department of Tourism, New Delhi, India, and the New York branch of the Government of India Tourist Office for enthusiastically endorsing our final research trip to India, especially Mr Ram Chopra (director), Ashok Sharma and Seema Shahi of the New York Office, as well as Mr N.K. Lakhanpal of the Department in New Delhi. We also thank all the staff in the regional offices where we were so warmly hosted, namely Raj Mittal (director), Vinod Kumar (assistant director) and Om Pal (assistant) of the New Delhi office; Ram Bali Sinha (director) of the Shillong, Meghalaya office; Dr Poornima Sastry (regional director) of the Madras, Tamil Nadu office; M. Sridhara (tourist officer) of the Bangalore, Karnataka office; as well as the staff of the Calcutta, Bombay and Gauhati offices who went out of their way to ensure a smooth journey. In addition, we thank Indian Airlines and Air India for their hospitality and help.

Additional thanks must also be given to Indian art specialist, Sabra Feldman, and textile historian and weaver, Desire Koslin, for reading the manuscript of the book and making many helpful suggestions and edits. Also to Dr Ruth Barnes (Ashmolean Museum, Oxford, England), Dr Stan Freed (American Museum of Natural History, New York, USA) and Dr Philip Gould (Columbia University, New York, USA) and his wife Nadia for their encouragement and support, and to Elizabeth Bayley Willis (Seattle, USA), whose extensive sari collection (and notes) at the Henry Art Gallery, Seattle, proved a goldmine for preliminary research.

Thank you, too, to all the people listed below who helped us in so many different ways: Eleanor Abraham (New York, USA), Shahajahan Ansari (Banaras, Uttar Pradesh); A. Prince Azariah (Madurai, Tamil Nadu); M. Bharkara (Karnataka Silk Industries Corporation, Mysore); Sylvanus Bhengra (Tribal Cultural Centre, Kagalnagar, Bihar); Neelu Chopra (Baltimore, USA); John Cort (New York, USA); Sharmilla Das (Calcutta); Chelna Desai (Bombay); Dr Glory Dharmaraj (United Nations, New York, USA); Lynn Felsher (Fashion Institute of Technology, New York, USA): Judy Frater (Bhuj, Gujarat); Ram Gandhi (New Delhi); Rina Gill (UNICEF, Kathmandu, Nepal); Dr Mattiebelle Gittinger (Textile Museum, Washington, DC); Susan Hay (Rhode Island School of Design Museum of Art, Providence, USA); Veena Girdhar (Baltimore, USA); C.R. Hembram (Tribal Cultural Centre, Kagalnagar, Bihar); Chhote Hembram (Jamshedpur, Bihar); Sally Holkar (Rehwa Society, Maheshwar, M.P.); Janakaammal and Rajalaxmi Iyengar (Amruthur, Karnataka); Dr Doreanne Jacobson (Springfield, USA); Jolen Kanduna (Muingutu, Bihar); George Kharkongar (Shillong, Meghalaya); Esther Lyngdoh (Meghalaya State Tourism Office, Shillong); Davina Lyngwa (Shillong, Meghalaya); Saro Mahli and family (Halubani, Bihar); Bud Mishra (New York University, New York, USA); Dr B. Mohanty (Bubhaneshwar, Orissa); Gillian Moss (Cooper-Hewitt Museum of Design, New York, USA); Runrekha Mushahary (Gauhati, Assam); Meera Nair (Trivandrum, Kerala); Geetanjali Narayen (Baltimore, USA); Nimi Oria (Muingutu, Bihar); Sunita Oria (Muingutu, Bihar); Pam Parmal (Rhode Island School of Design Museum of Art, Providence, USA); Anil Patel (Rajka Designs, Ahmedabad, Gujarat); Amy Poster (Brooklyn Museum, Brooklyn, USA); C.V. Radhakrishnan (secretary-general, The Indian Cotton Mills Federation, Bombay); Noormohammed Haji Abdul Rahim (Gamathiwala Cloth Centre, Ahmedabad, Gujarat); Sudha Rai (Bilaspur, Bihar); V.R. Srimathy Rajan (Madurai, Tamil Nadu): Lalitha Rajan (Madurai, Tamil Nadu); Larimi Rajan (Madurai, Tamil Nadu); Shanthi Rajan (Madurai, Tamil Nadu); A.K. Ramesh (A.B. Kuppusammy Manufacturers and Merchants, Madurai, Tamil Nadu); G.R. Rane (Ram Cloth Centre, Bombay); Tripura Rao (Hyderabad, Andhra Pradesh); Jon Eric Riis (Atlanta, USA); Susan Ritchie (New York, USA); Shirin Sabavala (Bombay), Rajiv and Poonam Sahi (New Delhi); Ashish Sharma (S.B. Sharma & Sons, Jamshedpur, Bihar); Nandita Singh (Raleigh, USA); Raka Singh (Patna, Bihar); Ritu Singh (Patna, Bihar); Sarojini Singh (Patna, Bihar); Shakuntala Singh (Dhankaul, Bihar); Archana Sinha (Bombay); Mahalakshmi Sinha (Patna, Bihar); Tara Sinha (Ahmedabad, Gujarat); Milton Sonday (Cooper-Hewitt Museum of Design, New York, USA); Judy Sourakli (Henry Art Gallery, Seattle, USA); Srinivasa (Karnataka Silk Industries Corporation, Mysore); N. Sundararajan (Bangalore); Bahleen Topno (Muingutu, Bihar); Roopak Vaidya (Bombay); Priyamda Varadachary (New York, USA); C.S. Varadan and C.S. Srivathsan (Shreenivas Silk House, Kanchipuram, Tamil Nadu); Lisa Whittal (American Museum of Natural History, New York, USA); Leela Wood (Michigan University, Ann Arbor, USA).

We also wish to thank the staff (whose names we did not record) of the following organizations for their helpfulness and patience: Handloom House (Bangalore); Kumaran Stores (Madras); Meghalaya State Emporium (Shillong); Meghalaya State Museum (Shillong); Ramakrishna Mission (Cherapunjee, Meghalaya).

For the studio and outdoor model shots, we wish to thank models Seema Chandna, Shelley Alexandra Diengdoh, Caroline Dkhar, Raka Singh, Ritu Singh, Archana Sinha and Iris Bass. And last, but not least, we wish to thank Catherine Blake, Avril Broadley, and the staff at Thames and Hudson, London, for making this book a reality.

Saris in Public and Private Collections
The saris featured in the colour plates were from the following collections:
Eleanor Abraham, Pls. 27, 82; Chantal Boulanger, Pls.146, 147, 148, 157, 158, 164, 166; Eliza Chakravarty, Pl. 168; Yasuko Chawla, Pl. 38; Neelu Chopra, Pls. 15, 87; Virginia Davis, Pls. 109, 111, 113, 114, 116, 121, 127, 128, 131, 132, 133, 134, 135; Sabra Feldman, Pl. 74; Ram Gandhi, Pls 122, 123, 206; Dr and Mrs Philip Gould, Pls. 28, 42, 43, 77, 80, 81, 125, 126, 129, 195, 196, 197; Roshan Kalapesi, Pls. 61, 199, 200; Desire Koslin, Pls. 46, 48, 57, 75, 83; Roshan Lala, Pl. 198; Davina M. Lyngwa, Pl. 20; Sillo Mistri, Pl. 60; Geetanjali Narayen, Pls. 21, 85, 103, 104; Tripura Rao, Pl. 169; Jon Eric Riis, Pls. 112, 203; Archana Sinha,Pls. 6, 39, 149, 171; Mahalakshmi Sinha, Pls. 13, 56, 79; Tara Sinha, Pls. 130, 142, 156, 159, 160; Nandita Singh, Pl. 162; Pushpa Singh, Pl. 165; Raka Singh, Pls. 14, 49, 51, 69, 73, 84, 140, 145; Ritu Singh, Pls. 16, 86, 88, 89; Sarojini Singh, Pls. 35, 78; Shakuntala Singh,Pls. 54, 67, 72, 76; Carol Westfall, Pls. 36, 91, 120, 152, 153, 154, 201, 202; New England Collector, Pl. 40. Henry Art Gallery, University of Washington, Seattle, USA, Pl. 29 (acc. no. 58.1-603), the Elizabeth Bayley Willis Collection, gift of Prentice and Virginia Bloedel; and Pl. 66 (acc. no. 92.14-1), gift of Linda Lynton. All other saris are in the collection of the author.

Photograph Credits
ACSAA Color Slide Project, Michigan University, Ann Arbor, Michigan, USA, Pl. 4; Richard Nicol, Pl. 29; Linda Lynton, Pls. 1, 3, 7, 25, 161, 163, 170, 182; Carol Westfall, Pl. 30. All other photographs were by Sanjay K. Singh.

Line drawings and maps by Linda Lynton.

Index

Numerals in *italics* refer to plate numbers

Abrawan 45, 56, 190; *82, 84, 85*
Adivasi 181 n1, 190; *see also* Tribes
Adyar mundhu 122, 127; *155, 174*
Afghanistan 9, 41, 189 n45
Agricultural groups 9, 26, 89, 94, 161, 171, 175, 190, 192
Ahmedabad 9, 26, 28, 32, 152; *29, 37*
Ahom 73, 75, 79, 175, 176, 184 n6, 189 n58, 190
Ajanta 10, 25, 28, 170, 171, 174, 177, 181 n22, n23, 182 n17, 189 n34, 190; *4*
Ajrak 31, 170, 190
Al-Fustat 26, 169, 177, 180
Alwar muslins 28
Ambara 44, 46, 162, 163, 183 n17, 188 n2, 190, 194
America 25, 54, 182 n12, 183 n6, n15, 187 n30, 188 n32
Amru 47-48, 55-56, 190; *60-62, 73, 74, 77, 80, 81*
Andhra Pradesh 9, 14, 46, 89, 90, 93, 94, 99, 100-104, 121-124, 126, 127, 148, 152, 166, 185 n3, n5, n29, 186 n38, n53, 187 n7, n9, n35, n43, 189 n21, 192, 193, 198
Appliqué 48, 49, 50, 53, 151
Bihar 48, 49, 50, 183 n37; *66, 68*
gota 50, 184 n41-42, 192; *67, 69*
Parsi 151; *195, 196*
sorahi 50, 195
wall hangings 53, 56
see also Embroidery
Arab(ia) 101, 187 n31
Arakku 123, 162, 190
Archer, W. 178, 189 n71
Aristocracy 7, 9, 27, 30, 31, 50, 73, 145, 148, 150, 166, 186 n33, n38, 193; *39, 89, 185, 187, 201-20*
Arni 123, 124, 125, 187 n20, 187 n43, 194; *150, 162, 165*
Arthashastra 43, 75, 78
Arunachal Pradesh 75, 184 n1
Assam 16, 42, 73-79, 174, 175-176, 182 n34, n36, 184 n1, n4, n6, 190-195
Assamese silks 42, 77-79, 184 n26, 185 n32; *93-95*
weavers 73-76, 184 n8, n9
Aurangabad 123, 148, 150, 188 n21, 194
Austro-Asiatic culture, languages 9, 73, 90, 181 n1, n12, 185 n21, 186 n53, 190-195
Austro-Tai languages 175-176, 189 n57, 190
Avatar, of Vishnu 99, 178, 189 n73, 190; *134*
Baluchar saris 6, 47-48, 161, 190, 199; *60-62*
Baluchistan 8, 189 n45
Bamboo 78, 80, 174, 191
Banabhatta 45, 79, 188 n2
Banaras 53, 54, 76, 104, 151
Banaras saris, brocades 42, 48, 50, 53-56, 184 n69, 199; *13-16, 74-89*
abrawan 45, 56, 190; *82-85*
amru 54, 55-56, 190, 199; *77, 80, 81, 73, 74*
bafta, pot-than 55, 56, 193; *75, 76, 78, 79*
designs 54-55, 56, 76, 124, 125, 146, 149, 179, 180, 182 n36, 191, 195; *13, 75, 77, 83, 85, 87, 89*
cutwork 56, 196; *83*
kincab 55, 79, 193; *13, 15, 16, 86-89*
tanchoi 56, 151, 195, 199; *14, 73-74*
tarbana, tissue 56, 195; *82-85*
weavers 54, 104, 190
Bandha 95-98, 99-100, 199; *120-130, 131-134*
Bandhani craftspeople, *see Bandhej*
designs, techniques 28-30, 32, 152, 178, 182 n16, 183 n26, 190-194, 197; *40-45*
saris, *odhnis* 28, 29-30, 103, 128, 199; *40-45*
Gujarat 28-30, 151, 182 n18; *40-44*
Machilipatnam 103
Parsi 29, 150, 151
Rajasthan 28, 29; *45*
south India 128
Bandhej 28, 182 n18, n19, 190
Bangalore 122, 124, 187 n23
Bangladesh 7, 41-44, 46, 49, 166
Barbosa 125, 187 n28
Bark, bast fibres 91, 189 n49; *112*
Bastar 90, 92, 94, 99, 101, 148, 186 n6
Bay of Bengal 89, 182 n30
Bayley Willis, E. 183 n40, 186 n4
Bengal 13, 14, 16, 41, 42, 51, 73, 74, 76-77, 79, 89, 90, 91, 98, 104, 127, 128, 148, 166, 171, 178, 180, 184 n18, 185 n5, 186 n29, n7, 189 n33, 190, 200
Bhat 31, 165, 171, 174, 190, 191, 194, 195
Bhatia 31, 190
Bhil tribe 14, 25, 26, 182 n2, n7, 190
Bhilala 26, 182 n2, n7, 190
Bhumihar 50, 184 n40, n42, 190
Bhuyan 73
Bichchitrapuri sari 96, 190; *121*
Bihar 8, 14, 41, 48-52, 56, 73, 77-79, 89-91, 152, 178, 181 n8, n14, 182 n40, 183 n1, n37, 184 n58, n61, n26, 185 n5, 186 n38, n43, 187 n29, 189 n21, 190, 192, 194, 195, 198
Block-printed designs 26-27, 32, 123, 171, 172, 178, 190, 191, 193, 194 *see also* printing
saris 25-28, 32, 103, 123, 199; *29, 31-34, 138, 139, 179-181*
Block-printing in Andhra Pradesh 103; *138, 139*
Gujarat 25-27, 32; *29, 31, 32*
Madurai 123; *179-181*
Rajasthan 26-28, 32; *33, 34*
West Bengal 178
Blouses 11, 16, 73, 80, 100, 151, 169, 185 n47, 191, 192; *11, 30, 101, 151, 163, 182, 186*
Bombay 9, 11, 55, 56, 145, 150-152, 181 n2, 188 n25, n32, 193, 195; *188*
Bomokoi sari 92, 96, 98, 123, 148, 165, 167, 190, 191, 194; *131*
Bondo tribe 90, 92, 190
Boro tribe 73, 75, 79, 190, 191, 194, 198
Brahma 170, 177, 180, 190
Brahmaputra river 7, 73-75, 175, 184 n4, 190
Brahmin 13, 26, 31, 50, 51, 79, 99, 125, 126, 162-163, 173, 176, 177, 183 n32, 184 n40, n42, 186 n3, 189 n74, 190-195
British, British Raj 9, 11, 41, 52, 55, 89, 103, 126, 150, 152, 182 n2, 184 n51, 187 n36, 195
Brocades, brocading 32, 42, 45, 47, 48, 50, 53-56, 76, 104, 124-125, 180, 183 n39, n6, n25, 185 n41, 190, 191, 194-197, 199; *13-16, 46, 55-62, 73-90, 93-97, 103-105, 110, 111, 136, 137, 152, 156, 159, 183, 201-203, 206; see also* Figured textiles
Bronzes 171, 189 n39
Brothers, brothers-in-law 30, 56, 102, 151, 183 n28, 194
Buchanan, F. 51, 52
Buddha, Buddhism 41, 51, 54, 73, 126, 161, 164, 169, 170, 173, 174, 176, 177, 179, 181 n2, n19, 185 n51, 190, 194, 200; *135*
Burma, Burmese 9, 73, 75, 76, 79, 80, 175, 181 n1, 182 n30, 184 n18, 190, 195
Calcutta 41, 50
Chadar 16, 73, 74, 77, 191, 192, 198, 199; *94*
Chanderi saris 148-149, 191, 195, 199; *204, 205*
Chhoi brothers 56, 151, 195
Chiffon saris 11, 32, 125, 151, 182 n28, 187 n25, 188 n26, 191, 195, 196; *38*
China 9, 30, 42, 56, 73, 74, 79, 150, 151, 175, 183 n26, 185 n34
Chinese embroidery 151, 188 n25, n27; *195-200*
silk 77, 151, 197
textiles, designs 56, 75, 151, 175-176, 188 n25, n27; *73, 74, 195-200*
Chintz 103, 128, 151; *138, 139*
Chota Nagpur 14, 89, 90-91, 185 n2, 188 n2; *115*
Christian 150, 181 n2, 186 n3
Chunari 128, 182 n16, 191, 195; *see also Bandhani*, Veil
Clothes, tailored 10, 11, 13, 16, 26, 48, 52, 73, 76, 79, 80, 177, 182 n44, 188 n29, 191; *11, 26, 30, 68*
see also blouses
untailored, *see Dhoti, Lungi*, Sari
Coimbatore 126, 128, 187 n8, n43; *183*
Colonialism, effects of 7, 150
Colour 12, 13, 25, 26, 30, 41, 46, 47, 54, 56, 74, 79, 89, 97, 122, 126, 127-128, 145, 150-152, 161-164, 181 n9, 187 n13, 188 n6, 191-197
black 29, 75, 80, 151; *42, 108*
blue 30, 44, 76, 147, 163, 188 n1; *29, 31, 54, 64-66, 90, 169, 170, 184*
gold 32, 42, 44, 54, 78, 91, 125, 150, 193; *16, 21, 39, 73, 82, 84, 93-96, 101, 103, 152, 156, 201*
green 163; *12, 57, 75, 155, 157, 166, 180*
multi-coloured 25, 27-30, 44, 48, 49, 56, 91-93, 97, 99, 101-103, 126, 185 n28, 192, 193; *12, 27, 28, 47, 48, 109, 112, 120-135, 140-144, 203, 206*
pastel 27, 47, 56, 149, 151; *38, 64-66*
pink 30; *8, 162*
purple, violet 56, 91, 151; *200*
red 12, 29, 47, 75, 76, 89, 91, 92, 123, 147, 151, 162-163; *15, 46, 53, 62, 67, 69, 86-89, 152, 175, 190, 198*
symbolism 12, 13, 28, 161-164
white 12, 29, 42, 47, 76, 89, 91, 125, 149, 151, 162; *9, 17, 18, 35, 53, 55, 115, 136, 171-174*
yellow/orange 29, 56, 93, 123, 161, 163-164; *14, 24, 25, 79, 81, 159, 161, 177, 187*
Coorg 16, 121, 182 n42, 191
Coromandel Coast 79, 121, 191
Cotton cloth 28, 41, 42-47, 51, 74, 75, 79, 80, 90, 93, 96, 103, 121, 125-128, 145-150, 152, 183 n31, 186 n67, 190-195, 196, 199; *10, 19, 36, 46, 172, 181, 206*
fibres 41, 45, 145, 197
embroidery 48, 50, 127, 147, 192; *64-68, 70, 71, 109*
Gangetic muslins 42-47, 183 n4, 188 n14; *9, 10, 55, 57*
handspun 52-53, 90, 188 n14, 199; *32, 112, 144*
high count 45-47, 95, 125-128, 148-150, 188 n14-15, 190, 193, 196, 199; *10, 54, 55, 171-175*
history 8, 54, 42-43, 172, 177, 181 n9, 183 n6, 186 n5
low count 13, 16, 89, 90-92, 93, 95, 99, 186 n32, n6, 196; *19, 46, 109-114, 176, 177, 206*
mills 9, 152, 182 n32, 188 n32, n1, 199; *8, 17, 186, 188*
muslins 13, 28, 30, 42-47, 50, 76, 104, 125-128, 145-146, 148-150, 174, 188 n14, 190-195, 197, 199; *9, 24, 55, 64, 65, 90, 171-177, 183*
unbleached 28, 42, 91, 93, 121, 174; *18, 49, 50, 54, 122, 136-137, 172*
Crepe 41, 125, 151, 187 n27, 191, 196, 197, 199; *69, 70*
Cuttack saris 96-98, 199; *124-130*
Dacca 43, 44-45, 56, 79, 183 n21, 193; *46, 50, 57; see also* Dhaka
Darbhanga 189 n71
Das phoolia saris 96, 191; *122*
Deccan 8, 9, 11, 14, 54, 123, 169, 181 n2, n12
central 163; *11*
east 16, 51, 78, 89-104, 166, 167, 170, 175, 180, 185 n1-74, 190, 195, 198, 199; *109-145*
west 121, 122, 145-152, 165, 166, 169, 187 n22, 188 n1-35, 190-195, 198, 199; *184-205*
Deccan saris 32, 51, 54, 89-104, 121, 122, 145-152, 170, 189 n7, 190-195, 199; *189-194*
Delhi 26, 182 n13, 183 n11; *38*
Deshi saris 42-44, 191; *49-54*
Designs, *see* Motifs
Devanga(n) 94, 101, 121, 122, 126, 186 n4, 187 n9, 191
Dhaka 49; *see also* Dacca
Dhaka cloth 73, 80, 185 n48, 191
Dhangar 181 n2, 191
Dharmavaram 76, 123-124, 194, 191; *2, 168*
Dhoop chhaon 146, 191; *189, 192*
Dhoti 49, 51, 79, 171, 191, 198
Do-chashmee 149, 191; *14*
Do-muha 93-95, 99, 191, 198; *114, 122, 134*
Dobby 95, 146, 190, 192
Domestic art, crafts 48, 99, 166, 169, 171, 184 n8, 190, 193-195; *17, 68*
Dravidian culture, languages 9, 90, 91, 93, 101, 121-128, 166, 167, 181 n1, n13, 182 n2, 185 n8, n21, 186 n53, n73, n1-2, 190-195, 198
Dupatta 26, 47, 101, 172, 191; *68*
Durga 4, 47, 166, 180, 191
Dyeing 44, 52, 74, 79, 93, 94, 126, 146; *see also* Colour, *Pitambar*
Dyeing, batik 103, 126, 186 n71, 196, 197
block-printing 25-28, 32, 103, 128, 195, 196, 199; *29, 31, 33, 34, 37, 45, 138, 139, 181*
dip-dyeing 30, 95, 123-125, 128, 152, 194; *40, 41, 45, 164, 168, 170, 180-183*
Gujarat 25-27, 28-31, 32-102; *29-32, 40-44*
history 8, 25-26, 28, 39, 164
ikat 30-31, 52, 90, 92, 95-98, 99-100, 101-103, 179, 186 n61, n63, 191, 196, 199; *27, 28, 114, 120-130, 132-134, 140-144, 182, 185, 206; see also Bandha*
kalamkari 103, 128; *138, 139*
Madurai 127, 195; *179-181*
Rajasthan 27-30, 32; *33-36*
resist 27, 28-31, 32, 90, 92, 95-98, 99-100, 101-103, 127, 147, 151, 182 n16, 186 n71, 190, 195, 197; *27-29, 31, 33, 114, 120, 130, 132-134, 140-144, 181*
tie-dye 28-30, 103, 128, 147, 151, 161, 182 n16, 190, 192, 193, 197; *40-43; see also Bandhani*
yarn-dyed thread 42, 43, 47, 52, 76, 127, 197; *36, 46, 52, 92, 95, 109, 173, 185*
Dyers 25, 28, 74, 90, 162, 191, 194
Chhipa 28, 91
Neelgar 28, 194
Rangrez 28, 194
Dyes, aal 91, 190; *111*
indigo 26, 162, 164, 196; *31*
lac 98, 123, 190, 193
madder (alizarin) 164, 186 n69, 196, 197
mordants 25, 181 n9, 186 n69, 197
synthetic 89, 93, 94, 186 n69, 196, 197
East India Company 9, 41, 51, 183 n6, 185 n2, 200
Embroidered saris, by type:
badla 32, 50, 151, 190
bel 51
broderie anglais 150, 196; *197*
chikankari 50, 191, 194-195, 197; *35, 64, 65*
Chinese 150-151, 188 n24, n25 n27; *195-200*
French 182 n28
gota 50; *67, 69*
kalabattun, kamdani 31, 192; *38*
kantha 49, 192; *70, 71*
karchopi 49, 192
kasuti 147, 191, 192, 194; *184*
machine 51; *72*
muga silk 49, 50, 79
muka 31, 193; *39*
on leather 31
reshme karchopi 49
silhahra 51
sujani 49, 195
tribal 77, 80, 92; *91, 109*
whitework 51, 191, 196, 197; *64, 65, 197*
zardozi 31, 44, 48-49, 50, 183 n35, 187 n32, 192, 195; *38, 39, 67, 69, 72*
see also Appliqué
Embroidery, major regions:
east 44, 48-51, 180, 191, 192; *35, 64-72*
east Deccan 92; *109*
south 126, 165
west Deccan 147, 150-151, 166, 188 n24, n25, n27, 191, 194; *184, 195-200*
west 25, 27, 31-32, 178, 183 n35, 190, 193, 195; *38, 39*
Endi, eri silk 74, 77, 191, 197
Erode 128, 188 n43
Ethnic groups 7, 10, 12, 14, 16, 26, 28, 29, 31, 73, 74, 79, 80, 126, 150, 152, 181 n2, 182 n42, 188 n27, n1, 191, 193-195
European influence 11, 48, 54-56, 73, 182 n28; *8, 25, 54, 74, 78, 188*
traders 9, 51, 121, 200
Evil eye 26, 161, 163, 165, 166, 169, 170, 194
Fariya 73, 79, 185 n44, n47, n54
Farmers 77, 80, 162, 176, 185 n2
Fertility concerns, symbols 42, 161-163, 166, 167, 169, 171, 173-179, 192, 193; *127, 132*
Festivals 29, 30, 47, 91, 100, 151, 169, 175, 191-195
Figured textiles 32, 42, 47, 48, 53, 54, 56, 76, 96, 98, 100, 124, 125, 127, 168, 172, 180, 183 n39, 190, 191, 193, 196, 197; *9-11, 55, 62, 73-90, 93-100, 101-105, 110, 111, 113, 114, 116-123, 131, 136, 137, 146-168, 183, 189-194, 201-203; see also* Brocade
Fisherpeople 101, 181 n2, 193
Fitch, R. 184 n51
Flowers 12, 164, 169-170, 185 n24, 189 n30, n34, 190-195; *33, 52, 54, 61, 92, 99, 117, 119, 134, 137, 156, 188, 195, 196, 198, 203*
bud 165, 193; *126*

see also Motifs
Forbes-Watson, J. 49, 79, 183 n9, n15, 184 n58
Gadaba tribe 90, 185 n7, 191
Gadwal saris 104, 148, 186 n38, 193, 195, 199; *145*
Gandhara 10, 11, 177, 181 n19
Gandhi 9, 52, 56
Ganga 7, 8, 41, 42, 44, 47, 73, 173, 179, 191
Garo tribe 73, 75, 78, 191
Gauhati 74, 184 n6
Ghaghra 11, 16, 182 n44, n45, 191, 198; *26, 30*
Ghara 151, 188 n24, 191, 198, 199; *198-200*
Gharchol(u)(a) 29, 178, 179, 191
Goddesses 45, 47, 100, 166, 169, 171, 176, 177, 179, 180, 183 n17, 190, 191, 193, 195; *161*
Gola nesana 182 n38, 191
Gollabhana 101, 186 n61, 191; *137*
Gond tribes 16, 90, 92, 104, 167, 174, 185 n8, n21, n22, n27, 186 n53, 191, 192
Gorad saris 47, 192, 199; *59, 63*
Gota saris 50, 184 n41-42, 199; *67*
Goyal saris 94, 192; *117, 118*
Greeks 9, 169, 182 n34
Gujarat 10, 14, 16, 25, 30, 89, 96, 102-103, 122, 128, 150, 151, 165, 173, 178, 179, 180, 182 n41, n44
communities 27, 28, 30, 56, 122, 128, 150, 181 n2, 182 n41, n44, 193
weavers, craftspeople 28, 30, 56, 151
Gulbadan 186 n61
Gupta period 10, 11, 161, 170, 171, 174, 180, 181 n21, 200
Gurung 80, 185 n42, n43, n47, 192
Hansabali kapta 186 n40, 192; *122, 123, 206*
Harsha, Harshacharita 45, 79, 169, 183 n23, 188 n2, 192, 200
Haryana 16, 25, 26, 29, 192, 194
Hindu art, culture, religion 11, 26, 41, 43, 46, 51, 73, 91, 121, 145, 162-164, 168-180, 181 n2, 182 n42, n19, 183 n28, 185 n2, n14, n51, 186 n3, 189 n45, n73-74 n79, 190-195
communities, traders 11, 25, 29, 31, 44, 89, 90, 95, 125; *see also* Weavers
wedding ceremonies 91, 168, 185 n24
Homespun cloth 9, 52-53, 80, 192, 199; *112, 144*
Hubli 188 n8, 192
Hublidhardi 188 n8, 192; *184*
Hsuen Tsang 42, 78, 200
Hyderabad 100, 101, 182 n28, 186 n67
Ikat saris of:
Andhra Pradesh 89, 101-103, 186 n61, n63, 190-192, 194, 199; *140-143*
Gujarat 25, 30-31, 194, 199; *27, 28*
history of 25, 30-31, 186 n43
Maheshwar *185*
Orissa 52, 92, 93, 95-98, 99-100, 178, 180, 190-192, 199; *114, 120, 130, 132-134, 206*
Ikat, history of 25, 30-31, 186 n43
technique 196, 197
Ilkal saris 104, 145, 147, 148, 192, 199; *184*
India, geography 7-8
history 8-10, 25, 41, 73, 76, 89, 121, 145, 152
maps 7-9, 25, 41, 73, 89, 90, 121, 145
maps of states 32, 42, 51, 52, 75, 76, 79, 95, 103, 122, 123, 126, 149, 151
languages 9-10; *see* Glossary

Indo-Aryan languages, culture 9-10, 73, 79, 90, 104, 121, 161, 168, 169, 171, 181 n1, n13, 190-195
Indonesia 12, 126, 166, 182 n16, 186 n71, 191
Indus Valley civilization 8, 25, 161, 170-180, 189 n45, 200
Industrialization, effects of 7, 9, 10, 25-26, 28, 41, 78, 89, 152, 187 n11, 188 n30
'Inlay' 32, 149, 150, 193; *203*
Jagannath 97, 100, 192
Jain 10, 25, 29, 31, 51, 52, 162, 173, 178, 179, 181 n3, 182 n44, 186 n3, 189 n39, 191, 192
Jaintia tribe 16, 73, 75, 192, 198
Jaipur 26, 27, 28
Jala, Jali 94, 165
Jamdani saris of cotton 41, 44, 45-47, 104, 127, 191, 192, 195, 199; *9, 10, 46, 55, 57*
Bangladesh 41, 46, 49; *46, 57*
history 42, 45, 50, 128, 183 n25
silk 47, 128; *58*
prices 45-46
Tanda 47
Venkatagiri 104, 127
West Bengal 43, 44, 46; *9, 10, 55, 58*
Jammu and Kashmir 25, 26
Jamnagar 28, 182 n18
Janani, junani sari 101, 102, 192
Japan, Japanese 184 n23, 187 n11
Jewelry 31, 146, 164, 165, 169, 185 n23, 187 n35, 189 n28, 191, 194; *67; see also* Motifs
Jewish community 126, 186 n3
Jot, Jote 148, 187 n22
Kalakshetra 123; *156, 159, 160*
Kalidasa 181 n18, 189 n70
Kameez 11, 47, 191, 192, 195; *68*
Kanchipuram 123-124, 148, 150, 166, 174, 187 n32, 194; *6, 147, 152, 157*
Kandy 126, 127, 166
Kantha saris 49, 176; *70, 71*
Karam kichri 175
Karnataka 14, 16, 104, 121-125, 128, 145-148, 166, 182 n38, n42, 186 n1, 187 n7, n9, n11, n13, n23, n25-28, 188 n4, 192, 195, 198, 199
weavers, communities 121, 122, 191, 192
Kashmir 25, 26, 171, 172, 182 n1, n11, 199
Kathmandu 73, 80, 184 n4, n5, 185 n49, n54, 192, 194
Kerala 16, 31, 121, 125-126, 127, 182 n33, n43, 186 n1, 187 n29, 194, 199; *171, 172*
weavers, communities 121, 122, 185 n49, 186 n3, n6, 187 n10, n31, 193, 194
Khaddar, khadi 9, 52-53, 56, 152, 192, 199, 200; *32, 47, 48, 144*
Khan blouse 100, 186 n60; *11*
Khan saris 100-101, 102, 186 n60, 191, 192, 199; *136, 137*
Khanda 91, 185 n21, 186 n53, n60, 192, 193, 198, 199; *115*
Khandua 97-98, 171, 186 n53, 193, 198; *127, 129*
Khanduva 186 n53, 192, 193, 198
Khapa 93-95, 116, 193; *206*
Khari 32, 193; *37; see also* Tinsel
Khasi tribe 16, 73, 75, 181 n12, 192, 193, 198, 199; *21, 22*
Khoja 29, 183 n24, 193; *42*
Khond tribe 16, 90, 92, 185 n29, 193, 198
Kinara 43, 80, 198
Kodalikarupur 128, 193
Kol(s) 181 n2, 193
Kollegal 123, 124, 125; *164, 166*
Koraput 89, 90-92, 174, 189 n49, 190, 191; *109, 111-113*
Kornad saris 104, 122-124, 147, 187 n12, n13, n20, 192-194, 199; *6, 149, 150, 152-161*

Kosa 79, 93, 184 n47, 192, 193
Kosara pudava 121, 125-126, 128, 174, 199; *171-174*
Kota saris 26, 28, 193, 199; *35, 36*
Krishna (deity) 178, 191, 192
Krishna (Andhra Pradesh) 103, 104, 185 n3, 188 n2
Lahariya 29, 183 n26, 193; *see also Bandhani*
Lakshmi 45, 162-163, 166, 169, 171, 179, 180, 191, 193
Lampas 54, 56, 180, 183 n39, 195-197; *73, 74*
Landscape saris 99, 100; *133*
Lanvin 182 n28
Limbu people 80, 185 n42
Lingayat 122, 181 n2, 186 n3, 193
Loom, backstrap 74, 80, 92, 196
bamboo frame 80, 191
Chinese 151
dobby attachment 95, 146, 190, 192
drawloom 45, 47-48, 54, 183 n26, 194, 196
handloom 9, 12, 43, 45, 53, 74, 77, 89, 95, 121, 126, 128, 152, 184 n8, 188 n33
jacquard 48, 74, 98, 196, 197
pitloom 197
powerloom 74, 80, 128, 197
simple frame 74, 80
sticks for supplementary warps 95, 164
Lucknow 41, 50, 191; *64, 65*
Lugade, lugda 145, 147, 188 n8, 193, 198
Lungi 12, 16, 73, 79, 80, 101, 126, 127, 166-169, 171, 182 n30, n44, 191, 193-195, 198; *151*
Machilipatnam 103, 128, 192, 194; *138, 139*
Madhya Pradesh 14, 25, 26, 27, 89, 90-94, 96, 98, 145, 148-149, 150, 165, 180, 182 n45, n2, 184 n26, 185 n29, 190-195; *117, 118, 185, 187, 204, 205*
Madras 123, 124, 187 n22, 194
Madurai 174, 187 n8, n43
saris 126, 127, 128, 199; *163, 179-182*
nineteenth century 127, 128
resist-dyed 127-128, 192, 199; *179-181*
Maha Devi 176, 183 n17, 191, 193, 194; *161*
Mahabharata 12, 78, 79, 182 n33, 193
Maharaja 99, 104, 188 n21
Maharashtra 10, 14, 51, 89, 93-95, 104, 121, 123, 128, 145-148, 150-152, 165, 181 n2, n22, 182 n38, 185 n1, n29, 186 n33, 187 n28, 190-192, 194, 195; *189-192*
Maheshwar saris 148, 149, 165, 188 n17, 190, 191, 193, 194, 199; *185, 187*
Maithili 178, 186 n43, 198; *17*
Malabar Coast 79, 121, 193
Muslims 187 n31
Malays 126, 189 n10
Manipur 42, 73, 75, 76-77, 78, 80, 184 n1, n18, n20, n22, n26, 193, 198, 199; *90-92*
Marco Polo 31, 200
Marwari community 31, 184 n42, 193; *38*
Mauryan period 41, 161, 175, 183 n4, 200
Medieval documents 43, 186 n43, 187 n32
Meghalaya 16, 73, 74, 77, 181 n12, 184 n1, 191, 192, 198; *21, 22, 97, 98, 100*
Mehrgarh 8, 189 n45
Mekhla 16, 73, 77, 174, 193, 198, 199
Merchants 51, 162, 179, 186 n67, 193
Middle East 11, 25, 54, 183 n6,

184 n69, 196
Mina tribe 25, 182 n2
Mirrors 25, 189 n74
Modesty, standards of 10, 181 n18
Mohenjo-daro 8, 164, 179, 181 n9, 189 n45
Moirang tribe 77, 184 n20, 193
Moirangfee saris 73, 76, 77, 80, 193, 199; *90, 92*
Motifs, designs, patterns:
aeroplane 92, 100, 102, 103; *133*
animals 31, 46, 49, 75, 76, 98, 101, 151, 168, 178, 179, 180; *47, 48, 71, 89, 105, 133*
auspicious 31, 98, 100, 163-165, 168, 169, 173, 179, 180, 189 n46, n74, 192, 193; *132, 134*
axe 92
barley grain 26, 27, 192
basket weave 31, 148, 164, 165, 171, 191; *142, 192, 202*
bel 26, 27, 44, 49, 51, 54, 164, 168, 174, 190, 194, 195; *13, 32, 52, 65, 89, 156*
bird 48, 50, 53, 75, 101, 151, 161, 175, 176, 177, 178, 192, 193; *39, 44, 54, 55, 62, 71, 105, 122, 144, 152-154, 156, 199, 200, 206*
bugdi 146, 164, 191; *190*
buta, buti, buteh 26, 27, 48, 77, 171-172, 182 n10, n11, 191, 192; *21, 23, 29, 31, 87, 99, 205*
centipede 94, 101, 146, 164, 165, 188 n7, 191; *185, 190*
chaas 164, 191
chatai 146, 164, 165, 191; *192*
chauk 91, 92, 94, 146, 164, 167-168, 185 n24, 186 n63, 191, 193, 194; *110; see also* square
check 43, 44, 75, 77, 90-92, 96, 101, 104, 122, 126, 127, 146, 147, 149, 164, 165, 183 n26, 187 n20, 188 n6, n18, 190-194, 198; *22, 51, 107, 157, 190, 194*
conch 96, 97, 99, 180, 195; *132, 134*
cotton flower 93, 146, 149, 170, 195; *117, 119*
creeping vine 30, 43, 49-51, 96, 98, 124, 149, 150, 168-9, 190, 193, 195; *32, 33, 45, 52, 57, 65, 66, 89, 124-126, 156, 198, 201*
cuckoo's eyes 165, 193
cumin seed 94, 165, 192; *206*
daant, danti 44, 48, 96, 166, 191; *50*
dabbi 30, 191, 192; *42*
dagger 146, 165, 192; *190*
dashes 94, 96, 146, 164, 165, 186 n61, 188 n17, 191, 192, 194, 195; *116, 206; see also* seed
diamond 75, 91, 96, 99, 164, 165, 167, 192, 194; *142, 192, 202*
elephant 29, 31, 54, 93, 96-98, 100-102, 124, 147, 163, 179, 180, 186 n43, 189 n74, n79, 190-193; *27, 40, 89, 127, 140*
eye 75, 149, 164-166, 188 n17, 190, 192-195; *149*
fertility-related *see* Fertility
fish 90, 91, 94, 96, 98, 167, 168, 178, 193; *113, 123, 129, 134, 206*
flower bud 98, 122, 165, 166; *124-126*
flower 29, 32, 44, 48, 75, 91-93, 94, 96, 99, 101, 102, 150, 156, 166, 167, 169-170, 175, 183 n25, 185 n48; *33, 52, 54, 61, 92, 99, 117, 119, 134, 137, 156, 188, 195, 196, 198, 203; see also phool*
fly 91
gavanti 147, 191
geometric 25-27, 29-31, 44, 46, 48, 75-76, 91-92, 94, 96, 98,

101, 102, 104, 126, 128, 147, 149, 164-168, 170, 171, 187 n20, 190-195; *91, 109, 110, 131, 185, 189-192*
goose 96, 171, 177-178, 182 n3, 186 n40, 192; *206*
gujroo 147, 164, 192; *184*
herringbone 94, 146, 147, 164, 165, 187 n14, 188 n7, 191, 192, 195; *185, 190, see* centipede
hills 75, 99-100, 194; *102, 133*
human beings 16, 29, 31, 48, 101, 176, 151, 180; *40, 60, 89, 134, 135*
hunting scene 29, 180, 195; *40, 89*
jaal 146, 164, 192; *13*
jasmine 79, 97, 126, 146, 165, 169, 170, 189 n28, 191-193; *124, 126*
jewelry 31, 146, 164, 165, 169, 185 n23, 187 n34, 191, 192; *184, 191-194*
jhaalar, jhul 26, 27, 54, 56, 146, 149, 164, 165, 191, 192, 194; *13, 61*
kalga 6, 26, 27, 44, 47, 48, 53, 54, 76, 101, 172-173, 193; *13, 15, 32, 37, 56, 57, 62, 64, 70, 87, 103, 203*
kampi 122, 164, 192; *184*
karavai 123, 166, 192; *153, 154*
karvat 94, 101, 146, 164-166, 192; *190*
katari 146, 165, 192
konia 172, 192, 193
kori 30, 193
kotakomma 104, 166, 193
kothi 146, 164, 191, 192, 193
kumbh(a)(am) 42, 47, 91, 92, 94-99, 101, 104, 148, 162, 163, 166, 167, 171, 185 n27, 186 n73, 193, 194; *59, 111, 116, 123, 126, 130*
kungri 26, 166, 193; *33*
kuyilkan 164, 165, 187 n20, 193
leaves 28, 29, 31, 32, 44, 47, 49, 50, 51, 54, 75, 78, 91, 92, 99, 101, 102, 124, 125, 150, 151, 172-175, 180, 189 n45, 190-192, 194, 195; *28, 39, 40, 44, 46, 65, 66, 74, 84, 89, 144*
lotus 27-29, 94, 96-98, 162, 163, 168-171, 192, 194; *41, 43, 66, 114, 127, 129, 132, 164*
lozenge 75, 91, 99, 165, 193; *149, 166, 202*
mango 26, 99, 162, 172-175, 192
mat-weave 149, 150, 165, 193; *142, 192, 202*
matsya, see fish
mayilkan 128, 164, 165, 187 n20, 193; *149*
Modern(ist) styles 30, 31, 46, 53, 54, 89, 99, 102, 103; *2, 21, 47, 48, 54, 70-72, 77, 105, 132-134, 140, 142, 144, 182, 183*
mokku 122, 126, 166, 193; *150*
mothra 183 n26, 193
muthda 149, 188 n17, 194; *185*
nari 31, 194
pankha 146, 164, 194
pareu megon 75, 194; *100*
parrot 29, 31, 101, 102, 150, 178, 180, 191, 194; *27*
peacock 29, 75, 96, 98, 99, 101, 124, 128, 150, 161, 165, 176-177, 180, 192, 193; *39, 44, 54, 55, 62, 71, 144, 156, 199, 200*
peacock's eyes 128, 165, 192; *149*
peepal 31, 125, 173-174, 175, 189 n45, n46, 190, 194; *28*
phool(a)(ia) 26, 91-94, 96, 98, 99, 146-148, 167, 169-171, 189 n26, 190-195; *117, 123, 124, see also* flower
pigeon's eye 75, 194; *100*
pomegranate 99, 149, 164, 165, 191; *149*
protection-related, *see* Evil eye, Goddesses
rattai neli 126, 194
reku 104, 122, 125, 147, 166, 186

n73, 194; *172, 184*
rhinoceros 76; *105*
rudraksha 93, 98, 146, 170, 187
n14, 194, 195; *123, 149*
sawtooth 123, 146-148, 165,
191, 192; *185, 190*
seed 8, 93, 94, 99, 165, 170, 171,
192, 195; *131, 149, 192, 206*
serrated 42, 94, 122, 123, 164,
166, 183 n31, 185 n27, 192, 193;
185, 190
singhaulia 91, 94, 167-168, 195;
19, 110, see also triangle
spot 28-30, 32, 182 n16, 183
n25, 190-195; *40-45*
square 29, 30, 53, 91, 96, 102,
146, 164, 167, 168, 186 n63, 188
n20, 191
stripe 10, 29, 30, 43, 44, 46, 47,
52, 76, 77, 80, 91-96, 104, 122,
124-127, 145-147, 149, 164, 183
n15, 185 n28, 186 n33, 187 n14,
188 n6, 190-195; *50, 53, 91,
116, 146, 155, 159, 174, 185*
sun 101, 146, 170, 177, 187
n14, 189 n74, 191, 194; *160*
sun tree 75, 175-176; *93*
tara 98, 164, 195
'temple motif' 9, 42, 76, 77, 80,
92, 97, 166, 189 n10, 194; *59,
90, 92, 110, 116, 119, 122-126,
150, 152, 162, 165, 172, 184; see
also kumbh, mokku
thikri, see* dashes
triang(le)(ular) 9, 30, 31, 47, 75,
76, 92, 96, 122, 166, 167, 183
n33, 185 n27, 193-195; *19, 90,
92, 102, 109, 110, 111, 140, 144,
162, 165, 194*
tribal, *see* Tribal sari designs
tortoise, turtle 94, 96, 98, 180,
189 n73, 192, 193; *117*
tumpal 8, 9, 30, 31, 126, 166,
183 n33, 189 n10, 195
vine 26, 27, 46, 47, 50, 51, 96-
98, 101, 124, 149, 150, 168-169,
177, 183 n35, 189 n20, 190, 192,
193-195; *13, 46, 52, 57, 65, 66,
89, 126, 127*
veesi 167, 195
vohra bhat 8, 30, 31, 102, 165,
195
weapons 123, 146-148, 165,
192; *190*
wiggly line 122, 126, 127, 194
zig-zag 125, 147, 193, 194
Mubhhagam sari 124, 193; *6*
Muga silk 42, 74, 77, 78-79, 193,
197; *21, 93-95, 103, 104*
Assam 42, 74, 78, 79; *21, 93-95,
103, 104*
clothing 79, 183 n15, 185 n41,
199; *93, 94*
embroidery 42, 49, 50
export 79
sericulture 74, 77, 78-79
Mughal Empire 9, 10, 31, 44,
145, 148, 150, 161, 177, 188 n3,
191, 200
style 25, 26, 29, 32, 44, 46, 48,
54, 74, 76, 100, 103, 145, 168,
172-173, 181 n26, 182 n36, 194;
13, 15, 29, 32, 87-89; see also
Motifs: *buta*, creeping vine,
floral, *kalga*
Muhajorhi 99, 148, 193
Muhurtham pudavai 126; *173*
Mukta saris 52, 96, 99, 194
Mulberry silk 28, 41, 42, 47, 49,
52, 74, 95, 96-98, 104, 121-125,
148; *27, 28, 40-43, 47, 48, 60-63,
73-89, 125-129, 140-143, 149-
161, 164-166, 168-170, 185, 187,
195-205*
characteristics 52, 77
history 79
noil, raw silk 77-78
prices 52, 78, 184 n60, 185 n41
production 52, 77-78, 95, 121,

186 n41
Multan 103, 182 n18, 194
Munda tribe 14, 16, 90-92, 181
n12, 185 n14, n16, n21, 186 n53,
190, 194; *18*
Mundu veshti 16, 126, 182 n43;
194, 198; *171, 172*
Murals, Ajanta 10, 25, 28, 170,
177, 181 n22, n23, 182 n3, 189
n34; *4*
Kandy 126, 187 n40
Madhubani 178, 183 n37; *17*
Murukku pattu 123, 194; *152*
Muslim dynasties, rulers 9, 45, 48,
73, 121, 150, 177, 181 n6, 186
n43, 187 n31; *see also* Mughal
Muslim communities, traders 10-
12, 25, 31, 32, 41-45, 48, 55, 89,
93, 101, 126, 145, 161, 163, 166-
169, 172, 177, 181 n2, 182 n44,
183 n24, 184 n69, 185 n2, 186
n43, 187 n31, 190, 192-3, 195, 200
Mysore crepe 122, 124, 125, 187
n11, n27, 199; *169, 170*
Nagpur 89, 92, 152, 185 n1, 188
n21, 190
Nagpur saris 93-95, 146, 148,
192, 195; *49*
Naidu community 126; *173*
Narayanpet saris 104, 148, 199;
191, 193, 194
Nayar 121, 125, 185 n49, 187
n10, 194
Neelambari sari 44, 46, 194; *90*
Neem reshmi sari 188 n16, 194
Neolithic 8, 167, 181 n8
Nepal 7, 16, 73, 79-80, 152, 183
n1, 184 n4
saris 73, 79-80, 152, 185 n47,
191, 198; *23, 106, 108*
tribes, communities 79-80, 185
n47-49, 192, 194, 195; *23, 106*
Nerege 182 n38, 194
New Delhi 26, 182 n13, 183 n11
Newars 80, 194, 198, 199
Jyapu 80, 185 n52, 192; *23, 106*
Nomads 8, 182 n44, 191
Gujarat 29, 178, 181 n2, 182
n44, 191, 194
Maharashtra 181 n2, 191
Rajasthan 178, 182 n44, 191
Sind 29, 178, 191
southern Deccan plateau 181 n2
North Arcot 128, 187 n8
North-East India 9, 16, 42, 44,
73-80, 90, 91, 166, 171, 175-176,
181 n12, 184 n1, 191, 199; *20-22,
90-107*
Nuapatna 97, 186 n47; *127, 128*
Odhni 11, 16, 25-32, 182 n45,
191, 192, 194, 198, 199; *26, 30, 31*
Onnariyum 182 n43, 194
Oraon tribe 16, 90, 91, 175, 185
n14, 194
Orissa 89-100, 152, 174, 179, 181
n6, 185 n1-59, 189 n21, 190-196
Pachhedo 182 n44, 194
Painted cloth 32, 103, 128, 177,
186 n71, 192, 194; *17, 138, 139*
Painting 161, 168, 177
Paintings, Ajanta 10, 164, 170,
174, 177, 181 n22, 190, 200; *4*
domestic, ritual 126, 161, 166,
168, 171, 190, 193, 194; *17*
Jain 10, 179, 182 n44
Madhubani, Maithili 178, 189
n71; *17*
Mughal 10, 161
Pottery 161, 176, 178
Rajput 27
South India 11, 12, 122, 126,
194
Sri Lanka 126, 187 n40
see also Murals
Paithani saris 99, 148, 150, 186
n33, 188 n21, 194-5, 199; *201-203*
Palamu 51, 185 n17
Pallo 79, 185 n44, 198
Panetar saris 29, 30, 194, 199; *41*

Parsi 25, 29, 56, 80, 145, 150-152,
181 n3, 188 n22-25, 195
saris 150-151, 188 n27-29, 191,
195, 198, 199; *195-200*
Pashan sari 91, 194, 198
Pat, pattu 123, 187 n20, 194; *see
also* Silk
Patan, Gujarat 30, 186 n67; *27*
Patan, Nepal 184 n5
Patasi 80, 185 n52, 198, 199; *23,
106-108*
Pathernu 182 n44, 194, 198
Patna 50, 184 n42, n60, 188 n2;
68
Patolu, patola 9, 16, 25, 30-31, 96,
186 n63, n67
designs 31, 102, 165, 166, 171,
174, 190, 191, 194, 195
Andhra Pradesh 102-103; *141,
142*
Gujarat 30-31, 173, 178, 179,
186 n67; *27, 28*
Pattern, *see* Motifs
Periplus of the Erythrean Sea 43,
183 n22, 186 n5
Persia 8, 26, 45, 48, 150, 172, 173,
181 n13, 183 n6, n25, n26, 191
Petticoats 182 n38
Petni technique 123, 124, 148,
150, 194; *153, 154, 202*
Pictorial saris 99-100; *132-135*
Piliya 29, 194
Pitambar(a) 163, 190, 194
Pochampalli 101-103, 190, 192,
199; *140-144*
Population 44
handloom weavers 12, 184 n61
rural 89, 126, 161
tribal 75, 76, 176, 185 n5
tasar silk rearers 184 n50
Porai 123, 124, 128, 194; *150*
Portuguese 48, 121
Pottery 42, 99, 101, 161, 166,
167, 169, 170, 173, 174, 176-178,
180, 189 n45
Potia 93, 184 n47, 194
Priests 162, 168, 186 n50, 190,
193
Princesses 77, 182 n28, 183 n35
Printed saris 13, 25-28, 32, 52,
53, 80, 103, 125-127, 152, 171,
172, 178, 183 n34, 185 n54, 199;
8, 29, 31, 32-34, 37, 47, 48, 188
Printing by hand 25-28, 32, 53,
103, 127-128, 169, 178, 180, 186
n69, 190-196; *29-34, 37, 180*
mechanical 26, 32, 42, 80, 125,
127, 152, 188 n34, 197; *8, 25,
32, 188*
screen-printing 28, 32, 53, 125,
127, 151, 152, 164, 195; *32, 45,
47, 48, 179, 188*
see also Dyeing, Block-printing
Puja 47, 100, 162, 164, 169, 194
Puja sari 47, 162, 164, 188 n2
Bengali 47, 183 n31, 192, 199;
59, 63
Gadwal 104; *145*
Tamil 165; *149*
Orissa 100; *134, 135*
Pukai Madrasi sari 194; *168*
Punjab 12, 25, 28, 50, 183 n35,
184 n6, 192
Puri 97, 100, 186 n48
Quilt 48, 49, 180, 192, 195
Rabari people 29, 31, 178, 181 n2,
182 n42, 194
Rajasthan 25, 26-30, 161, 181 n6,
n14, 182 n44, n2, 192-194, 198
Rajput 27, 29, 31, 50, 178, 181
n6, 182 n2, n7, n18, 186 n43, 190,
194, 195
Ramayana 48, 79, 194; *60*
Ranchi 51, 90, 104, 184 n50; *110*
Rehwa Society 188 n19; *185, 187*
Resin 32, 192, 193, 194; *37; see
also* Tinsel
Ritual(s) 47, 52, 91, 163, 164, 166,
173-175, 179, 182 n35, 183 n17,

186 n34, 189 n30, 191
domestic art 166, 168, 173, 190,
191, 193, 194
impurity 26, 162, 163
purity 47, 52, 163
saris 29, 30, 52, 91, 148, 162,
163, 183 n17, 186 n34, 188 n5,
190, 194, 195, 198; *18, 24, 25,
41, 59, 63, 77, 110, 119, 128,
133-135, 145, 161, 171-174;
see also* Puja saris, Wedding saris
Roman traders 43, 45, 121
Rumal 101-103, 186 n63
Sakachcha 182 n41, 195
Saktapar sari 96, 195; *120*
Salem 123, 125, 128, 187 n8, n20,
n43; *183*
Salwar kameez 11, 47, 191, 195
Sambalpur 95-97, 99, 199; *120,
121-123, 132, 133*
Sanskrit 11, 12, 45, 47, 97, 100,
161, 162, 164, 174, 176, 182 n38,
n41, 184 n47, 186 n3, 188 n5, 192
Santhal Pargana 51, 184 n50
Santhal tribe 51, 90-91, 181 n12,
184 n50, 185 n14, n15, n23, 189,
190, 195
Sarangu 125, 198
Sari designs *see* Motifs
diagrams of layouts 14, 26, 28,
31, 43, 45, 47, 48, 55, 74-76, 79,
91, 92, 95, 96, 99, 101, 122-125,
127, 128, 146-148, 150, 152
dimensions 13
Sari draping styles:
Assamese 16, 73, 77
Bengali 14, 42, 91; *8, 9, 24*
Bihari 14, 15, 91; *17, 18, 88*
Deccan 14, 15, 93, 182 n37; *11*
design 182 n36
Dravidian 14, 16, 91, 122; *5, 7*
Eastern Region 41; *8, 9, 14, 15,
17*
Gujarati 14-16, 32, 150; *26, 30*
history 10, 11; *4*
Kachchha 10, 13-15, 182 n41,
n5, 192, 195; *11, 12, 186*
Karnataka 16
Kerala 16
Meghalaya 16; *20, 22, 101*
Nepali 16, 73, 80, 185 n52, n54;
23, 106
nivi 11, 13-15, 80, 125, 127,
191, 182 n38, n5, 185 n54, 191,
194; *1, 3, 25, 35, 140, 170, 182*
north Indian 4, 15; *14, 15, 17,
18, 88*
Orissa 14, 93
Parsi 150, 188 n22
ritual 47, 186 n50
'round-wrapped' sari 182 n38
sidha 14, 15, 91, 195; *14, 15, 17,
18, 88*
South Indian 13-15, 122, 127;
3, 5, 7, 12
Tamil 15, 16, 122; *3, 5, 7*
tribal 16, 73, 79, 91, 185 n23,
192; *8, 18, 20, 22, 101, 115*
two-piece 12, 16, 73, 79, 92,
127, 191, 192, 198; *23, 26, 30*
ulta 14, 195; *see also nivi*
Sari history 10-13; *4*
Saris, by community, way of life:
aristocratic 9, 27, 30, 31, 50, 73,
126-127, 145, 148-150, 166, 186
n33, n38; *39, 89, 90, 92, 185,
187, 201-205*
Brahmin 26, 31, 50, 51, 99, 125,
163, 173, 183 n32, 191, 195; *12,
27, 59, 63, 67, 69, 79, 149, 152,
155, 157, 166, 167, 171, 172,
174, 191*
ethnic 9, 26, 28, 29, 30, 80, 89,
92-100, 104, 126, 146, 152, 166,
167, 175, 178, 180, 184 n9, 188
n1, 192-195; *11, 23, 43, 108,
114, 117-123, 132-137, 146-
148, 180, 184, 206*
fashion 9-11, 13, 32, 48, 54, 55,

89, 90, 128, 151, 172, 181 n26,
182, n28, n45, 186 n6, 188 n27,
191, 192, 199; *2, 21, 182, 183*
Janta 188 n33
modern, urban, designer 11, 16,
25, 26, 28, 30, 31, 32, 43, 46, 49,
52, 53, 54, 56, 74, 76, 89, 96, 98,
99, 101-103, 104, 128, 151, 163,
181 n2, 182 n38, 184 n9, 191,
198, 199; *21, 47, 48, 70, 71, 103,
104, 105*
mourning, widow 12, 29, 47,
162, 163, 183 n18; *35*
puja, see Puja saris, Ritual saris
temple 123-124; *161*
tribal, *see* Tribal saris
Saris, by style:
narrow-bordered 121, 122,
125-126, 127; *146-148, 169, 170*
nine-yard 13, 14, 123, 127, 181
n14, 191, 194; *11, 12, 146-148,
157, 158, 173, 186, 189-192*
skirt 125, 187 n24, 199; *162,
165, 166*
two endpieces 92-95, 99, 146,
149, 152, 191; *114, 189*
wide-bordered 75, 94-96, 102,
122-125, 128, 146, 149, 150,
165, 188 n7, n8, 190, 193; *6,
120-122, 140, 144, 145, 149,
150, 152, 155, 157, 159-166*
see also specific sari names
Saris, by textile:
cotton, *see* Cotton
mill-made, *see* Textiles
silk, *see Endi*, Mulberry, *Muga*,
Silk, *Tasar*, Wild silk
synthetic fibres, *see* Textiles
Saris by state (colour plates):
Andhra Pradesh *136-145, 175,
178, 191, 193, 194, 168*
Assam *21, 93-95, 98, 100,
102-105*
Bangladesh *46, 57*
Bihar *17-19, 56, 66-69, 72*
Gujarat *29-34, 37, 40-44*
Karnataka *155, 164, 166, 167,
169, 170*
Kerala *171, 172*
Madhya Pradesh *117, 118, 185,
187, 204, 205*
Maharashtra *119, 186, 188-192,
195-203*
Manipur *90-92*
Meghalaya *20, 22, 97, 98, 101*
Nepal *23, 106, 108*
Orissa *109, 111-116, 120-134*
Rajasthan *33, 35, 36, 45*
Tamil Nadu *2, 6, 146-154, 156-
163, 165, 173, 174, 176, 177,
179-183*
Tripura *99, 107*
Uttar Pradesh *13-15, 39, 47,
64, 65, 73-89*
West Bengal *9, 10, 49-53, 55,
58-63, 70, 71*
Sarong 12, 79, 195
Sassanian 183 n26, 196
Saudagiri 25, 128, 195; *34*
Saurashtra 28, 29, 32, 103, 182
n42; *30*
Scheduled castes 181 n2
tribes, *see* Tribes
Sculpture 10, 11, 161-163, 168-
171, 173, 177-179
Seals 170, 173, 174, 179, 189 n35,
n45
Selvage 146, 191, 197
Sequins 25, 50, 151, 182 n34, 184
n42; *39*
Shalabhanjika 173, 175, 181
Shallu, Shalu 145, 148-150, 188
n5, 191, 195, 198; *201-205*
Shan Ahom 75, 175, 189 n58, 190
Shawl 16, 73, 76, 80, 172, 182
n11, 186 n53, 191, 194; *94*
Sheer fabrics 7, 11, 45, 125, 127,
148-150, 192; *10, 38, 55, 58, 82-
85, 175, 178, 204, 205*

Shikargah brocade 180; *88, 89*

Shiva 170, 176, 191, 195

Shivaji 188 n3

Shunga 10, 14, 41, 168, 170, 173, 174, 200

Siddipet saris 100-101, 199; *136, 137*

Silk 7, 13, 16, 28, 29, 30, 41-42, 43, 45, 46, 47-48, 49, 50, 53, 96, 101, 103, 104, 122, 125-128, 148, 150-151, 175, 178, 182 n28, 183 n6, n29, n31, 184 n40, n60, n22, n23, n31, 186 n38, n41, n67, 187 n7, n11, n23, n24, 188 n11, n16, n18, 190-195, 196-197, 198, 199
weaving 29-31, 46-47, 54, 56, 74, 121-122, 123, 182 n19
'raw silk' 77, 122, 197
cocoon 196
figured silk 32, 42, 44, 47-48, 53-56, 74-76, 97, 98, 124-125, 128, 183 n6, 185 n41, 190, 196, 197; *13, 16, 56, 58, 62, 73-89, 93-95, 103, 104, 152, 156, 164, 201-203*
filament, thread 28, 48, 49, 56, 123, 145-147, 183 n31, 188 n15, 196, 197
gajji 29, 30, 151, 191, 199

Silver 31, 32, 50, 195

Sind 7, 28, 31, 182 n18, 190-195

Sindur 9, 91

Singhbhum 51, 184 n50

Sodha Rajput 31, 195

Sora tribe 174

South-East Asia 25, 31, 73, 74, 127, 166, 175, 182 n30, 186 n63, 187 n38, 189 n57, 194, 195

Sri Lanka 7, 16, 121, 125, 126-127, 165, 166, 186 n1, 187 n36

Srinagar 26, 28, 182 n1

Sualkuchi 74, 75; *93-95, 98, 103, 104*

Sudra 162, 163

Supplementary-warp 13, 43, 48, 89, 94, 124, 128, 197
-and-weft designs 13, 42, 73, 75, 89, 93, 100, 123, 196; *122, 159*
-bands in sari borders 90, 93-100, 104, 122, 124-128, 145-149, 164-166, 170, 180, 189 n7, 191-195; *117, 160*

Supplementary-weft 13, 42, 45-46, 76, 80, 92, 94, 96-99, 104, 124, 167, 171, 182 n36, 188 n20, 191, 192; *206*
-bands in sari endpieces, borders 54-55, 99-100, 95, 101, 122, 124-127, 147, 182 n36, 190, 193-195; *80, 83*
techniques 29, 42, 48, 54, 56, 91, 92, 128, 159, 193, 196, 197

Surat 30, 32, 56, 151, 188 n25

Swadeshi 9, 52, 152, 195, 200

Tamang 185 n42, n43, n54, 195, 198

Tamil Nadu 14, 42, 94, 99, 104, 121-128, 165-166, 169, 171, 178, 179, 186 n1, n3, 187 n7-9, n13, n17, n32, n33, n36, n37, 188 n45, 190-195, 199

Tamil/Telugu dialect 122, 166, 170

Tanchoi 56, 151, 184 n63, 185 n41, 195, 199; *14, 73, 74*

Tasar saris, Andhra Pradesh 104
Assam 74, 77-78
Bengal 46-49, 183 n15; *58, 59*
Bihar 51-52, 91, 184 n58, 193; *56*
Madhya Pradesh 93-95, 191, 194, 199; *118, 117*
Maharashtra 94; *119*
Orissa 51, 95, 96, 97, 186 n47, 199; *130*

Tasar silk 46, 51-52, 74, 77-78, 184 n47, 195, 197, 199
cooking 51, 52
export 51, 52

history 51, 78, 184 n58, 186 n38
mukta 52, 194
production 51, 78, 95, 184 n58, n25, n26, n31, 193, 199
ritual 47, 51-52
sania 51, 195
tasar-cotton mix 51

Tassels 182 n38, 193

Tavernier, Baron 45, 79

Telia rumal 101-102, 186 n63

Temples 10, 30, 97, 99, 100, 123, 124, 168, 169, 173, 174, 177, 178, 181 n22, 184 n5, 188 n2, 189 n21, 190; *3, 25, 163, 170, 182*

Teni 147, 148, 166; *184*

Terai 80, 183 n1, 195

Terracottas 10, 11, 14, 170, 178, 179, 181 n21, 189 n33

Textile mills 9, 10, 12, 32, 145, 148, 152, 188 n32

Textiles:
cotton, *see* Cotton
mill-made 9-10, 12, 13, 26, 32, 42, 43, 46, 55, 75, 80, 92, 145, 148, 152, 185 n54, 188 n32, n1, 199; *8, 186, 188*
polyester 121, 125, 185 n54, 196, 197, 199; *162*
rayon 121, 125, 196, 197; *148*
silk, *see* Silk

Thai market 128, 184 n23

Thali 126, 187 n34

Thanjavore 123, 126, 193
aristocracy 128, 193

Tharu tribe 80, 185 n52, 195

Thread:
contrasting colour 13, 44, 47-49, 92, 123, 126, 127, 146, 148, 149, 165, 186 n73, 187 n20, 188 n6, 191
cotton, *see* Cotton
count, texture 43, 46, 50, 52, 54, 55, 93, 100, 123, 125, 127, 149, 183 n31, 195, 196, 197
dyed, *see* Dyeing
gold-wrapped, metallic, *see* Zari
synthetic 41, 44
silk, *see* Silk
see also Warp, Weft, Supplementary

Tibet 9, 74, 79

Tibetan-style 16, 73, 76, 79-80, 183 n45

Tibeto-Burman culture, languages 73-80, 175, 181 n1, 184 n18, 185 n43, n46-47, 190-195, 198

Tinsel saris 25, 32, 50, 184 n42, 193, 194; *37*

Trade textiles 25, 31, 56, 75, 77, 79, 92, 103, 121, 151, 166, 186 n63, 195

Traders 7, 9, 31, 121, 150, 152, 162, 179, 181 n3, 183 n31, 187 n31, 188 n21, 190, 193, 195, 200

Trees 25, 78, 91, 174-176, 190, 192, 195
dyes from 91, 98, 190
fibre 189 n49
sacred 31, 173-176, 189 n30, n45, 194; *25*
sericulture 77, 78, 95
symbolic 26, 31, 75, 94, 96, 100, 125, 162, 168, 169, 172-176, 189 n30, n45, n79, 190, 192, 194, 195; *28*

Tribal art 161, 178, 179, 189 n74
communities 7, 9, 25, 51, 75-80, 89-92, 162, 181 n1, n12, 182 n41, n2, n5, 184 n10, n17, n18, n20, 185 n2, n5-7, n13, n22, 189 n73, 190-195; *18, 24, 115*
dress 13, 14, 16, 26-28, 73-75, 76, 79, 80, 91-92, 185 n23, n27, 188 n2, 189 n49, 198
history, migrations 7, 9, 89, 171, 185 n2, 190
kingdoms 9, 25, 76, 79, 89
weavers 74, 76-77, 90, 92, 95,

184 n9, 185 n18, 189 n49

Tribal sari designs:
Assamese 12, 73-78, 175-176, 182 n36, 184 n9; *93-96*
Boro/Garo 75, 78; *96, 97, 100, 102*
chauk(i) 91, 92, 146, 164, 167, 185 n24, 186 n63, 191, 193, 194; *18, 110*
eastern Deccan 89-92; *18, 19, 109-115*
Khond 167-168; *109*
maachee phool 91
Miri *see* sun tree
north-east 44, 73-75; *90-108*
pahar agat 75, 194; *102*
pareu megon 75, 194; *100*
phool cheeta chauk 92, 104, 167, 194; *111*
singhaulia 91, 94, 167, 168, 195; *19*
sun tree 174-176; *93*
'temple motif' 92, 166, 167; *90*
western India 26-28, 172, 182 n41; *29, 31*

Tribal saris:
Bhil 14, 26, 27, 182 n5, n41, 192, 194, 199; *29, 31*
Bondo 92, 189 n49; *112*
Boro *dokna* 73, 75, 191; *100, 102*
colour 26-27, 73, 89, 91, 92, 163; *24, 90, 93-96*
draping styles 13, 14, 16; *8, 24*
Dongaria Khond 92; *109*
Dhurua 92, 101
eastern Deccan 90-92, 104; *109-115*
Gadaba *kerong* 92, 192, 198; *113*
Garo *dakmanda* 73-75, 191, 198, 199; *97*
Gond *ganda* 92, 104; *111*
Jaintia *sempynwan* 73, 198; *101*
Khasi *dhara* 74, 75, 184 n16, 191, 193, 198, 199; *20, 98*
Khasi *jainkyrshah, jainsem* 73, 75, 191, 192, 198; *22*
Manipuri *enaphi* 73, 76, 198
Manipuri *Moirangfee* 76, 78, 80, 193, 199; *90, 92*
Manipuri *phanek* 73, 75, 76, 80, 198, 199; *91*
Munda *sangol paria* 91, 104, 198, 199; *18, 19, 110*
north-east 73-80; *20, 22, 90-107*
Oraon *kichri* 91, 175, 185 n21, 191, 193, 198
Santhali *khand(a)(i)* 91, 185 n21; 186 n53, n60; 192, 193, 198, 199; *115*
Santhali *sindur lugri* 91
southern region 121, 127; *146*
Tripura *pachera* 73-75, 198, 199; *99*
western region 35, 26-27; *26, 29, 31*

Tribes *see* specific tribal name

Tribes of Assam 73-74, 184 n10, 190-195; *97-107*
Bihar 51, 90-91, 190; *8, 18, 110*
Gujarat 25, 26-28, 190, 182 n2 n5, 190; *29, 31*
Manipur 76-77, 184 n17, n18; *90-92*
Meghalaya 73-75; *20, 22, 97, 98, 101*
Nepal 79-80, 192; *23, 108*
north-east 73-77, 79-80, 184 n9, n10, n17, n18, 190-195; *20, 22, 90-107*
Orissa 89-92, 104; *109-113*
peninsular India 89-92, 104, 184 n47, 190-195; *24, 109-113, 115*

Tripura 73-75, 184 n1

Umrer 95, 148, 195; *119*

Urdu 172, 173

Uttar Pradesh 25, 26, 41, 47, 50,

52, 56, 73, 183 n1, 189 n21, 192

Vaishnavite 73, 180, 195; *134*

Vaisyas 162, 163

Vandha 186 n43

Varanasi, *see* Banaras

Veil history 11, 12, 182 n33, n34 n44; *15, 26, 30*
types 11, 27, 29, 47, 98, 126, 127, 161, 182 n44, n16, 188 n5, 191, 193, 194, 198

Venkatagiri 124, 187 n32, 199

Veshti 16, 126, 194, 198; *171, 172*

Vishnu 99, 169, 170, 178, 180, 189 n21, n73, 190, 192-195

Warp patterns 42, 90, 93-96, 98-101, 104, 122, 124-125, 127, 128, 145-149, 165, 191, 192; *162, 165, 185, 190, 192*
-stripe 44, 104, 126, 145, 146, 183 n15, 194, 195; *152, 158, 160*
-threads 13, 43, 48, 52, 92, 99, 123, 125, 126, 146, 147, 148, 150, 164, 192, 194, 196, 197

Warp-lifting devices 45, 194

Warriors 11, 162, 169, 182 n42, 186 n3, n4, 191, 194

Watt, G. 27, 32, 45, 49, 148, 182 n13, 183 n20, 186 n40, n61, 187 n20, 188 n21

Weave, gauze-like 46, 150, 151, 191, 196; *67*
interlocked weft 42, 47, 76, 80, 91-92, 94, 96, 98, 101, 104, 122, 123, 124-126, 128, 147, 148, 150, 166, 183 n31, 186 n73, 187 n20, 193-197; *149, 150*
plain 42, 43, 196, 197; *19, 28, 36, 95, 206*
satin 29-31, 49, 56, 125, 126, 128, 145-151, 191, 196, 197; *63, 74, 164*
twill 42, 43, 80, 197; *108*
warp-faced 80, 197; *91, 99*
weft-faced 91, 94, 104, 121, 125, 127, 197; *110, 112, 148, 171, 172*

Weavers 8, 9, 51, 74, 162, 183 n26, 188 n19, n33, 196, 197

Weavers' communities:
Ansari 54, 149, 190
Buhlia 181 n6, 186 n43, 191
Jaggi 43
Julaha 43, 54, 149
Kaikkolar 186 n4
Khatri(ya) 28, 29, 182 n19, 192, 193, 198, 199
Meher 94, 95, 181 n6, 186 n43, 191, 193
Momin 149
Padmasali 101
Pank, Panr 90, 94, 194
Patra 97
Saaliya(r) 122, 195
Salvi 31, 186 n67, 195
Swansi 90
Tanti 43, 90, 195

Weavers' cooperatives 51, 95, 121, 188 n19

Weavers of Andhra Pradesh 101, 104, 122
Assam 74
Banaras 54-6, 151, 183 n26, 190
Bengal 13, 43-48, 77, 195
Bihar 51, 104
China, Chinese origin 30, 56, 151, 188 n25
cotton cloth 13, 43-47, 74, 76-77, 90-92, 99, 101, 104, 122, 126, 127, 149, 181 n6, 188 n6
Gujarat 28, 30, 31, 101, 182 n6 n19, 188 n25
Hindu 28, 43, 46, 90, 101, 122, 182 n19, 185 n18
Jain 30-31
Kandy 127
Karnataka 122, 192
Kerala 122, 195
Madhya Pradesh 93, 94, 149, 188 n6, n19

Maharashtra 148

Muslim 28, 43-45, 46, 54, 149, 182 n19, 183 n26, 190

Orissa 90-92, 95, 97-99, 181 n6
silk fabrics 28, 30, 31, 48, 51, 54-56, 74, 93, 94, 97-98, 101, 122-123, 148, 149, 182 n19, 188 n6, n25

Tamil Nadu 121-123, 126, 166
tribal textiles 74, 76, 90-92, 104, 185 n18, 187 n32

Weddings, motifs 14, 162, 163, 169, 171, 173, 174, 177, 185 n24, 186 n34, 187 n34, 188 n24, 189 n28, 190, 193, 195

Wedding saris:
aristocratic 31, 97; *39, 201-203*
Brahmin 182 n35, 183 n32, 184 n40; *67, 69, 152*
ethnic 27, 94, 96, 99, 100, 190; *120, 121, 132, 184*
Naidu 126; *173*
Parsi 150, 151, 188 n24; *197*
tribal 27, 91, 168, 175, 193; *111, 115*

Wedding saris from:
Banaras 55; *14-16, 75, 85-89*
Bengali 47, 183 n29; *62, 63*
Bihar 49-50, 184 n40; *67, 69*
Gujarat 27-29, 31, 166, 174, 178, 191; *27, 28, 39, 43, 141, 142*
Karnataka 184
Madhya Pradesh 94, 149, 175
Maharashtra 148, 150, 151, 195; *197, 201-203*
north India 31, 49-50, 194; *14-16, 39, 69, 75, 85-89*
Orissa 96-100, 171, 190, 193, 195; *120, 121, 127, 129, 132*
Rajasthan 31
south India 126; *152, 162, 173*
Tamil Nadu 126; *152, 162, 173*

Wedding saris, textile:
bandhani 28-29, 191, 193
brocaded 55, 94; *14-16, 86-89*
cotton 27, 29, 49, 91, 94, 96, 99, 100, 126, 184 n40, 193; *67, 111, 115, 120, 121, 132, 173, 184*
embroidered 31, 49, 50, 150, 151; *39*
ikat 31, 96-100, 166; *27, 28, 120, 121, 127, 128*
pitambar 94, 126, 163, 186 n35
plain-weave 47, 91, 94, 126, 149
printed 27
silk 28, 29, 31, 47, 49-50, 55, 97, 98, 148-151, 171; *14-16, 27, 28, 39, 43, 69, 75, 85-89, 127, 129, 141-142, 152, 197, 201-203*
synthetic 162

West Bengal 41, 42-49, 51, 89-91, 98, 166, 184 n61, 185 n5, n29, 187 n7, 189 n33, 191, 195

West Deccan saris 14, 104, 145-152, 165, 166, 187 n22, 190-194; *11, 184, 205*

Western deserts 7, 8, 16, 25-32, 194; *26-45*

Wild silk, *see* Tasar, Muga, Endi, Eri

Wool 28, 29, 56, 80, 182 n44, 194, 195, 197

Worship 169, 171, 176, 186 n50, 191, 192, 194, 195; *170, 182*

Wrap 12, 16, 73, 79, 92, 182 n31, n38, n43, n44, 189 n49, 191-195, 198; *23, 94, 109*; *see also* Chadar, Veil

Yaksha, Yakshi 169, 173, 174

Zari 25, 28, 29, 31-32, 44, 45, 47, 48, 50, 53, 55-56, 76, 79, 122-128, 145, 148-150, 174, 183 n31, 186 n33, 188 n20, n21, 190-194, 196-197; *13-16, 36, 38-39, 56, 67, 69, 72-73, 75-76, 78-79, 82-89, 98, 104, 127, 132, 142, 145, 148-149, 152-154, 156, 158, 162, 164, 165, 166, 168-172, 176-179, 181, 193, 201-205*